Functions, Methods and Concepts in
Evaluation Research

Functions, Methods and Concepts in Evaluation Research

Reinhard Stockmann
Center for Evaluation, Sociological Department, University of Saarland, Germany

and

Wolfgang Meyer
Center for Evaluation, Sociological Department, University of Saarland, Germany

Translated by

Gareth Bartley

First published 2013 by
PALGRAVE MACMILLAN

Palgrave Macmillan in the UK is an imprint of Macmillan Publishers Limited, registered in England, company number 785998, of Houndmills, Basingstoke, Hampshire RG21 6XS.

Palgrave Macmillan in the US is a division of St Martin's Press LLC, 175 Fifth Avenue, New York, NY 10010.

Palgrave Macmillan is the global academic imprint of the above companies and has companies and representatives throughout the world.

Palgrave® and Macmillan® are registered trademarks in the United States, the United Kingdom, Europe and other countries

ISBN: 978–1–137–01246–3

This book is printed on paper suitable for recycling and made from fully managed and sustained forest sources. Logging, pulping and manufacturing processes are expected to conform to the environmental regulations of the country of origin.

A catalogue record for this book is available from the British Library.

A catalog record for this book is available from the Library of Congress.

Contents

List of Figures

List of Tables

Acknowledgements

A work like this does not come about merely as a result of the efforts of the authors themselves. Numerous ideas and pointers were contributed by our colleagues at the Center for Evaluation (CEval), for all of which we are very grateful, though we lack the space to list all the relevant sources individually. Special thanks are, however, certainly due to the hard-working assistants who have played substantial roles in producing the manuscript and figures. In that regard, Linda Jaberg, Miriam Grapp and Angelika Nentwig, without whose support this book would not have been completed, deserve a special mention. Finally, the authors feel a particular need to thank Gareth Bartley for his accurate and dedicated translation work and Liz Holwell for her commitment and patience in the creation of this book.

Introduction

Reinhard Stockmann

This book is an introduction to evaluation, which has been the subject of a tremendous boom in recent years. While evaluation has been established as a profession in the USA for more than 40 years, it has only been possible to recognize a similar tendency in Europe since the beginning of the 1990s. Since the PISA evaluation at the latest, the term has become part of German vocabulary. It now occupies a regular place even in everyday usage. In a series of articles entitled 'How the world loves'[1] in *Stern* magazine, for example, it was asserted that '...women tend to evaluate more and more precisely who they are getting involved with' (*Stern* 32/2007: 102).

The use of this term is not only spreading in a positively inflationary manner; it now also appears in many contexts in which – at least from the point of view of its scientific meaning – it actually has no place at all, for not every form of assessment is necessarily also an evaluation.

Whilst some terms – such as social group, competence, qualification, institution, system – were consciously transposed from everyday usage into the language of science, subsequently having to be cleansed there of their everyday connotations and precisely defined in a scientific sense, the term evaluation has gone the other way. Being used in its everyday application to refer to just about anything at all, the term is rapidly losing its scientific precision, so that it is now time for it to be redefined more clearly.

This applies not only to the term itself, but also to the concepts originally denoted by it, which had by virtue of that connection become dissociated from other common procedures such as expert reports, inspections, performance reviews and other kinds of study. As the term evaluation is currently hip, chic and modern and has a scientific ring to it, it is increasingly used for procedures which themselves have by no means continued to develop in the direction of evaluation. It is therefore a good idea to make sure that evaluation is what is actually in the can when it says 'evaluation' on the label.

Of course, evaluation doesn't only appear in disguise; it is also used more and more often in all kinds of contexts in accordance with its scientific and political meaning. Even if, as Chapter 1 will show, there can hardly be said to be such a thing as an evaluation culture in Germany – or indeed in any other European country – so far, and even if evaluation is for that reason not a generally accepted procedure in social terms, or systematically applied in the political process and regularly used in rational decision-making, some early signs of the emergence of such an evaluation culture can at least be recognized. Evaluation has meanwhile advanced to become an important instrument of control: for example in ministries for verifying the effectiveness of programmes, in agencies for performance reviews, in government audit offices for ascertaining what amounts have actually been spent, in government and non-government organizations for programme control, and in companies for supporting quality management, and so on. In individual policy fields such as education and research there are firmly established government research institutions and subordinate authorities in most countries, such as the Institute for Employment Research (IAB) and the Federal Institute for Vocational Education and Training (BIBB) in Germany, which take care of these tasks to a large extent. In other policy fields, such as development cooperation, the ministry in charge, its implementing organizations and other aid organizations have in-house evaluation teams or agents, who conduct the majority of the evaluations themselves or assign a large number of individual experts, consulting firms and research institutions to do so – and they communicate keenly on evaluation in several national and international networks such as the OECD-DCD-DAC[2] or the Network of Networks on Impact Evaluation (NONIE).[3] In yet other policy fields, such as foreign, security, cultural, domestic, agricultural and environmental policy, evaluation leads more of a shadowy existence in most European countries.

Against this backdrop, it is important to get clear in one's mind not only what the concept of evaluation actually is and how it is distinguished from other concepts, but also what role evaluation plays in society. This book not only aims to provide a detailed introduction to the subject, but also to clarify the performance potential of evaluations. Its aim is to lay the scientific foundations for their professional execution and use.

Accordingly, the role of evaluation in modern society is analysed first, in Chapter 1. On account of the diversity of applications already hinted at, a systematization that refers to the different functions of evaluation in society is necessary. The section that follows outlines how those functions have developed historically, what characterizes the current situation of evaluation, and what challenges result from this for the future . Evaluation is faced with the dilemma that its significance is on the one hand increasing, i.e. that it must meet growing demand, whilst on the other hand the supply of professional evaluators continues to be limited, since there are still very few opportunities for basic and further training in Germany and Europe, to say nothing of most of the countries in Africa, Asia and Latin America. The world economic and financial crisis will further exacerbate the demand for evaluation, for whenever public funds grow scarce it becomes more important to increase the effectiveness and efficiency of programmes and measures and create rational decision-making platforms on the basis of which rational priorities can be set and selection processes implemented. Evaluation can make an important contribution to solving these problems.

For this to be possible at all, heed needs to be paid to professional standards and basic scientific principles in the field of evaluation. Yet this ambition is by no means easy to realize, for evaluation is not only part of empirical social inquiry, duly oriented toward the rules which prevail there, but also a field of activity that is very much under the influence of the policy-makers. Evaluation is predominantly assigned or commissioned research. And he who pays the piper usually also expects to call the tune; not necessarily as regards the actual findings, but at least in terms of the nature of the questions to be investigated. Since evaluation is defined not only by its scientific nature but also by its usefulness, a balance must always be found between these two aspirations. Chapter 2 looks into this area of twofold tension, between evaluation and politics and between applied and pure science, and introduces a research model that does justice to the various different demands made on evaluation. The CEval approach developed by Stockmann (1992, 1996, 2006, 2008, 2009) is described as an example. This approach makes it possible to conduct comprehensive (programme) theory-driven evaluations on the basis of various theoretical approaches, and it does so, in principle, in all policy fields and programme phases. First, the basic scientific principles of evaluation are explained as they relate to certain practical initial questions of the sort that must be answered in any evaluation, namely *what* (which object) is to be evaluated, *what for* (to what end), *applying what assessment criteria*, *by whom* (internal or external), and *how* (using what methods).

There seem to be almost as many evaluation approaches as evaluators. There is a veritable jungle of theoretical models and approaches which have at least one thing in common, namely that they are, strictly speaking, not theories. In Chapter 3 an attempt is made to put some structure into this diversity of concepts. For this, various different proposals for systematization are presented, and the authors' own model is then developed. Evaluations can for example be structured in terms of their historical development, in the form of 'generations', as suggested by Guba and Lincoln. Or they can be structured in the form of a tree, as proposed by Alkin, in which the individual approaches branch out as strong arms from a common trunk, subsequently splitting into ever more delicate limbs. A completely different kind of systematization was undertaken by Fitzpatrick, Sanders and Worthen, who sorted evaluation approaches according to the benefit they were intended to create. All these proposals have their pros and cons; yet when all is said and done none of them is really convincing. For this reason, a fresh attempt is made at systematization in Chapter 3, in which the four functions of evaluation identified in Chapter 2 are applied.

As comprehensive a knowledge as possible of the various evaluation approaches proves useful in identifying one approach that is adequate to cope with the complexity of the many different questions. The fact is that it is not necessary to create a new approach for each evaluation, further fuelling the diversity of evaluation concepts:it is mostly far more effective and efficient to adapt existing approaches.

In doing that, one is in fact already right in the middle of the implementational planning of an evaluation. In Chapter 4 an implementation schema is designed for planning, conducting and utilizing an evaluation or its findings, and the individual phases involved are explained: determining and defining the evaluation project, developing the evaluation conception, developing instruments, gathering and analysing the data, and writing the report and presenting the findings. The varied experience gained by the authors themselves in conducting evaluations over many years plays an important part here. To ensure the quality, utility and feasibility of evaluations and a fair procedure – as stipulated by the German Evaluation Society (DeGEval) and other associations in their standards – the active involvement of the groups affected by an evaluation offers many advantages. For this reason, Chapter 4 introduces the CEval participant-oriented evaluation approach, which combines a science-based evaluation concept (Chapter 2.3) with a participant-oriented procedure, as an example. What is special about this concept is that it strives toward the optimum integration of those involved without violating scientific standards. To this end, evaluators and stakeholders (including the evaluees) are defined as partners with complementary tasks in the evaluation process, partners who all bring their expertise and their specialized, concrete situational knowledge to bear.

Whilst those involved can be integrated in the planning and utilization processes to a great extent – depending on the degree of participation being aimed at – developing the evaluation design and the survey instruments and gathering and analysing the data are the responsibilities of the experts with the appropriate qualifications, i.e. the evaluators. In Chapter 5 the gathering and assessment of information is depicted in four chronological stages. First, the pros and cons of the relevant evaluation designs, particularly with regard to impact-oriented evaluations, are explained and attention is drawn to the special features that result from each specific evaluation context. In developing and deploying the data gathering instruments, flexibility and adaptations to the survey situation are necessary, though this applies equally to social scientific fundamental research too. The analysis of the data gathered also adheres unrestrictedly to the rules and standards of empirical social inquiry.

In data interpretation the special contextual conditions of the evaluation need to be taken into account. As assessments are made in evaluations, heed must be paid to the strict application of the previously stipulated criteria, and objective adherence to procedural rules must be ensured so that as far as possible the subjective attitudes of the evaluators, the clients or the stakeholders do not cloud the assessments. In order for evaluations to be able to do justice to the twofold aspiration of usefulness and scientific integrity, it is on the one hand necessary (as shown in Chapter 4) to integrate the stakeholders as fully as possible into the so-called discovery and utilization context of an evaluation process. In the research context, on the other hand, it is mainly the scientific know-how of the evaluator which is called for. On account of the complexity of the research questions, and also on account of the special conditions under which evaluations have to be conducted (e.g. pressure of time, scant resources, numerous different stakeholder perspectives, interests and expectations), it is absolutely necessary for every evaluator to be familiar with the full range of evaluation designs, qualitative and quantitative survey designs and statistical analysis procedures, since that is the only way in which he or she can ensure a combination that is as appropriate as possible to the issues being investigated.

In the area of tension between politics and science, these great scientific demands made on evaluators are also complemented by the necessity for special social competences in dealing with the various social factions involved in a particular evaluator context and their interests. Particular heed must be paid to the environment (i.e. the specific social context of an evaluation) when selecting the evaluation approach (Chapter 3), designing the implementation process and developing the investigation and survey designs (Chapter 5). Chapter 6 sheds light on the evaluation environment from three different perspectives. It deals first with the relationship between evaluation and the social institutions, since – as explained in Chapter 1 – evaluation as an important element of modern social life makes a necessary contribution to ensuring the rationality of political control and enlightening society. With a view to the function of social enlightenment, the focus is particularly on public and civil society institutions, which are both intended to serve to vet government action and mediate between the interests of the political system and those of the citizens. The complex relationships between the democratic state and its agencies and between the media and the actors of civil society often influence the way in which evaluations are conducted and their findings used.

Those involved do not act as individuals who are free to decide for themselves, but as representatives of collective units that combine the interests of certain social groups. Such organizations play a central role in modern societies; interests are formed and communicated via collective units such as parties, associations and other forms of civil society organization. Government agencies are primarily responsible for political control, though the latter is, on account of the increasing complexity of modern societies, an area in which civil society organizations are now more and more firmly integrated. Evaluations are commissioned by these organizations, and as a rule also conducted by organizations, not individuals. For that reason, particular attention needs to be paid to evaluation in organizational contexts.

This is done here by taking the example of three central aspects of organization: the relationship between individuals and organizations as reflected in various forms of membership, the modes of communication between functional units within an organization, and the implementation of such units within the formal structure of the organization. The influence of organizational features on the organization's relationship with evaluation is also illustrated. The commitment to the organization of those involved, the flow of information between its various departments, and the perceived importance of evaluation within the departmental hierarchy are all vital to the acceptance and support of evaluations being conducted within an organization.

As organizations not only fulfill routine tasks in firmly institutional-ized procedures but also carry out many activities as measures, projects or programmes that run for limited periods of time, evaluators too play an important role as part of project management. The relationships now extend to include groups outside the organization, which are involved more or less deeply or affected more or less strongly by the implementa-tion of measures, projects or programmes. The word 'stakeholder' has established itself as a generic term for this sometimes very heteroge-neous set of actors. The term will be looked at somewhat more closely with regard to its consequences for evaluation.

When all is said and done, these examples of the social components of evaluation and the diverse challenges they throw down to evaluators serve to illustrate the complex competence profile associated with this activity. Evaluation is most certainly not a 'sideline' for experienced prac-titioners within an organization, or for empirical social researchers who feel like making a bit on the side via assigned or commissioned research. If evaluation is to live up to its social tasks, it must be conducted seri-ously and professionally. Finally, the main aims of this book are to clarify the relevant tasks of evaluation and the special competences required of evaluators (the job profile, so to speak), and to provide an introduction to the current state of concepts and discussions.

Notes

1. Translator's note: the original title was *So liebt die Welt.*
2. See www.oecd.org/document/12/0,3746,en_2649_34435_46582796_1_1_1_1, 00.html (Feb 2012).
3. See www.worldbank.org/ieg/nonie (Feb 2012).

1

The Role of Evaluation in Society

Reinhard Stockmann

1.1   Evaluation – an invention of modernity

Modern societies are characterized by the replacement of traditionally and religiously determined beliefs regarding the world order by *faith in rationality and progress*. As early as the end of the 1960s, Daniel Lerner (1968: 387) produced an incisive summary of the features of modernity: they include a growing, self-sufficient economy; democratic participation in the political sector; a culture which orients itself toward secular, rational norms; a society that is performance-oriented, equipped with personal freedom, and is spatially, socially and intellectually mobile. Connected with this construct is the idea that modernity is a universal phenomenon, and that it can be shaped and governed (cf. for example Degele & Dries 2005; Hill 2001 for introductions). But that is not all: in view of the social, economic and ecological problems which accompany modernity and have noticeably come to a head in recent years, the idea has meanwhile established itself that social development is by no means a thing that will simply look after itself, but urgently needs to be steered resolutely toward 'sustainable development' (cf. Federal Government 2001).

However, for it to be possible to have an effect on social processes of change, their *determining factors* and *impact relationships* must be known. It is a matter of recognizing which impacts can be brought about by purposive interventions under given framework conditions, so that effective measures, programmes, strategies and policies can be designed and implemented. As modern societies are characterized by a plurality of different lifestyles and opinions and equality of rights with regard to the say citizens have in social development, these objectives compete with one another. The effectiveness of interventions and their contribution to the public good (i.e. the good of all) thus become crucial decision-making criteria. Having said that, it is not only a matter of learning from experience – in other words understanding correlations in retro-spect and seeing the rationale in them – and measuring ex-post changes and investigating whether or not they are actually consequences of the strategies deployed to bring about change. In view of the challenge of governing complex and extremely heterogeneous social systems and the risks associated with misgovernment, the task of shaping the main influencing factors of social processes as early as possible, on the basis of rational insights, becomes increasingly important. For this, too, sound and relevant data are required.

With the above, some of the *main tasks* of evaluation have already been outlined: evaluation is the instrument with which *summatively* observed social changes can be measured, analysed and assessed, and through which *formative* data for the rational control of processes generated. Thus the insights *from social science research* into social relationships and the *investigative methods* developed in order to gain those insights are utilized for the political practice of actively shaping social processes. A *culture of common learning about government impacts* is thus striven toward (cf. Chelimsky 2006). By making available up-to-date scientific informa-tion through public discussion, evaluation also contributes to the *ration-alization of political debates* about social objectives and thus shows what is feasible for all those involved in a clearly recognizable way.

Evaluation is an invention of modernity (for the relationship between evaluation and modernity see especially Dahler-Larsen 2011). It is on the one hand linked to the vision of economic and social progress, the pursuit of growth and continuous improvement, and on the other hand to faith in the feasibility and controllability of social develop-ment. Evaluation offers itself both as an *instrument of enlightenment* which sheds light on development processes, and as an *instrument of control* which aims to influence those processes purposively. Above and beyond that, evaluation is also suitable for reflexive use, as an *instru-ment for the criticism of modernity* itself. Because it can be used to record not only the intended impacts of interventions but also their unin-tended ones, evaluation provides the empirical basis for social self-reflection.

It has meanwhile become clear that in modern societies, which are becoming more and more complex, development strategies and policies must be questioned more radically than before, because of side effects which are undesired and in some cases decidedly harmful. This means that problems that up to now have only been treated as external (e.g. the environment), unintended consequences of purposively rational acts and the ability of those consequences to endure in the future (sustainability) must be integrated in the assessment to a greater extent. By these means, social action can be placed on a more rational basis and the public capacity for management increased.

From these considerations, the *conclusion* may be drawn that *evaluation has never been as necessary as it is today*. Evaluation does not merely support faith in progress by simply *comparing the targets and achievements* of the desired objectives with actual statuses. By also focusing especially on *side effects and unintended impacts* in its analyses, it detaches itself from a purely technocratic view of things, questioning progress itself. Only with a *holistic perspective* and a *comprehensive impact approach* can it pay heed to the sustainability of the solutions implemented.

1.1.1 Purposes

From the previous remarks, it becomes clear that evaluation can be carried on (1) in the service of *social enlightenment*. In this case it is primarily a question of assessing political strategies, programmes and measures with the instrument of evaluation to see whether or not they make a contribution to solving social problems. Creating transparency as regards the objectives and impacts of such strategies and measures enables assessments to be made on a rational basis. For example, by disclosing which political objectives are being achieved and which neglected, who benefits from such measures and who does not, which problems are solved and what risks are associated with solving them, evaluation can trigger public discussion. By doing so, it opens up the possibility '[of helping] society shape its own future in a qualified way through systematic, data-based feed-back. A society which seeks evaluation is one which prefers rational thought and critical inquiry to tradition, ideology, and prejudice' (Dahler-Larsen 2006: 143).

Be that as it may, evaluation must render its *assessment criteria transparent* in order not to be exposed to accusations along the lines of only having adopted the perspective of the political elites and decision-makers. Evaluation findings should be discussed in the *public sphere*, i.e. the central institution in which modern societies guarantee the exchange between the state and its citizens. Making evaluation findings accessible to the general public stimulates the debate about social problems and the political solutions proposed for them. Only if the assessment criteria are identified can evaluation promote an objective discourse, defuse ideologically motivated conflicts and contribute by means of solution-oriented recommendations to a consensus-oriented conclusion (cf. also Section 6.2).

Evaluation findings are always *assessive judgements*. It is not until the criteria applied have been disclosed that the rationale can be seen in the judgements made in an evaluation; only then does the possibility manifest itself of arriving at other assessments by applying other criteria. It is not the findings of an evaluation, based on systematically gathered data on specified aspects, that represent a *subjective value judgement*, but rather the assessment criteria stipulated in advance, and at the end of the day that judgement cannot be objectified. As long as the assessment criteria on which findings are based are made transparent in the relevant public discourse, evaluation contributes to separating these interest-guided value judgements from the objective realm of facts, thus making them accessible to social discussion.

By observing and assessing public action and rendering it transparent with the aid of its concepts and procedures, evaluation assumes a social enlightenment function which is similar to that of journalism. Eleanor Chelimsky (2006: 33), for many years director of the Institute for Program Evaluation at the U.S. General Accounting Office (now known as the Government Accountability Office) and thus familiar with the system of politics and evaluation from the inside, characterizes the special merit of evaluation thus: 'its spirit of scepticism and willingness to embrace dissent help keep the government honest'. By disseminating evaluation findings, it enhances the degree to which the public is kept informed about government action, but also about the activities of *civil society* with its many different non-government organizations (NGOs). It is only through the independent examination of the effectiveness and problem-solving competence of government programmes and measures that civil society is empowered to express competent criticism and to elaborate alternative proposals for solutions (cf. also Section 6.2).

Evaluation is not only part of society's control of the state, but also (2) an essential element of *democratic governance*. Evaluation is used on the one hand by *legislatures*, having been made compulsory in laws and ordinances for certain purposes and accordingly having to be implemented by the executive agencies. In other words the legislators use evaluation as a means of keeping an eye on the impacts of executive measures and thus of enabling themselves to make objective judgements in further developing legal framework conditions in parliaments and their subordinate (e.g. specialist) committees. Both the juridically fixed framework conditions, i.e. the extent of the obligation to evaluate, and the scope and type of the prescribed evaluations vary from country to country and are subject to change over time. This will be looked at more closely in the section that follows about the historical development of evaluation research. In general it can be said that in the last twenty years in particular there has, in all modern societies, been a clear increase in the number of public evaluation assignments and the degree to which they are binding.

Not only the *legislatures* however, but also the *executives*, in other words governments and their ministries and public administrations, are using evaluation more now. If these public institutions use evaluation to prove that they are achieving their set objectives (effectiveness), what impacts (including the unintended ones) have been triggered, what the ratio of cost to benefit is (efficiency) etc., the *credibility and legitimacy of policy* can be improved. If clear and logical reasons can be provided as to why certain programmes are being discontinued, cut or expanded, the acceptance of decisions, or at least people's understanding of them, increases. At the same time, the disclosure of the difficulties associated with political measures and a knowledge of correlations and the impacts caused by political strategies also promote the readiness of civil society to take part actively in solving these problems and support the government with contributions of their own for the good of all.

However, a prerequisite for this is that evaluation findings be used as a rational basis for political decisions. Donald Campbell (1969) picked up on this idea in his concept of the *'experimenting society'*, in which a kind of 'work sharing' between evaluation and political decision-making is propagated. According to that concept, the rational knowledge gained in evaluations should be translated directly and quasi-automatically into political decisions. This form of link between evaluation and politics has been harshly criticized as a reduction of political issues to technical ones and referred to as 'social engineering'. Not only that, but studies showed early on 'that the official political machinery did not actually behave according to the assumed rationalistic model' (Dahler-Larsen 2006: 143). The use of evaluation findings is a complex social and political process, which should be further rationalized in organizations for example by the introduction of knowledge management systems (cf. for example Becerra-Fernandez & Leidner 2008; Haun 2005; Amelingmeyer 2004; Götz & Schmid 2004a, b; Winkler 2004; Willke 2004; Ipe 2003; Alvesson & Karreman 2001 for an overview). Conducting evaluations is without doubt not adequate sufficient condition for *rational politics*, but it is at least a necessary one: unless the results achieved by governmental and administrative action are disclosed, it is very difficult indeed to form a democratic opinion on the basis of assessments which are really rational.

Evaluation can make a contribution not only to social enlightenment and to strengthening democratic participation and governance, but also (3) to improving the *manageability* of individual measures, programmes, organizations or even entire policy networks. The integration of evaluation into project management, for example by 'logic models' and the concept of 'project cycle management', already has a certain tradition in the modern industrial countries. In the past two decades, during the introduction of new management models in new public management and the establishment of far-reaching quality management models, evaluations have advanced increasingly to become an integral part of organizational structure and culture and of the work processes in organizations. Lastly, network management concepts have been under discussion for several years. Through the active involvement of civil society actors, these seek to establish a kind of 'institutional control' ('governance') as a complement to or perhaps even a replacement for government action.

Since evaluation can be organizationally integrated into *'feed-back' loops,* acquired knowledge, for example about the development and effectiveness of programmes, has again and again had an influence on its management. That knowledge can consistently support programme control in all phases of the political process and thus open up the potential for learning (see Chapter 2 for a detailed explanation). Thus the readiness and ability to integrate evaluation into the management structures of an organization have meanwhile become characteristics of modern organizations 'and a key to legitimacy, status, recognition, and sometimes funding' (Dahler-Larsen 2006: 147).

In Figure 1.1 the *three main purposes of evaluation* are presented again in an overview. It becomes clear that the three fields of deployment are closely connected.

These three perspectives are not to be understood as exclusive, but they do reflect different opinions and philosophies, some of which lead into fundamental discussions. Whether the point of evaluation is to be seen as the generation of knowledge, the further development of institutions or the maximization of the impacts of public programmes remains a matter of debate between evaluators (cf. Chelimsky 2006: 33f.). Here, the view is taken that evaluation by no means serves only a single purpose, but rather a variety of objectives, subsumed here under the three aspects of *democratic enlightenment, procurement of legitimacy* for policies and *control* of politics (by means of programmes, projects and measures). This close connection between evaluation and politics is not without its problems, as we shall see.

1.1.2   Institutionalization of evaluation

In order for evaluation to be able to develop its functions as an instrument of enlightenment, legitimacy and control, evaluation capacities

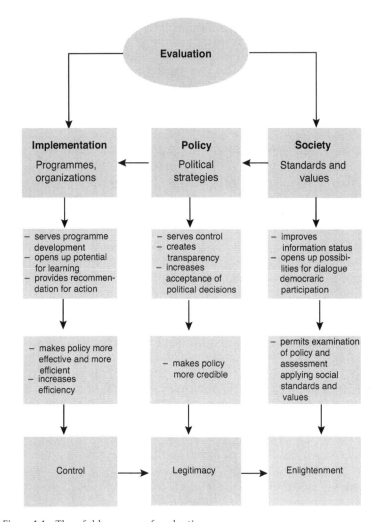

Figure 1.1   Threefold purpose of evaluation

are necessary in various fields: (1) to do justice to their enlightenment function, evaluation capacities need to be established *in society* such as can act as independently as possible of clients and entities which administer funding. In some countries (e.g. Sweden, the Netherlands, Great Britain, the USA) *General Accounting Offices* have undertaken these tasks. In accordance with Article 114 of the *Grundgesetz*,[1] the brief of the

German Federal Court of Auditors is to 'audit the account and determine whether public finances have been properly and efficiently administered'. Comprehensive evaluations, which investigate the effectiveness or even the sustainability of political strategies, are not among its original tasks. Meanwhile in Germany a number of independent institutions have come into being, and they are active in certain policy fields, e.g. the Institute for Quality in Schools in the Federal States of Berlin and Brandenburg[2] or the Institute for Research Information and Quality Assurance.[3] The idea of founding an international 'impact evaluation club' of the main donor countries in development cooperation in order to examine their effectiveness is also to be placed in this category.[4]

Evaluation capacities are also necessary at *political control level*, so that governments and their subordinate authorities can examine the implementation of their own strategies and policies and accompany them evaluatively. Evaluations can – as has been explained – serve not only (2) to *increase political legitimacy*, but also (3) to *improve control potential*, in order to make the work of implementing organizations and programme managers more efficient and more effective. This is a challenge not only for the government sector, but also, in view of its increasing involvement in policy networks, for the non-profit sector as a whole. Non-profit organizations in particular, which work with private donations, ought to have a particular interest in making full use of their control potential and proving, by means of evaluations, that they are doing effective work and that the donations they have received have been well invested (cf. Chapter 6 on the problems of evaluation in civil society organizations).

Recently, not only government institutions (e.g. ministries, authorities and administrative institutions of all kinds) but also private non-profit organizations (e.g. foundations, associations, clubs and relief organizations) have been seen using control and quality assurance instruments which were originally developed in the corporate sector of for-profit organizations. Whilst some instruments such as financial controlling can be transposed relatively easily, others run into great difficulties when used in non-profit organizations (cf. Stockmann 2006; Kuhlmann et al. 2004 for a summary). This is, as will be shown in Chapter 6, mainly because of the situative and organizational differences between for-profit and non-profit organizations (including government institutions). As these new management concepts become established, the non-profit sector is the very place where evaluation is becoming an indispensable instrument, providing and assessing the data necessary for management decisions.

In order to be able to fulfil these management tasks, both *internal evaluation capacities*, also present in the funding and implementing organizations, and *external evaluation capacities*, in the form of scientific institutes, private companies and individual experts, are necessary.

External evaluation capacities tend to be used more for independent analysis in the service of social enlightenment and democratic legitimation, whilst both internal and external evaluation capacities can be deployed for programme control. The advantages and disadvantages of internal and external evaluation will be covered in Chapter 6.

The *multi-functional use* of evaluation capacities makes it clear that there is no perfect mapping to the evaluation purposes defined here. External evaluation institutions can be called upon for all three purposes. The general view is that the more independent they are, the more credible their contribution to social enlightenment, democratic procurement of legitimacy and programme control will be. Internal evaluation institutions seldom contribute to social enlightenment – though courts of auditors can do so – and they are, on account of their restricted credibility, but little used in the portrayal of the legitimacy of government or non-government organizations which implement programmes; instead, they mainly serve the internal control of projects and programmes and sometimes also of policies, and the shaping of organizational quality and knowledge management (Figure 1.2).

1.2   Historical development of evaluation

As has already become apparent, evaluation is not only closely linked to politics and its institutions, but also, and to an even greater extent, *policy-driven*. This is made particularly clear by a look at its historical development.

Depending on how far back that look goes, various different roots of evaluation will appear. When all is said and done, it could be claimed that evaluation is as old as the world itself. The story of the creation, no less, tells of its use. When God created the earth, the light in the darkness, the firmament in the midst of the waters, the plants, the animals and finally man, we are told that at the end of the fifth day '...God saw everything that he had made, and, behold, it was very good' (Genesis 1, 31). He presumably applied criteria – unknown to us – and compared them with his impressions so as to arrive at an assessment and finally make a momentous decision, namely that of not scrapping it all and starting over.

Human attempts to find out which plants and animals are edible, which tools are best used for given activities, how welfare can be

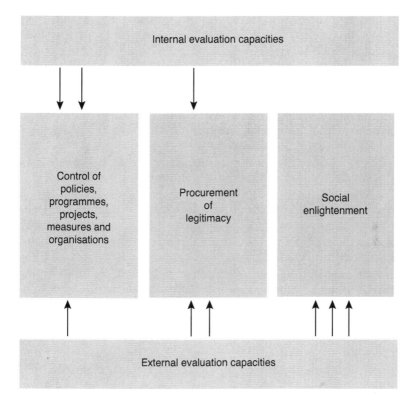

Figure 1.2   Relationship between evaluation purposes and capacities

augmented by farming etc., had evaluative – which at this point does not mean anything more than assessive – components. Empirical *data* are gathered and assessed according to certain *criteria*, and *decisions* then made, building upon them.

If however evaluation is not viewed as a commonplace process but a *systematic procedure* that follows certain *scientifically prescribed rules*, it is a relatively modern phenomenon closely connected with the development of the social sciences and with the political interests of those in government.

1.2.1   Development in the USA

The origins of evaluation in the USA can be traced back to early reform endeavours in the *19th century*, in which the government appointed external inspectors to evaluate publicly financed programmes in areas such as education and health or criminal justice (cf. Chelimsky 2006;

Mertens 2006; Fitzpatrick, Sanders & Worthen 2012; Madaus & Stufflebeam 2002). The investigations centred mainly on the effectiveness of these programmes. However, the real starting-point of 'modern' evaluations is depicted by most authors as being the evaluation of reform programmes to cut unemployment and improve social security in the context of the 'New Deal' in the *1930s and 1940s* (cf. Deutscher & Ostrander 1985: 17f.). The influential Western Electric study (at the Hawthorne Works) on the psychological and social consequences of technological innovations is also to be included here (Roethlisberger & Dickson 1934).

During the *Second World War* the U.S. Army attempted to take advantage of applied social research. Commissioned by the army, Stouffer and his colleagues (Stouffer et al. 1949) developed instruments for the continual measurement of mood among the troops and for the evaluation of certain measures in the area of staffing and propaganda (cf. Rossi et al. 1988: 5). However, studies from the early post-war period in particular are regarded as scientific pioneering works in evaluation research, for example Lewin's (1951) field studies and the work of Lippitt and White on democratic and authoritarian leadership styles (Lippitt 1940; White & Lippitt 1953).

The real boom in evaluation research began in the USA at the start of the *1960s* in the wake of comprehensive social, education, health, nutrition and infrastructure programmes. From the beginning, these were linked to the assignment of examining the impacts of these programmes. In the majority of cases, indeed, the evaluations were prescribed by law and special budget funds made available for them. The best known among them are the welfare and reform programmes of the Democrat presidents John F. Kennedy (1961–1963) and Lyndon B. Johnson (1963–1969). With the aid of the 'war on poverty', attempts were made to turn the idea of a 'great society' into reality. According to Hellstern and Wollmann (1984: 27), evaluation research was to be a witness, an instrument of justification and a stimulator for those policies.

With the *Economic Opportunity Act* of 1964, independent of the government ministries, an Office of Economic Opportunity was founded for the administration and financing of programmes such as Head Start (a pre-school programme for children from low-income families), Job Corps (a vocational training programme for young unemployed people), Manpower Training (vocational training), and health and legal services (legal advice). The 'Community Action Program' in particular attained great significance, being intended not only to relieve the material hardships of the population, but also to introduce new forms of democracy and participation at communal level (cf. Lachenmann 1977: 31).

Another important result during that period which had significant effects on the institutional development of evaluation was the passing of the *Elementary and Secondary Education Act* (ESEA) in 1965. The act provided for a tremendous accumulation of funds in the field of education, with the awarding of those funds being explicitly tied to the conducting of evaluations (cf. Fitzpatrick, Sanders & Worthen 2012: 44f.).

In the context of this legislative procedure, for example, *Head Start* became one of the best known, most intensively evaluated and most controversial socio-political programmes in the USA. About 7.5 million children took part in the programme, which was carried out between 1965 and 1980. More than 50 major evaluations were conducted and some 800 magazine articles published. By the time the first results were available, President Richard M. Nixon (1969–1974) was already in office, and he was determined to make major cuts to funds for reform programmes. The evaluation findings, hardly in a position yet to prove that the pre-school programme was having an effect, were thus exactly what he wanted to hear. The negative test results set off a further wave of evaluations and a wide-ranging methods discussion (cf. Hellstern & Wollmann 1984: 29ff.).

One very significant impulse for evaluation research emanated from the institution of a planning, programming and budgeting system, or PPBS, which was introduced in the Ministry of Defense by Robert McNamara and extended under President Johnson in 1965 to cover the entire government machinery and all the ministries. Wittmann (1985: 5) and Deutscher and Ostrander (1985: 18) see the introduction of the PPBS as a milestone in evaluation history: 'This concept and McNamara's influence are crucial to the history of evaluation research'. The PPBS was a variant of the then popular systemic (management) approaches, which aimed to improve system effectiveness and efficiency and fund allocation by linking explicitly defined organizational objectives to output and input parameters. These approaches, originally used by major industrial companies, were thus regarded as applicable to the public sector too. However, there were few advocates there, so under President Nixon a large part of the system was abandoned again in 1971.

Thanks to the reform programmes, a major *order market* arose, and it was one from which evaluation research benefited greatly. It is estimated that in 1976 $600m was already being spent on the evaluation of social service programmes (cf. Wittmann 1985: 9). The 'evaluation business' became a growth industry. Engagement opportunities for evaluators arose in numerous evaluation projects in a great variety of social areas, both in government institutions and in a large number of regional and local projects and organizations (cf. Fitzpatrick, Sanders & Worthen 2012; Madaus & Stufflebeam 2000).

As a reaction to the demand which had thus come about, a number of specialized *study programmes* sprang up in the university sector in areas such as 'educational research and evaluation', 'public administration' and 'policy analysis'. A dramatic general increase in the number of students who completed social science study courses was recorded along with this phase. For example between 1960 and 1970 the number of doctorates in economics, education, political science, psychology and sociology increased more than fourfold, with many of the graduates embarking on professional careers as evaluators in the public and non-profit sectors (cf. Shadish et al. 1991).

Numerous authors see the period from the *1970s to the mid-1980s* as the 'age of professionalization' (Madaus & Stufflebeam 2000: 14ff.). The following are cited as *essential features of professionalization:*

- the abovementioned major growth in demand for evaluation in the public sector
- the expansion of study courses with evaluation content which followed as a reaction to this
- the emergence of an independent evaluation literature, which particularly also developed theoretical-methodological approaches and models (cf. Chapter 3)
- the establishment of specialized professional organizations and networks.[5]

While this process of professionalization was still going on, the evaluation market changed dramatically. This change was sparked off by *criticism of social reform programmes,* already aired in the 1970s, but more so in the 1980s – and especially under the Reagan government. Funds for innovative model projects were reduced, but this did not detract from the importance of evaluation research. It was just that its focal point shifted. Increasingly, interest came to be focused on the cost-benefit ratios, management efficiency and accountability. Thus for example so-called 'sunset legislation' was passed, providing for automatic termination of programmes if proof of their effectiveness could not be provided within a specific period of time (cf. Rossi et al. 1988: 6).

In many areas, growth was thus recorded in the evaluation sector even in the Reagan era. Although most governmental and communal institutions did not occupy themselves with the subject until statutory regulations forced them to do so, a certain esteem for evaluation as an important means of planning and control did gradually develop among many of them.

A number of institutions, foundations, enterprises and even churches adopted evaluation as a routine instrument in their programme planning. Such programmes as were not publicly funded and in which there were no compulsory regulations whatsoever with regard to evaluation were among the ones affected by this. Engagement opportunities for evaluators in the USA thus became still more firmly established (cf. Fitzpatrick, Sanders & Worthen 2012: 51f.).

With the *Government Performance and Results Act* the role of evaluation research was yet again strengthened considerably. Mertens (2006: 55) says that this law, enacted in 1993 by Congress, 'shifted the focus of federal management and decision-making away from preoccupation with the activities that are undertaken under the auspices of federal funding to a focus on the results of those activities'. The GPRA[6] prescribes binding strategic plans designed to run for several years and annual performance plans and reports for the respective executive government institutions. The plans, each designed to run for at least five years, are to include mission statements of the respective institutions, general objectives and objectives criteria and the strategies for achieving them. These requirements almost inevitably resulted in it being necessary to conduct evaluations in all government institutions and programmes funded by them.

Against the backdrop of this strong institutional anchorage of evaluation in the public sector and its broad diffusion into society and its institutions, evaluation can be seen to have become an integral part of public action in the USA.

1.2.2 Development in Europe

In Europe, 'modern' evaluation research began ten years later than in the USA, at the end of the *1960s*. As in the USA, it gained in significance and profile with the emergence of comprehensive political reform programmes. Sweden, Great Britain and Germany were among the 'frontrunners' (cf. Leeuw 2006: 67).[7] Whilst this first wave of evaluation was powered by neo-Keynesian politics, the development of the welfare state and the improvement of government infrastructure institutions, and was still able to dip into full coffers, government finance bottlenecks began to occur as a result of the oil price increases of 1973 and the worldwide economic recession triggered by them. In the western industrial countries the discussion on the modernization of state and administration revolved increasingly around the problem of budget funding. Neo-liberal and neo-conservative trends propagated a stripping-down of the social and welfare state.

Until the middle of the *1970s,* evaluation research – as it had earlier in the USA – was mainly used to demonstrate the effectiveness of programmes and thus improve the chances of innovative measures being pushed through. Analytical interests and legitimational intentions often ran together. As from the middle of the 1970s – again as in the USA – cost-benefit considerations began to take on more significance and the administrators hoped that evaluations would provide rational aids to decision-making and aids to the prioritization and selection of programmes. Great hopes were invested in evaluation research:

> *The public* and *parliament* hoped to achieve improved control of government measures, taking into account side and follow-up effects; evaluation gave the *administration* chances of intervening, to improve the accuracy of the programmes and the efficiency of the measures and reduce costs; for *science,* this heralded not only the gain of additional resources, but also the possibility of an experimental test of its theories. (Hellstern & Wollmann 1984: 23)[8]

Under the heading *'new public management',* the reform and modernization debate took on new contours, at first in the Netherlands, Britain and in the Scandinavian countries, and brought about a revival of evaluation (cf. Wollmann 1994: 99). This was not a coherent concept, but rather a batch of organizational and procedural principles, the intention of which was mainly to achieve a reduction in state functions (particularly by privatization), a decrease in government regulation density (deregulation) and an increase in administrative efficiency (internal economies, value for money) via management reforms of inner structures and the introduction of competition. In principle it was a matter of imposing the private-enterprise company and market model, oriented toward economic rationality, on the public sector (cf. Schröter & Wollmann 1998: 59ff.). In this context, evaluation especially takes on the role of examining the efficiency of governmental measures.

Another essential factor that influenced the development of evaluation research is to be seen in *progressive European integration,* which led not only to the expansion of an administrative regime upon which there was a determining European influence (cf. Kohler-Koch 1991: 47ff.), but also to the initiation of a large number of very diverse programmes. This confronted evaluation research, which is mainly nationally organized, with some major challenges. Meanwhile it can be seen that 'In a variety of sectors – most notably for the EC Structural Funds – evaluation has been made legally or conventionally mandatory' (Pollitt 1998: 214). In general, the *European Union* has proved to be a major driving force behind evaluation in Europe (cf. Summa & Toulemonde 2002; Leeuw 2006 and others). As early as the 1980s, programmes funded by the European Community were being evaluated. An investigation carried out by Sensi and Cracknell (1991) shows that in the majority of the directorates-general of the European Commission at least rudimentary evaluation procedures were used, especially in development cooperation policy, research and technology policy and regional structural policy. The evaluation units in the Commission saw their work above all as useful for improving the efficiency of EC measures, and not so much as instruments of control for the Council or Parliament. Be that as it may, many experts see the pressure exerted by the Council as a major reason for the rapid development of the directorates-general of the Commission.

Leeuw (2006: 72) points out that a *new evaluation schema* was introduced in the mid-1990s, which combines an ongoing system of annual monitoring procedures and periodic five-year assessments of all research programmes and funding as a whole: 'These assessments can be understood as a combination of an ex-post evaluation of the previous program, an intermediate evaluation of the current program and an ex-ante appraisal of future activities' (ibid.). The advantages of this new system are perceived mainly as being the more prompt determination of programme developments and thus also improved possibilities for control. Having said that, some of the most influential EU measures have no programmatic character at all and are equipped with only modest funding, being mainly of a regulatory nature, as for example for market regulation, or consumer or environmental protection. Although in these areas too evaluations have been conducted again and again, Leeuw (2006: 72) says that 'EU institutions are not equipped with a formal evaluation system nor even with a database that would record the amount of work undertaken within the various Directorates General'.

With the *territorial expansion of the EU* in the 1990s and the enlargement of the EU budget (from 0.8 per cent of the GNP of the member states in 1980 to 1.2 per cent in 1993), the scope of the funding programmes also grew powerfully. At the same time, however, scepticism regarding the effectiveness and efficiency of such programmes increased in the member states. According to Leeuw (2006: 73), the European Parliament and the European Court of Auditors also played an important part 'in pushing the Commission to account better for what it spends'. It may also be that the admission to the EU of some Scandinavian countries, in which there was already a tradition of controlling and results-oriented public management, supported the will to reform.

From the middle of the 1990s, the so-called *Santer Commission* succeeded in introducing far-reaching reforms with a view to the planning and control of EU measures. One initiative, which related to the areas of finances and accountability, became known under the name of 'Sound and Efficient Management' (SEM 2000), whilst another, which occupied itself with internal administrative structures, went under the title 'Modernization of Administration and Personnel Services' (MAP 2000).

More systematic, prompt and rigorous evaluations were identified as one of the priority requirements for the improvement of internal finance structures. In this call for more systematic programme evaluations it was also possible to refer to Article 205 of the Maastricht Treaty, which requires that 'the Commission shall implement the budget (...) having regard to the principles of sound financial management' (Council of the European Community, 1992). This principle is explained in more detail in the financial regulations covering the Community budget. There, attention is drawn to the fact that the findings of programme evaluations should be taken into account in budget allocations, and that all proposed measures which affect the budget should be preceded by evaluations with estimates of their efficiency.

At the administrational level, a *decentralized model* was introduced to improve the practice of evaluation, according to which the operative directorates-general themselves are responsible for the development and use of systematic evaluation procedures regarding their respective programmes. The evaluation procedures used are explicitly not subject to any standardized specifications in terms of their shape, so that they can be adapted to suit the requirements of the evaluand in question. The Directorate-General for Financial Affairs took on the task of promoting and monitoring the dissemination of 'best practices', improving evaluation techniques and exercising general quality control.

1.2.3   Development in Germany

The development of evaluation in Germany was swept along and influenced by the abovementioned international and European currents. Having said that, a number of *national framework conditions* have also shaped it.

Following a *phase of 'institutional restoration'* (Alber 1989: 60) in the 1950s, the pressure increased considerably in the FRG during the 1960s. The so-called *bildungskatastrophe*,[9] a generally noticeable 'reform backlog' and concern about international economic competitiveness led to a broad social consensus to the effect that far-reaching reforms were necessary. The grand coalition of CDU/CSU and SPD (1966–1969) introduced a number of projects, which were then elevated to become elements of a government programme in the social-liberal coalition under Chancellor Willy Brandt (1969–1974) as part of an internal reform policy. A comprehensive modernization of state and administration was striven toward, based on the idea that 'the state should function as a central social control authority, pursue "active politics" and shape society by planning for the long term' (Mayntz 1997: 68). Particularly from the *introduction of new planning procedures,* it was expected that the ability of the state to act and shape would be extended, with evaluation being used as an important analytical instrument. Evaluation in Germany enjoyed an early heyday. Not only the institutions of the nation-state, but also the *länder* and municipalities were caught up in the zeal of reform and used evaluation as an instrument of management and control (cf. Wollmann 1994, 1998, 1999; Derlien 1976, 1990, 1994). Particularly in the areas of education, urban renewal and infrastructure, elaborate, large-scale evaluation studies were conducted.

The ministries mainly had recourse to *external evaluations,* for most of which public invitations to tender were issued. In most cases in-house evaluation capacities were not created. One of the few exceptions was the still young Federal Ministry for Economic Cooperation and Development, which set up an evaluation department of its own as early as 1972 (cf. Stockmann 2006b: 378ff.). The chancellery failed in its attempt 'to use evaluation as its analytical muscle for co-ordinating (and possibly controlling) the ministries "sectoral policies"' (Wollmann 1997: 4). So it was that the individual ministries remained relatively independent of one another, conducting their evaluations in a sector-specific way and geared specially to their own specific requirements and ideas.

The evaluation boom was supported by the *budget reform of 1970.* In the provisional administrative provisions (VV) covering §7 of the Federal Budgetary Regulations (BHO), performance reviews were expressly prescribed for wholly or partly completed measures. No. 1.3 of the VV-BHO stipulates that

1.3 By way of a performance review (measurement of results), the following in particular should be investigated.

1.3.1 During the implementation of measures lasting more than one year at least once annually, whether or not the interim results are according to plan, whether the plan needs to be adjusted and whether the measures are to be continued or discontinued.

1.3.2 Following the implementation of measures, whether or not the
result achieved corresponds to the original or adjusted plan,
whether or not the measures need to be revised and whether or
not empirical values can be secured. (Federal Court of Auditors
1989: 13 and Appendix 1: 49ff.)

Within a few years an evaluation market had grown in which the
universities were also participating, but it was, above all, dominated
by a rapidly expanding consulting economy. Hellmut Wollmann
(1997: 4) can be quoted on this, not only as a scientist, but also as
a contemporary witness: 'Commercial research and consultancy firms
mushroomed and succeeded to produce [sic] the lion's share of the
evaluation research funding'.

But this burgeoning of evaluation in Germany, as in many western
European countries, was brought to an abrupt end by the worldwide
economic and fiscal effects of the increase in oil prices in 1973. As
the *wave of modernization ebbed,* evaluation suffered a loss of importance. That the modernization euphoria wore off is, however, not only
to be attributed to fiscal constraints but also to a gradual disillusionment with reform successes, which were in some cases no more than
modest. Neither was evaluation able in all cases to fulfil the expectations
vested in it. Often, its findings were contradictory and insufficiently
implementation-oriented.

So it was – to cite but one prominent example – that the evaluation
studies carried out between the end of the 1960s and the beginning
of the 1980s at great expense in *pilot projects with integrated comprehensive schools* failed to come up with any clear recommendations. On the
contrary, the 78 individual studies, with regard to their methodological
approaches, their procedures and the data gathering methods used,
turned out to be so heterogeneous that it was not possible to come to a
conclusive verdict as to the effectiveness of the new form of schooling
as compared with the traditional, structured school system (cf. Aurin
& Stolz 1990: 269ff.; Fend 1982). Even if this 'failure' of what was the
costliest evaluation project to date is seen as a consequence of exaggerated expectations, its impact on decision-makers and administrators,
which went far beyond the borders of education research, must not be
underestimated.

In spite of the altered international and national framework conditions (fiscal constraints, strip-down of the welfare state, the emergence
of neo-liberalism and neo-conservatism, reform disillusionment, doubts
about the benefit of evaluations, the 1974 change of leadership in the

social-liberal coalition *['wende* before the *wende'],* the 1982 change of government [liberal-conservative *wende]*) evaluations were able to retain a certain significance. Having said that, the boom triggered off at the end of the 1960s did not by any means continue, let alone reach dimensions like those in the USA.

1.3 The current state of evaluation

1.3.1 International

The international status of evaluation research is strongly influenced by the American motherland not only in theoretical and methodological terms but also with regard to topics and trends. In the USA the highest degree of professionalization worldwide has already been achieved. There are a number of indicators of this. In the USA evaluation is firmly anchored in institutional terms, in legislation, in the implementation of public programmes and in impact assessment. In the American Evaluation Association (AEA), the USA has the association with the most members and certainly also the most influence. The 'Program Evaluation Standards' issued by the AEA in 1989 and revised in 1994, which were developed from the 'Standards for Evaluation of Educational Evaluations', were the force behind a large number of evaluation standards such as have meanwhile been issued by other national associations worldwide (cf. also Section 4.4.3). Other important efforts toward professionalization can be seen in the 'Guiding Principles for Evaluators', issued in 1995, and the lively debate on the possibilities for the certification of evaluators.[10]

The development of theoretical and methodological approaches and models in evaluation research is dominated by American authors. The training market for evaluators is also most well developed in the USA. Fitzpatrick, Sanders and Worthen (2012: 52) point out that 'many peple involved in conducting in-house evaluations have primary professional identifications other than evaluation. ... Expanded training opportunities and creative thinking by those in the evaluation field are needed to help these people develop their evaluation skills'. Training programmes for evaluators have expanded to cover the non-university sector, with many schools, state institutions, companies and different national professional associations offering such courses. There are also practical courses, pre-conference workshops, the Internet, journals and a deluge of practical guides and handbooks.

However, hardly anything is known about the quality of these basic and advanced training courses, since there are no studies on the results of the various forms of training. For this reason the call for such studies is loud: '(...) much more work – is needed in evaluating the outcomes of evaluator training' (Datta 2006: 420). This applies all the more to crash courses, which only last a few days and are supposed to empower programme managers to conduct evaluations themselves; a matter of some urgency, in view of the sharply rising importance of evaluations conducted 'in-house' by non-experts (cf. Datta 2006: 429).

Furubo, Rist and Sandahl (2002: 7ff.) made an attempt to characterize the evaluation culture of selected countries. They applied nine criteria, which do not, astonishing as it may seem, include capacities for basic and advanced training in the respective countries! In their ranking-list, only the USA achieves the maximum possible number of points. Canada, Australia, Sweden, the Netherlands and Great Britain follow. Even if their methodological procedure certainly does lay itself open to criticism,[11] the list compiled by these authors not only underlines the position of the USA at the head of the field, but also makes it clear that many countries are trying to establish an evaluation culture and have meanwhile initiated appropriate steps toward professionalization.

In Europe, professionalization in individual countries has progressed to very different degrees. Sweden, the Netherlands, Great Britain, Germany, Denmark, Norway, France and Finland are among those which Furubo, Rist and Sandahl (2002: 10) award a high or middling place on the ranking-list with regard to the degree of their evaluation culture. These positions have changed dramatically during the last ten years: Speer, Jacob and Furubo (2013) published most recently an update of this table, using the same criteria for the same group of countries. Finland and Switzerland are now on the top of the ranking-list, while the USA, Canada, Australia and Sweden slightly lost ground. In general, a dramatic increase can be recognized for most countries, especially those who were behind the others ten years ago (Japan, Israel, New Zealand, Spain and Italy). Stagnations characterize the situation in the leading European countries (UK, the Netherlands and Germany) and the gap between the pioneers and the rest has been closed during the last decade. Especially the two most important forerunners in Europe, Sweden and Germany, have dropped to being average (cf. Figure 1.3).

In general, but particularly in Europe, a *high degree of dynamism* with regard to the development of professionalization has made itself felt in the last two decades. As has already been shown, the European Commission and its individual departments are the strongest forces working towards the expansion and standardization of evaluation in the individual countries of Europe. Countries in which there has so far been no evaluation culture whatsoever must also gradually establish evaluation capacities in order to be able to meet the evaluation specifications tied to the implementation of EU programmes.

The current state of evaluation in the EU shows that the reform measures introduced by the *Santer Commission* in the mid-1990s have taken effect. A review carried out in 1999 came to the conclusion that the current evaluation systems (1) were fairly helpful for programme control and that they had (2) led to a certain extent to improved accountability, as seen in the increasing number of evaluation reports and an annual evaluation review. By contrast, the (3) objective associated with the newly introduced evaluation system, i.e. that of supporting budget decisions and resource allocation, had only been achieved with a modest degree of success.

A study carried out by the Directorate-General for the Budget[12] in 2005 reveals further positive trends. It emphasizes that 'evaluations have provided substantial input for policy-making both in formally established ways (...) and through ad-hoc procedures designed to take advantage of conclusions and recommendations (...)'. According to this study, evaluations have even greater significance with a view to shaping new interventions and controlling implementation processes in projects which are already running. Not only that, but some indications have also been found which show that evaluations are also used in allocation decisions. By contrast, 'accountability and awareness-raising' hardly play a role worth mentioning in EU evaluations.[13]

As a glance at the 'annual evaluation reviews' of the Directorate-General for the Budget shows, evaluations are meanwhile conducted in almost all areas of EU policy (www.ec.europa.eu/budget/evaluation). The number of evaluations has also increased considerably. In the three-year period from 1996 to 1998 the evaluation project count was 198, whilst there were almost three times as many (549) in the period from 2004 to 2006. In the last ten years mainly ex-post (approx. 40 per cent) and interim evaluations (approx. 40 per cent) have been conducted, with the share of ex-ante evaluations being far lower (approx. 20 per cent). Having said that, the importance of prospective (ex-ante) evaluations has recently risen considerably.

Internal evaluations conducted by the departments of the Commission are rather more the exception than the rule. The vast majority are awarded to external experts. Fault is sometimes found in subsequent reviews with the quality of the evaluation reports.

Summing up, it should be noted that both for most European countries and for the EU institutions there has been a clear increase in policy

	I		II		III		IV		V		VI		VII		VIII		IX		2002	R	2012	R	Trend
	02	12	02	12	02	12	02	12	02	12	02	12	02	12	02	12	02	12					
Finland	2	2	1	2	1	2	1	2	1	2	1	1	1	2	1	2	1	2	10	12	17	1	+++
Switzerland	1	2	1	1	2	2	2	2	0	1	0	2	2	2	0	2	0	2	8	14	16	2	+++
Canada	2	2	2	2	2	2	2	2	2	2	1	1	2	2	2	2	2	2	17	2	16	3	-
United States	2	2	2	2	2	2	2	2	2	2	2	1	2	2	2	2	2	2	18	1	16	4	- -
United Kingdom	2	2	2	2	2	2	2	2	1	2	1	1	2	2	1	2	2	1	15	6	15	5	=
Netherlands	2	2	2	2	2	2	1	2	2	2	1	2	2	2	2	2	1	1	15	5	15	6	=
Korea	1	2	1	2	2	2	2	2	2	2	0	2	2	2	1	1	1	1	12	9	15	7	++
Sweden	2	2	2	2	2	2	1	2	2	2	1	1	2	2	2	2	2	2	16	4	15	8	-
Denmark	2	2	2	2	2	2	1	2	1	1	0	1	2	2	1	2	1	1	12	8	14	9	++
Australia	2	1	2	2	2	2	2	2	1	1	1	1	2	2	2	2	2	2	16	3	14	10	- -
Norway	2	2	1	2	1	1	1	2	2	1	1	1	1	2	2	2	1	1	12	10	14	11	++
Germany	2	1	2	2	1	2	2	2	1	1	1	1	2	2	1	1	1	2	13	7	13	12	=
France	2	2	1	1	1	2	2	1	2	1	1	0	0	1	1	1	0	1	11	11	13	13	++
Japan	1	2	0	2	0	1	1	2	1	2	0	0	0	2	0	1	0	1	3	19	13	14	+++
Israel	1	1	1	2	1	1	2	2	1	1	0	1	1	2	1	1	1	1	9	13	12	15	+++
NewZealand	1	1	0	1	1	1	2	2	0	1	0	1	1	1	1	1	1	1	7	15	12	16	+++
Spain	1	1	0	2	1	1	2	2	1	1	0	1	0	1	0	0	0	1	5	18	11	17	+++
Italy	1	2	1	2	1	1	2	1	0	1	0	1	1	1	1	0	0	1	7	17	11	18	+++
Ireland	1	1	1	1	1	2	0	1	1	1	0	0	1	1	1	1	1	1	7	16	9	19	++
China	1	1	1	1	1	0	0	0	2	1	0	0	1	0	0	1	1	0	6		-		
Zimbabwe	1		1				0	0	1		0		0		1		0		4		-		

	I		II		III		IV		V		VI		VII		VIII		IX		2002	R	2012	R	Trend
	02	12	02	12	02	12	02	12	02	12	02	12	02	12	02	12	02	12					
Total	30	32	24	35	027	32	30	36	23	27	11	20	27	33	22	27	19	26	223	11	261	14	+++
Mean	1,6	1,7	1,3	1,8	1,4	1,5	1,6	1,8	1,2	1,5	0,6	1,0	1,4	1,7	1,2	1,4	1,0	1,4					

I   Evaluation takes place in many policy domains
II Supply of domestic evaluators in different disciplines
III National discourse concerning evaluation
IV Professional organizations
V Degree of institutionalzation – government
VI Degree of institutionalzation – parliament
VII Pluralism of institutions or evaluators performing evaluations within each policy domain
VIII Evaluation within the Supreme Audit Institution
IX Proprtion of outcome evaluations in relation to output and process evaluations
R Ranking

Figure 1.3 Ranking of countries on Evaluation Culture 2002 and 2012

Source: Furubo,Rist & Sandahal (2002: 10); Speer, Jacob & Furubo (2013)

and programme evaluations, that a large number of attempts to professionalize evaluation can be recognized, and that an 'evaluation culture' is spreading, a fact which led Christopher Pollitt (1998: 214) to say that 'these are grand days for European evaluators'.

This statement does not apply to Europe alone. With the aid of a number of observations (indicators) it can be shown that the importance of evaluation is on the rise *worldwide* (cf. Meyer 2002: 333ff.; Furubo, Rist & Sandahl 2002; Fitzpatrick, Sanders & Worthen 2012: 490ff.; Dahler-Larsen 2006: 141ff.):

(1) In many countries, evaluation is a fixed element in policy-shaping and a management control element in international organizations, national governments and their administrations and a wide range of non-profit organizations. Evaluation is also often a part of quality management or other procedures such as auditing, inspection, benchmarking etc. Datta (2006: 420) points out that 'scientific-research-based programs and evaluations', 'evidence-based resource allocation', 'program logic models', and similar terms of our trade have become widely institutionalized for all manner of programs'.

(2) The number of national evaluation societies has grown considerably in recent years. According to a worldwide Internet search by Dahler-Larsen (2006: 142),[14] the number of evaluation societies increased tenfold to 83 between 1984 and 2004. The strongest growth in recent years has been in Europe and Africa. The 'International Organisation for Cooperation in Evaluation' (IOCE)[15] was founded with funds from the Kellogg Foundation.[16] The former sees itself as a loose worldwide amalgamation of regional and national evaluation organizations, 'that collaborate to

- build evaluation leadership and capacity in developing countries
- foster the cross-fertilization of evaluation theory and practice around the world
- address international challenges in evaluation and
- assist the evaluation profession to take a more global approach to contributing to the identification and solution of world problems' (www.ioce.net).

(3) The increasing demand has given rise to a *broad demand market* for evaluation, which is continuing to grow (Leeuw, Toulemonde & Brouwers 1999: 487ff.). The number of consulting firms concerned with evaluation has also risen sharply. Small and very small companies are in the majority here. Alongside higher education policy, development

cooperation is probably – and not only in Germany – the policy field most often evaluated, with the evaluation of policies and even more so that of programmes and projects coming from a long tradition and a comprehensive evaluation system having been set up (cf. Borrmann et al. 1999, 2001; Borrmann & Stockmann 2009), and here in particular there are many individual experts. The major social research institutes, auditing companies and corporate consulting firms are only now beginning to discover the market for themselves.

Apart from consulting enterprises, there are a number of research institutions and universities active on the evaluation market that are attempting to combine research, evaluation in the service of the client, basic and advanced training and communication in a fruitful way. According to Frans Leeuw (1999: 487), an 'infant industry' has also arisen in the other European countries, characterized 'by many small companies entering a promising market, over-ambitious terms of reference, and unstable standards'.

(4) Above all thanks to the development of information and communication technologies and that of the World Wide Web, the *dissemination of evaluation findings* has been the subject of a tremendous surge. Even if many organizations still do not make their evaluation studies accessible to the general public, a host of findings from evaluations, audits and inspections are now already available on the Internet. Little is known about the extent to which this knowledge is used by others for shaping their own programmes or planning and conducting evaluations.

What is obvious – at least in Europe – is that the media take precious little notice of evaluation findings presented on the Internet. The fears of many government and non-government organizations that the media could latch on to negative evaluation findings and use them to their disadvantage – leading them to believe they should actually refrain from publishing their evaluation studies, let alone putting them on line – are therefore largely unfounded.

The Federal Ministry for Economic Cooperation and Development (BMZ), for example, trod this path. For decades, the ministry treated its inspection and evaluation reports as if they were top secret, so that not even the members of the parliamentary committee responsible (the Committee for Economic Cooperation [AwZ]) were allowed to look at them. Surprisingly, at the end of the 1990s, when it did finally make the reports accessible on line, the BMZ was forced to recognize that hardly anyone was interested in them, least of all the media.

Having said that, if evaluation findings are picked up on by the media on account of their politically explosive nature (e.g. the Hartz reform) or because the topic happens to be *en vogue* (e.g. PISA), this may often be seen to ' ... have an impact which outweighs all the other efforts an evaluator has made to produce a good, respectable, and useful evaluation' (Dahler-Larsen 2006: 149).

(5) *Training activities offered worldwide* have increased sharply. If in the USA – as has already been shown – there are numerous opportunities for training and advanced training, the range in Europe is also expanding. According to research carried out in 2006 by Wolfgang Beywl and Katja Harich (2007: 121ff.), there are 14 university programmes in ten countries (Belgium, Denmark, Germany, England, France, Ireland, Italy, the Netherlands, Switzerland and Spain), though they do vary greatly with a view to objectives, target groups and duration. The only 'full-value' masters course so far (four semesters, 120 ECTS credits) is the Master of Evaluation course (www.master-evaluation.de)[17] offered by Saarland University in cooperation with the Saarland College of Technology and Economics (HTW).

The World Bank[18] began in 2001 with evaluation training courses for people working in international development cooperation and founded the 'International Development Evaluation Association' (IDEAS)[19] to support evaluation in developing countries. This aid organization, registered in England and with an office in South Africa, has declared its aim as being 'to advance and extend the practice of development evaluation by refining methods, strengthening capacity and expanding ownership' (www.ideas-int.org).

With far more modest pretensions, needless to say, the activities of the Center for Evaluation (CEval)[20] also come into this category. In a university partnership, the CEval is currently not only supporting and further developing the Master of Evaluation study course offered by the Universidad de Costa Rica, but also establishing a Central American further education platform for ministries, authorities and development organizations. Other cooperation schemes with universities in Russia, the Near East and South-East Asia are in the process of being set up and the intention is to promote them in a similar way. In Southern Asia, UNICEF is making efforts to set up a worldwide evaluation network of universities, with the aim of strengthening evaluation training in the greater region. Moreover, with its courses worldwide, the central German basic and advanced training organization In WEnt contributes to boosting evaluation capacities in developing countries. More recently, the German Society for Technical Cooperation (GTZ) and other organizations have also been making increasing efforts to establish evaluation capacities in their partner countries.

These developments, observable worldwide, admit of the conclusion that following the years of expansion in the 1960s and 1970s a *second evaluation boom* can now be seen, though it is far more global in nature. The extent to which this affects Germany will be looked at below.

1.3.2   Germany

A number of clues suggest that the new *evaluation boom* observable worldwide and in the rest of Europe has also reached Germany:

- With the increased use of *'new public management'* concepts, 'the idea of a comprehensive control and management concept, together with the strategic accentuation and integration of the evaluation function, is experiencing a renaissance' (Wollmann 1994: 99, 2005: 502ff.).[21] In particular the orientation toward output and impact associated with this approach cannot manage without evaluation (cf. Stockmann 2008: 57ff.).
- As in other European countries, governments in Germany face notorious *budget problems* which make it necessary to prioritize and select measures more strongly. The need for evaluations has thus also increased so that data on the effectiveness and efficiency of programmes can be gathered. Pollitt (1998: 223) describes the situation of those in government fittingly: '...they can no longer call on the same reserves of legitimacy and authority which were available to them two or three decades ago. They have to do more with less and do it for a variety of more sceptical and less deferential audiences'.
- In laws or important programmes, the instrument of evaluation – other than for example in the USA – has hardly been integrated at all so far. Yet there are exceptions: for example in the German Social Security Code (SGB) II: 'Basic social care for job seekers', §55 (impact research) calls for prompt and regular investigation of the impacts of vocational integration services and services for subsistence maintenance. Even the practice of making laws valid for limited periods only (so-called sunset legislation) has found its way into the legislation of individual *länder* (e.g. Hesse, North Rhine – Westphalia). The extension of the validity of such laws is made dependent on the results they have achieved (impacts).
- Regulatory impact analysis, which in accordance with an agreement among the federal ministries has had to be carried out on each draft of a law or statutory instrument since the year 2000, can also be regarded as a form of evaluation. Regulatory impact analysis can be carried out ex-ante, ongoing or ex-post, in order to investigate

intended and unintended impacts, costs of enforcement, costs for the economy, effects on the budget, prices, consumers and other parameters. Although legally binding specifications do exist, there are some considerable shortcomings in their application (cf. Konzendorf 2009: 33f. on the causes).

- The *Federal Court of Auditors (BRH)* has developed to become one of the most important advocates of evaluation. It not only points with iron steadfastness to the performance reviews prescribed compulsorily in the Federal Budgetary Regulations, but also calls for the extension of public evaluation activities (especially to include examinations of the effectiveness of subsidies) and conducts impact evaluations itself.
- This change in the administrative provisions of the Federal Budgetary Regulations is putting the entities which receive funds from the ministries under increasing pressure to conduct evaluations in the form of performance reviews (cf. Section 1.4).
- As has already been shown, the evaluation obligations associated with the *implementation of EU programmes* are making an appreciable contribution to the spread of evaluation.
- Increasingly, there is a demand among NGOs, associations and foundations for evaluations of their programmes, in particular impact evaluations. This applies above all to organizations from the area of development cooperation.

In spite of all attempts at professionalization, according to Furubo, Rist and Sandahl (2002: 10) there is no well developed evaluation culture in Germany yet, as compared with countries such as the USA, Canada and Sweden. Whilst the expansion of evaluation in the USA not only created a new service market which offers social scientists 'chances to act and opportunities for vocational development on a scale which was previously unknown' (Wottawa & Thierau 1998: 59), but also led to a rapid increase in the amount of evaluation literature and the founding of journals and professional associations, and whilst evaluator training is firmly anchored at the universities, mainly in post-graduate study courses, a comparable development in Germany is only to be seen in its infant stages.

There are a number of impediments which contribute to this:

1) One main problem is the disciplinary segmentation of evaluation research.[22] There continues to be a lack of focus that would span the sectoral policy fields and integrate the various disciplines. Even in the German Evaluation Society, whose internal structure is

based on policy-field-related working-groups, this segmentation is reproduced.

2) In addition to that, evaluation research occupies a special position in science, as it is, to a large extent, obliged to rely on assigned or commissioned research. A university research landscape related to fundamental research is largely lacking.

3) Not only is there disciplinary fragmentation, but also corresponding institutional fragmentation into ministerial departments covering special sectors and fields, which award the majority of the funds for assignments. This is another reason why only very few goals have been able to develop which span more than one policy field.

4) This is exacerbated by the fact that in most policy fields there is a lack of transparency. Many studies and reports are drawn up, but as most of them are not made accessible to the general public (and not to the scientific public either), they do not become the subject of scientific discussion. For this reason too, the further development of evaluation theories and methods and the accumulation of knowledge which goes beyond the borders of the various disciplines are rendered more difficult.

5) The fact that the *evaluation market* is furthermore largely dominated by consulting and market research enterprises, which are not primarily interested in scientific discussion or the accumulation of knowledge, but to whom it is, on account of their situation on the free market, most important of all to process orders with a view to making a profit, has certainly not made much of a contribution to profiling evaluation as a scientific discipline either.

Nevertheless, it has in the past ten years been possible to recognize some remarkable changes and progress in professionalization. As shown at the beginning, a number of reasons have contributed to the establishment of a broad market for evaluations in Germany too. Neither is there any longer a severe lack of German-language textbooks and handbooks and interdisciplinary anthologies[23] in which evaluational knowledge is focused and integrated.[24]

In September 1997 the *'German Evaluation Society'* (DeGEval) was founded. Like comparable professional associations in Europe, it has set out to promote the understanding, acceptance and utilization of evaluations in society, developing principles for evaluation procedures, laying down quality standards and supporting interdisciplinary exchange (www.degeval.de). Although the association, with almost 600 members[25] today, has recorded some tremendous growth, it does not yet have an integrative force which could be described as blanket. However, an 'evaluation research community' is beginning to develop as a network of professionally active evaluation researchers.

The *'standards for evaluation'* (2002), elaborated by the DeGeval in 2001 and officially issued in 2004, are a further step toward professionalization (cf. Section 4.4.3 for details). Having said that, the standards have not yet become all that widespread among experts and clients. Further promotion work is necessary here (cf. Brandt 2009: 176ff.).

The mailing-list 'forum-evaluation' certainly makes a contribution to this. It has been made available by the Department for the Evaluation of Educational Services at Cologne University since 1997. This electronic discussion forum, in which some 400 people participate, was founded with the aim of promoting the German-language exchange of information in the evaluation sector (www.uni-koeln.de).[26]

With a circulation of some 600 copies, the German-language *Zeitschrift für Evaluation*[27] (www.zfev.de), founded in 2002, has spread notably five years on, but many articles on evaluation continue to be published in the journals of their specific disciplines. The expansion of the magazine is faced with the same problem as the association: as transdisciplinary ventures, both of them compete with the individual disciplines for contributions and subscribers or members, who see themselves primarily as professional evaluators and not as representatives of their disciplines. The new journal, listed in the Social Sciences Citation Index (http://apps.isiknowledge.com), provides a platform for professional exchange between science and praxis, for the interdisciplinary focus of specialized sector-related knowledge, for the diffusion of standards in evaluation and for the dissemination of insights into the theories and methods of evaluation research, among other things (cf. Stockmann 2002: 6f.).

Also in 2002, the *'Center for Evaluation'* (CEval, www.ceval.de) was founded at Saarland University. It combines the development of theories and methods, evaluation consulting and the conducting of scientific evaluations with the development of basic and advanced training courses (cf. Stockmann 2003: 4f.). In an external evaluation report on the CEval, this combination is highlighted as a special feature in the German evaluation landscape (cf. Frey et al. 2006).[28] Together with AGEG International Consulting Services,[29] the CEval has been implementing an annual seven-module (21-day) *further training programme for evaluators in development cooperation* (www.feez.org) since 2003. In Germany this continues to be the only systematic further training programme for people who are to be prepared for planning, conducting and steering evaluations in a selected policy field. In other areas of evaluation, there are in Germany – as far as the authors are aware – no purpose-built further training courses on offer so far which are that comprehensive. Today, there already exist a number of social science study courses – especially in psychology – in which courses on evaluation are integrated in the methods training. Since 2004, together with the Saarland College of Technology and Economics (HTW), a four-semester advanced study course '*Master of Evaluation*' (www.master-evaluation.de) has been on offer at Saarland University. Since 2008, the University of Bonn has also been providing a four-semester masters course in evaluation (www.zem. uni-bonn.de).

In contrast to the situation in the USA for example, no social science evaluation discipline has yet been able to develop in Germany in its own right, in spite of these tremendous successes in professionalization. Further efforts are required here. These will be looked at in the next chapter.

1.4 Fulfilment of evaluation's purposes and challenges

As shown at the beginning, evaluation can mainly serve to (1) promote social enlightenment, (2) strengthen democratic governance and (3) improve the manageability of programmes and organizations. For this reason, the question of the extent to which the *development trends* referred to here make these *evaluation purposes* feasible and what *challenges* need to be overcome.

A look at the *historical development* of evaluation has shown clearly that evaluation is *policy-driven*. Both the first boom in the 1960s and 1970s in the USA and somewhat later in most countries in Europe, and the second boom which began in the 1990s, were triggered by increased state demand. This second phase is no longer fuelled only by governmental (government and administration) and supra-governmental actors (in Europe the European Commission), but increasingly also by organizations of civil society. Not only the boom years, but also the evaluation doldrums of the 1980s which were to be seen at least in Europe, were attributable to policy, i.e. to considerably reduced demand.

From this, it can be seen just how heavily the development of evaluation depends on governmental – and nowadays also non-governmental – clients. This is no great surprise for an applied social science, for evaluation is supposed to make a contribution to solving certain problems. Accordingly, the demand for it increases when there is a greater need for problem-solving, for example when a large number of reform programmes are initiated in which it is hoped that evaluation will assist in planning (ex-ante), implementation (ongoing) or impact measurement (ex-post); or when, with a view to scarce budget funds, estimates of efficiency or information which will assist in selecting the right problem or problems are expected from evaluations; or when in new public management approaches management is to be carried out with the help of output and impact indicators. In other words the questions of whether evaluation is to take place or not, whether or not the market for it will grow, stagnate or shrink and even of what subjects are covered by it are, to a great extent, politically influenced – that is to say, they are influenced by the willingness of clients to deploy funds for evaluation.

However, if evaluation is also to fulfil the purpose of making a contribution to *social enlightenment*, this situation certainly does present a problem, for 'evaluation will tend to take place where money flows rather than where there is a societal need for evaluation' (Dahler-Larsen 2006: 148). This means that 'there is no guarantee, however, that important areas of life in society which need evaluation are actually evaluated' (ibid.). Of course evaluation carried out on behalf of government or non-government actors can also contribute to social enlightenment, but there is simply no guarantee for this, for there is of course – as has already been mentioned several times – no compulsion for clients to render their results public or investigate problem areas which have a high degree of social relevance.

Social enlightenment by means of evaluation can only be brought about purposively if the latter is not always strait-jacketed by clients' wishes. For this reason, on the one hand, *independent institutes* are *necessary*, which can decide freely where they consider social evaluation to be needed and what it is they wish to evaluate. Audit offices with a mandate of this kind can exercise such a function. However, institutions bound to certain policy fields, for example for ensuring quality in schools or quality of research services, or for examining the effectiveness and efficiency of job-market policy or that of development cooperation, can also bring about social enlightenment in the policy fields for which they were founded... but only if they are at the same time given a mandate which affords them access to the research object (for example to state, federal, communal or even EU programmes or statutory provisions).

The *provision of research funding* could, under these conditions, also contribute to social enlightenment. For this, funds would be necessary that could be applied for not only towards fundamental research projects but also to evaluation.

Evaluation research, which has something of a strained relationship with pure or disciplinary research – to be dealt with in the next chapter – has a tough time of it in the present research landscape. Its tasks and the topics it covers are often perceived in the world of science as clients' wishes, for the fulfilment of which said clients ought to pay. This impedes not only the theoretical and methodological progress of evaluation research – since the goals of a client with a very specific cognitive interest will hardly be concerned with that – but of course also its role as an instrument of enlightenment.

In Germany, particularly poor conditions prevail with regard to social enlightenment through evaluation, since there are hardly any independent evaluation institutions which can both select their evaluation goals freely while availing themselves freely of budgets worth mentioning. Apart from that, there has to this day never been a research fund from which evaluation research might be sponsored. In addition, the Federal Court of Auditors, whose functions are stipulated in Article 114 of the *Grundgesetz* – unlike many other European courts of auditors, to say nothing of the American Government Accountability Office – does not have an evaluation mandate. Its members, who are judicially independent, audit 'the account and determine whether public finances have been properly and efficiently administered' (*Grundgesetz* Art. 114 para. 2).[30]

However, if there are no independent evaluation institutions and if hardly any research funding is made available for evaluations which are independent (of clients), there is still a chance of finding other allies who have also taken up the cause of social enlightenment, namely the *media*. On the one hand the media are potential partners, but on the other they certainly do sometimes prove difficult (cf. Chapter 6). The media are not in principle interested in evaluation findings; indeed they sometimes entertain utterly erroneous ideas as to what evaluation is,[31] and of course they function in accordance with their own rules. Accordingly, information is filtered, reassessed and reinterpreted, so that evaluation findings can be turned into news of the kind which the representatives of the media assume will interest their audiences. No-one should feel surprised if, in the process, balanced evaluation findings suddenly turn into bold, one-sided statements. Dahler-Larsen (2006: 150) is therefore quite right in pointing out that ' … news exaggerates success or failure. News reports are more often negative than positive. They suggest blame or scandal, they emphasize or create conflict, and they have a short life'.

A small contribution every evaluation can make to social enlightenment thus consists at least in not leaving the right to analyse and publish at the discretion of the client alone, but actively advocating that the evaluation report be published. There may of course be reasons for suppressing the disclosure of evaluation findings, for example if competing organizations might use them to harm an evaluated organization, or if there is a risk that informants would be severely compromised by publication, or if the readiness of the evaluees to implement the evaluation recommendations would be substantially reduced. In such cases, clients, evaluators and affected parties must look for solutions together. For these reasons, the Standards for Evaluation not only recommend that the findings of evaluations be disclosed, but also that the type and scope of said disclosure be laid down in the evaluation contract (cf. DeGEval standard P5, see also Section 4.4.3).

The support of *democratic governance* has been cited as a further purpose of evaluation, particularly as evaluation can help to show whether statutory regulations, programmes or measures have actually been achieving the targets they set out to achieve, what effects they are having, whether they are sustainable and whether they are being implemented efficiently and really making a significant contribution to solving a socially relevant problem. By these means – so the theory goes – not only can the success of policy be publicly verified and made transparent, but people's understanding of the rationality of political decisions can be improved and the *credibility and legitimacy* of policy increased.

In order for evaluation to be able to realize this ambition, internal and – even more so – external evaluation capacities are necessary. This will make it to be possible to investigate these questions on behalf of governmental and administrational institutions, local authorities and civil society organizations and make the findings public. In Germany, carrying out the effectiveness checks called for in §7 of the Federal Budgetary Regulations would already enable the success of political strategies and regulations to be assessed. Yet German ministries – with a few exceptions – seem to have no interest in that.

A report drawn up in 1989 by the *Federal Court of Auditors (BRH)* on the *'performance review of measures with financial implications in public administration'*, came to a quite devastating conclusion:[32]

- there was a 'relatively well ordered procedure' (BRH 1989: 35) for carrying out performance reviews in only three of the departments investigated (the Federal Ministry of Post and Telecommunications, the Federal Ministry for Economic Cooperation and Development, and the Federal Ministry of Research and Technology)
- in almost all departments the prerequisites for performance reviews (formulation of objectives, stipulation of results, indicators for measuring success) already failed to be fulfilled in the planning phase (cf. BRH 1989: 26)
- attempts to ascertain the direct and indirect impacts of programmes or measures by means of evaluations were decidedly rare (cf. BRH 1989: 29)

- hardly any use was made of existing methods for determining the effectiveness of measures (ibid.)
- there was little or no implementation of evaluation findings (BRH 1989: 30)
- '... only a relatively poorly developed sensitivity to the purpose, significance and necessity of these investigations' was detected among staff responsible for performance reviews (BRH 1989: 38).

Some ten years later, the BRH (1998) issued a revised edition of this study, in which its more recent assessment insights on the subject of performance reviews in public administration were incorporated. The conclusions were certainly no more positive than before. Once again, the BRH came to the conclusion that

- very few performance reviews had been carried out, and that for that reason most departments were unable to judge the success of their measures adequately
- in almost all departments the prerequisites for a systematic performance review were lacking
- impact investigations, which also took into account unintended impacts and subjected the results to a cause-and-effect analysis, were more or less completely lacking
- existing methods for determining success and effectiveness had not been fully exploited (cf. BRH 1998: 22ff.).

For this reason, the *BRH recommends,* as it did in 1989, that organizational and methodological prerequisites be established for carrying out performance reviews, so that the granting of budget funds can subsequently be tied to the submission of such evaluations. For this, the BRH also recommends that

- support from external institutions be enlisted in performance reviews
- methods and procedures be developed that put the individual departments in a position to carry out performance reviews and
- staff who are to carry out performance reviews be qualified via basic and advanced training (cf. BRH 1998: 36ff.).

The federal ministries have welcomed the recommendations of the 1998 report (as in 1989), and the federal government has made a commitment to carry out the performance reviews prescribed in accordance with §7 of the Federal Budgetary Regulations. Having said that, there was hardly any mention of evaluation in the programme 'Modern state – modern administration' (www.staat-modern.de), enacted by the 'red-green' federal government at the end of 1999, which was intended to provide the basis for a comprehensive modernization process. Even the term 'performance review', often used in administration, did not play a central role in that programme.

Following the change of government in 2006, administrative modernization continues to be on the political reform agenda. The programme 'future-oriented administration through innovations' (www.verwaltung-innovativ.de), enacted in the Federal Cabinet on 13 September 2006, and 'E-Government 2.0', were intended on the one hand to cut unnecessary red tape, weed out avoidable administrative processes and improve strategic control. On the other hand, modern technologies were supposed to be used to implement government tasks more effectively, transparently and economically. The instrument of evaluation was also supposed to be used to this end.[33] Yet apart from a few guides provided by the BMWi, the government's Internet portal on the modernization of administration hardly offers anything on this subject.

In should also be emphasized that the evaluation function (in the concept of the performance review) has been strengthened by a change in the administrative provisions (VV) of the Federal Budgetary Regulations (BHO), very much in line with the criticism made by the BRH (cf. Dommach 2008: 282ff.).

In accordance with the new administrative provisions (no. 3.5 on §23 of the BHO), grants for project funding may now only be made if the objectives have been determined in terms of their content to the extent that a performance review is possible. In accordance with the new VV (no. 11a on §44 of the BHO), for all grants 'a performance review (...) is to be carried out by the uppermost federal authority responsible or an agency appointed by it'. A graduated procedure has been prescribed for this (ibid.). The 'simple performance review' prescribed for all individual project funding measures consists of a simple check on the achievement of targets. The 'comprehensive performance review', which applies to all project funding measures with superordinate objectives, provides for an accompanying and concluding performance review consisting of an examination of the achievement of targets, impacts and efficiency.[34]

Is it true that, with the modification of the administrative provisions of the Federal Budgetary Regulations, the basic prerequisites for performance review in public administration have been strengthened, but this is of course still a long way from being a guarantee that they will actually be applied. It may still be assumed that many ministries and subordinate administrative authorities are a long way off from using evaluation (in the form of performance reviews) in a purposeful way in routine operations.

Instead, evaluation seems to be a popular instrument of government action, above all when it is a question of legitimizing resolutions which involve economies and closures. Roth (2004: 6) thus criticizes evaluation as a 'means of domination', used to cloak unpalatable decisions with a degree of rationality. Since according to Roth (ibid.) government action is 'no longer a question of progressive social reforms, but instead the word reform has degenerated into a synonym for pre-announced deterioration (...) the fact that an evaluation is to be conducted means nothing good'. He thus reasons that 'evaluations have in Germany but few disciples and no good name' (ibid.). This position makes it clear once again just how closely political action and evaluation are linked, and how rapidly the negative image becomes applicable to the instrument itself in the wake of a socially unjust policy. Only if evaluations take into account the interests of the various 'stakeholder'[35] groups and do not exclusively commit themselves to governmental control is there is a chance of their outgrowing this image. Evaluation can only make a contribution to strengthening democratization processes if it is used open-mindedly in routine operation – just, indeed, as envisaged by the Federal Budgetary Regulations and their administrative provisions.

Having said that, dangers also lurk in the other direction. The more evaluation is used as an instrument of control to support democratic governance, the more the *routinization* of procedures can lead to fatigue, to a rule which is supposed to be complied with but no longer has any meaningful substance. This danger also looms if the stakeholders are regularly involved and the findings made public but no consequences – or insufficient consequences – are drawn from them. If evaluations make it clear that certain policies are not achieving the desired results and impacts, but are nevertheless maintained out of considerateness to a given clientele or on account of lobbyist pressure, evaluation proves to be nothing more than a time-consuming and costly undertaking without any added value. It is hardly likely that those involved will allow themselves to be won over a second time to an evaluation which was so ineffective.

This problem of course also occurs if evaluations are not conducted with the necessary expertise and fail to come up with any utilizable findings for that reason. Paradoxically, this risk is becoming greater and greater with the increasing popularity of evaluation – in other words with more and more 'laymen', i.e. insufficiently qualified experts, using the discipline. The situation is becoming even more conducive to this trend, with handbooks being written in 'cookbook style' and crash courses being offered for programme managers, all suggesting that evaluation can be used by just about anyone at all with relatively little effort. This belief is upheld particularly strongly if there is insufficient money available for the evaluations to be conducted professionally by experts: 'That is, while mandates for evaluation often exist, the money to hire formally trained evaluators often doesn't exist' (Datta 2006: 430).

'Lay evaluation' also emerges however when it is a question of strengthening the democratic function of evaluation, when it is intended to assist disadvantaged groups (empowerment) and improve the situation in which they live (see the discussion of the relevant approaches in Chapter 3). 'Those affected' are sometimes assumed to have special competence for assessing the consequences of policies and programmes. Professional competence is then replaced by social empathy, objectifying data collection procedures by personal experience and tales of concern. The result is a deprofessionalization of evaluation in practice and its reduction to an all-purpose procedure. As in the 'do-it-yourself' philosophy applied to manual work in the home, specialized knowledge, relevant work experience and skills acquired over years are sweepingly devalued and an appropriately intensive occupation with professional standards and methods discounted as unnecessary ballast. At the same time, there is a risk that the do-it-yourself evaluator will overestimate his own ability to perform and underestimate the difficulty of the task ahead.

Evaluations which are conducted unprofessionally and in which professional standards are ignored, and evaluations which have no political consequences because their findings are not integrated in decision-making processes, are inappropriate for improving the legitimacy and credibility of policy. Moreover, they also undermine the credibility of the value of evaluation itself. Accordingly, not only the way evaluations are conducted needs to be professionalized, but also the way people deal with them.

This combination of course also applies at the *programme control* level, where evaluation is intended to make a contribution to increasing the manageability of individual measures, programmes or entire organizations. If the procedure is abused for tactical purposes only, solidifies to become bureaucratic porridge or is used by incompetent 'evaluators', it cannot develop its potential.

The utility of evaluation in programme control, which – as has already been explained – consists in making available timely information to decision-makers, must thus be geared principally to their information requirements in order to make a formative contribution to programme development and improvement.[36]

More recent programme control approaches such as new public management pursue the aim of improving performance and the process of generating outputs in public administration. They avail themselves of various different strategic principles which are intended on the one hand to achieve an increase in orientation toward customers and competition, and on the other to do away with the kind of control which has a fixation with input parameters. Instead, orientation toward quality principles – such as are applied in the private economy – and a readjustment of political control to output and impact specifications are called for: 'It is no longer the means of production available but the outputs (products) or the impacts achieved with those outputs which should become a point of discussion and a yardstick for the orientation of administrative action' (Schedler & Proeller 2003: 62f.).

For public administrations or non-profit organizations as a whole to be able to gear their actions to outputs and outcomes, however, a number of methodological difficulties need to be overcome, for discovering and measuring impacts and attributing them to causes confronts empirical social inquiry with problems, some of which are major. Furthermore, both immediately and in the long term, intended and unintended impacts need to be discerned, identified and examined in complex impact structures for correlations and causal factors.

However, it is not possible to control administrative or non-profit organizations in general via outputs and impacts until this problem has been solved. It is unanimously agreed that this cannot be done using the traditional control and finance instruments. In other words, new assessment concepts and analysis instruments are required for impact-oriented management.

It is just to this purpose that the theoretical and methodological concepts and instruments of evaluation research lend themselves; with them, not only can the processes of planning and generating outputs be analysed, but the outputs generated, objectives achieved and impacts triggered can also be empirically examined and assessed.

In this way management is provided with the information it needs to make rational decisions. It is not possible to implement and apply new public management approaches – or quality management systems – at all without using evaluations.

Regardless of what control and quality management systems evaluation is integrated into, it is always a matter of providing management with information relevant to decision-making in a timely manner (cf. Stockmann 2006: 64). Thus evaluation makes a contribution to improving organizational structures and processes and increasing the manageability of organizations as a whole. Furthermore, evaluation is as a rule linked to the knowledge management system of an organization, in order to document evaluation findings in such a way that they are also utilizable for other departments and over time. In this way evaluation becomes an indispensable part of a learning organization in which knowledge is accumulated and made available in time to those parts where it is needed (see also Chapter 6).

In order to fulfil these tasks, information is on the one hand procured by external evaluators, in other words experts who do not belong to the organization which is implementing the programme (steering), and on the other by internal evaluators, i.e. experts who do (cf. Chapter 2). More and more organizations are creating internal evaluation departments or teams to this end. Although in many organizations evaluation is meanwhile part of the fixed repertoire of management instruments, there is still doubt as to whether this instrument can actually deliver what it promises. Datta (2006: 432), for example, offers the following thought for consideration: 'Evaluations indeed can benefit programs, a result devoutly hoped for, but unproven in practice'. However, more recent investigations (cf. Fitzpatrick, Sanders & Worthen 2012: 485; Stamm 2003: 183ff.) show that use certainly is made of evaluation findings by management and other stakeholders. The modest use made of evaluation findings by management (instrumental use), observed in many investigations of the 1970s and 1980s, is mainly attributed to periods of investigation which were too short and ways of looking at things which were too narrow. Going beyond this, comprehensive studies can show that evaluation has indirect impacts on further-reaching decision-making processes by influencing the general way people think about problems and learning processes (conceptional use). Evaluation findings also contribute to endorsing or refuting 'political' positions (persuasive use). This is for example the case if they are able to refute positions that were firmly anchored and no longer queried.

In studies on the utilization of evaluation findings, several factors that increase the chances of the practical implementation of those findings have been identified (cf. Fitzpatrick, Sanders & Worthen 2012: 485; Rossi, Lipsey & Freeman 2004: 414):

- the relevance of the evaluation for the decision-makers and/or other stakeholders
- the integration of stakeholders in the planning and reporting phases of the evaluation
- the reputation or credibility of the evaluator

- the quality of communication of the findings (promptness, frequency, methods) and
- the development of supporting procedures for utilizing the findings or providing recommendations for action.

1.5   Summary

If we visualize once again the development and current situation of evaluation and the challenges it faces against the backdrop of its role in society, it becomes clear that evaluation is widespread and that it is being used routinely more and more as an instrument of control for the *assessment of programmes, projects and measures* and as part of the *control and management system in organizations*. Evaluations are found much less often in the context of democratic governance for increasing the *legitimacy and credibility* of policy. Evaluations that cover such broad, whole policy fields (higher education policy, school quality, job-market policy) or sections of such fields are unusual. With a few exceptions, there is in Germany – unlike a number of other countries such as the USA in particular – no evaluation culture which ties political responsibility and evaluation together.

Evaluation is currently least able to do justice to the aspiration of making a contribution to *social enlightenment*. Especially in countries such as Germany, in which the BRH does not have an attested evaluation mandate, and in which (with a few exceptions) hardly any independent evaluation institutions exist that can evaluate under their own steam and are equipped with funds sufficient for the purpose, or in which there are at least research funds from which evaluation studies might be financed, evaluation is restricted to assigned or commissioned research. This means, in principle, that anything that government or non-government institutions see as being fit to evaluate can be evaluated. There is thus no assurance that that which is necessary from a social point of view will also be evaluated.

If evaluation is to make qualified contributions to all three function fields, a few *requirements for the future* can be derived from these observations.

In order for the quality of evaluation to be improved, (1) more needs to be invested in the basic and advanced training of evaluators and (2) the degree of professionalization of evaluation needs to be improved by making compliance with quality standards verifiable (e.g. via certification). Not until (3) the disciplinary fragmentation – which has so far continued to predominate heavily – has been overcome can a social science evaluation discipline with its own modified teaching canon come into being. To this end, and (4) to help with the further development of evaluation research theories and methods, it would be useful to establish areas of special research and core research areas. If evaluation is also to make a contribution to the legitimation of policy and to democratic governance, (5) the interests of the stakeholders need to be integrated more strongly and (6) an evaluation culture needs to be developed that sees evaluation not only as a instrument of control of 'those in power' or, to put it less dramatically, of those providing the funds, but as an instrument with which organizational activities, programmes and policies can be improved, i.e. with which solutions that are better adapted to the needs of the stakeholders can be developed. To strengthen the social enlightenment function of evaluation, not only do internal and external evaluation capacities need to be established, but (7) independent institutions also need to be founded or those that already exist need to be mandated in such a way that evaluations can also be conducted where they are perceived as particularly relevant in social terms. In other words: it is not until there has been a far-reaching professionalization and establishment of evaluation as a *scientific research discipline* that the previous status of a purely *policy-driven evaluation culture* geared to the interests and the demand of (mainly) public clients can be left behind.

Notes

1. Translator's note: Basic German Law.
2. Http://www.isq-bb.de.
3. Http://www.forschungsinfo.de.
4. In Germany, this idea of founding a centre for the independent verification of the effectiveness and sustainability of development cooperation was put forward for the first time by the author of this chapter during a conference on the 'sustainability of development cooperation projects and programmes' in November 1992 at the University of Mannheim. Cf. also the dpa [German Press Agency] interview of 2 December 1994 with the author, in which the proposal was reiterated. On 14 March 1996, Dr. R. Werner Schuster (member of the *Bundestag)* and the parliamentary SPD tabled a motion for 'systematic performance review', in which the founding of an evaluation institute was also called for (cf. BT document 13/4120). Having said that, these proposals were scuppered ahead of the political discussion, as governmental and private (charitable) non-profit organizations had no interest in an independent institution which would be able to evaluate their work. Instead, reference was made to evaluations carried out by those organizations themselves, conducted partly or wholly by external experts, though the independence of those experts has been queried time and again. Recently, a proposal was made to found an independent evaluation institute in the German development cooperation landscape, in a study commissioned by the Federal Ministry of Economic Cooperation and Development (BMZ) on the evaluation of German development cooperation organizations (cf. Borrmann & Stockmann 2009).

5. In 1976, the Joint Committee on Standards for Educational Evaluation formed as an amalgamation of several professional education and psychology-oriented organizations, in order to elaborate standards for evaluation. In 1981 the Standards for Evaluations of Educational Programs, Projects, and Materials were issued (cf. Section 4.3). The Evaluation Research Society and the Evaluation Network amalgamated in 1986 to become the American Evaluation Association (AEA), which has until today remained the evaluation society with the most members and certainly also the most influence worldwide.
6. Cf. the very instructive work of Reade 2004.
7. Cf. also Derlien (1990); Rist (1990); Wollmann (1997); Pollitt (1998); Wollmann (2000) on European developments.
8. Original italics.
9. Translator's note: a catchword from the 1960s meaning 'education catastrophe'. The term was coined following the publication of articles by Georg Pichl (1964) and Ralf Dahrendorf (1965). The latter considered that the state of education in the Federal Republic was so poor as to endanger German democracy itself.
10. Cf. in particular the contributions by Altschuld (1999); Jones & Worthen (1999); Smith (1999).
11. The most difficult problem with Furubo, Rist and Sandahl (2002) is that they form a national average although the individual sectors (disciplines) reveal major differences in the various countries. In many countries, for example, evaluations are conducted very often in university and development policy, so that an evaluation culture could be said to exist there, though this would hardly be appropriate for other policy fields. Thus individual sectors, viewed Europe-wide or even worldwide, sometimes have more similarities than different sectors in the same country (cf. Meyer & Stockmann 2006).
12. www.europa.eu.int/comm/budget/evaluation/studies/study_2005_eu.htm.
13. www.europa.eu/budget/evaluation/key-documents/evalguide_study_eu.htm.
14. Cf. also Donaldson & Lipsey (2006: 57), who arrive at different figures: 'In 1990, there were approximately five major evaluation professional associations, whereas today there are more than 50 worldwide.'
15. Http://www.ioce.net.
16. Http://www.wkkf.org.
17. The claim made by Beywl and Harich (2007: 126) that 'Saarland University offers a masters programme with 120 ECTS, a volume which makes it difficult to complete as an in-service study course', has no empirical basis whatsoever. On the contrary, the programmes implemented thus far have shown that there are hardly any dropouts and that the courses, which students only actually have to attend for three semesters, can be coped with by the participants. The Saarbrücken programme is not only a model for the Universidad de Costa Rica and Moscow's 'Higher School of Economics', but also serves as a template for competing German course options which are just in the process of being put in place.
18. Cf. Picciotto (2002) on the role of the World Bank as it relates to the funding of evaluation capacities in developing countries.
19. http://www.ideas-int.org.
20. www.ceval.de.

21. The reform and modernization debate carried on under the name of 'New Public Management' began in Europe mainly in the Netherlands, the Scandinavian and some English-speaking countries. Germany remained largely unaffected by this discussion for a long time. Cf. for example Pede (2000); Naschold and Bogumil (2000); Buschor (2002); Saner (2002); Reichard (2002, 2004); Mülbert (2002); Rehbinder (2002); Christensen (2002); McLaughlin (2002); Wollmann (2002, 2003); Ritz (2003); Schedler and Proeller (2000, 2003); Nöthen (2004); Dent (2004); Koch (2004a, b); Pitschas (2004); Mastronardi (2004); Lienhard (2005); Nolte (2005).

22. Cf. in particular Stockmann (2006a); Widmer et al. (2009) on the individual fields of evaluation.

23. Among others, Wittmann (1985); Wottawa and Thierau (1998); Bussmann et al. (1997); Vedung (1999); Flick (2006); Stockmann (2006b, 2007, 2008); Gollwitzer and Jäger (2007); Kuckartz et al. (2007); Aulinger (2008); Brandt (2009); Widmer, Beywl & Fabian (2009). Important anthologies: Stockmann (2006a); Hellstern and Wollmann (1984); Will, Winteler and Krapp (1987); Mayntz (1980c).

24. Even at the beginning of the 1990s, the keyword 'evaluation' was hardly to be found at all in many methods textbooks and social science reference works. Even in the standard work on methods training by Schnell, Hill and Esser, which has already appeared in several editions, the keyword evaluation research was still sought in vain in 1992. In the 7th edition of 2005 evaluation is dealt with in less than two pages under the sub-chapter 'Empirical social inquiry as political consulting', whereby the state of knowledge is not stated correctly and the current literature not acknowledged. In the textbook on 'Empirical social inquiry' by Andreas Diekmann (2007), evaluation research is only mentioned in the context of quasi-experiments. Bortz and Döring (2006) cover the special qualities of evaluation research in their textbook 'Research methods and evaluation' in a separate chapter. In his standard work on empirical social inquiry, Kromrey (2002) dwells only briefly on evaluation design in programme research.

25. Approx. 500 personal and approx. 90 institutional members.

26. Enrolments can be made directly to: Majordomo@rrz.Uni-Koeln.de.

27. Translator's note: 'Journal of Evaluation.'

28. This can be looked up on the Internet at: http://www.ceval.de/de/downloads/dateien/Gutachterkommission%20Bericht.pdf).

29. Translator's note: AGEG stands for the *Arbeitsgemeinschaft Entwicklungspolitischer Gutachter*, i.e. the development policy experts' working-group.

30. Cf. www.bundesrechnungshof.de on these tasks in detail.

31. One of the scientific editors at the *Frankfurter Allgemeine Zeitung (FAZ)*, for example, makes fun of basic and advanced training in evaluation in an article entitled *'Werdet Werter'* ('Become judges!') (12 September 2004), without even having begun to understand the difference between 'all-purpose evaluations' and scientifically based approaches.

32. There are however a number of ministries which have delegated evaluation tasks to subordinate authorities or institutions, including the Federal Highway Research Institute (BASt), the Federal Health Department (BGA), the Federal Institute for Vocational Education and Training (BIBB), the Federal Institute for Regional Research and Spatial Development, the Federal Environment

Agency (UBA), the Federal Institute for Population Research, and the Federal Institute for Occupational Safety and Accident Research.

33. In the coalition agreement of the grand coalition dated 11 November 2005, the German Evaluation Society (DeGEval) counted 28 uses of the term evaluation as compared with only four in the coalition agreement of the preceding red-green government. The DeGEval judges this to be an indicator of the increased significance of evaluation as an instrument for planning and management(http://www.degeval.de/index.php?class=Calimero_Article&id=329) [19 March 2009].

34. In order to render this task easier for public administration, an interdepartmental project group at the Federal Ministry of Economics and Technology (BMWi) has developed guides as general aids to work and made them available as downloads. The Federal Ministry for Economic Cooperation and Development (BMZ) is also working on appropriate aids. Sample terms of reference and an evaluation guide are to be found on the website of the BMZ (www.bmz.de/ de/erfolg/evaluierung/zep.html). The BMZ is currently working on 'basic principles of evaluation', which are intended to be binding on all implementing organizations and recipients of BMZ funding. Quality standards for evaluation reports, guidelines for evaluation criteria and on the process of evaluation.

35. According to Weiss (1998: 337) stakeholders are 'those people with a direct or indirect interest (stake) in a program or its evaluation.' Alongside sponsors and clients, stakeholders also include programme managers and employees, the recipients of programme outputs and their families, those groups of people who have been explicitly or implicitly excluded from the outputs, other organizations connected with the programme, interest groups and the public per se, i.e. all those 'who may otherwise affect or be affected by decisions about the program or the evaluation' (ibid.). Cf. also Fitzpatrick, Sanders and Worthen (2004: 174f.); Scriven (2002).

36. Cf. in particular Chapter 2 on programme evaluation.

2
Science-Based Evaluation
Reinhard Stockmann

2.1 Evaluation between politics and science

2.1.1 Evaluation and politics

In the previous chapter it was explained that the role of evaluation in society is to a large extent *politically ordained* and the development of evaluation history *policy-driven*. Phases in which evaluation boomed and stagnated have, primarily, followed from courses already set in politics. Even the main topics with which evaluation concerns itself are set politically: in the 1960s and 1970s the main question in the wake of large-scale reform programmes was whether the latter had 'functioned' and achieved their intended goals. In the economizing years, the 1980s, cost efficiency advanced to become the main topic. And the second boom of evaluation, since the late 1990s, has been attended by new control models and the increasing discussion of impacts. If the section which follows tends to emphasize the aspect of scientific integrity, sight must not be lost, on account of its paramount importance, of the complex web of relationships between politics and evaluation.

Karlsson and Conner (2006: 230ff.) use two dimensions to characterize the connection between evaluation and politics:

(1) 'whether it is possible operationally to separate evaluation and politics' and
(2) 'whether it is desirable conceptually to separate evaluation and politics'.

The starting-point of this classification is the consideration 'that the two main components of evaluation are providing information (the epistemological component) and providing judgement (the value component)'.

Table 2.1 Three positions on the inherent connections between evaluation and politics

Three positions	Possible to separate evaluation and politics?	Desirable to separate evaluation and politics?
First position	Yes	Yes
Second position	Yes, in providing information; not entirely when providing judgements	Yes, in providing information
Third position	No	No

Source: Karlsson & Conner (2006: 231).

According to this overview, there are three perspectives from which one can look at the relationship between evaluation and politics (Karlsson & Conner 2006: 237ff.):

(1) 'The first position sees politics as driven to protect its own interests and as harmful to evaluation. In this view, politics is at best a fickle partner, driven by many influences other than information and at worst an unsavoury one'. For this reason, the only advice to be given here is that 'evaluation can and should be kept apart from it'.

(2) 'In the second position on the connection of evaluation and politics, it is accepted that evaluation takes place in political environment and that evaluation and politics therefore cannot entirely be separated, specifically in the judging component of evaluation' (2006: 233). In the data gathering and analysis phase, according to this perspective, the evaluator should however not allow himself to be influenced by politics: 'evaluation is kept separate from politics in the implementation of the evaluation, to avoid biases in the information produced' (2006: 237).

(3) 'The third position views evaluation and politics as inseparable, both in the conceptual as *(sic)* operational aspects. Here, the evaluator accepts that evaluation and politics are connected in many intricate ways and acts accordingly'. For this, the evaluator must disclose his own ethical and moral standards during the evaluation process.

All three positions can be criticized variously. With regard to the first point of view, one might object that it has little to do with the real world. Politics, as its principal client, influences evaluation in many different ways. In the case of the second perspective, doubt might be cast on whether politics could be kept out of data gathering and analysis but readmitted for the assessment of findings. As for the third perspective, one might contend that it must eventually lead to the abandonment of scientific principles, in view of the evaluator's being forced into the role 'of an intellectual discussant on general political, ethical, and moral issues' (Karlsson & Conner 2006: 239).

On the one hand it is naive to suppose that evaluation can be carried on in a scientific ivory tower uninfluenced by politics and its ideals – even if the political sphere did not supply the main clients and independent authorities (comparable for example with the TÜV[1] or the accreditation agencies) were called into being. But to draw the conclusion that the aspiration of scientific integrity ought to be sacrificed in favour of the primacy of politics is equally wrong and would at the end of the day be tantamount to advocating the abolition of evaluation. It is rather the case that a model needs to be found which anticipates the social contextual conditions of evaluation while not depriving it of its scientific nature.

Having said that, anyone trying to hold this position runs the risk of falling between two stools, for on the one hand evaluation must commit itself as a science, just like pure research, to the latter's central values such as objectivity and neutrality, but on the other hand it must, as application and utilization-related research, also come to terms with non-scientific political and/or social values – which means that it may come into conflict with the postulate of value-free research. Before ways of solving this basic conflict can be suggested, some light first needs to be shed on the relationship between evaluation and science, which is not without its problems either.

2.1.2 Evaluation and science

Although evaluation *aspires to be of a scientific nature*, it is, as practical and applied research, not always recognized as a fully-fledged science by pure and discipline-oriented researchers, since it does not as a rule determine its own aims – the evaluand (e.g. a programme, project or measure), the aims of the investigation (and occasionally also the assessment criteria) being predetermined from outside instead.

Whilst fundamental research can strive toward insights in a relatively pure manner, any kind of applied social research – thus also evaluation – is designed to *solve practical socio-political problems*, in order systematically to provide a basis for non-scientific decision-making processes (cf. Clemens 2000: 215). To this end, evaluation uses the whole bandwidth of social science theories, concepts and research methods, and the rules for gathering valid and reliable data that are fundamental to science apply (cf. Rossi et al. 1988: 1ff.; Kromrey 1995: 314f.; Wottawa & Thierau 1998: 9f.; Bortz & Döring 2003: 3).

Whilst fundamental research aims to test theories and develop them further, multiply insights, provide explanations, convey an understanding of relationships, without asking whether or not this is useful for society, evaluation is *oriented toward concretely prescribed research targets* and has to allow its usefulness to be measured in terms of the achievement of those targets. Whilst it is society itself which makes available the funding for fundamental research, that funding being awarded via research communities or foundations in accordance with principles of excellence, evaluation is as a rule carried out as an order or assignment. The clients define the evaluand and targets, issue invitations to tender for evaluation projects and award contracts for them applying certain criteria, and consequently their scientific integrity is not always the most important thing. The definition and specification of their goals is thus geared to non-scientific cognitive interests and utilization contexts (cf. Kromrey 2002: 96f.).

The fact that fundamental research is not (at least in principle) carried out under *constraints of time*, as new insights ('discoveries') cannot be forced within a given period of time, can be viewed as a further difference. If results of evaluation research are to be able to unfold their usefulness, they must be submitted in a previously defined scope by a given point in time, as otherwise they can no longer be taken into account in decision-making processes (for example in programme control or for legitimizing funding decisions). Alongside *financial constraints*, constraints of time are among the main reasons why often only sub-optimal investigation designs are used in evaluations.

Kromrey (2003: 98) points out yet another major difference: fundamental research is allowed to 'err', which means that it is by all means acceptable for hypotheses to turn out to be 'false' during the course of the research. It is indeed regarded as particularly desirable to start the search for new insights from 'bold' assumptions. After all, a *failure that delivers plenty of information* may be the starting-point for new pioneering insights. In evaluation research, by contrast, the procedure in the conception of research designs is such 'that the assumptions and hypotheses on which the research is based are empirically well tried and tested and that the process of obtaining, assessing and interpreting all the information is backed up methodologically and accompanied by quality control' (Kromrey 2003: 8). Any false conclusion arrived at on the basis of incorrect data can have fatal consequences for those affected.

Another essential difference between evaluation research and fundamental research consists in the fact that evaluations are always linked to *assessments*. The assessment criteria are mostly derived from the programme being evaluated itself. In this case, the implementation of the programme and its impacts are assessed in the light of its own objectives. However, these are not subjective value judgements on the part of the evaluation researcher, but 'analytical judgements', which must be intersubjectively verifiable. The researcher as a rule proceeds by empirically investigating the statuses in the target areas of the programme before and after the measures implemented, and investigating which changes are to be attributed to which elements of the programme. Following a comparison of the empirical facts (actual status) with the target levels formulated in the programme (target status), deductive statements can subsequently be derived as to whether and in what areas the implemented programme was successful or unsuccessful, as the case may be. In order to arrive at a conclusive assessment, however, unintended impacts also need to be taken into account. Moreover, other or further assessment criteria can supplement the original ones, for example, those formulated by clients or affected target groups (e.g. political relevance or benefit for those groups).

There are, on the other hand, basically no differences between evaluation research and fundamental research with regard to selecting the research object or using data gathering and analysis methods to identify impacts and tackle the causality issue (cause-and-effect relationships). The differences between fundamental and evaluation research are recapitulated in Table 2.2. The latter thus hovers in an *area of tension between scientific integrity and usefulness*. On the one hand, evaluation is part of empirical social inquiry and has to comply with its rules and standards. On the other, it is geared towards providing utilizable findings for the improvement of social practice.

This aspect of being *geared to assessment and utilization* is one of the main prerequisites for evaluation's being useful. For this reason, evaluations (with a few exceptions) cannot be reduced to purely scientific aspirations, but are always oriented toward the interests and information requirements of those who initiate them, commission them or are affected by them in some other way. The main aim is as a rule not to advance general theoretical knowledge, but to use scientific procedures and insights to utilize existing knowledge in the investigation of client and target-group-related goals (cf. Kromrey 2001; Vedung 2000; Patton 1997; Shadish et al. 1991). How far scientific-methodological aspirations may be curtailed in favour of generating practical knowledge with a view to gaining insights as objectively as possible is a moot point; it cannot be resolved universally, but only from

Table 2.2   Differences between fundamental and evaluation research

Criterion	Fundamental research	Evaluation research
Cognitive aim	theory-oriented	utilization-oriented
Purpose	pure	applied
Evaluand	freely selectable	externally defined
Resources made available by	society	clients
Time frame	not subject to time constraints	subject to time constraints
Insights gained	for society	for decision-making
Conclusions	basis for new insights	positive or negative consequences for stakeholders
Benefit	everyone (whole world)	clients, target groups, generally: 'stakeholders'
Findings	interpretation	interpretation and assessment
Context	no problems as a rule	politically sensitive

case to case. However, it is clear that in practice recourse is very often had to solutions that are less than optimal from a social scientific point of view.

Evaluation research thus distinguishes itself by a special *'duality'*, expressed by the fact that it is on the one hand part of empirical social inquiry and avails itself of the latter's theories and methods, whilst on the other it is also part of the political process, which it itself influences with its findings. As an instrument for decision-making in political control, it is partly exposed to non-scientific demands. On account of this duality, various theoretical-methodological approaches have formed during the development of evaluation research. These approaches are oriented either more toward scientific standards or more toward the requirements of clients or the needs of target groups (cf. Chapter 3).

2.1.3   A research model for evaluation

It being the case that evaluation hovers uneasily in this niche between politics and science, what is a research model to look like if it is to allow scientific integrity, with its recognized standards such as neutrality and objectivity and valid and reliable findings, while not ignoring the political contextual conditions?

Here, it is useful to apply the *theory-of-science distinction between the discovery, research and utilization contexts*. According to Max Weber's (1968: 229–277) position on the freedom of science from values, there is no question but that all social science description and explanation of social circumstances is valuing in as much as the researcher selects certain goals from among an almost infinite conceivable number and works toward achieving them. This *selection of goals* is made against the backdrop of certain attitudes.

With evaluations, there is only a difference in as much as the evaluand is selected and the goals are formulated by the client. Politics, which decides what questions are to be investigated with the aid of evaluation and which criteria – against the backdrop of certain attitudes – are to be applied in the assessment, does not therefore pose a problem for the scientific integrity of the evaluation.

According to Weber (1968), the *objectivity* of the *description and explanation of facts* should continue to be assured, in other words they should remain value-free, such that anyone who has the specialist knowledge of the disciplines can see the rationale in them. Scientific statements should not be influenced by the value concepts of the researcher.

This requirement can also be fulfilled in evaluation. Once the research object and questions have been defined, it is the task of the scientist to develop a suitable investigation design that allows an objective procedure and makes it reasonable to expect reliable and valid findings.

The task of evaluation consists not only in gathering information, but also in *assessing* it. However, this assessment has nothing to do with value judgements, the findings being judged instead according to the criteria stipulated in the discovery context. By comparing a target value and an empirically determined actual value, for example, it can be ascertained whether or not certain programme objectives have been achieved. If the aim of a programme was to reduce the inequality of opportunities in society by increasing the share of working-class children who went to a grammar school from 20 to 30 per cent, it could be shown by gathering appropriate data whether or not the programme had made a contribution if the rise did occur and, if so, how much. An assessment could be made as to whether the programme had been successful, what had worked well (with regard to achieving the targets) and what had not. From that, recommendations that were theoretically sound (i.e. that took account of the correlations between variables) and empirically supported (i.e. data-based) could be derived as to how the programme's objective could be achieved more effectively and / or efficiently.

This procedure by no means contradicts Weber's postulate of freedom from value judgements in the research phase, for no value-related statements are made – for example to the effect that a 30 per cent share of working-class children at grammar schools is not enough to suggest equality of opportunities, or that equality of opportunities is not worth striving for anyway etc. These would be assessments based on social values such as individuality, justice etc., though they do not necessarily have to be the subject of evaluation. The admonition that evaluation must either make value judgements in the research phase, and that it otherwise chickens out of the process of evaluating (cf. Kromrey 2007: 113ff.), fails to recognize that evaluation does *not* aim to make *value judgements at all*.

Apart from that, it should be noted that fundamental research, in *interpreting its findings*, also has to carry out an assessment (cf. Chapter 5). The findings must for example be appraised with a view to their relevance, the significance test serving this purpose in the case of statistical procedures. The significance level arbitrarily set in advance by the researcher is nothing more than a decision rule that determines whether the findings are to be accepted or rejected (as a chance occurrence). The significance of subjective decisions made by the researchers in interpretive procedures becomes even clearer in qualitative social research, when for example the meaning is to be grasped in text interpretation and recourse has to be had to the researchers' own understanding of the text as a yardstick. These procedures are by no means value judgements in the sense Weber indicated either, however, and they are very similar to the assessment of circumstances by evaluators described here.

If evaluations were allowed to make value judgements, the field would mutate into a 'positive' (i.e. empirical) social science of the kind Auguste Comte (Littré 2005; see also Gane 2006) wished for in the mid-19th century: a science that provided the yardstick for decisions about what was good in social terms and what was right. But these verdicts cannot be arrived at by scientific methods. For this, value judgements are always necessary, and they cannot be derived with intersubjective validity from empirical data alone. This ambition was neither capable of being fulfilled by the sociology of the 19th century, nor can it be honoured by evaluation today. Yet it would not be true to say that sociology or evaluation had failed, since this simply cannot be their job.

That evaluation certainly can follow scientific principles and be a partner to politics at the same time is the basis of an idea referred to by Hellstern and Wollmann (1983: 1ff.) as *'experimental politics'*[2], according to which 'procedures of systematically gaining experience and insights' can be developed and used as a 'means of improving political decision-making' (Hellstern & Wollmann 1983: 1). For 'more systematic, more long-term' politics, 'programme renewals' should not be initiated and evaluated as 'at-random innovations', but rather as purposive 'social experimentation', 'in order to establish a 'process of cumulative and systematic political learning' (Hellstern & Wollmann 1983: 68).

To this end, the *decisional logic of the experimental procedure* is used for policy-making. Before programmes, statutory regulations or social services schemes are introduced across the board, and they are tested in individual pilot projects or limited regions. With the aid of systematic evaluations the results in those regions can be compared with those in which the measures have not yet been introduced ('control group'). If the programme proves itself as measured against the predefined objectives, then it can be extended; if there are no differences between the test region and the control region, then the programme must be modified or abandoned completely. With this approach, alternative versions can also be tested. Examples of large-scale pilot projects are the trials for the comprehensive-school concept, field experiments on TV text systems and cable TV, and the urban development programme 'socially integrative city'[3] involving both the federation and the *länder* (cf. Kromrey 2003: 105). In development cooperation, this approach is very widespread. Since the necessary funds are lacking, innovative solutions are as a rule first tested in pilot projects before being introduced across the board.

In such a procedure, evaluation, as an accompanying scientific study, supplies the data and makes the assessments necessary for such decisions. For this, it is necessary to *record the initial situation* (baseline) before programme interventions take place, and *measure the interventions* (input) and the *generated outputs* in the context of the programme, *the achievement of targets* (outcome) and the *impacts* brought about (cf. Section 3.5.3 for the 'logical models' on which this sequence of events is based). In measuring impacts, care should be taken that both the intended and the unintended impacts are recorded and assessed. Not least of these, the task of *attributing causes* also needs to be solved, – i.e. the question of which of the intended and unintended impacts observed are attributable to the programme interventions. Finally, the evaluation findings need to be assessed. For this, the criterion of achieving targets (effectiveness) is only one among several. The programme can also be assessed with a view to its efficiency, its impact balance sheet (between intended and unintended impacts), its sustainability (in the case of ex-post analyses), its ecological soundness etc. (cf. Section 2.2.4).

To make this clear once again: in an evaluation, an assessment is made by applying fixed criteria of whether and to what extent certain goals have been achieved and whether and to what extent the programme measures have contributed to this. Assessments are thus made about the extent to which a programme has contributed to the achievement of certain predetermined social objectives (and what intended and unintended impacts came about in the process). However, no value judgements are made as to whether or not certain social objectives ought in principle to be striven toward. These are political statements that are to be made in the utilization context of investigations. For this reason, decisions regarding the recommendations submitted by an evaluation

Table 2.3 Roles of politics and science in the research process

context of discovery	politics/society
research context	Science
utilization context	politics / society

and their implementation are no longer part of evaluation, but part of politics, administration and management.

As called for by Max Weber (1968: 229–277), findings from science are used to achieve political, social, economic and other aims, not within the research context but outside it, i.e. in the *utilization context* (cf. Table 2.3). This also applies to evaluation. Like scientists, evaluators do not determine the realization of social objectives. With their evaluations they merely provide options for action and assess them with regard to criteria that have previously been stipulated and rendered transparent by applying the method of systematic comparison with the help of empirically gathered data. These assessments are intersubjectively verifiable and anyone, applying different criteria, can arrive at different assessments.

Up to this point, no value judgements are involved, because the programme is only being assessed with regard to the *instrumental achievement of targets*, i.e. whether or not it makes a contribution to achieving a social target that has been selected on the basis of certain value positions. The value position on which that is based (for example: should society create equality of opportunities at all?), on the other hand, is not assessed by evaluation. This is a decision to be made outside the research process in the utilization context. According to this model it is neither necessary to link the act of evaluating (in the true sense) to anything outside the evaluation, nor to make value judgements in the research process.

This line-up is similar to the position of the 'value-sensitive evaluator' described by Karlsson and Conner (2006: 232ff.), according to which it is possible and desirable to separate politics and science: 'in the operational, information-finding aspects, however, the evaluator can and should stay separate from the political component' (2006: 233). The research model developed here goes beyond that, as it sees *instrumental assessment* as *part of the research process* too, and only allocates the *value-related judgement* of socially desirable circumstances and the decisions to be taken in making that judgement to the *utilization context*.

2.2   Fundamental principles

2.2.1   Definitions

The time has now come to define the term evaluation[4] more closely. It was pointed out at the beginning that evaluation goes a long way back in human history, that it is used for an enormous variety of purposes and can involve some very different procedures. Against this backdrop, it is hardly surprising to hear it said that 'evaluation' is an 'elastic word' which 'stretches to cover judgements of many kinds' (Weiss 1974: 19).

A review of the previous remarks about evaluation shows that the use of the term always includes an *assessment or judgement of a circumstance or object on the basis of information*. This meaning does indeed correspond to its Latin origin, which is put together from the word *valor* (value) and the prefix *e* or *ex* (from). This gives us 'to draw a value from something', in other words to carry out a valuation.[5] But there is also a third element: evaluations are conducted in a purposeful way. Information is gathered and assessed in order to make a contribution to decision-making.

It could thus be noted that evaluation is an *instrument for the empirical generation of knowledge*, which is *linked to an assessment* so that *purposeful decisions* can be made. These three aspects of evaluation are reflected in most popular attempts at definition, which render this basic paradigm more precisely. Donna Mertens (1998: 219), for example, suggests that 'evaluation is the systematic investigation of the merit or worth of an object (program) for the purpose of reducing uncertainty in decision making'.

This aspect of the assessment of the 'merit or worth' of an object (also generally referred to as an 'evaluand') is to be found in many definitions of evaluation, for example in Scriven (1991: 139), who defines it as follows: 'Evaluation refers to the process of determining the merit, worth, or value of something, or the product of that process'. Sometimes a distinction is made between 'merit' and 'worth', with the term 'merit' being used to denote the context-free qualities immanent to the evaluand (intrinsic). For example the value of a curriculum in itself, independent of its context-related application. 'Worth', on the other hand, is used to refer to the context-determined value, which duly varies depending on that context; for example the worth of a curriculum for teaching a certain child in a certain environment. On the basis of this distinction, Lincoln and Guba (1986a: 550) offer the following definition: an evaluation is 'a type of disciplined inquiry undertaken to determine the value (merit and / or worth) of some entity – the evaluand – such as a treatment, program, facility, performance, and the like – in order to improve or refine the evaluand (formative evaluation) or to assess its impact (summative evaluation)'.

In definitions of evaluation the purposes the evaluation is to serve are sometimes also specified. As for example the definition by Mertens (1998: 219) already quoted here, in which the purpose of reducing uncertainty in decision-making is cited. Patton's (1991: 139) definition contains a large number of possible functions for evaluation. 'Program evaluation is the systematic collection of information about the activities, characteristics, and outcomes of programs to make judgements about the program, improve program effectiveness, and / or inform decisions about future programming'.

Some definitions refer to the procedures to be used, as for example in Scriven (1991: 139): 'the evaluation process normally involves some identification of relevant standards of merit, worth, or value; some investigation of the performance of the evaluands on these standards; and some integration or synthesis of the results to achieve an overall evaluation or set of associated evaluations'.

Rossi, Freeman and Lipsey's (1999: 4) definition cites not only the methodological procedure but also a precise purpose:

> Program evaluation is the use of social research procedures to systematically investigate the effectiveness of social intervention programs. More specifically, evaluation researchers (evaluators) use social research methods to study, appraise, and help improve social programs in all their important aspects, including the diagnosis of the social problems they address, their conceptualization and design, their implementation and administration, their outcomes, and their efficiency.

As stated at the beginning, the term evaluation is in widespread use. Thus there are, apart from these scientific definitions, a large number of other meanings of the word in everyday life that can cause confusion if they are not clearly defined[6]. In its least specific form, evaluation means nothing more than that something is assessed by someone applying some criteria in some way (cf. Kromrey 2001: 106). In a procedure of this kind, neither intersubjectively verifiable nor uniform findings are to be expected. Depending on who gathers and assesses the information and what criteria and methods are used, different assessments will be arrived at for the same evaluand or circumstance.

It is true that in a political context considerably more specific definitions of evaluation are used, but it should be noted that some very diverse procedures are denoted by the same term. The measurement of efficiency in economic contexts, for example, is referred to as evaluation just as much as the analysis of the efficiency of organizations carried out by experts (e.g. the evaluation of scientific institutions), or even the involvement of evaluators in the process of developing or optimizing action programmes in a deliberative and moderating capacity. These days, people seem happy to refer to almost any form of report as an evaluation.

What with this inflationary use of the term, even 'common or garden variety' survey research appears to be dressed up as evaluation. The recording and analysis of assessive (i.e. 'evaluating') statements from respondents who have a calculable relationship to the evaluand such as customers, clients, affected parties, participants etc. is presented as evaluation. Although no specific evaluation design exists, subjective value judgements and assessments, utterances of satisfaction or information relating to acceptance are recorded. The only difference between this and popular opinion research is that it aims to record not opinions but assessments or estimates of people's satisfaction (cf. Kromrey 2001: 106f.).

If this use of the term is contrasted with the scientific understanding of evaluation presented above, it becomes clear in spite of the heterogeneity noted that *scientifically conducted evaluations* distinguish themselves by the facts that (1) they relate to a clearly defined object (e.g. political intervention measures, projects, programmes, policies etc.), (2) objectifying empirical data gathering methods are used to generate information and (3) the assessment is carried out explicitly on the circumstance to be evaluated and applying criteria that are precisely stipulated and disclosed (4) with the aid of systematically comparative procedures. The evaluation is (5) as a rule conducted by persons with appropriate special skills (evaluators) (6) with the aim of making decisions relating to the evaluand.

From the above remarks, it is clear that in an evaluation it is very much a question of *what is being evaluated, for what purpose, by whom and applying what criteria*. This fact is, however, often neglected in public discussion, when evaluation findings are brought to bear in all kinds of different explanation context and all kinds of different objective are thus pursued with them. If evaluations are not conducted professionally by suitably qualified people, applying scientific criteria and adhering to professional standards – in other words when they are *everyday evaluations* – they are encumbered with considerable *risk*. Circumstances can for example be presented one-sidedly or even 'falsely'; certain stakeholders' interests may be over- or undervalued; the criteria applied may not be uniform. It may also be the case that unsuitable designs or survey methods were used in asking the questions, that the real target groups were not the ones actually examined or even that the 'wrong' questions were answered. In such cases evaluations represent a *source of risk*, for the basis on which assessments or decisions are made only seems to be rational. In addition to that, evaluations conducted unprofessionally can more easily be abused for manipulative purposes than their professional counterparts, though of course the latter are not immune to abuse either.

To minimise this risk and exploit the utilization potential of evaluation in the best possible way, each professionally conducted evaluation should tackle the following *questions:*

(1) *What* (which object) is being evaluated?
(2) *For what purpose?*
(3) *Applying what criteria?*
(4) *By whom?*
(5) *How* (i.e. with what methods)?

Since the way in which these questions are answered has a very decisive influence on the respective evaluation result, they will be examined more closely in the section that follows.

2.2.2 What is to be evaluated? Evaluands

In principle, there are hardly any restrictions that apply to the selection of an evaluand. *Objects of assessment* can be laws, products, services, organizations, people, processes, social states of affairs of any kind whatsoever, or even other evaluations. Often, however, the objects investigated and assessed in evaluations are reform measures, projects, programmes or policies.

A *'policy'* can be defined as a self-contained strategy for action relating to a specific topic or problem (cf. Bank & Lames 2000: 6).[7] These strategies are sometimes rather nebulously worded and, looking far ahead, represent visions, though they do sometimes specify concrete operations. What they have in common is that they postulate objectives defined as being desirable, whatever their nature (cf. Bussmann et al. 1997: 66f., 83). In order to be able to achieve these objectives, detailed implementation plans are necessary, which are as a rule operationalized in coordinated programmes, projects and individual measures. An *intervention measure* is the smallest action unit. *Projects* consist of a group of individual measures, and *programmes,* in turn, of a series of interrelated projects. Together, they form the primary means with which governments and their administrations channel resources in order to realize their political strategies.

According to Hellstern and Wollmann (1984: 7), programmes are complex action models, 'which are geared to the achievement of certain objectives and based on certain strategies for action which seem appropriate to those objectives, and for the carrying out of which financial, human and other resources are made available'. Scriven (2002: 285) understands by a programme 'the general effort that marshals staff and projects toward some (often poorly) defined and funded goals'. Royse et al. (2001: 5) define a programme as 'an organized collection of activities designed to reach certain objectives'. Projects are referred to as 'the primary means through which governments (...) attempt to translate their plans and policies into programs of action' (Rondinelli 1983: 3). Regardless of how comprehensive or detailed development plans and strategies for action are, 'they are of little value unless they can be translated into projects or programs that can be carried out' (ibid.).

Viewed *instrumentally,* programmes and projects are groups of measures for achieving fixed planned objectives, by which the intention is to introduce innovations within social systems. From an *organizational* point of view, they are units equipped with material and human resources and embedded in an organization (the provider), which in turn is a component in a wider systemic context. Via programme/project interventions impacts can be triggered in the provider or its environment (e.g. the target groups, recipients of benefits [impactees] or entitled parties [awardees]).

According to Royse et al. (2001: 5ff.) the *characteristics of good programmes* include:

- qualified personnel
- a budget of their own
- stable allocation of funds
- an identity of their own
- an estimate of requirements based on empirical findings
- a 'programme theory' about the causal action of the programme
- a service philosophy and
- an empirically based evaluation system for the examination of programme results.

While the support of programmes is time-limited, institutional funding is not. This is obviously the most important difference between both kinds of support (cf. Kuhlmann & Holland 1995: 14).

When programmes are the subject of evaluations, the client is mostly interested in the question of whether the targets striven toward in the programme are achievable (preformative/formative) or have been achieved (summative). The target specifications are compared with the actual status, measured at the point in time when the evaluation is conducted. The more the actual value corresponds to the target specifications (or perhaps even surpasses them), the better the assessment of the result. There is however a number of problems associated with *objectives-oriented evaluations,* which can make it far more difficult to conduct them. This is particularly the case if programme objectives have not been clearly worded or are lacking altogether; if there are other, competing (informal) target specifications alongside the officially declared objectives; if not all the actors (for example in an organization which is implementing a programme) are pursuing the same aims or if the objectives turn out to have undergone major change over time.

Conversely, the evaluation itself can influence the *target formulation process.* If it is assumed in a programme that its success will be measured mainly in terms of how far it has achieved its targets, there is a great temptation either to formulate the targets loosely so that there is plenty of room for interpretation, or to set the thresholds for achievement of those targets very low so that they will be met whatever happens. Those responsible for the programme will tend to avoid demanding target formulations in order not to court failure. In such situations, evaluations based on mere comparisons of targets and achievements run the risk of serving as nothing more than a way of announcing that the evaluation has been conducted. Evaluations which stay at this level can thus cannot make very much of a contribution to solving implementation and development problems or increasing the effectiveness of projects and programmes, since they hardly have any capacity to bring about change (cf. also Section 3.4.1).

Regardless of these problems, objectives-oriented evaluations also carry a risk that unintended impacts may be systematically obscured from view (tunnel vision). Yet these impacts are just the ones which can prove interesting and important and thus vital to the assessment of the success, effectiveness or sustainability of a programme.

As a way of getting round these problems, *impact-oriented evaluation* may be a good *alternative. Impact-oriented evaluation* does not primarily investigate the objectives of a programme, but attempts, guided by hypotheses, to track down potential impacts. The evaluation approach developed by the CEval, for example, through which the search for intended and unintended impacts can be directed and structured, is suitable for this (cf. Section 2.3).

Although the term 'impacts' is a key factor in evaluation, it is not always clear what it actually means. It is often confused with the term 'output'. *Outputs* are the products or services made or rendered by an organization, such as the number of meals distributed, the number of patients treated, the number of consultations undertaken etc. *Impacts* are the changes which are consequences of those outputs – for example people who are no longer hungry, the improved state of health of those treated, or people who, having been advised, now know what to do.

When taking stock of the impacts of a programme, any *unintended consequences* must not be neglected, for the quality of a programme cannot be contemplated in isolation, but only in the whole of its complexity. This therefore also includes unexpected and undesired impacts. Impacts can then be categorized according to whether they are *intended (planned)* and in accord with the objectives of the programme or range of services, or *unintended (unplanned)*. Intended impacts will, as a rule, be assessed positively with regard to the achievement of targets, whilst unintended impacts can turn out to be both positive – when they support the achievement of the targets – or negative when they go against it. Intended negative impacts are certainly also possible – for example if certain anticipated disadvantages connected with a programme are consciously tolerated. Whether an impact is assessed as intended or unintended, positive or negative, of course depends on the objectives of the programme, and not least also on the point of view of the observer.

There would, for example, be positive intended impacts if an injection of funds into the school system led not only to more teachers being engaged, but also to smaller classes, so that the pupils could learn more. An undesired effect might be that fewer qualified teachers were engaged because not enough of them were available, so that the quality of education at the schools actually dropped instead of rising as intended.

Impacts can manifest themselves in the changing of *structures, processes* or *individual behavioural patterns*. There would for example be a change in structure if the Education Act or the curricula were changed in order to increase the amount of practical work done in class. Process impacts would be brought about if, for example, the syllabus were imparted more interactively and less didactically. For this to happen, the individual behavioural patterns of the teachers would also have to change – for example by their adapting the style of their lessons and teaching according to the new curricula.

According to this concept, impacts can be classified analytically in three dimensions (cf. Table 2.4):

1st dimension: structure – process – behaviour
Impacts can relate to structures (e.g. of organizations or social subsystems), processes and/or individual behavioural patterns.

2nd dimension: planned – unplanned
Impacts can occur as planned (intended) or unplanned (unintended).

3rd dimension: positive – negative
Impacts which occur as planned or unplanned can either support the objectives of the programme or output (+) or go against them (–).

Table 2.4 Impact dimensions

Impact dimension	Planned	Unplanned
Structure	+ –	+ –
Process	+ –	+ –
Behaviour	+ –	+ –

As the *aim of impact-oriented evaluations* is to ascertain with the greatest possible degree of reliability whether or not an intervention is having the intended impacts, the influences of other factors that might also be responsible for the changes measured need to be eliminated. Causes thus need to be attributed very carefully in the network of observed impacts. This is one of the greatest challenges that an evaluation faces. The main reason is that the social world is highly complex, which is to say that most social phenomena have many different causes. In addition, interventions as a rule have only a rather limited area in which to operate and a low potential for bringing about change. Often, the outcomes of programmes or outputs are only poorly developed and there is a risk, even if the analyses are carried out professionally, that they may, in the general hubbub, not even be recognized at all (cf. Section 5.4).

A distinction needs to be made, in the identification of outcomes and their causal factors, between *'gross outcome'*, which comprises all outcomes, and *'net effects'* such as are to be attributed to the intervention alone: 'Net effects are the changes on outcome measures that can be reasonably attributed to the intervention, free and clear of the influence of any other causal factors that may also influence outcomes' (Rossi, Freeman & Lipsey 1999: 240ff.).

There are also *effects* that are caused by *other factors* ('extraneous confounding factors'). These include all the outcomes which have come about in addition to and independently of the intervention. Apart from these there are also *design effects*, i.e. measurement errors and artefacts which can be attributed to the investigation process itself. This circumstance can be illustrated as follows (cf. Figure 2.1).

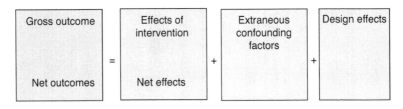

Figure 2.1   Impact formula

The objective of an evaluation consists in cleansing the gross outcome of these extraneous confounding factors and design effects so that the net effects and their causes can be isolated. In this way, erroneous rival explanations of the outcomes observed can be excluded.

These may also be the results of endogenous and/or exogenous change or the occurrence of 'historical events'. There will be an *endogenous* explanation when a critical status which was to be remedied by means of certain intervention measures disappears of its own accord. Many people recover from acute illness without being treated by a doctor, for example. This endogenous change is referred to in medicine as 'spontaneous remission'. If new medication is tested in pharmacological experiments, the self-healing powers of the human body are therefore taken into account – as part of the 'gross outcome'.

In a road-building project the intended aim might be to increase the welfare of certain farmers by enabling them to get into town more easily using the new road, thus increasing their sales market and bringing about an improvement in their welfare. However, an endogenous process of change could also be responsible for the increase in welfare observed, –for example if the farmers planted crops that yielded more or were more marketable, developed new sales markets for themselves or found new sales channels.

The increase in welfare among the farmers' families could furthermore be the consequence of an *exogenous* change. General structural trends such as an overall economic upturn may have led to an increased demand for agricultural produce and thus be responsible for the boost to the farmers' welfare. Or a prolonged period of favourable climatic conditions may have brought better harvests.

Finally, a *sudden event* may also render the outcomes of an intervention stronger or weaker. The construction of another road, for example, might simultaneously make it easier for people from another region to make their way to the market and thus bring about a surplus, causing prices to fall. Or a storm might damage the road, rendering it impassable. A positive scenario is equally conceivable: if for example after a change of government, some privilege is granted to the farmers in the region concerned on account of their political allegiance or for family or ethnic reasons, and their earning capacities improve for that reason.

It should be noted here that some very diverse objects and circumstances can be objects of evaluation (evaluands). Often, it is programmes and other politically ordained measures, in the evaluation of which the achievement of targets is mainly to the fore. Having said that, a number of problems can occur, so that it may well be a good alternative to orient the evaluation toward the impacts brought about by the evaluand. Whatever happens, it is necessary to come to terms with the meaning of the term 'impacts'. Here the suggestion has been made that impacts be determined analytically in three dimensions and that a distinction be made between gross outcome and net effects.

2.2.3 For what purpose is the evaluation being conducted? Objectives and tasks

As explained in Chapter 1, evaluation can serve three superordinate purposes:

- *social enlightenment,* in order to examine the relevance of policies applying generally accepted standards and values
- the *procurement of legitimacy for democratic regimes,* in order to put the credibility and acceptance of political decisions on a rational, verifiable basis
- the *optimization of programme management* in order to increase the effectiveness, efficiency and sustainability of projects and programmes.

In the section that follows, it is mainly *programme evaluation* which is highlighted. Its main task is to procure and assess information for decisions in control and management processes.

In this context, evaluations can fulfil four functions, which can be kept apart analytically although they are closely connected. Having said that, it does make sense to distinguish between them, because depending on the topic or topics selected different approaches and concepts may be used. The four functions referred to are as follows:

(1) the gaining of insights
(2) the exercising of control
(3) the initiation of development and learning processes

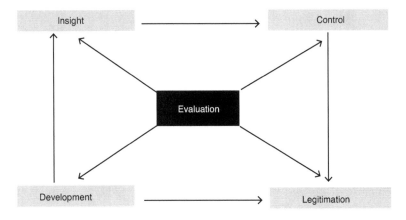

Figure 2.2   Main functions of evaluation

(4) the legitimation of the measures, projects or programmes
implemented.

In detail:

a) Evaluations are intended to supply *insights*, for example in order to put
management decisions on a rational basis. Someone may for example
be interested in knowing whether or not the programme is developing
smoothly, what the requirements of the target group are, whether the
measures are actually reaching the target group, how things are going
with regard to the acceptance of the programme, whether the implementing organizations are in a position to implement the programme
effectively and efficiently, how the framework conditions have changed,
what effect this has had on the development of the programme or
the achievement of targets and the programme impacts, what contributions the programme has made to solving the problem concerned,
what degree of sustainability the programme has achieved, whether or
not the changes observed really can be attributed to the programme
or to other factors etc. The information is gathered with the purpose
of gaining insights, so that these can be judged by applying the agreed
assessment criteria, or the assessment criteria already prescribed in
the programme and management decisions derived from them. The
insights presented by the evaluators and their assessments do not
necessarily have to be in harmony with the assessments made by the
entities implementing the programme or the target groups, and the
latter may, in turn, also differ from one another.

It is true that evaluations are often – but not always – commissioned by sponsoring or implementing entities. Scientific evaluations distinguish themselves mainly by having a cognitive interest. It is then not primarily a matter of gaining information in order to rationalize a decision or decisions, but of analysing internal structures and processes in the politico-administrative system. Such insights, gained in the immediate social field, feature a degree of external validity that can hardly be achieved in any other way (cf. Kromrey 2001: 114).

b) Without gaining insights, in other words knowledge about the development of structures and processes, no evaluation would be able to create benefit. Yet it is not always the decision-making that is to the fore in the utilization of the insights, but the *control*. In this case it is above all a matter of ascertaining whether or not the objectives stipulated in the planning phase have been achieved. 'Success' criteria such as effectiveness, efficiency, acceptance or sustainability can be used for this. Alongside legitimacy control (courts), political control (politics) and efficiency control (courts of auditors), 'control' evaluations are a further way of examining administrative action (cf. Kromrey 2001: 115). Even if evaluations are not primarily intended to serve the purpose of control, they do as a rule reveal whether or not all those involved in a programme are fulfilling their tasks, meeting the obligations to which they have committed themselves, and whether or not their qualifications and competence are sufficient etc. In other words, directly or indirectly, some form of control is associated with every evaluation.

c) Both insight-oriented and control-oriented evaluations provide findings that can be used for the *development* of a programme. When findings are disclosed, a *dialogue* between various different stakeholders (sponsors, the implementing organization, target groups, other stakeholders) becomes possible. On the basis of the findings, for example, a summary can be made, jointly and in a way that is transparent for all, of how successfully the cooperation is going, in what areas the greatest successes can be recorded and where deficiencies have occurred, so that conclusions can be drawn as to how to proceed. In this function of evaluation, *learning processes* are to the fore, and these are intended to be used for the further development of programmes. As will be shown later, this function plays a pivotal role in formative (programme-shaping) evaluations.

d) Another function of evaluation consists in *legitimizing* programmes or measures that have already been implemented. The data obtained with the aid of an evaluation make it possible to prove in a verifiable way what outputs and impacts have been achieved over time, and with what inputs. This makes it possible for funding and implementing organizations to demonstrate how efficiently they have handled funds and what degree of efficiency their projects and programmes have achieved. With ex-post evaluations, statements can also be made about the sustainability of programme impacts. Particularly when funds are scarce, this function of evaluation becomes more important, since programmes often compete with one another and policymakers have to set priorities and make choices. Applying evaluation criteria (e.g. effectiveness, efficiency, relevance, sustainability etc.), the legitimation of programmes or measures can be demonstrated and communicated. However, it is often the case that evaluation findings are put to internal use only, i.e. not made transparent to the general public and not used for legitimizing the work of clients or policymakers.

e) Very often, evaluations are also attributed with *'tactical' functions*. This is said to be the case if their findings are only to be used to legitimize certain political decisions (sometimes even after the event), for example because a programme is to be continued or discontinued. Meanwhile, it has also become 'chic' for politicians 'to use evaluations as baubles or as bolsters' (Pollitt 1998: 223), as decorative symbols of modern politics, without actually intending to put their findings to any use. This kind of 'tactical' function can however hardly be reconciled with the real purpose of evaluations. It would be nearer the mark to say that it represented their pathological side.

Specifying a priority function governs the approach and determines how evaluations are designed and conducted. Evaluations may not only perform different functions, but they may also, in the individual phases of programme development, pursue different analysis perspectives and cognitive interests (cf. Table 2.5). They can be used to

(1) improve the planning of a programme or measure (ex-ante evaluation) (cf. Rossi, Lipsey & Freeman 2004: 336ff.)
(2) observe implementation processes (ongoing evaluation) or
(3) determine the effectiveness and sustainability of interventions ex-post (ex-post evaluation) (cf. Rossi, Lipsey & Freeman 2004: 360ff.).

(1) If an evaluation is oriented toward the *programme development phase*, including its conceptualization and planning, its main task is to examine 'the material, human, institutional, financial, theoretical framework conditions of a programme', in order to make a

Table 2.5   Dimensions of evaluation research

Phases of programme process	Analysis perspective	Cognitive interest	Evaluation concepts
programme draft/ planning phase	ex-ante	'analysis for policy' 'science for action'	preformative/ formative: actively shaping, process-oriented, constructive
implementation phase	ongoing	both possible	formative/ summative: both possible
impact phase	ex-post[8]	'analysis of policy' 'science for knowledge'	summative: summarizing, recapitulating, results-oriented

contribution to the programme design (cf. Brandtstädter 1990: 217). Estimates should be made as early as possible regarding the negative effects of the programme and its chances for sustainability, in order to find out whether or not it is sustainable in the long term and will continue to have the desired impacts after the end of the funding period. Such investigations are referred to as *'ex-ante'*, *'input'* or *'preformative evaluations'* (Scriven 1991: 169).

(2) During the *implementation phase* the evaluation primarily supports the programme managers in management. As information about the way the programme is going and the programme results is collected, systematized and assessed, the intention is to provide aids to decision-making for implementation and enable corrections to be made to the programme design (cf. Rossi et al. 1988: 12, 31, 63; Wottawa & Thierau 1990: 54). Such evaluations with the pressing aim of providing management with information relevant to control by monitoring programme development and the implementation of the planning specifications and verifying the achievement of targets, are referred to as *'ongoing'* or *'formative evaluations'* (Scriven 1991: 169) or as 'accompanying research' (Rossi et al. 1988: 11). They concern themselves with the same phase of the political process as implementation research and pursue similar aims.

(3) *After the conclusion of the implementation* of a programme, the evaluation has the task of recording and assessing the full scope of the impacts triggered by the programme, discovering correlations, and minutely investigating the causes of the impacts observed (causality

issue) (cf. Scriven 1991: 340). Such *'ex-post evaluations'* also have the important task of investigating the sustainability of projects and programmes.

Evaluations can thus be more *formative*, i.e. actively shaping, process-oriented, constructive and communication-promoting, or more *summative*, i.e. recapitulating, summarizing and results-oriented.

As there are hardly any opportunities for a summative evaluation in the planning and design phase of a programme, any evaluation at this stage can only be of a formative character. In the implementing phase both formative and summative evaluations are possible. Ex-post analyses are as a rule summative, there being no shaping aspect. With the appropriate information feedback loops for follow-up projects they can however also take on formative significance.

This observation is also a good indication of the *benefit* the evaluation of projects and programmes can create:

(1) Evaluations can (preformatively) serve to examine the *prerequisites for implementing a programme* and then (formatively) to observe the *work processes*. This is a question of identifying problems in the implementation of a programme and of whether or not schedules can be adhered to. In this context it is also necessary to find out whether or not the measures are accepted by the various stakeholders, what conflicts of interest arise, whether or not qualified staff are available in sufficient numbers to implement the measures, how the communication and coordination of the executive entities with one another and with the target groups of the programme functions, whether or not the technical and financial equipment is sufficient for the achievement of the targets, whether or not the innovations introduced with the programme are likely to lead to the right results etc.

(2) One prominent task of evaluations, as has already been explained, consists in drawing up an *overall balance sheet of the impacts*. This balance sheet comprises an examination of the extent to which the *targets have been achieved,* by means of a *'comparison of targets and actual achievements'* involving the target values stipulated in the planning phase, and actually goes far beyond this by recording as many as possible (ideally all) of the impacts triggered by the programme interventions. It is not until an *overall balance sheet of the impacts* has been drawn up that it becomes clear whether it is the positive or negative effects of a programme that predominate.

(3) Evaluations are not only supposed to ascertain whether or not one is 'on the right road' *(process observation)*, in other words whether or not one might expect that the targets can be achieved to the extent planned, with the material and human resources envisaged, in the prescribed period of time, but also whether or not one is 'doing the right things'. That is to say that evaluations question the very objectives of a programme or measure. It is a matter of investigating whether or not *relevant development or innovation outputs* can be generated with the programme at all, or if it would be better to set off in a completely different direction.

(4) It is of course not sufficient to register impacts and assess their contribution to development; the question of whether or not the intended and unintended impacts observed are to be attributed to the programme at all *(attribution problem)* or to external factors *(causality problem)* is also of vital significance.

2.2.4 What assessment criteria are to be applied?

Before circumstances or objects are assessed by one or more people, the criteria according to which the assessment should be carried out need to be determined. The fact that the *assessment criteria* selected can of course vary greatly is already one reason to expect a great variety of evaluation results. If for example someone gets his friends ('evaluators') to assess a film ('evaluand') so that he, as the 'user of the evaluation results', can make a decision on whether he wishes to see it or not, the assessments will be dependent on the criteria applied to a crucial extent; for example on whether the 'evaluators' apply criteria which involve the dramaturgy, the most impressive action sequences, how convincing the respective actors were, the principal gags, the logic of the plot etc., or indeed a combination of all or any of these.

Unlike *series* of standards such as those posted by the ISO[9] and the parameters laid down in quality management models such as those of the EFQM,[10] evaluation cannot have recourse to a fixed canon of assessment criteria (cf. Stockmann 2008: 21ff.). Indeed, in view of the great variety of tasks evaluation faces and objects it investigates, this would not make much sense. Very often, however, the assessment criteria are oriented toward the benefit of an object, circumstance or development process for certain people or groups. For example, the following criteria might be suitable for the assessment of a funding programme to improve equality of opportunities in the education sector:

- an increase in the proportion of children from lower social strata or with an immigrant background who succeed in passing from primary to secondary school (e.g. middle school, grammar school etc.)
- a reduction in the number of those children who have to repeat a school year
- an improvement in the performance of those children in school performance tests in the various different types of school
- an increase in the proportion of those children who have middle school or grammar school leaving qualifications
- an increase in the proportion of those children who begin and complete studies at a university
- an increase in the proportion of girls in the group who make the transition to a middle or grammar school etc., obtain leaving qualifications there and enrol for and complete studies at a university.

After Dror (1968: 28); Vedung (2000: 224) cites the following points of reference for assessments in evaluations:

(1) *Historical comparison:* how does the output achieved compare with that achieved in the past?
(2) *Intranational comparison:* how does the output achieved measure up to that of similar institutions in the same regional or national area?
(3) *International comparison:* how does the output achieved measure up to that of similar institutions in other countries?
(4) *Standard values:* how does the output observed stand as compared with the best empirical practice?
(5) *Targets:* does the output measured meet the formulated target dimensions?
(6) *Target group expectations:* does the output achieved fulfil the expectations of the target groups (audiences)?
(7) *Stakeholders' expectations:* does the output achieved come up to the expectations of other stakeholders?
(8) *Professional standards:* do the outputs correspond to widely accepted professional standards?
(9) *Minimum:* is the output achieved high enough to meet minimum requirements?
(10) *Optimum:* is the output achieved as high as it could be when compared with an optimum model?

Binding evaluation criteria have been established in individual policy fields. This applies particularly to development cooperation, which is among the best evaluated areas. Of particular importance here is the Development Assistant Committee (DAC) of the Organization for Economic Cooperation and Development (OECD), toward which many national organizations orient themselves. The DAC applies the following criteria for the evaluation of development cooperation programmes:[11]

Relevance: The extent to which the aid activity is suited to the priorities and policies of the target group, recipient and donor.

Effectiveness: A measure of the extent to which an aid activity attains its objectives.

Efficiency: Efficiency measures the outputs – qualitative and quantitative – in relation to the inputs. It is an economic term that signifies that the aid uses the least costly resources possible in order to achieve the desired results. This generally requires comparing alternative approaches to achieving the same outputs, to see whether the most efficient process has been adopted.

Impact: The positive and negative changes produced by a development intervention, directly or indirectly, intended or unintended. This involves the main impacts and effects resulting from the activity on the local social, economic, environmental and other development indicators. The examination should be concerned with both intended and unintended results and must also include the positive and negative impact of external factors, such as changes in terms of trade and financial conditions.

Sustainability: Sustainability is concerned with measuring whether the benefits of an activity are likely to continue after donor funding has been withdrawn. Projects need to be environmentally as well as financially sustainable.

The criteria to be applied for the assessment of information in an evaluation can be stipulated in different ways. If there are standards such as those of the DAC, they are often stipulated *directively* by the client. Sometimes, however, it is left to the evaluator to determine them, as he or she is considered to be an expert who ought to know best what criteria need to be applied to judge a given programme. This selection of criteria could be referred to as *knowledge or experience-based*. It is relatively rare for the assessment criteria to be stipulated by the target group, in other words those who are supposed to benefit from a programme. In such an – emancipatory – procedure, the interests of the target group (which may be disadvantaged) are brought right to the fore. The subjective view of those affected in the selection of the criteria is intended to ensure that their needs and requirements receive priority in the assessment of evaluation findings. A procedure could be referred to as *participant-oriented* in which the clients, evaluators, representatives of the target groups and other stakeholders stipulate the assessment criteria for the evaluation jointly, in order to cater to as many perspectives as possible.

2.2.5   Who is to conduct the evaluation?

Evaluations can in principle be conducted by internal or external experts. Evaluations are referred to as *internal* when they are conducted by the same organization that is implementing the programme or project. If this internal evaluation is conducted by members of the department who are at the same time entrusted with the operative implementation of the programme, the evaluation is a *'self-evaluation'*. If members of a different department in the organization (e.g. an evaluation or quality assurance department) conduct the evaluation, it is an internal evaluation but not a self-evaluation.[12]

'In-house' evaluations have the advantages that they can be conducted quickly and at low cost, that the evaluators as a rule have plenty of relevant know-how, and that the findings can be implemented immediately. The main weaknesses of internal evaluation are considered to be that the evaluators mostly lack sufficient methodological competence, independence and detachment and that they may be so wrapped up in their programme that they fail to recognize more promising alternatives (cf. Figure 2.3).

External evaluations are conducted by people who do not belong to the funding or the implementing organization. As a rule external evaluators thus have a greater degree of independence, profound methodological competence and professional evaluation knowledge, and are familiar with the area to which the programme or project belongs. External evaluations can also endow the reformatory forces within an organization with the extra legitimacy and strength of influence they need to set processes of change in motion (cf. Pollitt 2000: 72).

On the other hand, external evaluations sometimes have to face the problem that they trigger feelings of apprehension among the evaluees and lead to defensive reactions. During the subsequent implementation of evaluation findings too, problems may crop up if those findings are not accepted by the affected parties. It is true to say that external evaluations cause extra costs, but this does not necessarily mean that they are always more expensive than internal ones. If the calculation also includes the costs incurred by those internally occupied with the evalu-

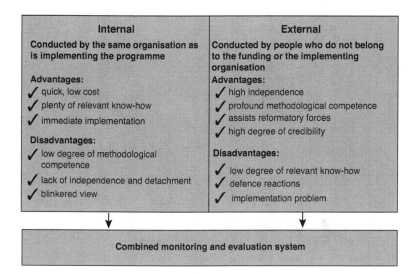

Internal	External
Conducted by the same organisation as is implementing the programme	Conducted by people who do not belong to the funding or the implementing organisation
Advantages:	**Advantages:**
✓ quick, low cost	✓ high independence
✓ plenty of relevant know-how	✓ profound methodological competence
✓ immediate implementation	✓ assists reformatory forces
	✓ high degree of credibility
Disadvantages:	
✓ low degree of methodological competence	**Disadvantages:**
✓ lack of independence and detachment	✓ low degree of relevant know-how
✓ blinkered view	✓ defence reactions
	✓ implementation problem

Combined monitoring and evaluation system

Figure 2.3 Internal and external evaluation

ation in the context of their activities, the financial difference between external and internal evaluation can in fact be relatively slight.

On the contrary, for smaller organizations in particular, it is often far more economical in financial terms to count exclusively on external evaluation expertise. Instead of setting up and maintaining expensive in-house evaluation teams or departments, organizations can outsource this task in its entirety. In this way, smaller organizations can purchase evaluation services from qualified professionals. This means that tasks such as monitoring and controlling, which entities prefer to organize internally, can also be carried out at reasonable cost and always in a way that is right up to date from a professional point of view. So far, this practice of outsourcing tasks in order not to have to maintain expensive capacities themselves, common practice in many private-sector enterprises, has hardly been used at all by non-profit organizations, which avail themselves of the instrument of evaluation more often than companies. On the other hand, internal and external evaluations are often seen *combined*, so that the two views can be brought together and the advantages of both procedures exploited (Figure 2.4).

This depiction is of course a *general typification*, which means that the advantages and disadvantages of internal and external evaluation do not always have to apply like that. Especially when independent evaluation departments have been set up in organizations and qualified experts

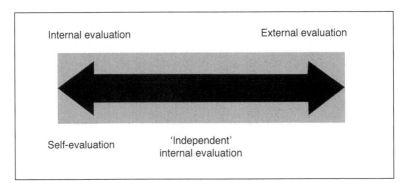

Figure 2.4   Evaluation spectrum

work in those departments, it should not be assumed that the disadvantages of internal evaluations as mentioned above will still manifest themselves with the same intensity. Depending on the degree of their internal independence, they usually have not only a high degree of methodological competence, but also more credibility, a greater degree of professional detachment and a greater potential for reform. At the same time, the disadvantages mentioned in respect of external evaluations can also occur, – for example defensive reactions, implementation problems etc.

Conversely, external evaluations do not automatically guarantee a high degree of independence and credibility. Especially when external experts work repeatedly for the same client and are dependent on only a few clients, their credibility may suffer. For this reason, the typification chosen here is not so much of a dichotomy as a continuum, with external, independent evaluation at one end of the spectrum and internal self-evaluation at the other. Somewhere in between, depending on the degree of organizational independence, is *internal 'independent' evaluation.*

With reference to the objectives of the evaluation it should be noted that evaluations in which the development function (learning) is mainly to the fore are often conducted internally. Insight and control-oriented evaluations are conducted both internally and externally. Evaluations mainly intended to serve the purpose of legitimation are almost exclusively commissioned as external evaluations, so that the greatest possible degree of objectivity and credibility can be attained. Sustainability evaluations, in which the legitimation aspect is very often central, are also mostly external.

Monitoring is closely connected with the instrument of evaluation. In fact, it can be viewed as a special form of internal evaluation, though not every internal evaluation is a form of monitoring. It is true that monitoring tasks are sometimes outsourced or undertaken by external actors (often at national level), but monitoring programmes and projects is mostly an internal activity. Monitoring can start at the level of the system as a whole, or at the level of a policy field, a programme, a project or individual intervention measures. Input, output and impact data can be gathered. A well-known example of a monitoring system at *policy-field level* is environmental monitoring, which supplies measurement data describing the status of our environment. At the whole-society level, for example, a social indicator system provides information on the development of living-conditions in Germany, complementing the official statistics.

At *project and programme level,* a monitoring system has the task of providing management continually with data on progress and the achievement of targets. Rossi, Freeman and Lipsey (1999: 231) duly define it as follows: 'Program monitoring is a form of evaluation designed to describe how a program is operating and assess how well it performs its intended functions' (cf. also Rossi, Lipsey & Freeman 2004: 171). Unlike evaluations, which are conducted singly at a given point in time, monitoring is an ongoing task, a progressive, routine activity aimed at keeping an eye on whether or not the planning specifications and objectives being striven toward are being achieved as efficiently as possible, using the available resources and within the prescribed period of time. Monitoring thus verifies scheduled performance. The programme or project plan and the development hypotheses on which it is based are not questioned. This and the analysis of impact relationships are the task of evaluations. In monitoring, the causal allocation of changes observed plays but a subordinate role. Monitoring is a largely descriptive activity, with which the most reliable data possible are to be collected periodically, continually producing time series from which development trends can be recognized (cf. Kissling-Näf & Knoepfel 1997: 147). This is often either difficult or impossible with individual evaluations.

The difference between monitoring and evaluation consists primarily in the fact that monitoring looks more into routine questions and serves more as a kind of stock-take. Evaluations mainly investigate the impacts of a programme and attempt to get to the bottom of their causes. As well as a stock-take and an assessment, an evaluation will as a rule include an analysis of causes and consequences; monitoring will not. Evaluations are broader and deeper and have other points of emphasis. Unlike monitoring, evaluations also query the concept as a whole; they are of a fundamental nature.

2.2.6   How is the evaluation to be conducted?

The selection of the research paradigm is fundamental to the question of how the evaluation is to be conducted. Broadly speaking, there are *two main tendencies*.[13] Some see evaluation as an *empirical-scientific procedure* which follows critical-rational research logic and in principle considers all the known empirical research methods deployable. Evaluation is thus to be understood as applied social research, which must take account of special research conditions and has a specific cognitive interest in insights and their utilization, in which the use of the findings for praxis is the primary consideration (cf. Vedung 2000: 103ff.; Kromrey 2001: 113).

The second main tendency ascribes a different aspiration to evaluation and starts from different assumptions. The existence of a world which really exists, one which can be recognized as a matter of principle and 'objectively' recorded with the aid of empirical-scientific procedures, even if such instruments may be incomplete and partly defective, is contested. Instead, the assumption is made that *'reality'* is *socially constructed* from various different perspectives that may conflict. For this reason, the disciples of this approach call for 'qualitative' thinking, in order to able to record the various views and interpretations of 'reality'. According to the epistemological position of constructivism, it is as a matter of basic principle not possible to make any statements about the actual nature of the world; '...they merely show whether an insight is compatible with the nature of the world, whether or not it 'fits in' – but not that it is 'true' (in the sense of being the 'only correct version')' (Meinefeld 1995: 100). In evaluations too, therefore, this attitude necessitates a scientific procedure that differs from that used in analytically-nomologically oriented empirical science (cf. in particular Guba & Lincoln 1989; Patton 1987; Stake 1983; see Chapter 3 for a detailed explanation).

Even if the 'cold war of the paradigms' is no longer fought no holds barred, and even if in recent years it is more the similarities between them that have been stressed than the differences, these two tendencies are still not compatible. The premises on which they are based differ too markedly for that. This is a point that should be discussed in somewhat more detail.

On the basis of epistemological realism, the aim of empirical science is to recognize the 'true' structures and laws of reality and document them in theories. Starting from central ex-ante hypotheses, empirical knowledge is gathered systematically, so that (objective) reality can

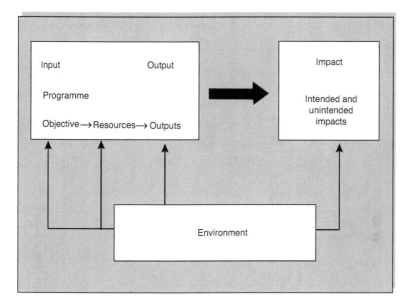

Figure 2.5 Correlations in programme evaluation

be confronted with (subjective) perception data. An attempt is made to control the subjectivity implied by this procedure by applying strict methodological rules in order to eliminate conditions that would influence perception in the empirical gaining of insights as thoroughly as possible ('objectification of procedures'), so that said insights can be verified intersubjectively. The separation of descriptive – and thus 'objectifiable' – statements from normative ones takes on a special significance here, the subjective character of the latter being irrevocable in methodological terms, so that their intersubjective validity cannot be established by empirical means. Resolving this dilemma consists in dividing the normative elements of the gaining of insights into those which form the normative basis of the research (i.e. the values which are immanent to science and upstream of the research) and the non-scientific interests and values, which are shifted to outside the scientific explanation context and relegated to the discovery and utilization context of the research project (cf. Kromrey 2007: 116).

This strategy for dealing with the problem of value judgements used in fundamental research is precisely where the (re)solution of the assessment dilemma in evaluation research is also seen. Kromrey, for example, (2007: 116) comes to the conclusion that the research logic of a science

Table 2.6 Deductive–nomological explanation model

	Hempel-and-Oppenheim deductive-nomological explanation model (1948)	Deductive-nomological programme evaluation model
Explanans	(1) There is (at least) one nomological law (e.g. if A and B, then C)	(1) The manner in which the intervention is to be carried out is based on cause-and-effect hypotheses (theoretical basis) (e.g. if A and B are carried out, C will ensue)
	(2) The framework conditions cited in the then component are empirically fulfilled (e.g. A and B are fulfilled)	(2) Interventions in the current framework conditions (measures) (e.g. A and B have been carried out)
Explanandum	(3) Single sentence which describes the circumstance to be explained (e.g. C is fulfilled)	(3) Programme objective describes future situation (e.g. objective C has been achieved)

which commits the researcher to freedom from values can be applied to evaluation research seamlessly, as long as the evaluand is a programme that has been elaborated.

In a programme, objectives are laid down and resources made available in order to carry out certain measures (i.e. generate outputs) that are aimed at producing certain impacts. This impact structure is influenced by 'confounding variables' in the programme environment.

In evaluation research, the Hempel-and-Oppenheim deductive-nomological explanation model (1948) can be applied analogously (cf. Table 2.6). According to Hempel-and-Oppenheim, the single event to be explained (the *explanandum*) is given (3), whilst the *explanans* needs to be found (1 and 2). In this kind of explanation, the *explanandum* (3) must follow deductively logically from the *explanans* (1 and 2), whereby (2) is derived from the if component and (3) from the then component of the nomological law (cf. Kromrey 2007: 114f.).

Table 2.7 shows a simple example. The circumstance to be explained (3) is why pupils show increased motivation to perform well. The explanation avails itself of a 'law' (1) of motivation theory, which states that rewards can lead to increased motivation to perform under certain conditions. Sentence 2 of the explanation model shows that these conditions have been fulfilled.

Table 2.7 Example of a deductive–nomological explanation

	Explanation model for the power of rewards in motivating pupils to better performance	Explanation model for the effectiveness of a programme aimed at people wishing to set up a business
Explanans	(1) If a pupil performs well (A) and is rewarded for it (B), this increases his motivation to perform well (C)	(1) If unemployed persons (A) take part in a programme aimed at people wishing to set up a business (B), they subsequently go into business for themselves (C)
	(2) The pupil has performed well (A) and been rewarded for it (B)	(2) Unemployed (A) have participated in a programme aimed at people wishing to set up a business (B)
Explanandum	(3) Pupil shows increased motivation to perform well (C)	(3) Unemployed persons have gone into business for themselves (C)

In the explanation model of the evaluation which follows this (cf. Table 2.6), the *explanandum* (3) is not given, but is the status being striven toward (i.e. the programme objective). In the conception of the programme, consideration must be given to the question of how this status can be achieved. The way in which the interventions are to be carried out under certain conditions, in other words which measures are to be implemented for the achievement of the targets (2), is based on cause-and-effect hypotheses (1).

In the example in Table 2.7, this means that the objective of getting unemployed persons to go into business for themselves (3) is achieved by their taking part in a programme aimed at people who wish to set up a business (2), since it is assumed that said programme (1) empowers people to go into business for themselves. As empirical experience shows, this is in fact seldom the case, even if the programme does prepare the unemployed persons excellently for future independence, since many factors in the environment of the programme (confounding variables), such as the lack of a market for their business idea, no financing on account of poor creditworthiness etc. may impede the achievement of the programme objective.

From this alone, it becomes clear that the explanation of programme impacts, in particular that of unintended ones, calls not for one of these deductive-nomological derivations, but several. The complexity of social circumstances is one of the very characteristics of applied social research and thus also of evaluation. Whilst fundamental research, with objectives such as theory test and theory development, attempts to solve the problem of complexity by systematically simplifying the investigation situation – going so far as to design laboratory situations which are far removed from reality – in order to isolate the influence of individual impact factors, such a procedure is hardly an option in applied research: *'Real social circumstances* are not a field of experimentation which can be simplified; they are, and continue to be, complex reality. In this framework, a *reasonable description and diagnosis* can *only ever be complex* – either that, or it must be wrong and must equally lead to wrong conclusions' (Kromrey 2003: 97).[14]

As shown in Chapter 1, it is true that the object to be assessed in the evaluation is neither neutral nor 'pure' as an object. Quite the opposite: the programme explicitly aims to bring about change in order to achieve a defined objective. But the value problem associated with that is solved by being transferred to the context of discovery, so that the actual research phase takes on a neutral character (cf. Kromrey 2007: 117).

The assessments made in evaluations – despite what Kromrey (2007: 113) says – are not regarded as violations of neutrality, since no value judgements are made, but rather as instrumental assessments relating to criteria laid down in the discovery context of the evaluation (cf. Chapter 1).

In spite of its stringency – or indeed perhaps just because of it – this research model can often only be realized for evaluations with great difficulty, because a number of conditions associated with it cannot be complied with. A programme, for example, is not a static formation with immutable objectives; the evaluand evolves over time. With ex-post evaluations, this is not a major problem, as a certain baseline can be stipulated retrospectively, serving as a starting-point for the impact research to be undertaken. With formative evaluations, which aim directly to change the evaluand, the reference points for the analysis vary. Moreover, criticism might also be levelled at the research model to the effect that it concentrates closely on the impact path 'programme objectives → measures for their implementation → impacts', neglecting those involved and central environmental factors by declaring them to be 'confounding variables' that can be controlled statistically. Those involved are only given a shaping role in this research model in the discovery context and then once again in the utilization context. That may not be a problem with summative (or in particular with ex-post) evaluations, but in formative evaluations the research model quickly reaches its limitations.

From the criticism of this model and under the postulate that evaluations ought mainly to serve the interests of those affected, a research position has developed that sees evaluation more as a political process than a scientific one...one which in extreme cases resembles an 'art' (Cronbach 1982) more than a science.

Action research takes up this idea and postulates that evaluation must not only include quality control with regard to innovations, 'but at the same time the design, optimization and legitimation of the model measures' (Lange 1983: 256). Methodologically, the procedure is that the programme development is evaluated in an iterative, loop like procedure. Each of these 'loops' is divided into three main phases: identification of the evaluand, gathering of information, dissemination of findings. With as many stakeholders as possible being involved, this process of questioning and querying, answering, assessing, informing and negotiating is repeated again and again while the programme develops, with the aim of achieving the greatest possible benefit for those affected or targeted by the programme (cf. Kromrey 2001: 129).

In this concept, evaluators take on the role of moderators, becoming active in the discourse of the groups involved in the project as gatherers and managers of information, enlighteners regarding correlations, imparters of specialist knowledge, conflict managers, coordinators and consultants (cf. Cronbach et al. 1981; Cronbach 1982; Wottawa & Thierau 1998: 33). Kromrey (2001: 129) thus refers to this form of evaluation as the *'helper and advisor model'*. He points out that this form of evaluation, as accompanying consultancy, is certainly not to be regarded as a 'softer' or less demanding variant than the concept of programme research. Evaluators in the function of moderators and consultants, says Kromrey, first of all require all the knowledge and skills usually imparted in social science study courses (especially the empirical quantitative and qualitative survey methods and the various different data analysis procedures), and over and above that also other qualifications, only some of which can be learnt, the others having instead to be gained by experience, such as interdisciplinary orientation, the ability to communicate, force of persuasion, scientifically precise and politically comprehensible usage, empathy, moderation, and techniques for presentation and public speaking. Having said that, these are all qualifications that evaluators must have at their disposal anyway if they are proceeding according to critical-rational research logic.

The following methodological consequences follow from the evaluation model borrowed from action research, and they run counter to the conventional social science research paradigm:

- It is not the falsification of theories or hypotheses that is the primary scientific objective, but the indication of alternative actions for solving problems that may arise.
- The detachment between evaluators and their evaluands is revoked. The scientists abandon their detached position with regard to the evaluand and become equal-footing partners of those directly involved in the evaluation and those affected by it (evaluation research with strongly participant-oriented components, in extreme cases action research).
- It is not the research questions of the evaluator on which the interest is focused, but the information requirements of the target groups.
- It is not neutrality which is striven toward in the statements; on the contrary, judgements are called for which are prepared to take a stance.
- The quality criteria of the evaluation are no longer primarily validity, reliability and objectivity, but communication, intervention, transparency and relevance. (Cf. Gruschka 1976: 142–151; Weiss 1972: 6f.; Rein 1984: 179; Lachenmann 1987: 320; Staudt et al. 1988: 27f.; Gagel 1990: 45ff.; Schneider-Barthold 1992: 379ff).

The participant-oriented approaches, as represented for example by Stake (1967); Guba and Lincoln (1989); Patton (1994); Cousins and Earl (1995) and House and Howe (1999), to name but a few protagonists, attempt systematically to put these positions into practice in evaluation (see Chapter 3 for more detail). They do not seek merely to ensure that the stakeholders are involved but actually 'assist in conducting the evaluation' (Fitzpatrick, Sanders & Worthen 2012: 189). Assuring stakeholder involvement is one thing that other evaluation approaches can also do. It is much more a question of bringing about a complete change of perspective. In order to ensure 'that all relevant interests are represented in the evaluation and given full expression', the advocates of participant-oriented approaches suggest that one should proceed in a certain way: 'representation of views and interests should not be dominated or distorted by power imbalances, such as powerful interests curtailing the less powerful in the evaluation (...) evaluative conclusions should emerge from deliberation, from careful reasoning, reflection, and debate' (House & Howe 2000: 409). In order to achieve the evaluator must abandon his position, which was as objective and neutral as possible, and become part of a team 'whose members collaborate to conceptualize, design, and test new approaches in a long-term, ongoing process of continuing improvement, adaption, and intentional change.

The evaluator's primary function in the team is to elucidate team discussions with evaluative data and logic, and to facilitate data-based decision making in the development process' (Patton 1994: 317).

In its most radical form, evaluation turns into a constructivist combination of negotiations, organizational development and group therapy which by no means searches for superordinate scientific explanations, but serves to emancipate and empower deprived stakeholders (cf. Pollitt 2000: 71).

Starting from the various different 'science philosophies' and the concepts of the role of evaluation in society and the purposes for which it ought to be used, a large number of evaluation theories, models and approaches have developed. They will be dealt with in detail in Chapter 3.

2.3 The CEval evaluation approach after Stockmann

From among the diversity of the various evaluation approaches, the CEval approach, basically oriented toward critical-rational research logic, will now be introduced. This approach has been used in the past fifteen years in numerous policy fields and for all kinds of evaluation purposes. It has proved very versatile, having been used for formative, summative and in particular ex-post evaluations.

In order to be able to deal with the two main tasks of every single evaluation, namely (1) recording as many as possible (ideally all) of the (intended and unintended) impacts and (2) clearing up their causality, an evaluation approach through which the most important relationships between programmes and their impacts can be shown and investigation parameters derived is useful. It is assumed that programmes, looked at in terms of time, follow a phase pattern which resembles the life-course of an individual. Thus (1) the conceptual assumptions of *life-course research* can be applied to clarify programme development. It is also assumed that projects and programmes are as a rule carried out by organizations. Thus (2) *theory-of-organization approaches* are a good idea for analysing relationships between programmes and their areas of impact and developing goals central to the investigation. As on the other hand programmes are often instruments for the introduction of innovations, (3) *theory-of-innovation* and *theory-of-diffusion approaches* can also be utilized.

2.3.1 Life-course model

Programmes are, as has already been emphasized, ideally derived from a political strategy, planned and implemented in individual stages, and as a rule funded for a limited period of time in order to bring about certain desired impacts. The *time axis* connects the various individual phases with one another, in each of which the implementation of specific plans and operations ensures that resources are accumulated successively. In addition to that, programme courses are a multi-dimensional process; they are made up of different programme areas (e.g. development of programme strategy, organizational development, financing etc.), which are interrelated and influence one another mutually. As in the life-course of an individual, the various individual 'areas' are more or less significant, depending on the different 'life situations' and the individual's age.

Moreover, the course of a programme is embedded in sophisticated social multi-level processes. A programme is not developed independently of other existing or planned programmes. Different actors will often pursue different aims with the same programme. Programmes are developed depending on existing social, institutional and organizational framework conditions; social and regional contexts need to be taken into account and they have to adapt to economic, social, political, legal and cultural changes.

Having said that, programmes can of course also have a shaping effect on structures and processes, and as they themselves are, in turn, exposed to external influences, the way they will develop is not always predictable. However, they are *planned* and attempts are made to control them in such a way that the programme objectives are achieved, if possible, within the prescribed periods of time. Programme courses thus differ from life-courses in as much as they are often planned rationally right through from the very beginning in all their individual implementation phases – sometimes in the 'ivory tower' of a planning institution, and sometimes in a participant-oriented way, together with those affected.

Once the programme conception has been developed and the funds made available, the *implementation* can begin. Those responsible for the programme – like an individual in his or her own personal life-course – make sure that their 'life' (i.e. the programme) – is organized in the best possible way. Monitoring and evaluation instruments are used for this, in order to obtain data for 'replanning' and (re-)directing the programme. The programme does not always follow a linear course. On the contrary, sudden events and altered framework conditions not only call for the occasional change of course, but also sometimes even make it necessary to question the intended programme objectives themselves.

With increasing age, i.e. as the programme continues, the desired impacts as regards achievement of the objectives should come about increasingly, so that the programme – if it is designed to run for a limited period of time – can be brought to a *conclusion*. If a programme is designed to be sustainable, the intended impacts should continue beyond the end of the funding period. Very often, funding programmes have been initiated specially for the purpose of bringing about long-term change in structures or behavioural changes in certain target groups. For example, an energy-saving programme should persuade people to carry on using energy frugally after the end of the funding period; a programme for the integration of handicapped persons in the work process should offer entrepreneurs the chance to gain positive experience with the handicapped, so that they alter their employment behaviour in the long-term; a programme for increasing efficiency in fiscal administration should alter the existing administrative structures and sequences in such a way that the objective continues to be achieved after the end of the programme.

To sum up, the *life course* of a programme can be divided roughly into *three main phases* (cf. Figure 2.6): the (1) *planning* and (2) *implementation phases* during the course of the actual programme, and (3) the period following termination of the funding *(sustainability phase)*. The beginning of the life-course of a programme can be characterized by the formulation of a programme idea (t1). The various 'life' phases – such as the programme check, the development of concepts, the individual phases of implementation (t4–tn), the preparation for the end of the funding phase (tF) and the period following funding (tNF) – to name but a few – are each characterized by typical problems. They can be delimited from one another and lend themselves well to analysis using a large quantity of process-produced data available, for example, from applications, tenders, programme descriptions, operational plans, progress reports, monitoring documents, evaluation and final reports etc.

The heuristic advantage of the life-course perspective has two main aspects:

(1) On the one hand, the life-course working hypothesis makes it possible to recognize the phase that comes after the end of the funding period, in which the sustainability of a programme is revealed, as an integral component in the life course of a programme. Like the sequences in the life course of an individual, the individual programme phases are built on one another and arranged in such a way as to implement the aims of the programme successively over time.

(2) On the other hand, the life-course perspective emphasizes the causal interconnection of the individual phases. It becomes clear that the sustainability of a programme is already influenced by the programme selection and that the material and immaterial structures created during the period of funding form the foundation of the long-term programme effects.

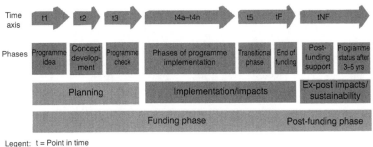

Legent: t = Point in time
tF = Ending of funding
tNF = Post-funding phase

Figure 2.6 Life-course model

2.3.2 Organizational model

Innovations introduced by a programme can be aimed at producing *internal changes* both in the organizations implementing the programme and in other (external) social systems (e.g. other organizations or social subsystems). The more extensively this works, in other words the more the innovations introduced by a programme are adopted by others, the greater the *diffusion* and the more successful the programme.

A concrete example can be used to illustrate this view: the chambers of industry, trade and commerce (providers) decide to run an environmental consultancy programme. Its aim is on the one hand to establish sustainable consultancy structures in the chambers, and on the other to advise companies effectively on environmental issues so that they alter their procedures and structures.

To implement the programme, special organizational units (the chambers' environmental consultancy units) are formed, which carry out consultations in the companies. In this way, the aim is to introduce innovations in the companies advised (e.g. energy-saving production methods, the use of environmentally sound building materials etc.). The more companies introduce these innovations, the greater the diffusion effects. Additional diffusion effects (multiplying effects) would come about if these innovations were also adopted by companies which had not been advised (for example because they proved to be profitable or cost-saving for those that had).

Since it is *organizations* that implement programmes or provide services intended to produce impacts, they and their relationships with

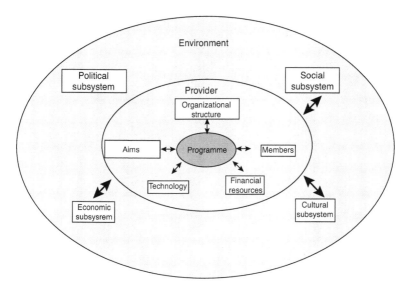

Figure 2.7 Impact model[15]

other organizations or social subsystems are of special importance in impact evaluations. This interdependence is illustrated in Figure 2.7. At the centre of the 'model' is the programme, which – perhaps as part of an organizational unit – is embedded in a provider. Within the framework of the programme's objectives, the aim is to introduce innovations both inside and outside the provider with the aid of coordinated groups of measures. The impact possibilities of the programme are influenced on the one hand by the provider – the internal environment – and on the other by the systems which surround the provider and thus also the programme – the external environment. The external environment areas can have a supportive effect on the objective or act as 'counterforces', hindering or preventing the achievement of the aims.

From among the host of theory-of-organization approaches, an explanatory model presents itself here that understands *organizations as open social systems*, which are, *in terms of their intention, rationally* organized *in order to achieve specific aims* (cf. Thompson 1967: 66ff.; Kieser & Kubicek 1992: 4ff.; Kieser 2002: 169ff.; 1993: 161ff.; Kieser & Walgenbach 2003: 6ff.; Müller-Jentsch 2003: 20ff. Scott 2003: 33ff., 82ff., 141ff.). They have a *formal structure* and use a certain *technology* to gear the activities of their *members* to the *aims* being pursued.[16] The popular sociological organization concepts do not cover the *financial resources* available to an organization. However, since this dimension is of central importance in ensuring that an organization fulfils its tasks and thus continues to survive, it will be included in the analysis here. From it, the elements which constitute an organization can be derived. They are: its aims, its members (i.e. those involved), its formal (i.e. organizational) structure, its technology and its financial resources.[17]

The impact model, as part of the evaluation conception being presented here, admits of *various different causal ways of looking at the situation*. Two analysis perspectives can be taken up, one after the other: first, the programme interventions are viewed as independent variables (IV) and the organizational elements as dependent variables (DV), in order to verify whether or not the interventions (inputs) – under given framework conditions – have brought about any changes in the various different dimensions of the implementing organization. For example, the creation of acceptance of the aims of the programme within the organization, the basic and advanced training of staff for the achievement of those aims, the improvement of communication structures, the optimization of the coordination or division of labour (organizational structure), the provision of technical instruments and the ensuring of financial resources may be prerequisites for achieving the aims of the programme.

If the individual organizational elements could be designed effectively by the programme interventions, this result is also an internal programme output that relates to the implementing organization.

In the ensuing analytical perspective, the internal programme outputs (i.e. the organizational dimensions changed by the programme inputs) become independent variables via which the aim is to bring about changes in areas outside the provider. These external areas (e.g. the employment or education system, the ecological system, the legal system) now assume the role of dependent variables. The diffusion effects of the implementing organization in these specified (external) areas, which can be measured with the aid of indicators, then become a yardstick for the effectiveness of the implementing organization. This would, for example, be the case if an educational institution were successful in supplying the employment system with qualified employees in a qualification programme.

2.3.3 Innovation/diffusion model

According to the theory-of-organization concept developed here, programmes diffuse *innovations* in and through organizations. *Diffusion research* concerns itself with the conditions under which diffusion processes take place.

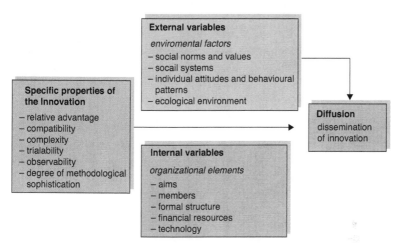

Figure 2.8   Diffusion model
Source: After Mohr (1977: 43)

An *innovation* is understood here to mean any form of new development, described by Schumpeter (1947: 151) in a much quoted and succinctly worded definition as 'the doing of new things or the doing of things that are already being done in a new way'.

Diffusion research[18] concerns itself with the conditions in which the diffusion of innovations takes place. According to Rogers (1995: 5), diffusion is 'the process by which an innovation is communicated through certain channels over time among the members of a social system'. Mohr (1977) developed a basic model for the factors that may influence the diffusion process positively or negatively. He differentiated between four groups of variables: (1) The first group refers to the specific properties of the innovation itself. (2) The second is composed of environmental variables. (3) The third group occupies itself with those who latch on to an innovation idea, make the decision to introduce it and, if appropriate, enforce its implementation. (4) The elements of the formal structure of the organization which introduces the innovation make up the fourth group of variables (cf. Mohr 1977, 19ff.).

In accordance with the organizational concept used here, those who latch on to an innovation, enforce it and work on its implementation are treated as members of organizations. For this reason – after Mohr (1977: 43) – we differentiate here between *three groups of variables* only (cf. Figure 2.8):[19]

(1) The first group of variables relates to the *specific properties of the innovation* itself (e.g. an environmental consultancy programme). Numerous investigations have meanwhile been able to show that an innovation is more likely to adopted 'the more relatively advantageous, the more compatible with existing production conditions, the less complex, the more trialable and observable the innovation appeared to the user' (Mohr 1977: 60).[20]

(2) As organizations are regarded in diffusion research as dynamic-complex constructions which exist in a symbiotic relationship with their environments, (cf. Mohr 1977: 64), which in turn consists of other organizations, networks and social constructions and systems, the *variables external to the organization* are of special importance in the diffusion of innovations. Depending on the evaluand (programme), various different systems may be of importance (in the case of an environmental consultancy programme, for example, companies, environmental legislation, the waste disposal system etc.).

(3) The *elements of an organization* that introduces an innovation make up the third group of variables and have already been determined and described in the organizational model.

Guidelines for the evaluation of programmes can be developed from theory-of-organization considerations and considerations that relate to the theory of innovations and their diffusion. The various individual fields of investigation depend on the variables used in these theoretical considerations. The identified organizational parameters are applied for the investigation of the *'internal areas of impact'* (i.e. the changes in the organization in charge of the programme) (cf. Figure 2.2). For the 'measurement' of the impacts in the *'external areas of impact'*, the changes in the target systems (policy fields) and target groups (e.g. people or other organizations) are investigated in which changes were supposed to be brought about. From the life-course perspective presented in Section 2.1.3, furthermore, it follows that the individual *phases of a programme* need to be observed in order for it to be possible to assess the planning and implementation process. These analytical chapters are preceded by a section in which the programme to be evaluated and its contextual conditions are described (cf. Stockmann 2008: 116ff. for more detail).

2.3.4   Sustainability

The CEval evaluation approach, suitable for preformative, formative and summative evaluations, is supplemented by a *sustainability model*, which distinguishes between sustainability at the macro level and sustainability at the programme level.

At the *macro level,* the evaluation approach follows on from the concept of sustainable development, which is based on the insight that economic, social and ecological development processes are inseparably connected with one another and must be balanced in such a way that the natural foundations for the existence of subsequent generations are not destroyed.[21] There are, meanwhile, a great variety of concepts for the operationalization of these three target dimensions. Here, a simplified, easy-to-use operationalization has been selected. Mainly suitable for the evaluation of programmes (cf. Stockmann 2008: 122ff., 142ff. for more detail), it is shown in an overview in Table 2.8.

These criteria, which are kept abstract consciously, need to be operationalized further in their respective contexts of course, so that it then becomes possible to gather measurable (quantitative and/or qualitative) data.

In order for it to be possible to realize the future vision of a society in which economic, social and ecological objectives are in accord with one another, political strategies and programmes are called for that contribute to the implementation of sustainable development. The question arises as to whether measures are only effective for as long as they are funded, or whether structures can be created and behavioural changes brought about which will effect long-term change in a given problem situation. Sustainability is achieved when these new organizational structures and behavioural changes continue after the end of the period in which the measures were funded. Four dimensions are identified here with which the *sustainability of programmes* can be determined:

The *first dimension* contains the element common to all definitions of sustainability – that of *durability*. The effect can be described as durable when the target group and/or the provider *perpetuates* the innovations achieved with the project/programme *in the long term* without any outside assistance. This dimension of sustainability follows the project/programme closely, and denotes the 'long-term impacts' which continue after the end of the programme or the end of the funding period and can thus be referred to as *project/programme-oriented sustainability*.

The *second dimension* takes into account the *range* of the impacts or the benefits of a project or programme. The *output* is considered to be an indicator for this, i.e. the number of users (recipients of benefits or 'impactees') or the type of user group. The crucial question is whether people other than those in the original target group have adopted the innovations introduced by the programme in the long-term in their own interest and for their own benefit or not. This dimension can be referred to as *output-oriented sustainability*.

The *third dimension* comprises the change in the system in which the innovation was introduced (e.g. in organizations in the health-care,

Table 2.8 Dimensions of sustainability at macro level

Target dimension	Operationalization	Criterion fulfilled if
Economic	efficiency	an optimum of output and if possible all the intended impacts (outcomes) are achieved with the least possible input.
Social	socio-political relevance	the (intended and unintended) impacts of the outputs can on the whole be classified as socio-politically relevant and useful.
Ecological	low environmental impact	the resources for providing the outputs are handled in an environmentally sound way, and if the outputs and their (intended and unintended) impacts have a low environmental impact.

education or economic system). The central thrust of this dimension is thus not merely the expansion of the user group, but the *evolution* of the *entire system*. This means that there is not only regional diffusion – not only the provider that was once funded and other organizations use the innovations – but that the entire system to which the target groups and providers belong is affected by them. That being so, *sustainability* can be referred to as being *system-oriented* when innovations introduced by a programme lead to an improvement in the performance of an entire system via diffusion processes.

The *fourth dimension* of sustainability takes account of the fact that outputs are not simply reproduced in the same way, but that a target group, a provider or even a system can *adapt* to changing environmental conditions in a *flexible and appropriate* way. Sustainability does not consist in perpetuating that which has been created or introduced, but in the ability to continue to develop innovations further. In other words the provider or target group must have a potential for innovation in order to be able to bring about adjustments and changes consciously. If outputs are reproduced again and again in the same way although the environmental conditions have changed, they will soon cease to meet the needs of the target groups. If there is no longer any demand for the outputs or products, then sustainability is in jeopardy.

To sum up, it should be noted that the evaluation approach presented here adopts various different theoretical perspectives one after the

Table 2.9 Dimensions of sustainability at programme level

Dimension	Type	Feature
I	Project-/programme-oriented	The target group and/or provider perpetuates the innovations in its own interest and for its own benefit.
II	Output-oriented	Other groups/organizations have permanently adopted the innovations in their own interest and for their own benefit.
III	System-oriented	By processes of diffusion, the innovations lead to an improvement in the performance of the system as a whole (e.g. the health-care or education system).
IV	Innovation-oriented	The target group/provider has a potential for innovation with which it can react to altered environmental conditions in a flexible and appropriate way.

other, each of which concerns itself with different aspects of projects and programmes. The starting-point is a *life-course model*, which focuses on the time perspective and the process character of a project or programme. According to this model, the time perspective and process character of these consist in a series of successive, discrete phases, in each of which the carrying out of specific planning and implementation stages is intended to lead to successful implementation of the programme, i.e. so that the targets can be achieved. The individual phases are connected up along the time axis and placed in causal connection with one another. This facilitates hypothesis-guided cause-and-effect analyses.

As programmes are as a rule carried out by organizations, which are interdependent on their environment as open social systems, a *theory-of-organization concept* is used to analyse these relationships between programme, organization and environment. Programme interventions are regarded as innovations that are introduced into organizational or specific environmental systems (e.g. the education, health or job-market system). An attempt will now be made to explain the extent to which these innovations are adapted and implemented and the extent to which they diffuse across an organization and, beyond that, in the (external) systems that surround it, with the aid of *theory-of-diffusion considerations*.

If it is an ex-post evaluation, the *sustainability* of a programme can also be investigated. To this end, a model geared to the macro and micro (programme) level has been developed, in which the three theoretical perspectives (life-course, organizational and diffusion model) are combined.

The structure of the evaluation guide in terms of its content follows these theoretical considerations because

Table 2.10 Structure of guidelines for the evaluation of programmes

1. Programme and environment
    1.1 Programme description (including programme data and conception, innovation conception, resources)
    1.2 Environmental/contextual conditions (incl. description of the area of practice/policy field or of the social subsystem, target groups)

2. Course of programme
    2.1 Planning
    2.2 Control
    2.3 End of financial support
    2.4 Post-funding support

3. Internal areas of impact
    3.1 Acceptability of aims to the implementing organization and/or politically superordinate organizations (e.g. sponsors)
    3.2 Personnel (especially qualification)
    3.3 Organizational structure (especially functionality and operability)
    3.4 Availability of financial resources
    3.5 Technology: technical infrastructure (particularly equipment)
    3.6 Technology: organizational programme/conception

4. External areas of impact
    4.1 Acceptability of aims to the target groups
    4.2 Ability to reach target groups
    4.3 Benefit for target groups
    4.4 Impacts affecting more than one target group
    4.5 Impacts in the policy field of the programme
    4.6 Impacts affecting more than one policy field

5. Sustainability
    At macro level
    5.1 Efficiency
    5.2 Social relevance
    5.3 Ecological soundness (low environmental impact)
    5.4 At programme level
        – project/programme-oriented
        – output-oriented
        – system-oriented
        – innovation-oriented

(1) questions are first asked about the programme (evaluand) and its situative environment

(2) as in the life-course model, the chronological sequence of the individual programme stages and their causal interconnections are investigated

(3) in accordance with the parameters developed in the organizational model, questions are asked about the structures, processes and changes within the organization in charge of implementing the programme

(4) the status and the changes in selected policy fields and in the target groups intended to benefit from the programme interventions are investigated, and finally

(5) sustainability at macro and micro (programme) level is determined applying the developed set of criteria or system of categories.

The structure of the guide is shown in Table 2.10. A sample guide and a comprehensive explanation of the individual evaluation fields, the use of the guide and the assessment procedure are given in Stockmann (2008).

Notes

1. Translator's note: German Technical Inspection Agency (Technischer Überwachungsverein)

2. A working-group was organized under the keyword 'experiments in politics' at the 1979 annual conference of the German Organization of Political Science (GVPW). This group endeavoured to achieve some conceptual clarification of the terms 'pilot project', 'pilot test' and 'experimental politics', the use of which was expanding at the time in a positively inflationary manner.

3. Translator's note: this refers to a programme named *Soziale Stadt,* run by the Federal Ministry of Transport, Building and Housing (BMVBW). See www.bmvbs.de

4. The terms 'evaluation' and 'evaluation research' are used here synonymously.

5. In the 'forum-evaluation', the central Internet forum of the German evaluation community, there has been some very intense argument in the past years about whether the word 'evaluation' is to considered as derived from Latin or from English. It is certain that today's evaluations cannot be derived directly from activities in ancient Rome. Instead, there is no doubt that the specialist term 'evaluation' found its way into German usage via the USA. However, this does not make it an 'essentially American' word; it is, in its English root 'value', related to the Latin word *valor*. Neither is it a scientific novelty created to demarcate items in conventional usage (such as Luhmann's term 'autopoiesis' – which is of course by no means 'essentially German' either), but a word which has simply been adopted from everyday language. Whether the term 'evaluation' in German should be pronounced more like a Latin or more like an English word, or should even perhaps be 'germanized', is a matter that each of its users should decide for him- or herself.

6. Just how much the term evaluation has already diffused into everyday usage is shown for example in a series of articles in *Stern* magazine entitled 'How the world loves' *('So liebt die Welt')*, in one of which it was asserted that ' ...women tend to *evaluate* more and more precisely who they are getting involved with' *(Stern* 32/2007: 102).

7. After the English-language usage of the term *politik*, distinctions are as a rule made between three dimensions: (1) policy, (2) politics and (3) polity. (1) *Policy* circumscribes the dimension of the term *politik* as regards its content. This primarily concerns all interactions between government and society, for example how problems are perceived by the politico-adminis- trative system and dealt with, and which purposive or purposeful activities the state intends to use to implement solutions. Policy studies and policy field analyses investigate such questions. (2) The term *politics* refers to the procedural aspect of *politik*. In political research it is a question of which rules are applied in solving a conflict, what role institutions play, how interests are pushed through etc. (3) *Polity* comprises the formal aspect of *politik*. This is the form in which *politik* unfolds (cf. Druwe 1987: 393ff.). Jann (1994: 308ff.) wrote an excellent introductory article on policy-field analysis. Cf. also Dye (1978); Windhoff-Héritier (1983, 1993); Hartwich (1985); Feick & Jann (1988); Schmidt (1988); Derlien (1991); Schubert (1991, 2003); Dunn (2004) and others.

8. Final evaluations ought also to be included in this category. They are conducted directly after the termination of a project or programme.

9. URL: http://www.iso.org.

10. URL: http://www.efqm.org/en.

11. Http://www.oecd.org/document/22/0,2340,en_2649_34435_2086550_1_1_1 _1,00.html (last viewed February 2012). See also OECD (1991). Very similar criteria are proposed by Bussmann, Klöti and Knoepfel (1997: 100ff.); Posavac and Carey (1997: 42ff.); Vedung (1999: 223).

12. Cf. Vedung (1999: 104ff.); Scriven (1991: 159f., 197f.); Widmer (2000: 79f.); Caspari (2004: 32).

13. Cf. Campbell (1969); Cronbach et al. (1981); Cronbach (1982) on these origins; cf. Mertens (2006) for a summary.

14. Italics by Kromrey.

15. A selection has been made of the subsystems. Which ones are important in a given organizational model depends on the kind of programme being carried out.

16. Cf. Barnard (1938: 4); March and Simon (1958: 4); Blau and Scott (1963: 5); Etzioni (1964: 3); Hage and Aiken (1969: 366ff.); Mayntz and Ziegler (1976: 11); Mayntz (1977: 36, 40); Scott (2003: 19ff.); Kieser and Kubicek (1992: 4); Bea and Göbel (2002: 2); Abraham and Büschges (2004: 109ff.) and others.

17. Each of these elements in turn has been identified by individual authors in organizational research as the most significant feature, to the neglect of the others (cf. Scott 2003: 24).

18. Cf. Tews (2004); Rogers (1995, 38ff.); Kortmann (1995, 33ff.); Mohr (1977, 33ff.) and others on the various directions taken by diffusion research. Cf. for example Rogers & Kim 1985 on the diffusion of innovations in non-profit organizations.

19. Cf. Rogers (1995: 11, 20ff.) on the development of the diffusion process over time and the various types of adoption.
20. Rogers (1995: 15f.) cites the following as criteria which explain the various different adoption rates of innovations: relative advantage, compatibility, complexity, trial ability and observability.
21. For the facets of the sustainability concept cf. Meyer (2000); Meyer (2002a, b); Meyer et al. (2003); Caspari (2004) and others.

3

Evaluation Approaches and Their Fundamental Theoretical Principles

Wolfgang Meyer and Reinhard Stockmann

3.1 Introduction

The science-based evaluation concept presented in the previous chapter and the CEval approach built upon it are procedures that, in terms of their theoretical foundations, have a number of things in common with other concepts and approaches, but also some aspects in which they differ from them quite markedly. Although evaluation research, as compared with most scientific disciplines, has a relatively short history, various development tendencies have already formed. These will be presented briefly in the section that follows, so that the approach developed here can find a place in the theory-of-evaluation discussion.

In order to be able to structure the immense diversity of fundamental evaluation approaches, three different systems are selected here, each applying dissimilar criteria for its attempts at classification. Whilst the *generation approach* of Guba and Lincoln (Section 3.2) is oriented toward a linear historical sequence and clearly sees the generations of evaluation it identifies as a developmental sequence, this only applies to Alkin's *tree model* (Section 3.3) with certain restrictions. It is true that here too, the 'growth' of the tree suggests a development tendency, but the way the individual approaches are ordered by no means follows the historical sequence, relating instead much more to conceptual similarities and differences than to chronology. Finally, the systematization of Fitzpatrick, Sanders and Worthen (Section 3.4) breaks completely with the historical view of things and applies a uniform classification criterion, that of the *purpose of the evaluation* and its utilization.

The authors' own systematization, covered after these (see Section 3.5), attempts on the one hand to synthesize the classification systems proposed by the authors cited, and on the other to look beyond that at the *social function* of evaluation presented in Section 2.2.3, and to use this criterion as a principle for classification.

3.2 Systematization according to Guba and Lincoln: the generational model

For a long time, the diverse disciplinary origins of evaluation were a tough obstacle to the classification and systematization of evaluation approaches. Within the various social science disciplines (especially the educational sciences, psychology, sociology and economics), evaluation studies were understood exclusively as applications of the researchers' own theories and methods and duly allocated to existing systematizations.

Having said that, several systems of categories were proposed in the 1970s and early 1980s, and they provided an overview of the various approaches from the point of view of interdisciplinary evaluation research (see for example Glass & Ellett 1980; House 1978; Popham 1975; Worthen & Sanders 1973). These early attempts also include the *generation model* of Guba and Lincoln (1989). The use of the term generations suggests progressive development, although the individual generations, built upon one another, are characterized by new developmental phases, which differ fundamentally from the progress made within any one generation. The emergence of a new generation does not necessarily mean that the existing one is replaced[1] – the sequence being non-linear and overlapping – but the latter does at least surrender its pacemaker's role and the new generation absorbs it (or at least the main insights it has yielded). However, this picture of the generations has been selected rather illustratively and does not see itself as a further development of existing generation concepts.[2] There is no systematic distinction of generations applying specified and verifiable criteria; on the contrary, the grouping together of certain approaches as a 'generation' and their allocation to it would seem more or less arbitrary.

Neither do Guba and Lincoln attempt to allocate all the known evaluation approaches meaningfully to the various individual generations or to distinguish the procedures classified as evaluations systematically from other scientific procedures. On the contrary, there is a noticeable 'bias' with regard to educational science papers, which ignores other research directions and evaluation studies in other areas of work.

In spite of that, the generation model is presented here as a first attempt at systematization, since it did have some indisputable advantages and attained a certain degree of popularity because of them. The first advantage of this classification system lies in its simplicity and thus in its clearness. It is easy to see the rationale for the division of the complex world of evaluation into four successive generations with easily comprehensible labels (measurement, description, assessment and negotiation). The distinctions, made with the aid of certain activities that are necessary to all evaluations, have considerable appeal, particularly with a view to the universal applicability of such a system of categories. Drawing boundary lines between these four activities, however, is not particularly selective for all approaches, and regrettably Guba and Lincoln did not even attempt to classify them all. Nevertheless, certain core features of the evaluation concepts introduced below can be recognized with regard to the activities of measuring, describing, assessing and negotiating.

This will be looked at still more closely later on (cf. Section 3.5). In the section that follows now, the model proposed by Guba and Lincoln will first be depicted and a brief description given of the generations using their examples.

3.2.1   The first evaluation generation – measurement

The *first generation* of evaluation was identified to by Guba and Lincoln in terms of 'measurement'; they asserted that in the early phase of evaluation it was exclusively a matter of gathering (quantitative) data. The examples given to illustrate this relate to the first empirical research work in educational science in the 19th century and the attempts made by researchers such as Wilhelm Wundt and Francis Galton to use psychometric testing procedures for the *measurement of pupils' performance*. The authors did not query whether or not these measurement procedures really were evaluations or why they were different to other measurements, quite usual at the time, in the social sciences. None of the authors named (Rice, Binet, Otis, Hildreth) actually referred to his / her own work as 'evaluation', and for this reason alone it may be doubted whether classifying these works as 'evaluation approaches' is justified. Having said that, there is no question but that the empirical educational science that had begun to emerge by the end of the 19th century – following on from the scientific school of educationalism founded by Johann Friedrich Herbart – had, and continues to have, a marked influence on today's school evaluation.

This applies especially to the works of *Joseph Mayer Rice,* cited by Guba and Lincoln as their first example. Rice was an American of German origin and (especially during his studies in Leipzig and Jena) the more recent developments at the Herbart school (among others by Wilhelm Wundt and Wilhelm Thierry Preyer), which were particularly strongly influenced by psychology, most certainly left their mark on him. In the spirit of this science-oriented, positivist educationalism, Rice carried out several investigations of the American school system in the 1890s (of which a summary is to be found in Rice 1893), and these contained the first comparisons of learning performance carried out by independent researchers involving more than one school. However, these early works still relied exclusively on participatory observations of class teaching and not on performance tests. Rice did not become the 'father of school evaluation' (cf. for example Albjerg 1966; Stanley 1966; Oelkers 2008) until he had carried out a further study in the year 1895, in which the first comparative spelling tests at schools in the USA were used in a survey of more than 30,000 pupils (Rice 1897).

In allocating Rice to the first generation, Guba and Lincoln refer to this study only. Yet in this work Rice was by no means aiming to *develop a (measurement) procedure for school evaluation*, but to reveal deficiencies in the American school system and make a plea for the establishment of progressive educationalism. His life was not distinguished either before or after by methodological research work on evaluation. In spite of all the significance this study had, and still has, for the development of school evaluation, Rice was not a pioneer of evaluation research and he certainly did not develop a methodologically oriented evaluation concept.

Even if it is difficult to place the research work of Joseph Mayer Rice among the evaluation conceptions, it is beyond doubt that right up to the present day *empirical performance tests* have been an important part of evaluations at schools, universities, vocational schools and extracurricular and advanced training courses. The best example of this is undoubtedly the comparative education studies initiated by the OECD in the 'Program for International Student Assessment' (PISA). The performance tests in the PISA programme – like the test procedures Rice used – relate to basic skills and not to knowledge of facts. The focus is on measuring and drawing up a balance sheet of central competences that are necessary for participating in life in modern societies. (See for example OECD 2010, 2009, 2006; Prenzel et al. 2012; Kunter et al. 2002; Stanat et al. 2002; Baumert et al. 2001; for the UK see Bradshaw et al. 2010a, b, c and the National Foundation for Educational Research (NFER) for actual results; for the USA see Fleischmann et al. 2010 and the National Center for Educational Statistics (NCES) for actual results; for Germany see Klieme et al. 2010; PISA consortium Germany 2008, 2007, 2006, 2000 and the newly founded Zentrum für Internationale Bildungsvergleichsstudien (ZIB) at the TU Munich on the methodological conception of the PISA evaluations, the survey instruments and the German extensions.)

It should be noted that the psychometric procedures for performance measurement introduced by Rice are still used (and in recent years considerably more so, thanks to international efforts). The procedures referred to by Guba and Lincoln as the 'first evaluation generation' of school performance measurement have by no means been 'superseded', but are in fact currently enjoying considerable public attention: no other scientific (evaluation) project in recent years has given rise to such an intense political debate as the PISA programme, which, for example, in Germany triggered off nothing short of a 'PISA shock' and duly intense efforts to improve national education results. Having said that, measurements of school performance are more part of regular educational monitoring, which only affords a limited amount of information about the impacts of educational measures and hardly provides any assistance for the concrete further development of the performance of individual schools. These are functions assumed more by parallel procedures of school evaluation (cf. Section 3.5.2), though these do not represent a 'further development' of performance measurement. It is far rather the case that a certain parallelism in the development of monitoring AND evaluation can be recognized. Even Rice, cited by Guba and Lincoln as (unquestionably) the most important author for the development of the measurement of school performance, by no means had a fixation about the establishment of quantitative test procedures, but actually made earlier use of qualitative observation methods and methods that involved more intensive subjective reconstruction. In the case of Rice, in fact, the causal connection is quite clearly reversed: on account of criticism of his methods, he tried to support his findings objectively by means of newer test procedures.

3.2.2 The second evaluation generation – description

There must furthermore definitely be some doubt as to whether or not 'measurement' is really to be placed historically before 'description', as the *second generation* of evaluations is labelled, and whether or not description really does represent a significant 'further development' of measurement. The sole example of this second generation as cited by Guba and Lincoln also comes from school educationalist research; only *Ralph W. Tyler* is cited as a representative, on the basis of his work in the 'eight-year study' (begun in 1933). Guba and Lincoln argue that his approach is characterized by the *'description* of patterns of strengths and weaknesses with respect to certain stated objectives'* (Guba & Lincoln 1989: 28; original italics), and that description were thus allocated to the evaluator as the latter's main task. 'Measurement was no longer treated as the equivalent of evaluation but was redefined as *one of several tools* that might be used in its service' (ibid.)

Without doubt, Tyler's works on education evaluation in the 1930s and 1940s (Tyler 1935, 1938, 1942, 1950; Smith & Tyler 1942) were important milestones in school evaluation. His aim was to make a *comparison* between clearly formulated (educational) objectives and (education) results that could be measured as exactly as possible: the success of the (educational) measures implemented could then at the same time be measured in terms of the *difference between performance and the objectives that were originally set*. The description of the strengths and weaknesses of a project is certainly an important element and result of this comparison, but it does seem rather too much of a curtailment if Tyler's works are reduced exclusively to this aspect of description.

His methodological contribution consisted on the one hand in developing classification procedures for education results, and on the other in occupying himself with the problem of 'outcome measurement'. He availed himself of a procedure that even today can still be described as fundamental to the *evaluation of the achievement of Objectives* (see Section 3.4.1 for more detail on these objectives-oriented approaches). In this respect, his work goes far beyond the purely descriptive aspirations attributed to it by Guba and Lincoln. It also seems somewhat exaggerated to insinuate that Rice, unlike Tyler, understood measurement not so much as a tool of evaluation but more as an end in itself.

Procedure for evaluation of the achievement of objectives after Tyler

(1) Establish broad goals or objectives
(2) Classify the goals or objectives
(3) Define objectives in behavioural terms
(4) Find situations in which achievement of objectives can be shown
(5) Develop or select measurement techniques
(6) Collect performance data
(7) Compare performance data with behaviourally stated objectives

Source: Fitzpatrick, Sanders & Worthen (2012: 155)

Unlike Rice' school performance measurement, which is to be allocated primarily to educational monitoring at international and national level, the comparison between objectives and results relates more to the actual implementation level in the individual schools and was thus mostly implemented as an element of self-evaluation (cf. Section 3.5.2). There is however certainly no indication that the 'second' generation of evaluation superseded, displaced or subsumed the 'first' in any way. Furthermore, it would be necessary to prove that Tyler's work was 'more informed and sophisticated' than that of Rice. The reasons given for putting Tyler in a class of his own are therefore less than convincing; the use of the term 'generation' is surely inapt for this individual example alone.

What is more, the *chronological order* – as already mentioned at the beginning – is also rather questionable, the more so if one breaks with the purely school-related perspective and takes into account the *economic basis* of the perspective of achieving objectives and the comparison of targets and achievements (cf. Section 3.5.3 for more detail). The latter term – which Tyler did not use – comes from *bookkeeping*, and can be traced back to the Mesopotamia of 9000 B.C. Today's 'double-entry bookkeeping', a comparison between debit and credit (and double-sided booking of all entries), was already common practice in the 14th century. The comparison between targets and achievements emerged as an important element in *deviation analysis*, which put the planned target costs and the calculated actual costs into proportion, enabling statements to be made on deviations in consumption and thus also on the (current) efficiency of the measures. This is done in a similar way in the works of Tyler, though he does break away from a purely economic, cost-oriented view and focus more on the target dimensions.

This comparison between outputs and objectives as an element of evaluation is one of the very things that would be most likely to justify allocating Tyler to a category of his own. Once again, it is not appropriate to speak of the 'outdatedness' or 'supersession' of a 'second evaluation generation' but, on the contrary, of the introduction of an important new element that has clearly made its mark on today's evaluation activities.

3.2.3   The third evaluation generation – assessment

Guba and Lincoln see the next development stage in the transition from description to 'assessment', which in their view characterizes the *third generation* of evaluation. 'Assessment' is indeed the central basic element of evaluation, distinguishing it from scientific fundamental research (cf. Section 2.1.2). The special significance of some of the authors named by Guba and Lincoln and their approaches (Stufflebeam, Provus and in particular Scriven, see Section 3.3.3) will be dealt with later on. The remarks that follow here are limited to *Robert Stake* as one of the cited examples of this generation, and once again their primary aim is to list the special features of his approach and classify them with regard to the aspect of assessment which Guba and Lincoln considered essential.

Robert Stake was among the first evaluation researchers to be seriously troubled by the 'dominance of program evaluation by what he saw as parochial, objectivist, and mechanistic conceptions and methods' (Fitzpatrick et al. 2012: 191). In his influential essay 'The countenance of educational evaluation' (1967), he dissociated himself from the scientific view of evaluation that had prevailed until then. First, he developed a simple schema, which compares the two behavioural components ('countenances') which are in his opinion essential to each and every evaluation: description and assessment. It was, he said, the task of the evaluator (1) to provide a *description of the logic on which a programme was based* and of the identified needs ('background, justification and program description of the program rationale'), (2) to list the *intended programme structure and programme conditions* (antecedents: inputs, resources, existing conditions, *programme activities and processes* (transactions) and *record* the (intended and unintended) *outcomes* (3) *empirically*. Once (4) the *standards or criteria used for the* assessment have been *explicitly named*, then (5) the *programme structure / conditions, activities / processes and impacts* can be assessed. Using the matrix developed by Stake (cf. Figure 3.1), the expected values (intents) are compared with the ones actually observed (observations) in the *'description matrix'* for congruence, and the correlations with the programme conditions, processes and impacts traced (contingencies). The judgements are then recorded in the *'judgement matrix'*.

This early work by Stake thus displays a certain parallelism with the LogFrame approach explained below, even if no direct connection can be made between the two (cf. Section 3.5.3). There can be no doubt that the introduction of the judgement aspect was an important contribution, which does indeed differ greatly from the approaches of Rice and Tyler as emphasized by Guba and Lincoln. By introducing the comparison with external criteria and standards that were established outside the evaluand as a central element of evaluation, Stake does indeed go beyond the work of Rice and Tyler. True, it is not the case that the latter did not make any judgements, but the judgement criteria are not stipulated so systematically or explicitly. In spite of that, it does seem questionable whether this development stage – at least in the case of Stake – suffices to justify talking about a new 'evaluation generation'.

In his subsequent works (Stake 1972, 1975, 1980), Stake himself provides a good argument for this critical view of things by introducing a further, considerably more significant innovation into his evaluation concept and placing the focus more heavily on *paying heed directly to the problems and interests of those involved*. The aim is responsively to devote time and attention to the reactions of those involved in the programme while the evaluation is being conducted. Accordingly, Stake (1975: 11) defines an

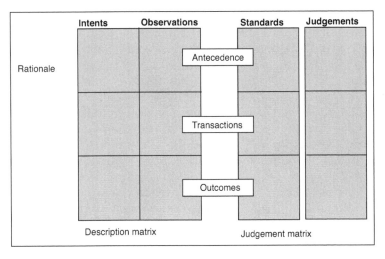

Figure 3.1   Stake's description and judgement matrices
Source: cf. Stake (1967: 529).

Talk with Clients,
program staff,
audiences

Assemble formal   Identify program
reports, if any   scope

Winnow, format for   Overview program
audience use   activities

Validate, confirm,   Discover purposes
attempt to disconfirm   concerns

Thematize: prepare   Conceptualize issues,
portrayals, case studies   problems

Observe designated
antecedents, transactions   Identify data needs,
and outcomes   re, issues

Select observers, judges,
instruments, if any

Figure 3.2   Evaluation clock after Stake (1975)
Source: Quoted from Fitzpatrick et al. (2012: 194).

evaluation as *responsive* 'if it orients more directly to program activities than to program intents; responds to audience requirements for information; and if the different value perspectives present are referred to in reporting the success and failure of the program'. Responsive evaluation aims on the one hand to promote *insights into the programme contexts among those involved* and on the other to *improve communication with them*. For this, the evaluator has to enter into a continual exchange with the various stakeholder groups. Stake (1975: 20) arranged the individual functional stages in a responsive evaluation clockwise (cf. Figure 3.2).

Advantages of responsive evaluation after Stake

(1) 'It helps target groups of evaluation to understand the programme if evaluators try to accommodate the natural ways in which those target groups understand things and communicate them to one another.

(2) Knowledge gained by experience (tacit knowledge), facilitates human understanding and expands human experience.

(3) Naturalistic generalizations, on which we agree by recognizing the similarities between objects and interests inside and outside the context, have developed through experience. They help people to obtain an extended view of things and to understand the programmes.

(4) In studying individual objects, people gather experience, which can be used in recognizing similarities with other objects. Individuals contribute to existing experience and human understanding'.

Source: adapted from Stake (1978: 4ff.)

With the concept of 'responsive evaluation', Stake added another important feature, apart from highlighting the judgement process explicitly, and it presumably represented the greater change for evaluation conceptions. It is true that Rice and Tyler also took the groups of people involved seriously and made use of them as resource subjects; but they certainly did not place this group anywhere near so near the centre of their evaluation approaches. The significance of these participant-oriented components of evaluation will be looked at more closely later on (cf. Section 3.4.4).

3.2.4 The fourth-evaluation generation – negotiation

First, however, tribute is to be paid to the approach of Guba and Lincoln as self-appointed representatives of a 'fourth-evaluation generation'. The first thing noticeable here is that Stake's participant-oriented perspective and so-called *'responsive constructivist evaluation'* have more in common than a 'difference between generations' would suggest. In their various

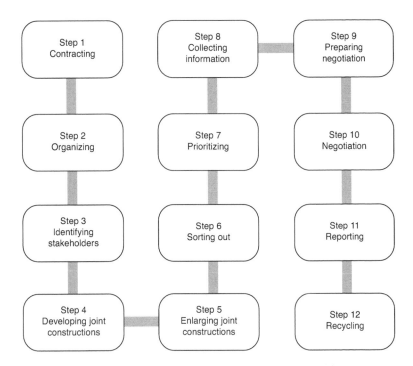

Figure 3.3   Implementation plan of 'fourth-generation evaluation'
Source: Guba & Lincoln (1989: 186f.; abridged version by Stockmann/Meyer).

studies and theoretical discussions, Guba and Lincoln (1981, 1989, 2000); Lincoln and Guba (1985, 2004) associated the central ideas of responsive evaluation after Stake with so-called *'naturalistic' data gathering methods* (cf. House 1983, quoted from Fitzpatrick et al. 2012: 197), which are rooted in ethnological tradition. The essential role of a 'fourth-generation evaluation' consists in devoting time and attention to the information requirements of the potential audiences of the evaluation and also taking into account the various different value perspectives of those involved.

Fitzpatrick, Sanders and Worthen (2012: 198) sum up this approach as follows: 'By taking a naturalistic approach to evaluation, the evaluator is studying the program activity in situ, or as it occurs naturally, without constraining, manipulating, or controlling it'. According to the ideas of Guba and Lincoln, the evaluator becomes a learner and the evaluees advance to take on the role of teachers. 'The dominant perspective is that of the informant, because the evaluators learn their perspectives, learn the concepts they use to describe their world, use their definitions of these concepts, learn the 'folk theory' explanations, and translate their world so the evaluator and others can understand it' (ibid.).

Guba and Lincoln presented the procedure of 'fourth-generation evaluation' in a detailed flow diagram with a total of twelve steps (Figure 3.3).[3] Some of these steps (1 and 2, 8, 11) are not necessarily specific to a certain form of evaluation and can also be found in other approaches. The following depiction concentrates solely on the main elements of this approach.

The starting-point of 'naturalistic evaluation' is the *identification of all the potential stakeholders* (step 3) whose perspectives are to be taken into account. The main questions are elaborated together with the stakeholders in hermeneutic circles[4] (step 4) and then enlarged and / or substantiated by means of qualitative interviews, observations and literature studies (steps 5 to 7). The following kinds of information (step 8) are adduced in answering the questions (cf. Fitzpatrick et al. 2012: 197f.):

- descriptive information on the evaluand and its context
- information which caters to interests (matters concerning documents, the search for reasons and consequences and the identification of possible sequences of events)
- information on elucidating problems and identifying potential ways of overcoming them
- information on impacts (clarifying impacts, finding out their causes, degree of persuasion)
- information on standards used for the evaluation (identification of criteria, expectations and requirements).

Qualitative instruments (interviews, observation, document analysis and non-reactive procedures) are used principally for data gathering. One main contrast to other evaluations is the way in which the information gained is processed. True, in 'fourth-generation evaluation' too, the findings are summarized in reports geared to the information requirements of the respective audiences (step 11), but the oral presentation is made in a joint negotiation process with the stakeholders and is not exclusively an interpretation on the part of the evaluators (step 10). Through this joint 'reconstruction' of the view elaborated jointly at the beginning, the perspectives of the stakeholders can be picked up again and integrated in the report. The evaluation process is not then considered to have been completed, but should now instead start again from the beginning in order to be able to arrive at a sharper interpretation (step 12).

With regard to the *quality criteria* of such an evaluation, Guba and Lincoln point out that it is not – as in the classical scientific approach – the quest for 'objective' truths (internal validity) which primary, but credibility. To improve this, data cross-checks and triangulation are used. If it is a question of the transposability of evaluation findings into other contexts, it is, accordingly, not their external validity that is decisive, but their accuracy.

The special reason for Guba and Lincoln's regarding their approach as a new evaluation generation in its own right is (1989: 8) is its emphasis on *negotiation* with the stakeholders: 'We have called this new approach fourth-generation evaluation to signal our construction that this form moves beyond previously existing generations, characterizable as measurement-oriented, description-oriented, and judgement-oriented, to a new level whose key dynamic is negotiation'. It thus centres around the consensually elaborated joint 'construction' of an assessment of the evaluand by the evaluators and all the stakeholders, i.e. an *assessment* which is not only ascribable to the subjective opinion of the former. From this point of view in particular, Guba and Lincoln – see Section 3.2.3 – are not all that far removed from Stake. As emphasized here, the introduction of naturalistic methods seems much more typical, though it hardly justifies allocation to a 'fourth-evaluation generation' in its own right.

3.2.5   Summary and assessment

Summing up, it can be said that the choice of the term generations for the categorization of evaluation approaches by Guba and Lincoln is at the very least unfortunate, and inadequately justified by the examples they give. It would certainly have been meritorious to present a comprehensive history of evaluation approaches and the individual stages of development and arrange their main elements in historical order (cf. Madaus and Stufflebeam 2000 for a good example of this; see also the presentation by Rossi et al. 1999: 9ff.). Guba and Lincoln do this, at best, rudimentarily in relation to school-oriented educational science research.

On the other hand, Guba and Lincoln were not primarily concerned with writing a treatise on evaluation theories or the presentation of as perfect a classification schema as possible, but above all with the presentation of their own approach. Their claim of being able to present that approach as the forerunner of a new 'evaluation generation' is certainly exaggerated. However, the merit of their systematization consists in their emphasizing four different central activities which are to be pursued in an evaluation and which are indeed reflected in the individual evaluation approaches in various forms. Whether or not the measurement, description and assessment of the evaluands and negotiation with the stakeholder groups on the evaluation findings really did come into being in that order (thus justifying the choice of the term generation) is less relevant. This is shown not least by the next example of a systematization of evaluation approaches, which picks up on at least two of the terms (measurement and description) and places the focus much more strongly on the various lines of development and the distinctions between them.

3.3 Systematization according to Alkin: the tree model

The 'tree model' of Marvin C. Alkin and Christina A. Christie for the systematization of evaluation theories has received much attention in recent years (Alkin & Christie 2004, cf. Figure 3.4).[5] Unlike Guba and Lincoln, Alkin and Christie do not follow a chronological principle of classification, emphasizing instead the kinship of the approaches in terms of their content, which they accordingly place on a primary or secondary branch. This vivid depiction in the form of a tree suggests a process of growth from 'bottom' – the roots of 'accountability' and empirical social inquiry, which at the same time represent the 'trunk' of the tree – to 'top', which suggests a progressive diversification of

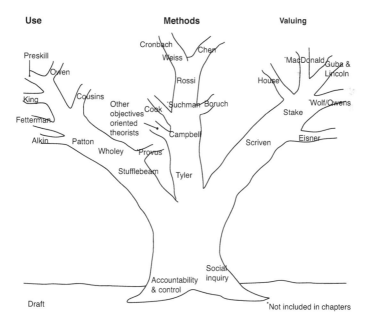

Figure 3.4 Tree model of Alkin and Christie
Source: Alkin & Christie (2004: 13).

approaches, with more and more branches giving a visual representation of individual theory lines.

Unlike Guba and Lincoln, Alkin and Christie thus emphasize the importance of the accounting tradition (as in Section 3.2.2) and the various different social inquiry activities as important starting-points for evaluation development (without restricting themselves to any particular disciplines or objects). They see the first major stage in terms of the diversification of evaluation approaches into three 'primary branches': those that concern themselves mainly with 'methods', 'use' or the valuing process respectively, which differ fundamentally from one another in accordance with that image and subsequently form 'schools' of their own with further ramifications. These primary branches and their ramifications will be looked at somewhat more closely in the section that follows.

3.3.1   The 'methods' branch

Alkin and Christie (2004) allocate a 'progenitor' to each of the three primary branches, which they have identified as being central to the further development of the related evaluation approaches. In the case of the *primary branch of methods development,* which has proceeded mainly from empirical social inquiry, that progenitor is Ralph W. Tyler, whose work – as already mentioned (Section 3.2.2) – was cited by Guba and Lincoln as characterizing the second, more descriptive generation of evaluations. Alkin and Christie, by contrast, acknowledge this work as the theoretical foundation of objectives-oriented evaluation. Without wishing to detract from Tyler's undoubtedly great merit in the development of theory, especially in the field of educational evaluation, the role allocated to him by Alkin and Christie, namely that of the key figure in methods-oriented evaluation theory, must be given a critical look.

For this assessment, Alkin and Christie put forward the methodological innovations of the 'eight-year study' – significant and formative for the further development of evaluation research as they were (Alkin & Christie 2004: 18; cf. also Madaus & Stufflebeam 1989: xiii) – particularly Tyler's article on 'outcome measurement' and his pioneering thoughts on objectives-oriented evaluation. The latter in particular were further developed by a number of authors (Alkin and Christie name in particular Bloom, Hammond, Metfessel and Popham), who are assigned to a secondary arm of the methods branch under the heading 'other objectives-oriented theorists'. In general, however, it is noticeable that although a number of evaluation theorists – above all Stufflebeam – discuss the theoretical deliberations of Tyler and use them in the development of their own theories, these do not include Campbell, Suchman or Rossi, who are placed on

Alkin's methods branch. Unlike the textbooks of Fitzgerald or Stufflebeam, the work of Rossi, Freeman and Lipsey does not feature the name Tyler at all, other studies being cited there as pioneering for the 1930s and 1940s (Dodd on the public health system, Stephan on the evaluation of the 'New Deal', the Hawthorne study and the work of Lewin, Lippitt and White; see Rossi et al. 1999: 10f.).

Let us assume that this placement of Tyler is correct as regards content; the tree model and the central position allocated nevertheless suggest that Tyler played a role in the development of a certain line of evaluation theory, and that is a role he never actually played. This already applies with reference to the psychologist D. T. Campbell, who is classified as a direct 'successor' of Tyler on the main arm of the methods branch. Some authors would even argue with citing Campbell as an evaluation theorist at all – presumably even Campbell himself. There is no doubt about the fact that Campbell's pioneering article on field research and the development of 'quasi-experimental designs', written together with J. C. Stanley (Campbell & Stanley 1963), represented an important basis for the development of evaluation methodology, and that it also had a certain influence on the development of theory. However, neither that article nor the other writings of Campbell are to be judged as *contributions to evaluation theory in their own right*. Neither are they by any means to be seen as sequels to the studies of Tyler, to which no heed is paid, at least not in Campbell's main writings on evaluation (Campbell 1969, 1975, 1991; Campbell & Boruch 1975).

The same applies to the works of Edward Suchman, whose principal work 'Evaluative Research' (Suchman 1967) was an initial attempt at the theoretical integration of the evaluation field. It is from Suchman that the important distinction originated between *evaluation in general usage* as a social process for the judgement of the value of an object and the *scientific understanding of 'evaluation research'*, which distinguishes itself by the use of scientific research methods and techniques. Accordingly, Suchman occupies himself in great detail with the scientific procedure and design questions in which Campbell was interested at the same time. Thus it was Suchman who rendered Campbell's works utilizable for evaluation and integrated them into a theoretical concept for conducting evaluations. Apart from that, since he also had a definite influence on the works of Peter Rossi (cf. Alkin & Christie 2004: 22), it would certainly have been more apt to give Edward Suchman the central position in the methods branch of the tree of evaluation theories.

The existence of a common, methodologically oriented tradition of theories of evaluation can certainly not be derived from the virtually independent works of Tyler and Campbell, but rather from the upper third of that branch and the constellation of the authors Suchman, Rossi, Chen and Weiss. In particular, the introductory book 'Evaluation: A Systematic Approach', written by *Peter Rossi* together with Howard Freeman at the end of the 1970s, attained a high degree of popularity and is still available today in its seventh edition (Rossi, Lipsey & Freeman 2004). It can at the same time be regarded as a seminal work of 'theory-driven evaluation', even if that term was primarily coined in the cooperation of Rossi with Huey-Tsyh Chen in a number of other publications (Chen 1990; Chen & Rossi 1980, 1983, 1987).

The central idea in *theory-driven evaluation* is the design of a programme theory, with the help of which the evaluation can then be driven. The reasoning is as follows: 'Every program embodies a conception of the structure, functions, and procedures appropriate to attain its goals. This conception constitutes the 'logic' or plan of the program, which we have called program theory. The program theory explains why the program does what it does and provides the rationale for expecting that doing things that way will achieve the desired results' (Rossi et al. 1999: 156). In accordance with these remarks, a *'programme theory'* does not by any means have to meet the scientific requirements imposed on theories, neither does it have to correspond to the current state of research. In most cases, it will be an implicit theory of the actors (especially of the programme client), which has not been taken to its logical conclusion or put on a detailed logical basis in the form of hypothetical statements and causal chains. In a more elaborate form this is a 'logical model' not based on sound scientific results, designed during a planning workshop and for example put down on paper in the context of a 'LogFrame approach' as the consensual result of that workshop (cf. Section 3.5.3).

The first task of evaluation is thus to conceptualize this *programme theory in accordance with scientific standards*, making it accessible to scientific investigation. Unlike fundamental research, in an evaluation the guiding theory is thus not developed from the scientific standards but from the basic assumptions of the programme actors, and the concrete investigation design is derived from it (cf. Section 5.2).

Processing and evaluation of programme theory after Rossi et al.

(1) 'Every program embodies a program theory, a set of assumptions and expectations that constitute the logic or plan of the program ….

(2) Program theory is an aspect of a program that can be evaluated in its

own right. Such assessment is important because a program based on weak or faulty conceptualization has little prospect of achieving the intended results.

(3) ... evaluability assessment [is] a preevaluation appraisal of whether a program's performance can be evaluated and, if so, whether it should be.

(4) Evaluability assessment involves describing program goals and objectives, assessing whether the program is well enough conceptualized to be evaluable, and identifying stakeholder interest in evaluation findings....

(5) To assess program theory, it is necessary for the evaluator to articulate the theory, that is, state it in a clear, explicit form acceptable to stakeholders. The aim of this effort is to describe the 'program as intended' and its rationale, not the program as it actually is...

(6) The evaluator describes program theory by collating and integrating information from program documents, interviews with program personnel and other stakeholders, and observations of program activities....

(7) The most important assessment of program theory the evaluator can make is based on a comparison of the intervention specified in the program theory with the social needs the program is expected to address....

(8) A complementary approach to assessing program theory uses stakeholders and other informants to appraise the clarity, plausibility, feasibility, and appropriateness of the program theory as formulated....

(9) Program theory also can be assessed in relation to the support for its critical assumptions found in research or documented program practice elsewhere....

(10) Assessment of program theory yields findings that can help improve the conceptualization of a program or, possibly, affirm its basic design...'.

Source: Rossi, Freeman & Lipsey (1999: 187f.); abridged version

An important step is taken with the integration of methodological procedures into a basic theoretical concept, and it is one which goes beyond the purely methodological considerations of Campbell and the highly application-oriented works of Tyler. With the call for the formulation of a programme theory as a basis for evaluations, which postulates the methods to be deployed not as ends in themselves – as the label in Alkin and Christie's classification would suggest – but as a strict derivation from that theory, evaluation research approaches the principles of fundamental research more closely, liberating itself at the same time from the corset of integration into various different fundamental research disciplines. Tied to the thought patterns of individual social science subjects is just what the programme theory fundamental to evaluation is not; on the contrary, it must present itself in the service of the evaluation task as interdisciplinary, and must be able to substantiate the various different aspects of the explicit and implicit assumptions of a programme. More so than the authors described thus far, Chen and Rossi therefore contributed to the establishment of evaluation as a research discipline in its own right, even if most subsequent authors followed a different understanding of theory and science.

Few authors have attempted to develop a programme theory that goes beyond the form of specific theory formulation oriented toward the respective programme intentions envisaged by Chen and Rossi and that is generally applicable. One such, however, has been provided by *Reinhard Stockmann*, who has translated solid insights from fundamental research into a connecting overall concept and uses that concept to derive evaluation criteria (Stockmann 1996, 2008). This general programme theory and its use in evaluations have already been covered (cf. Section 2.3). At this point let it simply be said that these evaluation approaches can hardly be dealt with under the heading of 'methods', but have taken up the very cause of the theoretical integration of the various branches and ramifications of the 'evaluation tree'. Regrettably, no tribute is paid to this integrative counter-movement in the tree model, which is oriented toward progressive diversification (see Section 3.4 for more detail).

3.3.2 The 'use' branch

The second primary branch of Alkin and Christie's evaluation tree embodies the *use-oriented theories*. Here, *Daniel L. Stufflebeam* is cited as the key figure. Unlike the authors referred to in the previous section, Stufflebeam focuses his theory on the *decision-makers* and sees evaluations as a procedure for gaining information on their behalf. In his CIPP model (Stufflebeam 1983), he differentiates between four types of evaluation – context, input, process and product evaluation. Judging the *context* helps the decision-makers to design realistic objectives and objectives systems. Examining the *input* is intended to underpin decisions on strategies and programme designs. In *process evaluation*, the strengths and weaknesses of existing programmes are weighed up, so that the implementation of the measures can be improved. And in *product evaluation*, finally, the impacts of the measures are investigated and an improvement of effectiveness and efficiency duly striven toward. This model has been further developed in various different stages and meanwhile has ten elements instead of four. The contractual component (at the beginning) and the meta-evaluation and reporting components (at the end) have been added, and product evaluation has been split up into impacts, effectiveness, sustainability and transportability see the brief presentation in the box below).

Stufflebeam's CIPP model

(1) *Contractual agreements:* CIPP evaluations should be grounded in explicit advance agreements with the client, and these should be updated as needed throughout the evaluation.

(2) *Context evaluation:* Context evaluation assesses needs, assets and problems within a defined environment.

(3) *Input evaluation:* Input evaluation assesses competing strategies and the work plans and budgets of the selected approach.

(4) *Process evaluation:* Process evaluations monitor, document and assess programme activities.

(5) *Impact evaluation:* Impact evaluation assesses a program's reach to the target audience.

(6) *Effectiveness evaluation:* Effectiveness evaluation documents and assesses the quality and significance of outcomes.

(7) *Sustainability evaluation:* Sustainability evaluation assesses the extent to which a programme's contributions are institutionalized successfully and continued over time.

(8) *Transportability evaluation:* Transportability evaluation assesses the extent to which a programme has (or could be) *(sic)* successfully adapted and applied elsewhere.

(9) *Meta-evaluation:* Meta-evaluation is an assessment of an evaluation, especially its adherence to pertinent standards of sound evaluation.

(10) *The final synthesis report:* Final synthesis reports pull together evaluation findings to inform the full range of audiences about what was attempted, done and accomplished; what lessons were learned; and the bottom-line assessment of the programme.

Source: CIPP Evaluation Model Checklist (Stufflebeam 2007) found at http://www. wmich.edu/evalctr/archive_checklists/cippchecklist_mar07.pdf

---

In this early work, Stufflebeam describes evaluation as a process and understands evaluation design not primarily as a product of theoretical considerations but as the result of an interactive process with the decision-makers. Evaluation is understood here as a *service* which needs to adapt itself to changing requirements and decision-making situations. The evaluation must ensure that it can satisfy the information requirements of a programme's decision-makers, and it must continue to verify during the data gathering phase what those requirements actually are. In this respect, evaluation differs strikingly from fundamental research, the interests of third parties being among the very things the latter will not take into account; ideal-typically, the latter also pursues only its own research interest, completely independent of the clients of a study, and aims to test the hypotheses derived from theories as exactly as possible.

This view of things does not however mean that Stufflebeam rigorously rejects the use of programme theories or abandons the scientifically exact use of research methods in favour of a dialogue-oriented process. Particularly in his most recent work, Stufflebeam deals very extensively with programme evaluation theories and acknowledges their importance both for the consolidation of evaluation as a scientific research field in its own right and for the practical conducting and utility of evaluation for decision-makers (Stufflebeam & Shinkfield 2007: 57ff.). As in the distinction introduced above, Stufflebeam and Shinkfield differentiate between *a general and a specific form of programme evaluation theory:*

> A general theory of program evaluation would characterize the nature of program evaluations, regardless of subject matter, time and space. Such a general theory would cover a wide range of program evaluations, denote their modal characteristics – including logic and processes of evaluative discourse – and describe in general how program evaluations should be assessed and justified. Specific theories of program evaluation would have many of the same characteristics as a general theory but be delimited to account for program evaluations that are restricted to particular substantive areas, locations, or time periods. (Stufflebeam & Shinkfield 2007: 58)

It becomes clear that Stufflebeam and Shinkfield strive to develop a general theory of programme evaluation, but that they then understand that theory as only one element of a general evaluation theory. They see the exchange with praxis as the cornerstone of the development of such a theory, the aim of which should be 'to produce a science of program evaluation – one that is grounded in ongoing conceptualization and rigorous testing of theory-based propositions and continually improves' (Stufflebeam & Shinkfield 2007: 59). This aspiration is certainly shared by Chen, Rossi, Suchman and Weiss, who were allocated to the methods branch of the evaluation tree.

With regard to their aspirations, Stufflebeam and Shinkfield are even more radical and call for more scientifically formulated *theories* which contrast more clearly with the *models* that have dominated so far. Whilst each idealized conceptualization formulated by the evaluators for conducting a programme evaluation is classed as a model, the demands they make on a programme evaluation theory are considerably higher: 'A program evaluation theory is a coherent set of conceptual, hypothetical, pragmatic, and ethical principles forming a general framework to guide the study and practice of program evaluation' (Stufflebeam & Shinkfield 2007: 63). Accordingly, they would like to see the *quality of evaluation theories* judged by applying six central criteria: 'overall coherence, core concepts, tested hypotheses on how evaluation procedures produce desired outcomes, workable procedures, ethical requirements and a general framework for guiding program evaluations practice and conducting research on program evaluation'.

At this point it should be noted that Stufflebeam, in his theoretical thought processes, by no means differs fundamentally from the authors of the 'methods branch'. As mentioned above, he gets to grips much more intensively with the works of Tyler than, for example, Rossi does. Moreover, he does not fundamentally reject a theory-driven procedure, but considers it an important element in the further development of evaluation research as a discipline in its own right. Nevertheless, it should be noted that Stufflebeam does indeed occupy himself much more intensively than the theorists cited on the methods branch with the question of the utilization of evaluation findings for decision-makers. Whether this is enough for him to be able to lay claim to the outstanding position of the 'progenitor' of a theory development branch in its own right is another matter.

Much is to be said for preferring to allocate this role to *Michael Patton*, whose *'utilization-focused evaluation'* model is in much stronger contrast to the ideas of theory-driven evaluation research (Patton 1978, 1997, 2003, 2012).[6] The procedure in a 'utilization-focused evaluation' consists ideal-typically of five different phases:

(a) the identification of the intended users (target groups) of the programme to be evaluated
(b) the attitude of those users to the objective of the evaluation being striven toward and to the utilization of the insights gained
(c) the involvement of the users in methods, design and measurements
(d) their commitment with regard to the active and direct interpretation of the findings and their assessment
(e) the making of decisions on future dissemination measures.

Thus the *'stakeholders' of the evaluation* are in the centre of the procedure, and the evaluators' first important task is to identify them. Patton emphasizes the personal role of the evaluators, who should, according to his dictum, behave 'actively – reactively – adaptively'. The evaluators need to act to identify the users and focus the goals. Reactive behaviour calls for a continuous learning process relating to the social situation of the evaluation. After all, the aspiration of adaptability is derived from the continual adaptation of the evaluation goals and the evaluation design to the changing situation or, as the case may be, the continuously expanding understanding of that situation.

By introducing the term *'developmental evaluation'* Patton even goes a step further: 'The evaluator becomes part of the program design team or an organization's management team, not apart from the team ... but fully participating in decisions and facilitating discussion about how to evaluate whatever happens' (Patton 1997: 106). The most important features of Patton's approach are shown in the overview below.

Features of Patton's utilization-focused evaluation approach

(1) *Stakeholder orientation*: evaluation is a service for 'stakeholders'. A careful 'stakeholder analysis' which takes due account of the varied and different interests of those involved in the programme is the starting-point of an evaluation.

(2) *Use orientation*: evaluation must focus on its use. This is a task which continues from the beginning to the end, and it must adapt to the requirements which may change depending on the situation. Standardized approaches do not have the necessary flexibility.

(3) *User involvement*: the users of an evaluation are to be involved in the important decisions. It is not the frequency but the quality of the participation which is paramount. Personal contact plays a key role.

(4) *Shaping function of the evaluators*: conducting an evaluation is the responsibility of the evaluators, whose credibility and integrity depend on the quality with which they cope with this task. They must behave actively, reactively and adaptively and contribute to the assessment of the merit of a programme (summative evaluation), to its improvement (instrumental use) and to the generation of knowledge (conceptional aspect). They must support the stakeholders in utilizing the evaluation findings.

(5) *Dissemination of evaluation findings*: the utilization of the evaluation is not necessarily to be equated with the reporting and dissemination of its findings. This task is to be separated from those of decision-making, programme improvement and generation of knowledge.

Source: After Stufflebeam and Shinkfield (2007); Patton (2003)

Finally, it remains to be noted that the notion of a 'use' branch makes considerably more sense than that of a 'methods' branch. The latter features, on the one hand, empirical social researchers who are interested in methods development and do not see themselves as evaluators or, if they do, only to a certain extent. On the other hand, the (programme) theory-driven authors are subsumed here, who were not primarily concerned with the development of methods (or at least no more than the authors in other parts of the tree). Their allocation here would rather seem to be due to a common theory-of-science understanding. So this is where the links with the 'methodologists' on this branch would be found: all the authors placed here by Alkin and Christie share an understanding of evaluation which seeks to test theories by means of empirical procedures. (See Donaldson & Lipsey 2006 on the various attitudes to the role of theories in evaluation approaches).

The authors on the 'use' branch do indeed differ from this, placing prime emphasis on service for the client and preferring not so much a scientific view as a pragmatic one. In Michael Patton – and also in Daniel L. Stufflebeam – the most important protagonists are indeed allocated to the primary branch, whereby Patton in particular can be distinguished from authors such as Chen, Rossi or Suchman.

3.3.3 The valuing branch

Finally, there remains the third primary branch of Alkin and Christie's evaluation theory tree, which centres around *valuing procedures*. *Michael Scriven* (1967, 1974, 1980, 1983, 1994, 1997, 2003) is cited as the main protagonist of this line. Scriven is – also in the opinion of Shadish et al. (1991: 94) – the sole leading evaluation theorist to have an explicitly worded and general *theory of valuing* at his command (similarly also Mark et al. 2000: 3f.; Stufflebeam & Shinkfield 2007: 369f.).

This already becomes clear in Scriven's much quoted definition of evaluation: 'Evaluation is the process of determining the merit, worth and value of things, and evaluations are the products of that process' (Scriven 1991: 1). For Scriven, therefore, the principal task of the evaluator consists in carrying out assessments and stating clearly what is 'good' and what is 'bad' about a programme (or other evaluand). In so doing, he acts and judges in the public interest and his task cannot be reduced to that of obtaining and processing information for decision-makers. Scriven dissociates himself expressly from the orientation of an evaluation toward the objectives of a programme and calls for *'goal-free evaluation'* (see in particular Scriven 1974; cf. Section 3.4.1). It is, he says, the task of evaluation to seek out all the effects caused by the activities and then to assess them. A restriction to or even just a priority orientation toward the programme objectives carries the risk that side effects, unintended consequences of action and side impacts may be overlooked or underrated.

Features of Michael Scriven's 'goal-free evaluation'

(1) In 'goal-free evaluation' the evaluators are completely blind to the objectives of a project.
(2) The evaluators have the task of finding and investigating all the impacts a programme has (intended and unintended) – regardless of the planned objectives.
(3) The impacts detected are compared with the needs of the target groups and assessed on that basis.

(4) The use of a programme is assessed exclusively on the basis of the empirical data on the impacts of the programme intervention.

(5) During the phase in which the evaluation questions are worded, the 'goal-free evaluator' avoids contact with the programme managers, as they could have a tendentious influence on his point of view.

(6) An investigation of the objectives has nothing meaningful to say about the social use of a programme and should not therefore be carried out. The evaluator's gaze must be directed beyond the objectives so as also to include the unexpected impacts.

Source: After Scriven (1976: 137)

The *advantages of goal-free evaluation* are said to be that

- there is no longer any need for the costly, time-consuming and difficult determination and weighting of programme objectives
- it interferes less with the ongoing implementation of the programme, because the actors are not accountable for the objectives
- the evaluators are less likely to be influenced socially, perceptually and cognitively since they have less contact with the programme managers and the staff
- it is reversible, in other words it can subsequently lead into an objectives-oriented evaluation, though the converse is not possible (cf. Scriven 1991: 180).

However, since *all programmes* always have a certain *relationship with values and objectives* (cf. Brandtstädter 1990b: 221), even if it is not always explicitly worded, the concept of completely goal-free programmes, not to mention goal-free evaluations, would be a very naive one indeed (cf. Weiss 1974: 22). Owen and Rogers (1999: 269) also point this out: 'Practically, the notion of deliberately ignoring the intentions of a programmatic intervention borders on the bizarre. Commissioners and clients are almost always interested in whether program objectives have been met, and the evaluator would need to go to extremes to ignore information about how the program is meant to operate'.

Following the theoretical style of contemplating the evaluand in a way completely detached from the objectives of programme managers, Scriven concentrated on the *analysis of the requirements of the target groups* and occupied himself in particular with various *forms of assessment procedure*. The effects of an intervention, having been ascertained, must be assessed by comparing them with the needs of the beneficiaries of those intervention effects, for which reason the investigation of those needs should be a cornerstone of the evaluation. For comparative assessment, four different methods are available: 'scoring', 'ranking', 'grading' and 'apportioning'. In the *scoring procedure* numerical values are allocated to the evaluand (or one of its sub-dimensions); these are intended to depict the quality of the effects and thus of the 'value' of the intervention on a predetermined scale. The object of the *ranking procedure* is to make possible a comparison between different options or evaluands. It is not strictly necessary to award values on a scale. The *grading procedure* forms classes or groups from existing numerical values or other information features, by which means certain similarities and differences can be emphasized. With the *apportionment procedure,* the distribution of existing resources or effects over different evaluands or alternative actions is investigated.

Scriven's allocation to the 'valuing branch' of Alkin and Christie's evaluation tree is indisputable and can be justified relatively simply and conclusively. As compared with the other authors cited (Stake; Eisner; Wolf & Owens, Guba & Lincoln; MacDonald; House), Scriven's outstanding significance for this line of theory can certainly be understood clearly, also in comparison with Stake, whose approach was presented in Section 3.2.3. Tribute is paid to the great significance of the assessment aspect for the development of evaluation approaches in practically all attempts at systematization, the generic term 'valuing' selected by Alkin and Christie appearing more apt for covering the various aspects than the term 'judgement' as used by Guba and Lincoln.

On the other hand, it should be noted that Scriven not only made a major contribution to the valuing discussion, but also provided many stimuli for the 'use branch' (cf. the remarks in Section 3.4.3). The efforts he made toward customer orientation are reflected, among other things, in a series of evaluation check-lists and the publication of an evaluation thesaurus (Scriven 1991). So let the question at least be asked here whether the 'bifurcation' between valuing and use as a development tendency in evaluation approaches came about because of Scriven.

3.3.4 Summary and assessment

In general this classification model has some indisputable advantages, above all, of course, its visual comprehensibility and the *clear principle of classification* on which it is based, by means of which the most important evaluation theorists can be classified very conclusively. The identification of three main lines by the central topics of 'use', 'methods' and 'valuing' and their basis in the area of accountability and empirical social inquiry is decidedly valuable. Unlike Guba and Lincoln, Alkin and Christie refrain from introducing a separate branch for 'description', which seems justified in view of the former's weak evidence in support of such a 'generation'. On the other hand, the term 'use' of evaluation approaches points to an important line of thought, which is not appreciated in that way in the generation model.

However, when it comes to *classifying individual names*, there are at least a few points of criticism to be raised. This applies particularly to the question of who is to be referred to as an evaluation theorist and duly featured in a tree of evaluation research – or, as Alkin and Christie would have it, even specifically of 'evaluation theories'. When all is said and done, such classification would be tenable if it were adhered to systematically on all branches. But this is not the case: in Michael Scriven, for example, the beginning of the assessment branch undisputedly features a leading evaluation theorist who has made a major contribution to the development of this line of thought. On the other hand, the important works of Scriven's forerunners, which cannot necessarily be allocated to evaluation theory, such as the value judgement dispute led by Alkin and Christie (cf. Albert & Topitsch 1990 for an overview) and all the economic research on problems in decision-making, which led after all to several procedures – very much in use today – such as multi-criteria analysis (cf. Section 5.5), are neglected. In the methods branch the procedure is the reverse: in Campbell's case at least, allocation to the 'evaluation theorists' is debatable, whilst – conversely – in the case of the authors who occupied themselves more with theory of evaluation in that branch (such as Rossi) the question needs to be asked what exceptional contribution they made to methods development which distinguishes them clearly from others such as Patton or Scriven.

Things become particularly difficult when the principle of classification designed primarily for the evaluation theories developed in the USA (or at least in those parts of the world where English language and culture hold or held sway) *is applied to developments in Europe and is supposed to depict not only the theories but the entire evaluation landscape.* In view of the many diverse national, sectoral and discipline-related backgrounds and developments which were for a long time largely independent of one another, it is hardly fitting to refer to a common tree of development, the image of an impenetrable 'thicket' or jungle seeming much more appropriate (cf. Meyer & Stockmann 2007 on this; see also the other contributions in the documentation of Peterson and Vestman 2007 on the overall discussion of the transferability of Alkin and Christie's schema to Europe within the European Evaluation Society).

It is not only because of these problems that the *tree metaphor as a whole* – striking though it is – can be cast into doubt. As made clear in the preceding section, taking Scriven as an example, it is certainly not the case that the branches split early on and that further ramifications are now taking place inside the various schools. On the contrary, the various authors pick up on impulses from other authors and attempt to integrate them into their approaches. There are for example parallels, not only between Scriven and Stake (within the valuing branch) but also between Scriven and Patton (who are a very long way apart in the tree model). A similar situation has already been shown to exist for Stufflebeam and the methods branch, and one might certainly argue similarly for a number of other authors.

Of course it is not easy to find a simple and convincing principle of classification for the diversity of evaluation approaches which have meanwhile been developed. It is further evidence of the increasing importance of evaluation that, especially in recent years, there have been considerably more attempts at such classification and some very different criteria have been applied in their making (cf. Donaldson & Lipsey 2006; Lee 2006; Madaus & Kellaghan 2000; Owen & Rogers 1999: 39ff.; Cook 1997; Shadish et al. 1991 as a selection). For this reason, a further attempt at systematization will now be presented in the section that follows. It is in clear contrast to the two systems introduced above: systematization according to Fitzpatrick, Sanders and Worthen.

3.4   Systematization according to Fitzpatrick et al.: the use model

In recent years an attitude mainly characterized by pragmatism has established itself in evaluation research, according to which the focus is not so much on the theory-of-science roots, the theoretical approaches or the methods deployed but rather on the usefulness of the evaluation findings for the individual stakeholders. Chelimsky (1995: 6) describes this more recent development thus: 'We think less today about the absolute merits of one method versus another, and more about whether and how using them in concert could result in more conclusive findings'. The real evaluation questions come more to the fore: 'We have learned that the choice of methods (and measures and instruments and data) depends much more on the type of question being asked than on the qualities of any particular method' (ibid.). Over and above all theoretical and methodological issues, there is more and more agreement on the fact that it depends mainly on evaluation findings being put to use by the stakeholders. For this, it is necessary for evaluations to do justice to their functions.

This aspect of the *practical orientation* of evaluation is used by Fitzpatrick, Sanders and Worthen (2012) as a structuring criterion for the classification of evaluation approaches:

'Our classification is based on what we see as the driving force behind doing the evaluation: the factors that influence the choice of what to study and the ways in which the study is conducted' (Fitzpatrick, Sanders & Worthen 2012: 124). Applying this yardstick, the authors differentiate between four different forms of evaluation, these being shown in the box here and discussed in more detail in the section that follows.

Systematization after Fitzpatrick, Sanders and Worthen

(1) *Approaches oriented to characteristics of the programme*, including *Objectives-based approaches*, in which the focus is on identifying programme objectives and judgement, *Standards-based approaches*, using generally agreed standards and benchmarks for evaluation, and *theory-based approaches*, in which programme theories are tested.

(2) *Approaches oriented to decisions to be made about the programme*, in which the focus is on providing information to improve the quality of decisions made by stakeholders or organizations (*Management-oriented approaches*).

(3) *Approaches oriented to comprehensive judgements of the quality of the programme or product*, including *Expertise-oriented approaches*, in which the evaluation is carried out by selected experts from a given area of practice, and *Consumer-oriented approaches*, the main task of which consists in providing product-related information and assessments, for example in the form of product check-lists.

(4) *Approaches oriented to participation of stakeholders (Participant-oriented approaches)*, characterized by particular emphasis on the integration of the various interest groups involved in or affected by an evaluation (stakeholders) in the planning and conducting of that evaluation

Source: Fitzpatrick, Sanders and Worthen (2012:123)

3.4.1 Approaches oriented to program characteristics

Example: Objectives-oriented evaluation approaches

The main emphasis in objectives-oriented approaches is – as their label indicates – on answering the question of whether and to what extent the specific objectives of a programme, project or measure have been achieved. Objectives-oriented approaches thus serve mainly purposes of control by examining whether or not the proclaimed target status is matched by an appropriate actual status. The findings from the evaluation can then be used to modify either the objectives or the processes.

Ralph W. Tyler, already presented in detail in Section 3.2.2, who carried out studies on the improvement of the educational success of students at the end of the 1930s, is regarded as an early champion of this approach. *Sanders and Cunningham* (1973, 1974) enriched the objectives-oriented approach by adding the insight that not just the achievement of targets can be empirically investigated; the objectives can also be assessed with regard to their logical structure and their compatibility with one another. Thus the coherence of the arguments on which an objective is based can be verified, or the conformity of objectives with superordinate values. The consequences which ensue from the achievement of an objective can also be derived logically and compared with the potential consequences of competing objectives. The 'logical models' explained in more detail in Section 3.5.3, and planning procedures built upon them such as the 'LogFrame approach' (cf. NORAD 1999) or the 'objectives-oriented project planning' (ZOPP) of the German Society for Technical Cooperation (GTZ) (cf. GTZ 1988) follow a similar design principle.

In Tyler's tradition, Malcolm Provus (1971) developed a 'discrepancy evaluation model' (DEM), which focuses on the differences between the programme objectives being striven toward and the actual achievement of targets. Starting with the assumption that a programme has four phases, to which Provus adds a fifth, appropriate tasks are allocated to evaluation:

Evaluation tasks in the discrepancy evaluation model after Provus

(1) During the *definition or development phase,* the main work is on defining objectives, processes and activities and identifying the necessary resources and actors. Target dimensions (standards) are to be developed for each of these components, and these standards must be able to be verified during the evaluation. The task of the evaluator in this phase consists in taking care that a complete set of design specifications is produced, said specifications then forming the basis of the evaluation.

(2) During the *implementation phase* the defined target dimensions (standards) or design specifications are used as yardsticks for assessing the development of the programme. The main task of evaluation consists in carrying out a series of congruency tests, in order to identify any discrepancies between the implementation of the programme as striven toward and the implementation as actually achieved.

(3) During the *process phase,* the evaluation concentrates on gathering data about the progress of the programme participants in order to find out whether or not their performance has improved or, as the case may be, whether their behavioural patterns have changed as desired.

(4) In the *product or production phase* the evaluation aims to investigate whether or not the long-term programme objectives (terminal objectives) have been achieved. For this, a distinction is made between intermediate and long-term outcomes, which are recorded in follow-up studies.

(5) In an optional *fifth phase,* cost-benefit analyses and a comparison of the findings with those from cost-benefit analyses of similar programmes can be carried out.

Source: After Provus (1971)

Provus' evaluation model could also be referred to as an early form of the management-oriented approach, since it aims to ensure effective programme development. The intention is that any discrepancies found should be used by the programme managers together with the evaluators to research the causes, so as to be able to make corrections. Many elements of the discrepancy model are also to be found in current models – especially programme logic models – (e.g. the 'LogFrame' approach', see Section 3.5.3).

Orientation toward the objectives of a programme has been leaving its mark on evaluation since the 1930s and is thus *considerably older* than the approaches of Tyler and Provus. The procedure of turning predefined objectives into a yardstick for determining the success or failure of a programme and for the improvement, continuation or termination of programme measures has proven particularly attractive.

The particular *strengths of the approach* include its (alleged) simplicity: 'It is easily understood, easy to follow and implement, and produces information that program directors generally agree is relevant to their mission' (Fitzpatrick et al. 2012: 166). Apart from that, the approach has provided impulses for a large number of technological and methodological developments that have contributed to the better specification of objectives, and the adequate development of indicators and methods for their measurement. It is said in favour of the objectives-oriented approach that it admonishes programme managers and programme participants to reflect on their real intentions and specify their programme objectives explicitly. Finally, the evaluation of a programme with regard to its previously specified objectives also provides a basis for assessment in which the rationale can easily be seen.

Having said that, this is one of the very features that might be perceived as a *weakness of the approach*, as there is no real assessive component (going beyond the objectives of the programme themselves), using which the general merit of a programme might be determined. Besides, it is often not all that easy to determine the programme objectives – the starting-point of all objectives-oriented approaches – since these are often only nebulously worded and of a very general nature. Note should also be taken of the fact that the official objectives – for example those mentioned in the programme documents – and the objectives actually being pursued may be a very long way apart. Target specifications are often only part of a political and sometimes nebulous legitimation rhetoric, and have but little to do with actual programme developments.

Another problem of which mostly *no account is taken* is that objectives tend to change in the course of time, so that there is a risk of judging achievement in terms of objectives that are actually no longer relevant at all. As numerous actors are involved in the implementation of a programme, and in view of the fact that they may all be pursuing different, sometimes even contradictory aims, the question arises against whose objectives the achievement of the outputs is to be measured. If target dimensions are focused on, there is a risk that information about the merit of a programme that does not reflect its objectives and unintended impacts may be systematically neglected. This constraint may lead to a 'tunnel-vision evaluation', in which the real potential is not exploited (cf. Weiss 1974; Lange 1983; Brandtstädter 1990b; Vedung 1999; Fitzpatrick et al. 2012).

3.4.2 Approaches oriented to decision-making

Example: Management-oriented evaluation approaches

The management-oriented evaluation approaches are related to the objectives-oriented approaches in as much as the programme managers have an interest in achieving the planned programme objectives in order to be able to intervene in an appropriate way. Having said that, the management-oriented approaches do not exhaust their potential in answering these questions. In particular, the question 'why?' is much more to the fore; in other words the question of which internal (programme-inherent or organizational) and external reasons are responsible for the achievement or, as the case may be, non-achievement of targets. Moreover, in these approaches the evaluation may also come to focus on other issues, for example work processes, personnel or resource problems, organizational structures etc. Put in general terms, management-oriented evaluation approaches are characterized by the fact that they provide decision-makers with information so that the latter can make decisions on a rational basis. Evaluations of this kind are duly oriented toward the information requirements of management and thus become an important component of decision-making processes in organizations.

Major contributions to the management-oriented approaches have been made by such as Daniel Stufflebeam (1971, 1973, 2000), whose CIPP model has already been discussed in Section 3.3.2 above, and Marvin Alkin (1969, 2004). Alkin (1969: 2) defines evaluation as 'the process of ascertaining the decision areas of concern, selecting appropriate information and collecting and analysing information in order to report summary data useful to decision-makers in selecting among alternatives'. When Alkin was director of the Center for the Study of Evaluation at the University of California, Los Angeles (UCLA), he developed an approach that closely followed Stufflebeam's CIPP model. It involves five evaluation goals:

(1) *system assessment*, in order to obtain information about the whole system to be evaluated (comparable with context analysis in the CIPP model)
(2) *programme planning*, to enable specific programmes to be selected with a view to their effectiveness in satisfying certain needs (comparable with input analysis in the CIPP model)
(3) *programme implementation*, to obtain information as to whether a programme has been implemented in accordance with the planning specifications (comparable with process analysis in the CIPP model)
(4) *programme improvement*, to generate information on how a programme is functioning, whether or not interim targets have been met and whether or not any unanticipated impacts have come about (also comparable with process analysis in the CIPP model)
(5) *programme certification*, to obtain information about the merit (use) of a programme and about the potential for deploying that programme in other contexts (comparable with product analysis in the CIPP model).

Even if it might look as though these operations should follow one another sequentially, both Stufflebeam (CIPP model) and Alkin (UCLA model) go to some trouble to point out that this need not be the case by any means. For example, an evaluation designed to examine programme improvement can manage without a prior assessment of the system, planning or implementation, and vice versa. According to these models, the procedure and the question of which operations are integrated into an evaluation depends solely on the information requirements of the decision-makers.

Basic assumptions of the UCLA model after Alkin

(1) Evaluations are a process for obtaining information.
(2) The information obtained with the aid of an evaluation is used mainly to assist in making decisions on possible alternative procedures in the further shaping of the programme.
(3) This information should be oriented toward the information requirements of the decision-makers and presented in a form they can actively use.
(4) Different decision-making problems require different forms of evaluation.

Source: After Alkin (1991: 4)

The operations and principles proposed in the CIPP model, and very similarly in the UCLA model (named after the university), are also to be found in the same or comparable form in other (more recent) management-oriented evaluation approaches.

The other evaluation models that Fitzpatrick, Sanders and Worthen (2012: 172ff.) classify as 'decision-oriented' include the 'utilization-focused evaluation' approach of Michael Patton (see Section 3.3.2) and the works of *Joseph Wholey* (1983, 1994), which concentrated on the practical use of evaluation in the field of public administration.

One main *strength* of the decision-oriented evaluation approaches is seen in the clear orientation of evaluation toward the information requirements of the decision-makers. However, this a mixed blessing: 'the focus on managers and their informational needs could restrict the information that evaluators seek, the types of data they collect, and the dissemination of the results' (Fitzpatrick et al. 2012: 185).

The management-oriented approaches emphasize the utility aspect of evaluations by linking decision-making requirements explicitly with information requirements. Furthermore, these approaches already made it clear early on that programme managers do not have to wait until a programme shows impacts to conduct evaluations, but that it makes sense to evaluate in any phase of a programme. This in particular has strengthened the formative function of evaluations (cf. Section 2.2.3).

To that extent, these approaches also represent an extension of the objectives-oriented approaches, since they can focus not only on the achievement of targets, but also on questions of programme planning, implementation and development. Moreover, the management-oriented evaluation approaches emphasize the special importance of taking information into account in good time in order to render a prompt reaction on the part of the decision-makers possible at all.

Having said that, the management-oriented evaluation approaches also have a number of *weaknesses:* it is true that on the one hand focusing on the information requirements of the decision-makers is a strength, since in this way the evaluation is shown clearly what direction it needs to go in, yet disadvantages also arise from this. It may for example be the case that critical aspects of the topic are consciously neglected, important perspectives are not taken into account and stakeholders' interests are neglected or even deliberately suppressed. There is a risk that the evaluators may be taken in by the client to such an extent that they see only the client's point of view, with the result that "the evaluator can become the 'hired gun' of the manager and program establishment" (Fitzpatrick et al. 2012: 185). A narrowing of angle, to say nothing of a unilateral client perspective, can lead not only to the 'falsification' of evaluation findings and the suppression of important opinions and perspectives, but also from the outset to severe curtailment of the evaluation goals. The assumption on which the approach is based – that those responsible for the programme would already know in advance exactly what information they required to make their decisions – is empirically untenable and fails to do justice to the complexity of programmes and their environment. In addition, this concept can lead to evaluations that are equipped with only very modest financial budgets and a rather short period of time to carry them out. This can lead to considerable deficiencies that seriously impair their quality. For this reason, management-oriented evaluations should also make sure that other stakeholders are factored into the evaluation plan, that the evaluation goals are not too narrow, that various different perspectives are admissible and that time-and-resources arguments are not used to prevent evaluations that are thorough from a conceptual and methodological point of view.

3.4.3 Approaches oriented to comprehensive judgements

Example: Consumer-oriented evaluation approaches

What the management and consumer-oriented evaluation approaches do have in common is that both of them are mainly intended to serve certain stakeholder groups. Whilst the one provides solid information and assessments for management decisions, the other serves to render purchasing decisions easier for consumers. Both approaches thus achieve their focus mainly by being oriented toward the information requirements of individual – different – groups of evaluation audiences.

The *consumer-oriented evaluation approach* is a reaction to the increasing diversity of competing products and services, which are now such that an individual can hardly hope to keep track of them. It aims to support consumers in judging the merits of products and services offered. As a rule, wide-ranging 'evaluation check-lists' are provided for this, with which products and services can be compared. The best known in Germany are probably the product tests of *Stiftung Warentest*,[7] in which comparative assessments are made applying open criteria.

In the USA, consumer-oriented evaluation approaches were mainly developed for the classification of educational services. Michael Scriven (1967, 1974, 1991, 2004), who has made some significant contributions to this approach and concerned himself particularly with the assessment of educational products, developed an appropriate *check-list*[8] in 1974 and later extended it. This evaluation grid comprises 15 generally worded checkpoints. Scriven points out explicitly that these criteria do not represent a maximum-requirements list that can be shortened at will, but 'indispensable' test criteria. In the USA the consumer-oriented evaluation approach is mainly used by government institutions and independent consumer-oriented institutions (particularly in the field of education, for example the Educational Products Information Exchange (EPIE), www.epie.org).

Key evaluation check-list after Scriven

- background and context of a programme
- descriptions and definitions
- consumers of the product ('impactees')
- resources of the programme ('strengths assessment')
- values to which the programme refers
- process
- outcomes
- costs
- comparisons
- generalisability
- synthesis
- (possible) recommendations and explanations
- (possible) responsibility and justification
- report and support
- meta-evaluation

Source: www.wmich.edu/evalctr/checklists/kec_feb07.pdf

One of the main *strengths* of the consumer-oriented approaches is that they structure and comparatively assess the plethora of products and services offered, of which individual consumers can hardly keep track, according to selected criteria. The consumers are provided both with assessment criteria for their own analysis and the findings of the product evaluations. This creates market transparency. On the one hand the purchasing decisions of the consumers are thus put on a sound information basis, and on the other the findings can be used for quality improvement on the part of suppliers and manufacturers. The evaluation check-lists are thus useful, easy-to-use instruments for both provider and consumer.

Having said that, the criteria are developed without any involvement whatsoever on the part of the stakeholders (providers or consumers), so that too much or too little importance may be attached to certain criteria, whilst others may even be lacking altogether. Moreover, there is *criticism* to the effect that carrying out product tests can lead to increased product costs. Once stipulated, the criteria (standards) may also have an inhibiting effect on the development of production innovations. It is also pointed out that there is a risk that local products – which cannot all be tested on account of the cost – may be ousted by products tested over a wider area (cf. Fitzpatrick et al. 2012: 148f.).

All in all, it should be noted that the consumer-oriented evaluation approach is a very special case which covers only a very narrow group of functions. True, its evaluands are mostly products or services, yet it can – at least in an adapted form (cf. Scriven's checklist) – also be used for the evaluation of programmes and policies and for meta-evaluations. As it is based on a fixed catalogue of assessment criteria, this approach is mainly summative. However, if the criteria are already applied in the planning and implementation phase, they can also take on a formative character.

Example: Expertise-oriented evaluation approaches

Another group of evaluation approaches classified by Fitzpatrick, Sanders and Worthen (2012: 127ff.) differs in terms of its logic from the rest of their system. As shown at the beginning, the authors determined 'the driving force behind doing the evaluation' (2004: 124) as a classification feature. However, this feature does not apply to this type of approach. *Expertise-oriented evaluations* are not an evaluation purpose like those discussed previously, but a survey method. Indeed, one might strictly speaking doubt whether review procedures like those described below are evaluations at all.

Expertise-oriented evaluation approaches use the professional assessments of experts for judging institutions, programmes, products or activities. Even if the other evaluation approaches outlined above cannot manage without professional expertise, this approach relies primarily on the assessment of circumstances by experts. Since as a rule a single person will not possess all the skills necessary for a comprehensive assessment, teams with complementary qualifications are usually deployed for reviews.

Fitzpatrick, Sanders and Worthen (2012: 128) point out that there is a variety of such evaluation processes, comprising such diverse procedures or facilities as a doctoral colloquium conducted by several professors, an expert commission on a certain subject, accreditation units of professional organizations, governmental supervisory institutions for compliance with certain standards or peer reviews in the selection of articles submitted to a journal.

In order to reclassify these various processes, the authors differentiate between *four types of expert-oriented evaluation*, which can be distinguished in accordance with five dimensions (Table 3.1):

Table 3.1 Types of expert-oriented evaluation approach

Type of expert-oriented evaluation approach	Existing structures	Published standards	Set rhythm	Opinion of several experts	Canbe influenced by findings?
Formal review procedures	yes	yes	yes	yes	usually
Informal review procedures	yes	rarely	sometimes	yes	usually
Ad hoc panels	no	no	no	yes	sometimes
Ad hoc review	no	no	no	no	sometimes

Source: Fitzpatrick, Sanders and Worthen (2012: 128).

1st Is there a formal structure for the review procedure?

2nd Are there any published standards for the procedure?

3rd Are reviews carried out at specified intervals?

4th Does the review procedure include the assessment of several experts?

5th Do the results of the review procedure affect the status of the evaluated circumstance?

Formal, professional review processes come nearest to the procedures and intentions of evaluations, which is why the presentation below is restricted to this sector. For this kind of review procedure certain features can be determined and a clear trend toward standardization recognized.

Characteristics of formal professional review procedures

(1) Existence of a structure or organization that carries out periodic reviews
(2) Published standards (and possibly instruments) used to that end
(3) A set rhythm for regular reviews (e.g. every five years)
(4) The combining of several expert opinions to reach an overall assessment
(5) The results of the review procedure have an effect on the circumstance evaluated.

Source: Fitzpatrick, Sanders & Worthen (2004: 114)

The best known form of this type of expert-aided evaluation is the *accreditation procedure*, which is defined as a process 'whereby an

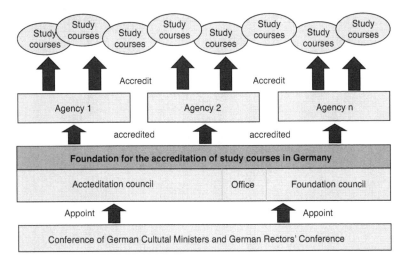

Figure 3.5   The German accreditation system

Source: www.akkreditierungsrat.de/fileadmin/Seiteninhalte/Akkreditierungssystem /
Organigramm/Schaubild_Akkreditierungssystem.pdf

organization grants approval of institutions such as schools, universities, and hospitals' (ibid.). In the education sector particularly, accreditation procedures in many states have been recording a tremendous boom. In Germany, for example, in 1998, following a resolution passed by the German Rectors' Conference and the Conference of German Cultural Ministers, an *accreditation council for the higher education area* was set up, the task of which is 'to make a contribution to the development of the quality of studies and teaching in Germany and to contribute accordingly to the realization of the European Higher Education Area' (see www.akkreditierungsrat.de).[9] The statutorily regulated German higher education accreditation system is depicted schematically in Figure 3.5.

According to its resolution of 29 February 2008, the German accreditation agency applies the following *criteria* for the accreditation of study courses:

(1) Systems management of the university (incl. quality assurance concept and drafting of quality objectives)
(2) Qualification objectives of the study course concept (incl. empowerment to take up a qualified occupation)
(3) Conceptual placement of the study course in the study system (incl. the standards for structural specifications common to the *länder)*

(4) The study course concept (incl. whether or not it can be studied within the normal period of time)
(5) Implementation of the study course (incl. staffing and equipment)
(6) Examination system
(7) Transparency and documentation
(8) Quality assurance.

Accreditation is carried out by accreditation agencies such as the *Hanover Central Evaluation and Accreditation Agency* (ZEvA). The ZEvA was set up in 1995 by the State Universities Conference of the Federal State of Lower Saxony as a joint institution for the universities of that state and developed a concept of its own for the implementation of the accreditation procedure in 1998. Since February 2000, the ZEvA, the first agency to be certified by the German Accreditation Council, has been carrying out accreditations throughout the Federal Republic in accordance with that procedure, though the latter does frequently need to be amended to fit in with the changing statutory background and the resolutions of the Conference of German Cultural Ministers, the German Rectors' Conference and the Accreditation Council.

Accreditation procedure of the ZEvA

1st phase: application
(a) Application made by the university to the ZEvA
(b) Counselling and contract
(c) Preliminary examination

2nd phase: external peer review
(a) Appointment of experts
(b) Peer review
(c) Assessment report by experts to the ZEvA

3rd phase: deliberation and decision by the SAK[1]
(a) Assessment report to the SAK
(b) Adoption of resolution
(c) Announcement of resolution

[1] SAK = Foundation for the Accreditation of Study Courses in Germany

Source: www.zeva.org/akkred/verfahren/ablauf.htm

Some public *criticism* of this accreditation procedure has been quite severe. The accreditation of jurists, for example, is castigated as an 'unlawful parallel administration' (Lege 2006) and described even by auditors as 'bureaucratically puffed up'. On account of the 'disproportionately high cost' and not very reliable results occasioned by the fact that the discretionary powers of the agencies are rather wide-ranging, the Thuringian Court of Auditors (2008) adjudged that the accreditation procedure was 'no longer acceptable or practicable'. However, the Bologna Process involving the introduction of accreditation procedures at universities throughout Europe is progressing, even if the concepts actually used do still differ greatly in spite of the laws on which they are based[10] becoming more and more uniform.

Having said that, some *basic structures* have formed. These were summarized by Scriven (as early as 1984) as follows:

- published standards
- a self-evaluation of the institution being investigated
- a team of external evaluators
- a site visit
- a report based on that visit, as a rule with recommendations
- a review of said report by a specially qualified panel
- a concluding report and accreditation by the accreditation agency.

Formal accreditation systems are moreover based on the shared assumption that 'experts are in the best position to make the judgements and provide the advice institutions need, because they know what can be accomplished in the environment of such an institution – and how to accomplish it' (Fitzpatrick et al. 2012: 135). For this reason, the external reviewers who for each evaluation carry out the site visit and the review panel which assesses the report are selected from among the members of the profession whose work they are supposed to be judging. Moreover, the standards and assessment criteria for the reviews are also determined by members of this group – without any contribution from the other stakeholders.

With regard to the *examination criteria,* the main issues are adequate equipment, qualification of the staff and the appropriateness of the organizational processes. Whilst there are already a number of attempts to record the achievement of targets too (for example in the scientific sector using indicators such as the number of publications or citations, the number of occasions on which external funds have successfully been raised etc.), the measurement of impacts is still in its early stages. If, finally, the *strengths and weaknesses* of this approach are again compared, it must be said that the outputs of expert-aided evaluation procedures are to be seen mainly in the development of standards and assessment criteria. The conducting of self-assessments, as a rule permitted in accreditation procedures, makes it necessary for those assessing themselves to look closely at their own structures and processes, and can thus also serve to expose their own strengths and weaknesses, which in turn offers opportunities for improvement. Furthermore, the external angle of the reviewers makes an independent perspective possible, which can be compared with the results of the self-assessment thereby facilitating learning.

At the same time, however, the expert-aided assessment approach also features a number of striking weaknesses. As mentioned above, the experts who set the criteria for the reviews, the experts for the site visits and the experts for the assessment of the reports which have been drawn up all come from the same professional pool, so that there is not only a risk of one-sided assessments (as in 'birds of a feather flock together'), but also a risk that the external perspective that is supposed to produce new ideas is not actually as external as it was thought to be (as in 'everyone is stewing in the same juice'). Moreover, accreditations often cover only a very limited range of questions. Unintended impacts are almost completely neglected. Not only that, there is also a strong predilection towards quantitative indicators because they are easier to measure. Qualitative indicators are thus often neglected. In addition, the standards on which the accreditation is based are as a rule not weighted, so that factors which are about to become very significant may not stand out among trivial ones.

Furthermore, the implicit assumption on which every review procedure is based, namely that the experts consulted for carrying out a review actually possess the professional and other skills necessary to enable them make a judgement, is difficult to verify using objective yardsticks. To make matters worse, it cannot be ruled out that in spite of published standards the assessments of the individual experts may lead to distortions on account of their personal preferences and subjective horizons of experience.

For these reasons, the review process is also *criticized* because 'the closeness of the experts to those being judged and possible competition between institutions or departments present serious conflicts of interest that can lead to biased judgements' (Fitzpatrick et al. 2012: 135). Scriven (1984: 73) pulls no punches with his criticism of these review procedures either, calling accreditations 'an excellent example of what one might with only slight cynicism call a pseudo-evaluative process, set up to give the appearance of self-regulation without having to suffer the inconvenience'. Last but not least it should also be borne in mind that accreditation processes are associated with considerable burdens of budget and time, which can lead to institutions' not being able to afford the costs. This can then automatically lead to devaluations, although the quality of the non-accredited institutions or their products is of course not necessarily poorer than those of accredited ones.

3.4.4   Approaches oriented to participation of stakeholders

Example: Participant-oriented evaluation approaches

As shown at the beginning, the early years of evaluation research were marked by a *methodological rigour determined by positivism*. Evaluators were concerned not only about identifying the impacts of programmes but also above all about discovering the 'true relationships' between causal forces (cf. Cook & Matt 1990: 20), so that programme decisions would not be made on the basis of 'false' assertions. Against the current practice of applying social science methods to evaluation goals, there was criticism to be heard as early as the mid-1960s, criticism which according to Fitzpatrick, Sanders and Worthen (2012: 190f.) related in particular to the evaluators' predominant occupation with explicating programme objectives, developing elaborate evaluation systems and sophisticated instruments and writing lengthy reports. This, they said, sidetracked them from recognizing what was really going on in the programmes they were supposed to be evaluating. Not only the experimental methods used at the beginning, but also the conventional use of surveys began to be criticized more and more: 'with long questionnaires tended to be drawn-out, tedious, a headache to administer, a nightmare to process and write up, inaccurate and unreliable in data obtained, leading to reports, if any, which were long, late, boring, misleading, difficult to use, and anyway ignored' (Chambers 1994: 956). It was even claimed that many large-scale evaluation studies had been conducted without the evaluators' actually being present! This criticism culminated in the accusation that the 'human' component was lacking in the conventional investigation designs that had been adopted from science, and that it was therefore necessary to integrate those involved in the programme more intensively in the evaluations. From this call for the greater *participation of affected parties,* an abundance of approaches developed, leading to one of the most extensive discussions in the history of evaluation research.[11]

Some aspects of this aspiration to involve stakeholders in general and affected parties in particular have already been covered in other parts of this book (see Sections 3.2.3, 3.2.4 and 3.3.2). A number of the authors cited by Fitzpatrick, Sanders and Worthen (Stake; Guba & Lincoln; Patton) and their evaluation conceptions have also already been presented. The *empowerment evaluation* approach goes beyond the call for the involvement of the stakeholders in an evaluation, which is inherent in all these *participant-oriented approaches*. Like the *participatory evaluation approaches* – not covered here[12] – this concept is rooted in action research and requires "that evaluators should not only facilitate citizen participation in evaluation, but also become advocates for societies' disenfranchized and voiceless minorities". The evaluator, as the advocate of the disadvantaged, helps the latter to acquire more skills (not only with regard to evaluation), so that they can gain more self-determination and self-responsibility.

The empowerment approach, in the development of which David Fetterman (Fetterman et al. 1995; Fetterman 2000; Fetterman & Wandersman 2005) played a decisive role, consciously throws the classical quality criteria such as objectivity, validity and reliability overboard, saying that science in general and evaluation in particular have never been 'neutral' and that there is no such thing as a scientific truth anyway. Instead, it says, evaluation should be used to strengthen the skills of those involved in such a way that they are in a position to improve their situation themselves.

Strengths of the empowerment approach after Fetterman

(1) After suitable training from the evaluators, the stakeholders can conduct evaluations themselves (training).
(2) The evaluator thus takes on the role of a helper (facilitation).
(3) He also functions as an advocate of the disadvantaged (advocacy).
(4) Those involved gain a better understanding of the programme (illumination).
(5) Empowerment evaluation contributes to the liberation of those involved from their traditional roles and the expectations associated with them.

Source: After Fetterman (1994: 3ff.)

Of course, by no means all evaluators agree with this redefinition of their role and the concept of evaluation based upon it. Stufflebeam, for example, (1994: 323) points out that 'helping people help themselves' is a lofty enough goal, but that it is not the task of evaluation.

A useful feature for the internal distinction of participant-oriented approaches is the understanding of participation on which they are based. The questions of *who is to be involved in what and to what extent* receive very different answers in the various individual approaches; the range includes consultation with those involved (responsive evaluation), active participation (naturalistic approaches) and even scenarios in which the participants conduct the evaluation themselves (empowerment approaches). Their understanding of participation can be seen to change, from the question 'whose reality counts?' to the question 'who counts reality?' (cf. Caspari 2004: 102). The plea for explicitly taking into account the perspectives and values of the individual stakeholders turned into a call for the extensive involvement of the stakeholders, all the way to their taking over responsibility for the evaluation.

An alternative to this understanding of participation is provided for example by the evaluation concept of Melvin M. Mark, Gary T. Henry and George Julnes (Mark et al. 2000, 1999; Henry et al. 1998; Henry 1996; Julnes et al. 1998; Julnes 2012; Chen et al. 2011).[13] The key concept of these authors is *'social betterment'*, and they set it against the aspiration of usefulness and thus against the stakeholder-based approaches (above all those of Patton and Weiss): 'social betterment, rather than the more popular and pervasive goal of utilization, should motivate evaluation' (Mark et al. 2000: 19). In contrast to the situation in the participatory approaches, the decision-makers are clearly the intended targets for the 'social betterment'goals and not the affected parties themselves. It is a matter of designing programmes which help people get over emergency situations, and it is the aim of evaluation to provide information for improving them. This is the task of experts and not of the affected parties themselves.

On the other side, these three authors do not in principle oppose a participatory evaluation approach, though they would like it to be integrated into an overriding concept:

> Evaluation success should not be defined solely in terms of method, theory, direct utilization, or staff or client empowerment. ... The alternative we present might be called betterment-driven evaluation. That is, decisions about an evaluation and the definition of its success should be driven by an analysis of the potential contribution that the evaluation can make, in the particular circumstances, to the democratic processes that define and seek social betterment. (Mark et al. 2000: 11f.).

In other words, Mark, Henry and Julnes are searching for an integrative concept, which combines the components introduced here and deploys them in such a way as to correspond to social needs. At the same time, they oppose the idea that only a participant-oriented approach that trains the affected parties as well as possible to themselves become the evaluators could be useful for this. They make it clear that evaluation not only acts on behalf of the target groups but also has a social function – and therefore also a social responsibility – toward political bodies, taxpayers and people who are not integrated into the programme or cannot benefit from it.

Tasks of betterment-driven evaluation after Mark et al.

(1) *Assessment of merit and worth:* the development of warranted judgments, at the individual and societal level, of the value of a policy or a program.
(2) *Program and organizational improvement:* the effort to use information to directly modify and enhance program operations.
(3) *Oversight and compliance:* the assessment of the extent to which a program follows the directives of statutes, regulations, rules, mandated standards or any other formal expectations.
(4) *Knowledge development:* the discovery or testing of general theories, propositions, and hypotheses in the context of policies and programs.

Source: Mark et al. (2000: 13)

Those in favour of participant-oriented approaches emphasize as *advantages* above all the explicit consideration of the 'human' component in planning and conducting evaluations and the clear focus on the needs of those who are, when all is said and done, supposed to benefit from them. Their conceptual amplitude that can encompass the diversity of the various interest perspectives is said to be another strength of these approaches, since it could enable novel insights into the programme contexts. Apart from that, they say, it also makes it easier to identify possible unintended impacts. The use of multiple methods, the great flexibility of the approach in conducting evaluations and especially the training aspect in the context of accumulating skills (empowerment approach) for conducting evaluations oneself are cited as further advantages (cf. Fitzpatrick et al. 2012: 223ff.).

Having said that, there is also plenty of *criticism* of this kind of evaluation. The objection that that the participant-oriented approaches fail to meet scientific quality criteria such as objectivity, validity and reliability on account of their political component (especially the empowerment approach), and that they are for that reason not scientific approaches at all is the one that must be regarded as the most fundamental. And the transfer of the assessment component from the evaluator to those involved in the programme – as envisaged in some participant-oriented models – is also seen by some evaluation researchers as a kind of estrangement from the true concept of evaluation.

In view of the fact that the approaches are, from the point of view of their basic theoretical understanding, fairly complex, they are difficult to implement in practice, so that there is a risk of their being used in an over-simplified, unconsidered way. The introduction of principles such as that of 'optimal ignorance' (unnecessary accuracy should be avoided), 'good enough' (adequate accuracy is sufficient) or 'reasonable inaccuracy' (cf. Laderchi 2001: 5) in some participant-oriented approaches, and the view (at least in the empowerment approaches) that anyone involved can quickly learn about the development and application of the neces- sary evaluation instruments themselves, support this tendency.

A further problem is posed by the *lack of representativeness* of findings and their low generalizability, since the participant-oriented approaches are heavily oriented toward the individual case and representativeness does not seem so important to them: 'Participatory approaches are more relaxed about sampling, assuming that if there is enough consultation and good will, the right voices will be heard. (...) But here is where the participatory practice falls short, and for a simple reason. Being relaxed about sampling often means falling back on the judgement of local groups, village governing bodies and user committees about who should and should not be consulted, and this is risky' (Freedman 1997: 776).

The question of the extent to which the participants in an evaluation are representative of those involved or the groups for whom they speak is addressed surprisingly little in the participant-oriented approaches. However, since it is clear that there are hardly likely to be any evalu- ation projects in which all conceivable interest perspectives are taken into account or all stakeholders integrated in the process, there is a risk that predominantly non-organized interests, as often the case with disadvantaged sections of the population, may not be represented suffi- ciently. Questions may be asked about who those involved actually represent and whether or not they are legitimized to speak for others. It will not always be the case that representatives can be found at all. In such cases, the suggestion – which comes from empowerment evalua- tion – that the evaluators should act in the interest of the disadvantaged, does not help much either. Such a procedure would require the evalua- tors to be familiar with the actual needs of the disadvantaged sections of the population who were not represented. But such an assumption could hardly be made with any seriousness (cf. Mertens 2004: 45ff.; Lee 2004: 135ff.).

In spite of all this justified criticism of participant-oriented evaluation approaches it should not be forgotten that they have enriched evalua- tion research enormously, not only by the development of a new form of evaluation form, but also particularly by the *change of perspective* it has brought about in evaluation research as a whole. The involvement of stakeholders in planning and conducting evaluations, the consideration of their assessment criteria and interests, the recording of their various perspectives, estimates and assessments have – to different extents – become part and parcel of most evaluations. Basically, there is only serious dissent with regard to the scope of the participants' involvement.

3.4.5 Summary and assessment

In contrast to the other systems for classifying evaluation approaches presented here, Fitzpatrick, Sanders and Worthen look more at the practical orientation of the evaluation than the activities of the evaluators. They identify four different categories with two clear-cut principles for selecting the studies. They do not succeed in classifying the approaches with good selectivity either. In other words there are at least some individual authors / concepts that could justifiably be allocated to two or more categories because they contain aspects of both.

By refraining from metaphor, Fitzpatrick, Sanders and Worthen avoid implying a development tendency: it is just as conceivable that a new, fifth category might be formed on the basis of evaluation praxis as it is that two of them might merge into a single class.[14] Whilst the tree model suggests a continuous process of differentiation from a common trunk and two roots, ramifying out into ever finer branches, and the generation model postulates a linear growth process which transcends previous development stages, the utilization model of Fitzpatrick, Sanders and Worthen remains neutral on this point.

There is a broad consensus on the conceptions and authors who and which are to be included in such a classification schema: the central conceptual contributions of authors such as Tyler, Scriven, Stake, Stufflebeam, Rossi, Chen, Patton, Guba and Lincoln, Fetterman and several others besides are not disputed within the evaluation community as regards their importance. Nevertheless, there does seem to be a 'bias' here, both in favour of educational science research and psychological research and in favour of the North American subcontinent: heed is not paid to European, Asian or African evaluation research – small and insignificant as their contribution may be – and just as little as to developments in economics, political science and even – with some reservations – sociology.

In spite of the change of perspective, the concept of Fitzpatrick, Sanders and Worthen does still have something in common with the other classification systems introduced here: this classification principle assumes that it is possible to allocate each approach to exactly one of the predetermined classes and thus implies that the classes are optimally distinguished from one another. For example, there is said not to be a 'decision-oriented' approach that is at the same time also 'expertise-oriented'. On account of the fact that there are hardly any evaluation approaches that do not take into account both perspectives to at least some extent, the classification schema loses some of its selectivity and must therefore accordingly accept accusations of a certain arbitrariness.

In the section that follows, an attempt will be made to avoid these fixed positions, and classify the evaluation approaches solely in relation to their social functions. Thus this principle of classification is actually not all that far removed from the ideas of Fitzpatrick, Sanders and Worthen – there too, it is a matter of the objectives and tasks of evaluation – but it follows a predetermined theoretical framework concept. As stated in Section 2.2.3, evaluations fulfil four different main functions, namely the gaining of insights, the exercising of control, the initiation of development and learning processes and the legitimation of implemented measures, projects or programmes.

This implies that the different approaches are variously suitable for the fulfilment of individual evaluation purposes. In the section that follows these four functional dimensions are used to structure existing evaluation approaches.

3.5   Systematization according to Stockmann and Meyer: the function model

The starting-point of the function model is the question of why there are evaluations at all. As shown at the beginning of this book, evaluations are a 'child' of modern societies, inextricably tied to their emergence and further development. They are the result of a certain management consciousness, which carries, as important elements within itself, basic principles such as rationality, justice, transparency and participation. Feudal society, for example, did not have to legitimize itself to its citizens; not until after the age of enlightenment was there an increased interest in gaining insights.

Only modern societies endeavour to achieve transparency and are prepared to allow the relevance of their policies to be verified by applying generally accepted standards and values. Only democratic regimes require legitimization of political decisions for their citizens, whose interests they represent for limited periods of time. And it is not until that legitimation has been undertaken that there is a need to optimize programme control, in order to be able to make an actively shaping contribution to social improvements as effectively as possible.

It was pointed out in Section 2.2.3 that the four main functions of evaluation are by no means independent target dimensions that are separable from one another. However, it was asserted – and demonstrated with at least a few examples – that the topics involved suggest different approaches, which are then reflected in various evaluation concepts. Accordingly, the aim of the section that follows is to show how the conceptions introduced here can be classified to with regard to these four functions.

The borders between the four functions are not viewed as fixed or insurmountable; on the contrary, the individual functions are understood as overlapping dimensions. For exact allocation, they would need to be positioned four-dimensionally with the help of interval scales. Since there has been no such operationalization, the two-dimensional graphic illustration below is only to be understood as such and not as scientifically sound findings. The graphic is structured as follows: the four different functions of evaluation are to be found in the respective corners, and allocation of an evaluation conception to one of those corners means that the function in that corner is strongly highlighted in that approach, the other three being of little or no importance. If all four functions are emphasized approximately equally, the allocation is central. The stronger the orientation toward one of the four functions, the more marked the placement towards the respective corner, and vice versa.

Another problem consists in defining what is to be classified in this schema. In some individual cases it was certainly difficult to determine with good selectivity what the function of an evaluation conception is, or when the investigation concerned even becomes an evaluation or to what extent it is still fundamental research. Alkin and Christie even talk of theories of evaluation, which – if scientific standards were to be applied to 'theories' – would dramatically reduce the number of allocatable contributions. When all is said and done, all the classification systems covered here have primarily allocated *people,* keeping quiet to a greater or lesser extent about the development processes of the various different authors with regard to their concepts, or at least placing these background.

If in a first step the same logic is pursued here, this is mainly to ensure that this classification system is comparable with those already introduced and to demonstrate the effectiveness of our own principle of classification. However, our proposal for systematization, introduced in the next section, does not escape the basic problem of failing to take account of subsequent developments in their individual conceptions of the people we classify.

3.5.1   People-related systematization

The systematization according to the four functions presented below relates to the authors referred to in this chapter and thus lays no claim to being a complete presentation of all evaluation concepts. On the other hand, it should be noted that there is a broad consensus about the importance of the authors and concepts listed here for the development of evaluation, and an introductory book ought of course to concentrate primarily on this. In principle, however, it is possible to classify any other author (or concept) on the basis of the four functions without any problems, and this does not require any changes to be made to the principle of classification. So universal applicability is postulated, which cannot be said of the other classification systems covered here.

A first glance at the graphic illustration (Figure 3.6) should be aimed at the insight function in the upper left-hand corner, i.e. those authors/ concepts that are clearly identifiable as research-oriented and hardly have any significance for the other functions. Of the authors introduced here, Campbell is certainly the one most firmly anchored in *fundamental research* and the one whose conceptions were primarily oriented toward (his own) *cognitive interest*. Of course, a large number of other authors could also be cited here, authors who did not commit themselves to evaluation, but to *applied field research* in their respective disciplines. Depending on where the line is drawn, for example, the Chicago School of Sociology, the Hawthorne study or authors such as Paul Lazarsfeld could be counted as evaluators here. For all their differences, the authors in this group do have in common that their scientific cognitive interest dominates and that they did not see themselves as service providers in the sense of assigned or commissioned research.

From this 'pole' of classical empirical fundamental research, applied and carried out in the field, especially after Suchman, a kind of evaluation research that was oriented toward *programme theories* developed, and it was one which increasingly integrated not only insights, but also participatory and legitimizing elements in its conceptions. Whilst the earlier authors (Suchman, Rossi, Chen) felt even more strongly committed to a positivist scientific ideal and to the use of quantitative survey procedures, the more recent approaches (Stockmann, Mark et al.) endeavour to pick up on the contributions to the evaluation discussion which start from a 'counterpole' and incorporate them into their concepts.

Fetterman, whose empowerment approach clearly focuses on *learning (on the part of those affected)* and would thus probably be more prepared to drop down a gear or two as regards the gaining of insights, can be seen as the 'counterpole' here. Having said that, the empowerment approach does not see itself as a 'service' for clients either, but rather

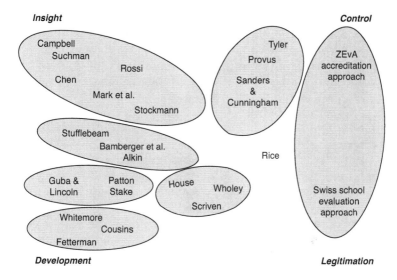

Figure 3.6   People-related systematization of evaluation approaches*

* All the authors and concepts listed here have at least been referred to in this chapter. Exceptions are Bamberger et al., whose approach will not be introduced until Section 5.2, and our own approach, which has already been described in the previous chapter. The bubbles illustrate the groups of authors mentioned in the text. The grouping is – to say the least – arbitrary and not based on any systematic clustering procedure.

as an advocate for affected parties. Any form of self-evaluation that is for exclusively internal utilization is to be placed at this pole. Then again, there are problems of distinction, for example from approaches involving organizational development or learning in groups in general, if the protagonists no longer see themselves as 'evaluators'.

A different attitude is held by the group of evaluators centred around Michael Scriven (House and Wholey), who emphasize primarily the aspect of assigned or commissioned research and define themselves more or less emphatically as *service providers for the client (who is mostly governmental)*. Unlike the attitudes of the two groups already referred to at the upper and lower ends of the scale, this attitude definitely does greater service to the legitimation function of evaluations – in other words the ambition of public budgets to justify the expenditures connected with measures in the light of the results achieved. They are thus in contrast to a further group of authors (Stufflebeam, Alkin, Bamberger et al.), who see the outputs they generate as being related to the *programme or project management of the implementing organizations* rather than to the government authorities, which mostly only provide the funds.

Contrasting with these again are those authors (Guba and Lincoln, Patton, Stake) who focus their approaches primarily on *those involved in a programme or project* (in other words not only clients and management, but also employees, target groups, beneficiaries and people barred from the outputs). Their ambition involving the active integration of the clients of a programme or project does not however go as far as that of the participatory and empowerment approaches, which concentrate exclusively on this group. (Alongside Fetterman, Cousins and Whitmore have been listed as representatives of the latter).

Beyond this 'mainstream' in the current evaluation debate, the older *objectives-oriented approaches* (Tyler, Provus, Sanders and Cunningham) remain. These are alone in placing the emphasis on the control function of evaluations (in the sense of monitoring the achievement of targets). They thus resemble more closely the evaluation concepts that predominate on the right-hand side, which are initiated and implemented by government institutions. It is noticeable that here in the meantime there are practically no individual evaluation researchers to be found, but rather mainly development teams and committees acting on behalf of the public authorities in order to fulfil the control and legitimation functions.

Another problem of the previous systematizations thus comes into view: with all this concentration on those authors who publish on evaluation in scientific journals or books (and in addition to that, exclusively in the English-language areas), sight tends to be lost of all the evaluation approaches that do not avail themselves of these media. This may, in view of the advanced institutionalization of evaluation, be less of a problem in the USA than it is in Europe, where in many *policy fields* the term evaluation is also used outside the relatively young evaluation community and the state sees itself more as an actor and motor of social change in its own right. The accreditation approach introduced in Section 3.4.3 cannot be allocated to an individual person or institution, yet it is among the most influential evaluation concepts of recent years. Furthermore, the intensive exchange between the different accreditation agencies at home and abroad leads to a harmonization of the various alternative concepts and promotes a dialogue beyond the existing evaluation societies.

In spite of all the links of accreditation with evaluation elements (as shown in the example of the ZEvA), it is definitely the concept of control which dominates in accreditation. For example, in the law on the establishment of a 'foundation for the accreditation of study courses in Germany', the mission of the foundation very clearly emphasizes *control functions,* which centre in particular around 'monitoring the accreditations carried out by the agencies' (§2, para. 1, no. 4). The accreditation department of the ZEvA also brings the concept of control to the fore in seeking to 'ascertain and verify minimum professional standards and standards of content by judging the concepts submitted for bachelor, masters and further education programmes' (quoted from www.zeva.org/uploads/media/Leitfaden_Systemakkreditierung.pdf).

On the other hand, however, the accreditation system for the universities is by no means typical of the implementation of evaluation in the various different policy fields. On the contrary, the differences in scope and form and in the degree of institutionalization of the evaluation vary a great deal. Special committees assigned with the accreditation of institutions by law have only been formed for the universities, and that already represents a striking difference to the procedure with regard to other education institutions such as schools. Having said that, there are examinations of the outputs of implementing organizations that work on behalf of the (federal) ministries in all the policy fields. These are carried out by the ministry itself (e.g. by implementing an evaluation department as in development policy), by subordinate authorities (e.g. the Federal Environment Agency [UBA]), by scientific institutions attached to those authorities (e.g. the Institute for Employment Research [IAB]) and by suitably empowered private organizations (e.g. the German Technical Service Corporation).[15] The section that follows outlines the classification of approaches within one policy field using the example of school evaluation. The function model, unlike the other classification systems, can be used here without any problems as a framework for orientation and thus makes it possible to draw comparisons between various different policy fields. As an example of this, the special emphasis on the legitimation function of school evaluation (in contrast to that of the universities) will now be looked at.

3.5.2   Policy-field-related systematization

Viewed historically, the start of the development of evaluation in the *policy field* of schools worldwide lies in the *supervision of schools by the education authority,* which in its early form served exclusively *bureaucratic control* and was designed to ensure that education authorities had access to the schools. The aim of this was to guarantee a certain degree of uniformity in the implementation of the teaching and educational assignments in the individual schools, which was supposed to be carried out as intended by the superordinate agencies. This form, clearly oriented toward control, was the starting-point of development in this policy field (top right in Figure 3.7).

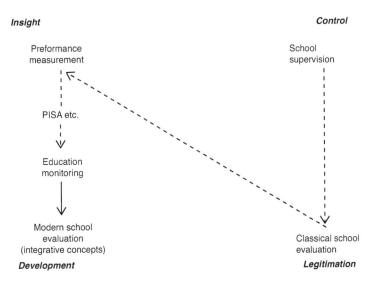

Figure 3.7   Policy-field-related systematization (taking schools as an example)

Criticism of the education authority's supervision of schools, which found expression in lively public debate as early as the 19th century, related to its lack of ability to ensure the necessary improvements with a view to imparting skills. In the USA, it was the work of Joseph Mayer Rice on the *measurement of pupils' performance* that underpinned this criticism with empirical data (cf. Section 3.2.1, top left in Figure 3.7). This scientifically based criticism, primarily oriented toward *cognitive interest*, increasingly divested the existing school system and its controlling authority, the education authority, of their *legitimation*.

To this day, this legitimation deficit has been the bedrock for the establishment of school evaluation (bottom right in Figure 3.7), which is intended to serve mainly a quality assurance communicable to the outside world, by involving external experts and scientific procedures. With reference to the PISA debate, an effect similar to that in the 19th century can also be observed today: following the international comparison of pupils' performance and the relatively poor score of German pupils in the first round of data gathering, the quality of the German school system was questioned fundamentally. One of the reactions was to try harder to establish a *school evaluation scheme* that went beyond the measurement of performance in the various schools.

Table 3.2 Basic quality assurance model of the Canton of Zürich

Quality management	Self-evaluation	External evaluation
Teacher level	Individual self-assessment (forms of individual feedback)	Individual external assessment (forms of staff assessment)
School level	Self-assessment of the school (systematic, criteria-guided self-evaluation)	External assessment of the school (systematic, criteria and standards-guided external evaluation)
Whole *volksschule*[16] system level	Self-assessment by cantonal teaching and educational directorates (educational statistics)	Education monitoring (independent scientific system evaluation)

Source: Educational Directorate of the Canton of Zürich (2001); quoted after Brägger et al. (2007).

Whilst many researchers on school topics may be familiar with the systems in use in the USA, the UK, Germany (and perhaps other major players in the arena of world politics), the most recent developments in (the German-speaking areas of) *Switzerland* (see Ruep & Keller 2007 on the introduction of school evaluation in Germany, used here as an example, are presumed to be little known. Yet efforts made towards a comprehensive reform of school supervision (by the education authority) are in fact even greater in Switzerland than in Germany, the intention being particularly to redefine completely the roles of the inspectors, authorities and schools (cf. Brägger, Kramis & Teuteberg 2007). More so than in the previous forms of school supervision and school evaluation, the aim is to implement a closed system, which is intended to serve the *ongoing further development* of each individual school (bottom left in Figure 3.7).

At the centre of the reforms in Switzerland, there is a *two-tier evaluation concept* at three levels of investigation (Table 3.2), which – in accordance with the official objectives – is intended to enhance accountability for public legitimation and build confidence in the institution on the one hand, and quality development in order to optimize school performance on the other. Just like education monitoring (including performance measurements in the PISA studies), external school evaluation is thus part of a comprehensive quality assurance concept that complements internal quality management at the schools.

The *overall concept* also includes the implementation of an inter-cantonal 'working-group for the external evaluation of schools' (ARGEV), which has been ensuring an exchange of experiences on the utilization of external evaluations among the Swiss cantons since 2002. Education monitoring was institutionalized as a federal task under the responsibility of the State Secretariat for Education and Research, the Federal Statistics Office, the Federal Office for Professional Education and Technology and the Swiss Conference of Cantonal Ministers of Education (EDK), and led in 2006 to Switzerland's first education report, drawn up by the Swiss Coordination Department for Educational Research (SKBF) in Aarau. Furthermore, independent specialist departments for school evaluation were set up in the departments of the education authority responsible for school supervision, and these were designed to assist the schools in conducting self-evaluations.

External school evaluation contracts are as a rule not awarded to freelance experts, but to independent evaluation agencies or university institutions via an invitation to tender and conducted by them using their own methods. Mostly, the cantonal offices responsible have put in place appropriate evaluation agencies, which prepare, organize, implement, analyse and publish school evaluations independent of the schools and authorities (and in particular independent of the education authority). An example of this is the Department of School Evaluation (FSE) of the Canton Lucerne, which externally evaluates some 50 of the approximately 200 school units in the canton once a year. The assignment of this department is not to supervise the schools (which continues to be the responsibility of the education authority), but to support them in their own quality development. Apart from external evaluation, the department thus also offers advice on self-evaluation and, on the basis of the accumulated expertise, recommendations for measures for the further development of school and teaching quality (for further details see Brägger et al. 2007). School evaluation has also been implemented in similar forms in other cantons (cf. Oelkers 2008; Landwehr & Steiner 2007; Schönig 2007; Abs et al. 2006).

Particularly in Europe, the initiative to establish school evaluation came to a very great extent from the state, and the state has continued to view this primarily as a task of its own until the present day. In contrast to other policy fields, an institutional solution in its own right is sought for the evaluation of schools instead of contracts being awarded to the freelance expert market. This difference can be explained by the special (self-)commitment of the state with regard to the school education assignment and the particular pressure on the state to justify itself to the public that results from that commitment. For this reason, today's school evaluation concepts (as shown in the Swiss example) also refer explicitly to the legitimation of the school system in the public eye as one of the main aims of the evaluations.

By contrast, the *control ambition* of school evaluation is less well developed, since the education authority was and still is responsible for it. The education authority resembles the accreditation agencies, which govern the awarding of titles using predetermined check-lists and also act relatively independently of the university evaluation authorities. Unlike the accreditation agencies at the universities, however, the education authority came into being very early on and is not a product of the most recent developments. Accordingly, school supervision and evaluation are, in institutional and conceptual terms, less strongly linked to each other than university evaluation and accreditation (see the example of the ZEvA in Section 3.4.3); indeed, efforts are being made to separate them largely in institutional terms.

As well as school supervision and evaluation, education statistics have existed for a long time as a basis for regular *educational reporting* and continuous *education monitoring* on the basis of performance tests. (See Böttcher et al. 2008; Weinert 2001 on education monitoring and performance measurement in schools in general. See for example Bos et al. 2008a, b, 2007, 2005, 2003; Bos, Gröhlich & Pietsch 2007; Bos & Pietsch 2006; Mullis et al. 2003 on other current school performance tests such as IGLU and TIMSS). Unlike institutionalized school evaluation in this sector, university educational research is much more heavily involved and the initiative comes more from international organizations than from national ones (as for example in the PISA programme).[17]

The most recent developments include the recording of impacts at individual school level. These can be supplemented by disaggregate data from educational statistics and thus also used in a *quality management system at school level*. By the transposition of these concepts, which originated in industry, the *development and learning component* of evaluation at school level is emphasized for the first time. Whilst school supervision (and the accreditation model) are based on a clear 'top-down' approach to quality assurance, school evaluation is developing increasingly towards 'bottom-up' management for the production of quality. This is accompanied by a greater degree of autonomy for the school administrations, which is in turn expressed in the integration of *self-evaluations* in the overall conception. The newly institutionalized systems for the evaluation of schools mostly involve a combination of school supervision (as the governmental control authority), external school evaluation (as the independent specialist authority for the legitimation of the school system), internal school evaluation (for quality assurance and further development of the school organization by the school itself) and education monitoring (as a regular feedback of new insights into the skills imparted to the pupils and the framework conditions of curricular work in scientific research papers) in a comprehensive quality management concept.

This is of course only one example of how, in a given policy field, evaluation has gained a toehold in the area of tension between the four functions of insight, control, legitimation and development. In other important social areas such as that of social politics, job-market policy, environmental policy, regional politics and development policy, separate evaluation philosophies and conceptions have been generated largely independently of one another (and independently of the discussions in school education), and established themselves more or less firmly in different forms. Having said that, the example of school evaluation shows two different things: firstly, the four function dimensions are very suitable for classifying historical developments, and they can thus contribute to a better understanding of the differences in the various evaluation cultures in the individual policy fields. Secondly, however, the development in school evaluation also underpins the theory that the way these international activities are interwoven within a given policy field has a greater influence on the development of practical evaluation than national effects, which span more than one policy field.

It is however not only the distinctions between the various policy fields and departments that have contributed to the emergence of different evaluation concepts because of diverse aspirations and functions. Another important influence emanated (and continues to emanate) from the *disciplinary origin* of the authors, who have access to the topics that fit in with their discipline and feel committed, consciously or unconsciously, to certain traditions of content in the way they think. However, thanks to the increasing interdisciplinary exchange in evaluation research, these models diffuse over time into other specialist areas and policy fields. Since with quality management reference has already been made to one aspect, it would seem logical to deal somewhat more closely in the next section with the development of economic concepts for evaluation and the philosophies behind them.

3.5.3   Scientific-field-related systematization

Most of the authors introduced in this chapter – for all their differences as regards content – have one thing in common: they were trained as social scientists, mostly as educationalists, psychologists and sociologists. Having said that, there are within these scientific fields some considerable differences with regard to the establishment of evaluation as a sub-discipline in its own right (cf. Meyer 2003a, b for an overview). In the evaluation organizations and journals that exist, meanwhile, only some of the researchers who conduct evaluations have committed themselves to this, whilst many focus more on the institutions of their own discipline. On account of the still very limited opportunities for studying evaluation at universities, there are hardly any scientists with appropriate training so far. For these reasons, there is as yet no clearly distinguishable, recognized evaluation research tradition that unites all the main scientific works on their topic under a single umbrella.

This means that there have, also aside from the mainstream of the evaluation debate, been contributions that were or are more or less influential and significant for the development of the theory and methodology of evaluation. In accordance with the remarks made by Alkin and Christie (2004: 14f.), *accounting* can be shown to have had a significant *influence* on the development of practical evaluation. These *economically* oriented connecting lines include bookkeeping, social and economic reporting, project and programme planning tools and quality management instruments, all of which have made a significant contribution to the integration of monitoring and evaluation in the implementation of major (government) projects. This remark is of course not intended to advocate dominance on the part of economics; on the contrary, its purpose is to indicate that the history of evaluation cannot be described from the point of view of a single discipline. Nonetheless, these economic connecting lines can also be depicted with the aid of the function model (Figure 3.8).

The *comparison between targets and achievements,* which originated in accounting (see Section 3.2.2; cf. Gölz 2002; Löffelholz 1993 for an introduction to the economic procedures of comparing targets with achievements) broke with a purely cost-oriented view of things, which was geared to improving efficiency, by extending its perspective to include the results (or the benefit) of measures (for example in cost-benefit analyses, cf. for example as an introduction Brent 2008; Mühlenkamp 2008; Drummond et al. 2007; Florio 2007; Lewin & McEwan 2007; Mishan & Quah 2007). Tried and tested economic procedures were thus available to verify the achievement of targets. This is done by observing the target values set at the beginning of a given period for the end of that period with the values ('results') actually achieved at the end of said period. In many policy fields, such comparisons of targets and achievements were, very early on – especially in project and programme planning – an important *element of investigation* and thus also the starting-point of practical evaluation. Within evaluation research this procedure was mainly made known by Ralph W. Tyler (cf. Section 3.2.2).

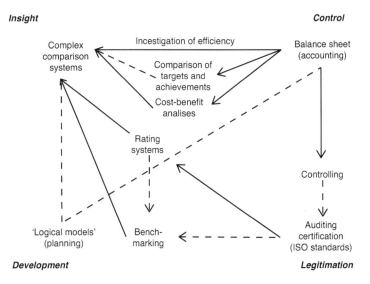

Figure 3.8   Scientific-field-related system (as relating to economics)

In comparing targets and achievements – just as in bookkeeping as a whole – the *concept of control* is to the fore: the aim of such comparisons is to investigate whether certain objectives have been achieved or not. No direct contribution is made to explaining the reasons for the result observed or improving it. The contribution made by the investigation to legitimation is also only indirect, (which is why it is placed at the top right in Figure 3.8).

Nevertheless, the spectrum of *comparing*, which has developed from this economic tradition and from the planning sector, has become considerably broader and more versatile over time. For target values to be compared with results, it is generally necessary to specify indicators and use measuring procedures, allowing reliable measurements to be made at two different points in time (see Meyer 2011 for more detail; cf. also Section 5.3). If this difficulty is still fairly easy to overcome when the perspective is purely one of cost (as in accounting), mostly on account of the common monetary calculation base, the contemplation of benefit particularly in *'performance measurement'* makes very high demands on the standardized description of the object to be investigated, to allow not only a comparison between different investigation units (e.g. two schools) but also between different points in time (e.g. the beginning and end of a planning period). At the same time, the standardized descriptions, classifications, indicators and measuring instruments cannot be transposed to other areas of application as simply as one might think, and that is the reason why various different conceptual solutions have been developed for carrying out the comparison between targets and results.

It is no longer (financial) control on which these observations focus, but increasingly the *gaining of insights* as regards the efficiency and effectiveness of measures, which is made possible by comprehensive *reporting systems* (above all national income accounting) with complex indices, comparative figures, time series and suchlike being recorded continually and comparably. This in turn is not so much an evaluation system as a (social) monitoring system, and it is meanwhile regularly submitted in various different forms (e.g. social reporting, family reporting, health reporting, environmental reporting). In spite of all the differences between them, these reporting systems have in common that they primarily make available to the public data and numerical measurement values on certain social aspects in a comparable way. Accordingly, these complex comparison systems have been allocated to the 'insight' pole in Figure 3.8.

Following this economic tradition, there are also attempts to integrate evaluation in internal organizational *controlling* or to utilize controlling instruments for evaluations (or in the area of monitoring). Among other things, – staying with school evaluation for the moment – approaches have been proposed for the development of education control.[18] Unlike accounting (and unlike accreditation too), the audit and certification procedures resulting from this development tendency (for example in accordance with ISO standards) put more emphasis on the *legitimation character:* by participating voluntarily in a test scheme that prescribes the implementation of certain management practices, organizations demonstrate their readiness and ability to assure quality to the outside world.[19] Auditing and certification procedures therefore make up the 'legitimation' pole in Figure 3.8.

Finally, the *learning and development perspective* has also become increasingly important in this economic tradition of thought. This relates on the one hand to *benchmarking approaches,* which enable a comparison to be drawn with the 'best-practice' competitor and are thus intended to lead to a continuous improvement in quality. Particularly important for evaluation, however, was the development of modern planning procedures, which envisage the integration of monitoring and evaluation systems for monitoring project progress in 'logical models'. These efforts to generate innovative and very sophisticated programmes

Table 3.3   World Bank LogFrame model

Cause and effect (causal logic)	Performance indicators	Monitoring and evaluation	Assumptions
Program goal	Measurement system of performance indicators	Monitoring and evaluation system (supervision)	Program to development goal
Project impacts			Project impact to program goal
Project output (deliverables)			Project output to project impacts
Project input (activities)	Required resources		Project input to project output

Source: World Bank (publication date unknown: 15; slightly modified).

and projects (mainly in development cooperation) centred very much around the (further) development aspect. There are various different kinds of *'logical model'*, though they cannot necessarily be traced back to a common origin. They are applied in such diverse areas as corporate work organization and information science. Mostly they are an element of *project planning management* and provide information about how the individual elements (measures, investments, resources etc.) are, theoretically, to contribute to the achievement of targets. Especially in complex programmes or projects, they serve to systematize the deployment of resources and interim steps or interim results that are supposed to be achieved during implementation.[20] As the development perspective dominates in 'logical models', they have been allocated to that dimension in Figure 3.8.

In a *'LogFrame'* model such as has been used for the planning of development projects by the World Bank since 1997, monitoring and evaluation are a central element (Table 3.3).

The systematic monitoring of the planned project development is part of the LogFrame model. By means of a measuring system of *'performance indicators'*, the aim is to keep an eye on the way pace is kept with the planned project progress and measure it with a *monitoring and evaluation system*. The World Bank gets to the heart of the difference between monitoring and evaluation with a simple variation on the central question: whilst monitoring aims to follow up the control-oriented question *'Are we doing the project right?'*, evaluation is concerned with the question of its meaningfulness: *'Are we doing the right project?'* (World Bank, publication date unknown: 49). Accordingly, evaluation is assigned with the central *development task,* which can, on the basis of the experience gained during the course of the project, lead to modifications to the basic assumptions developed in the planning phase, and thus also to changes with regard to the resources, activities and results required to achieve the targets.

Certainly not all the economic procedures that have had an influence on the development of evaluation have been cited here. And of course concepts from other specialist areas have also attained some significance – a fact of which sight should not be lost when concentrating on economic development.

3.5.4   Summary and assessment

Summing up, it should first be noted that a systematization of evaluation approaches must not – unlike fundamental research – be restricted exclusively to theories within a single discipline, but must much rather keep an eye on the different threads of development within various areas of science and the internal dynamics of individual policy fields. Here too, the special association of politics *and* science with evaluation is seen again, and this itself has an effect on the way that the conceptions are presented.

It is also necessary to find a principle of classification that can be used universally for these various areas and that is oriented toward criteria which are clearly distinguishable from one another. Our own systematization design is the first attempt in this direction. All the other classification systems covered here restrict themselves to a large extent to the allocation of authors and theoretical concepts, in other words to the scientific perspective. Moreover, with regard to their sorting criteria, the systems are not stringent, and suggest to some degree, by the forms of their presentation (and the metaphors associated with them), a certain developmental tendency. The generation model suggests that there has been a continuous improvement in the approaches, though this assumption does not actually hold water. The 'old' approaches were not absorbed by the 'younger' ones and further developed; the latter in fact rather represent new, independent threads. This picture corresponds with the implicit assumptions of the tree model, which postulates an increasing ramification of evaluation approaches. But this model too has two obvious weaknesses, saying nothing about the opposite process – i.e. the attempt by mainly younger authors to integrate the various aspirations and concepts – and postulating a common 'trunk' as a starting-point.

Here, rather the opposite assumption is made, namely that evaluation first grows together in the course of the professionalization process, so that some very different evaluation traditions (distinct according to disciplines and policy fields) gradually begin to come together. With these integrated concepts an attempt is made to combine the aspirations of evaluations, which in some cases are diametrically opposed, thus building bridges not only between individual theory-of-science lines of thought (see Section 2.2.6), disciplinary traditions of thinking and fundamental methodological positions (see Section 5.2) but also between different participatory ambitions (for example as regards the connection between 'top-down' and 'bottom-up' management), and between aspirations and possibilities for utilization.

Meanwhile, especially in the procedure and methods deployed – apart from a few radical positions – it is the things the evaluation approaches have in common which predominate. Neither the evaluators' orientation toward programme theories, nor the involvement of the stakeholders in the evaluation process, nor the orientation of the evaluation toward its utilization context are fundamentally questioned any more. The discussions are more about weighting these factors and the question of how much science is possible and necessary, how much influence politics should be allowed to have and, above all, for whom evaluation must generate outputs and to what extent. It is true to say that the area of tension between science and politics has not been resolved in the more recent evaluation approaches, but there are at least some approaches that aim to balance it out in design-technical terms and in so doing cater to all the aspirations as far as possible.

To a notable extent, the trend is towards standardization for the development of evaluations, which are being harmonized more and more on account of the experience gained and coming closer together thanks to the increasing exchange between evaluation communities. The next two chapters aim to clarify these statements on the general development of evaluations and on the procedures of gathering and assessing information.

Notes

1. Donna Mertens (2000: 44) claims that Guba and Lincoln viewed the sequence of generations as exclusive. There is no proof of this, and it cannot be inferred in that form from the original. Having said that, Guba and Lincoln (1989: 22) do stake the claim that each successive generation, on account of the historical framework conditions, its emergence and continuous social change, has been was 'more informed and sophisticated' than the one before.

2. For example, the works of Karl Mannheim, who emphasized the experiences that we share and which form us as characteristics of a generation; see Mannheim (1964). See also Parnes et al. (2008) on the popularity and history of the term 'generations'.
3. Guidelines and check-lists that facilitate the implementation of the procedures of Guba and Lincoln are also available on the Internet. See Guba E. G. and Lincoln Y. S.: Guidelines and Checklist for Constructivist (a.k.a. Fourth Generation) Evaluation: www.wmich.edu/evalctr/checklists.
4. Cf. Section 5.5 on hermeneutic methods.
5. We refer here to the original version from 2004. There are three revisited versions available that slightly differ from the first issue (Alkin & Christie 2013; Carden & Alkin 2012; Christie & Alkin 2008). The value branch received the most substantial revisions both in ordering and in adding new authors. The reason for doing revisions is quite simple: "As theorists modify their views over time, we propose changes to the evaluation theory tree…, which reflect some substantive changes in our thinking" (Christie & Alkin 2008). One may doubt these changes being as substantial as the authors think: the basic structure and the ordering of key authors have not been changed and the new ordering is not more convincing than the earlier one.
6. Stufflebeam too appears to share this assessment, devoting a chapter all its own to Michael Patton's utilization-focused evaluation concept in his most recent book and dissociating himself in the foreword from Alkin and Christie's allocation of himself as the 'progenitor' of this line of thought (Stufflebeam & Shinkfield 2007: 431ff.).
7. Translator's note: a neutral German consumer check magazine similar to the British *Which?* or the American publication *Consumer Reports*.
8. Downloadable with all its details at: www.wmich.edu/evalctr/checklists. Apart from those developed by Michael Scriven the site also has other checklists from the evaluation center at Western Michigan University.
9. Nowadays accreditation systems for universities can be found in almost all Western countries and they vary significantly. For a short introduction to the US system see Eaton (2011). For the UK system see the informative website http://www.accreditedcolleges.co.uk/accreditation-system.php
10. See for example the French variant of accreditation as compared with the German one, cf. the description of the procedures followed by the Comité National d'Evaluation (CNE) (www.cne-evaluation.fr).
11. Particularly in the evaluation of development cooperation, participatory approaches have enjoyed tremendous popularity, though here particularly the boundaries between project planning approaches, implementation approaches and evaluation approaches become blurred. Cf. Caspari (2004: 101ff.) for a summarizing appreciation.
12. Cousins & Earl (1995, Cousins 2004); Whitmore (1998) are regarded as the main proponents of the participatory evaluation approaches. Not to be confused with the generic term 'participant-oriented evaluation approaches' used here.
13. The pragmatic 'RealWorld' approach of Bamberger et al. introduced in Section 5.2 is another variant. There, 'empowerment' relates exclusively to the project managers and not to the target groups.

14. This is precisely what the authors did by updating the book in the fourth edition in 2012: the third edition used five classes that have now been reduced to four. Consumer-oriented and expertise-oriented evaluations were merged to a single class.
15. Translator's note: TÜV (Technischer Überwachungsverein)
16. Translator's note: a *volksschule* in Switzerland is a combination of primary and secondary schools encompassing the first nine compulsory school years.
17. The Federal Republic of Germany did not, for example, participate in these international performance tests for many years. It has indeed only very recently become active in that respect, albeit on a remarkable scale.
18. Cf. for example Brauwer & Rumpel (2008) for general information on the educational controlling approach based on human resources management. See Lehmann et al. (1997) particularly on schools and the connection with school evaluation.
19. Cf. Stockmann (2006, 2002) for a detailed account of the difference between auditing, accreditation, certification, quality management and evaluation.
20. Cf. AUSAID (2005); World Bank (publication date unknown); GTZ (1997) on the planning procedures in development policy which have been taken as examples here.

4
The Evaluation Process

Reinhard Stockmann

4.1 Introduction

The way the planning and implementation process in evaluations is structured depends primarily on the type of evaluation and not so much on the evaluand or on clients or contractors. As already shown in Chapter 2, every evaluation must come to terms with the basic questions of *'who is to evaluate what, how, and applying what criteria?'* What is essential is that the evaluand be limited from the beginning, with the objectives of the evaluation clearly defined and the circle of those who are to be involved stipulated (cf. Alkin 2011 on most essential questions to be answered during the evaluation process). What purpose the evaluation is to serve is of central importance along with which phase of the programme process it is to refer to and therefore which analysis perspective is to be adopted. Once these questions have been resolved, investigation goals and assessment criteria must be laid down and the questions answered as to who is to conduct the evaluation and how, in other words using which investigation design.

Once the planning issues have been settled, a start can be made on gathering and analysing the data, this being followed by the assessment of the results and, if appropriate, the derivation of recommendations for action. Since the uppermost aim of every evaluation is to create benefit, of whatever kind, the utilization and implementation of the findings in the course of the evaluation should also be taken into account and the process as a whole organized in such a way that conditions conducive to this are created.

Ideal-typically, evaluations (like other research projects) can be divided into three work phases, which follow one another logically and are causally connected:

(1) Planning phase
(2) Implementation phase
(3) Utilization phase.

It must however be borne in mind that the planning and implementation of every evaluation are connected with its specific context and that there may be considerable overlaps between these three individual

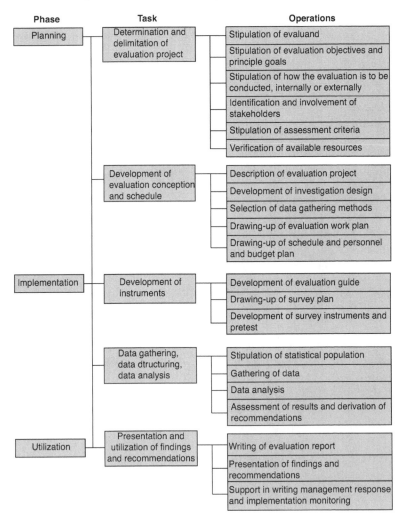

Figure 4.1   Evaluation course

phases. This is particularly the case when the evaluation is a formative one in which planning, implementation and utilization are arranged in iterative loops, so that the individual phases merge and are mutually interdependent. Figure 4.1 shows an ideal-typical evaluation course. It is intended to serve in the section that follows as a basis for elucidating the three evaluation phases and the individual evaluation stages.

4.2 Planning phase

4.2.1 Determination and delimitation of the evaluation project

Every evaluation begins with a goal. Sponsors, those who have commissioned the evaluation, along with scientists or other actors want to use the instrument of evaluation to analyse and assess an evaluand. For this reason, at the beginning of each and every evaluation, the questions about how this evaluand is defined and for what purpose it is to be investigated need to be answered. These two questions are closely connected.

As already explained in Chapter 2, there are hardly any restrictions on the *selection of the evaluand*. Often, however, it will be a project, programme or other measure. In such cases, the question first needs to be asked as to what aspects, phases and situative conditions of a programme are to be covered by the evaluation. This of course is directly related to its *objectives*. If its purpose is to procure information about the efficiency, effectiveness, sustainability and socio-political relevance of a programme, the evaluand needs to be defined more broadly than if the goal covers only the work processes in a programme or only the cost-benefit ratio.

The selection of the evaluand and the investigative goals associated with it depend on the benefit that those responsible for the evaluation expect to obtain from the findings about the evaluand. In accordance with the four functions of an evaluation, this benefit may consist in (1) gaining insights into structures, processes and changes and the correlations between them, (2) initiating learning processes which can be used for the further development of the area being investigated (e.g. programmes), (3) exercising control, for example in order to ascertain whether or not the objectives stipulated in the planning phase have been achieved and whether or not all those involved have met the commitments they made, and (4) legitimizing the work done, for example by showing that the funds spent have been deployed effectively and efficiently.

At the beginning of every single evaluation, the initiators must investigate whether it should be conducted internally or externally. Depending on the purpose it is to serve, the pros and cons of these two procedures (listed in Section 2.2.5) are to be weighed up: if the learning aspect is central, the advantages of an internal evaluation, namely that the implemented programmes and the objectives, problems and situative conditions associated with them are well known and recommendations can be implemented directly by those responsible, outweigh the disadvantages. If however an evaluation is to be conducted more for purposes of control and legitimation, the disadvantages of internal evaluation mean that an external procedure should probably be recommended. This may make it possible to escape the potential risk that internal evaluators, on account of their propinquity to the actors and the organizational structures into which they are integrated, may lose their detachment with regard to the evaluand, may not be sufficiently open to alternative explanations, models and procedures, may be afraid to make critical utterances (lest their careers be damaged), and may thus take insufficient account of stakeholders' interests, etc.

The first operations in the planning phase of an evaluation – the stipulation of the evaluand, targets and principal goals and the form of implementation (internal or external) – may be carried out in a highly formal way, or they may be organized quite openly.

In the *formalized procedure,* the clients of an evaluation decide the issues mentioned above. In an external evaluation, as a rule, an invitation to tender is issued, which is either public (i.e. in principle open to anyone) or restricted to a certain group of applicants. An important element of any invitation to tender is the concrete tasks, known among other things as the 'terms of reference', which are to be carried through in the context of the evaluation. They describe the expectations of the client, state objectives and goals and sometimes even contain information on methods and on the feedback of findings and communication. Not only that; invitations to tender often include deadlines by which the findings are expected and, less often, about what budget framework will be available (cf. Silvestrini 2011: 108ff. for more detail).

However, evaluation can also – especially if it is formative – run along less strictly formalized lines, that is to say in *open processes,* in which the most important parameters are successively determined in such a way as to involve as many as possible of those affected and involved, so-called stakeholders.

A *participant-oriented procedure* – either prior to the invitation to tender, in order to develop a goal that will be appropriate to the various stakeholders' interests, or once the contract has been awarded – can make a major contribution to increasing the worth and the benefit of an evaluation. If the various stakeholders participate in formulating the objectives and investigation goals of the evaluation and later on in selecting the assessment criteria etc., the chance increases that they will actively support the evaluation and be more likely, when the findings and recommendations have been submitted, to accept and implement them. Furthermore, this ensures that the valuable bodies of knowledge of the various actors can be put to good use. What such a participant-oriented model can look like is shown in this chapter.

Before it can be decided who (apart from the immediate client) is to be involved in planning an evaluation, a *stakeholder analysis* needs to be carried out. This can – if it is an internal evaluation or if this operation is carried out prior to an invitation to tender – either be done by the entity that is implementing the programme itself or defined as a function of the external evaluation.

Regardless of the above, it needs to be determined, by means of an analysis of the programme to be evaluated, who is involved in the programme or affected by it (even if indirectly). This list of stakeholders can soon become quite lengthy.

Those *responsible for the programme* can be identified quickly, i.e. those who manage the programme and make decisions (e.g. managers, members of the board, members of advisory committees etc.) and the programme staff, who carry out the planned activities. Mostly, these people form a sub-unit in a larger organization, which is referred to as the (programme) provider or implementing organization (cf. Figure 2.7 in Section 2.3). Other departments, which are not involved directly with the programme, though they may be affected by it, are more difficult to identify. Yet they must not be neglected, for there is a risk that they may jeopardize the successful implementation of a programme and its evaluation as well if they do not feel that sufficient heed has been paid to their interests.

Those responsible for the implementation and the implementing organization itself do not work in isolation, but in the context of other organizations, so there is a need to investigate which of them should be involved, either because important contributions are expected from them, or simply to keep them informed so that they do not torpedo the evaluation project.

Last but not least, of course, the so-called *target groups* need to be taken into account, i.e. those whom the programme activities are supposed to benefit directly. Here too, however, it may be very important to integrate groups of people who will have to bear the indirect consequences of the programme activities, especially if there is a risk that those consequences will be negative.

Which of the stakeholders are actively involved depends not only on their importance for programme development and the evaluation process, but also on quite practical considerations such as

- their being available in terms of time
- their being interested in making a contribution to the evaluation and getting involved
- their having the right to represent a given stakeholder group
- the size of the planning committee in terms of its members and
- agreement on the part of the client that certain stakeholders should be integrated.

Once the question of who is to be involved in the clarification of objectives and assignments has been answered, the *function* this *'committee'* is to have should be stipulated. It may for example simply meet once and hold a 'clarification workshop', or it may be constituted as an *'advisory committee'* that is to be consulted before any important evaluation decision is made.

One of the main functions of an initial meeting is to disclose and discuss the various interests associated with the evaluation. It will become clear at the meeting whether or not the participants' individual expectations are compatible. Often, diffuse ideas that are not capable of being realized in the context of a limited evaluation are rife among the stakeholders. Often enough it is also necessary to dispel unfounded fears and anxieties with regard to the planned evaluation. In order to prevent disappointments, it is also important to adapt the aspirations of the clients and/or other stakeholders to what is actually feasible under the given constraints of time and budget.

This is all the more important in as much as in some policy fields fairly unrealistic *expectations* hold sway *as to the possibilities evaluations offer* – for example if an evaluation is expected to be able to 'provide information across the board, soundly and without delay as to the success of a certain programme, measure or even a policy' (Widmer 2001: 9f.). As an important indicator of this, Widmer (2001: 10) cites the texts of invitations to tender for evaluations, which, he says, often feature a scope statement that is much too extensive, i.e. one which could not possibly be covered properly with the means available. The periods of time allowed for conducting the evaluation are, he adds, also often much too short. Not only that, but invitations to tender sometimes include 'specifications for the implementation of the evaluation [...], which can only be described as methodologically absurd' (ibid.).

These observations agree with the findings from a survey of evaluation contractors carried out at the European level. On the one hand they reported unrealistic expectations and ideas on the part of clients, but on the other they also admitted that they themselves made promises that they were not, against the backdrop of the resources available, in a position to keep at all (Leeuw et al. 1999: 493; cf. also Leeuw 2004: 65–69). However, *unreasonable evaluation agreements* lead inexorably to quality problems and, in the worst case, to major conflicts in the conducting of the evaluation and the acceptance of the job by the client (cf. Widmer 2002: 11; Summa & Toulemonde 2002: 422).

Limiting the goals often proves particularly difficult: 'It is quite common for clients such as a steering committee, a school council or a middle-level manager to put forward a long list of issues which they would like addressed. The evaluator may need to work with the client to reduce this list' (Owen & Rogers 1999: 69). In order to do this, the goals essential to the evaluation need to be separated from those that are less important. Against the backdrop of the objectives and tasks of the evaluation and the information requirements of the client and other stakeholders, the questions *'Who wants to know what and for what purpose?'* may help to make the selection easier.

If important questions are erroneously discarded, this may detract considerably from the benefit of an evaluation. By contrast, a large number of 'unimportant' questions puts undue strain on time and budget resources, which are as a rule scant. In both cases, the credibility of the evaluation findings (and thus also that of the evaluator) may suffer. In the worst case, the evaluation may produce misleading findings.

Stipulating the evaluation goals becomes a particularly difficult undertaking if the stakeholder groups involved in the planning process are unable to reach agreement because of their divergent interests, or if sponsors and/or clients refuse to take into account those interests of other stakeholders that run counter to their own. In these cases, the evaluation is mostly exclusively conducted from the perspective of the sponsors or clients, which confronts the evaluators, especially at the beginning, with the problem of creating sufficient acceptance among the other stakeholders.

Because there are so many diverse questions at the beginning of an evaluation, it is a good idea to hold a *'clarification workshop'*, at which the expectation structures of the various stakeholders should be discussed and the main goals of the evaluation elaborated. Furthermore, attempts should be made to achieve agreement about the assessment criteria to be applied, the methodological approaches, the question of resources and the schedules. The tasks of the client (for example enlightenment of those affected by the evaluation as to its objectives, logistical support), those of the individual stakeholders (for example information procurement) and those of the evaluators can also be laid down in such workshops. Often, however, not all these questions can be dealt with in a single workshop, so that during the course of the evaluation project further conferences or coordination meetings, for example in the context of design development, may be necessary.

Right at the beginning of an evaluation process, however, it is absolutely necessary to obtain a clear picture of the *resources* available. Important aspects to be taken into account here are the scope of the funds envisaged, the timeframe allowed, the availability of staff and the existence of data material (e.g. documents, statistics, monitoring data etc.) that which can be used in the evaluation.

It is the task of the evaluator to put the available resources in relation to the objectives and goals in order to be able to judge whether, and to what extent, the evaluation is actually feasible.

Particularly clients with little experience often lack clear ideas of what resources are necessary for dealing with certain questions. Sometimes it is not clear to the clients or stakeholders involved either what output potential an evaluation realistically has. For this reason it is the task of the evaluators to advise clients and/or stakeholders and enlighten them as to alternative procedures and investigative approaches. If clients and/or stakeholders have already had bad experiences with evaluations, it will surely be difficult to persuade them otherwise. It is thus all the more important for evaluations to be well thought out in the planning phase and conducted professionally while adhering to qualified standards.

Often, however, the evaluation is not planned in this kind of open and participant-oriented way; instead, the clients issue very restrictive specifications for the available financial resources, time-frame conditions, general objectives and tasks of the evaluation. Sometimes, indeed, entire lists of questions will have been drawn up, stipulating the nature and scope of the stakeholders' involvement and the survey methods to be used. In such cases, there is of course only very little room for negotiation of the planning issues outlined above between the sponsor/client, the other stakeholders and the evaluators.

Yet in these cases too it is advisable to hold a joint evaluation workshop at the beginning, in order to sensitize all those involved to the evaluation, explain to them the objectives and tasks, promote acceptance and active involvement and exploit the possibilities for cooperation which still exist.

The results of the *clarification of the assignment,* negotiated either in a dialogue with the client or in a participant-oriented workshop with all the important stakeholders, are in any case to be recorded in writing, for they not only represent the foundation on which the evaluation is planned, but also safeguard the evaluators against any 'new' expectations that may crop up later on.

In clarifying the assignment, the evaluators must not only investigate whether or not the evaluation can be conducted at all adhering to professional standards (cf. Section 4.4.3) and within the framework of the time and budget resources estimated by the client and the given situative conditions.

It would be *inadvisable to conduct an evaluation* if

- it looked likely to produce only trivial information, for example because an evaluation had just taken place and no new findings were to be expected
- it could be foreseen that the findings were not actually going to be utilized, for example because the decision-makers rejected the evaluation
- the available financial resources and/or the time frame allowed were not reconcilable with conducting an evaluation in accordance with the requirements and expectations of the client, for example because comprehensive analyses were called for although the requisite budget and time resources had not been provided
- no valid or useful findings were to be expected, for example because the situative conditions had changed so much (e.g. as a result of natural disaster or war) that it were no longer possible to ascertain any programme impacts, or because a programme was so badly delayed that a given development phase which was supposed to be evaluated had not even been reached yet
- the evaluation approach requested by the client were unsuitable with regard to the programme or measured against professional standards, for example if a request were made in an impact-oriented evaluation that the target group be allowed to gather their own data, or if other professional rules were violated
- the way the evaluation was to be conducted were determined by political considerations alone (tactical evaluation), so that proper implementation and subsequent adequate utilization of the findings could not be expected, for example if the decision on the continuation or termination of a programme had already been made and were now merely to be legitimized in retrospect with the help of the evaluation.

In cases like the above it is better to refrain from conducting the evaluation altogether, because either the expectations of the client will be disappointed or professional standards will not be able to be adhered to.

To sum up, it should be noted that in the planning phase the evaluand is fixed and the objectives and principal goals of the evaluation stipulated. This needs to be done not only in internal but also in external evaluations. This process can be participant-oriented, the most important stakeholders first being identified and then involved in the process to an appropriate degree. Alternatively it can be directive, with the client alone calling the tune. In external evaluations the evaluators may be involved in this process, or they may not, if for example for the purposes of an invitation to tender, the decisions on the evaluand and evaluation objectives have already been made beforehand. In any case it is the task of the evaluators to judge whether or not an evaluation can be conducted under the prescribed time, budget and situative conditions. If an evaluation is to be able to develop the greatest possible benefit, it is necessary for the available resources to be sufficient for processing the tasks in hand.

4.2.2 Evaluation conception and implementation planning

Once the specifications for an evaluation have been settled and fixed in a written document, work can commence on the elaboration of the evaluation conception and the investigative design. Furthermore, an *implementation plan* must be developed. This should contain the chronological sequence, the deployment of human resources and the cost calculation.

The *evaluation conception* presents the implementation of the objectives and the principal goals. In detail, it should contain the following:

- a description of the evaluand
- the objectives and tasks of the evaluation
- the form of implementation (internal or external or a combination of the two)
- the names of the principal stakeholders to be taken into account
- the audiences for the findings
- a clear statement of the individual evaluation goals (and assessment criteria)
- an investigative design from which it becomes clear how the questions are to be processed empirically
- a selection of the methods with which the required data will be gathered and

- a description of how the evaluation process will be organized (directive vs. participant-oriented procedure).

This is complemented by a schedule and a plan for human and financial resources.

Starting from the basic design elaborated early on, in the first stage of planning, it is now a matter of developing an *investigation design* with which the identified questions can be processed empirically, and selecting the *data gathering methods* with which the information required can be collected (cf. Section 5.2 for more detail on this).

Heed needs to be paid in the evaluation work plan to how the *evaluation process* is to be organized: more participant-oriented (i.e. involving all the important stakeholders if possible) or more directively (i.e. as a rule determined by the client). If the evaluation is to be conducted in a participant-oriented way, attention needs to be paid to taking suitable measures to inform and involve the stakeholders. For example, these may consist in (1) setting up an advisory committee for the evaluation which meets on a regular basis, (2) holding workshops about the involvement of the stakeholders in decisive phases of the evaluation (e.g. kick-off meetings, workshops on the clarification of the evaluation conception and design, interim workshops at which initial findings are presented, a final workshop for the assessment of the findings and the derivation of recommendations for action), (3) creating an evaluation website, on which all the important planning documents, agreements, survey instruments, findings etc. are posted and information is provided about current and forthcoming events.

The evaluation conception is supplemented by a *schedule and a plan for the deployment of human and financial resources,* in order to clarify which outputs are to have been generated by whom and by when, and what amount of funding has been planned for this.

The *schedule* can easily be presented with the aid of bar charts or using network planning techniques (cf. Wottawa & Thierau 2003: 114ff.). Estimating realistically how much time will be required for certain operations is more difficult. Often, various different activities need to be organized parallel to one another. Care should then be taken to ensure that they mesh together and are compatible. For example, while a standardized written questionnaire is out in the field, i.e. while its return is being awaited, oral guided interviews can take place. With postal, e-mail or on-line surveys two or three waves of 'reminders' need to be included in the plan. Overall, the challenge consists on the one hand in developing a work plan which takes into account the constraints of time imposed by the clients, i.e. the deadlines by which the initial findings, interim and final reports are to be submitted, and on the other hand incorporating as many time-in-hand phases ('buffers') as possible, so that problems which crop up unexpectedly can still be overcome within the time agreed.

In *planning the deployment of human resources* the question of who is to carry out which tasks needs to be answered. It is true that first and foremost this involves the allocation of tasks among the evaluators, but it should also take into account whether and to what extent staffing inputs may be necessary: on the part of the client (e.g. for meetings and workshops), on the part of the programme provider, the target groups and other stakeholders (e.g. for the collation of material and data, procurement of addresses for surveys, logistical support in conducting interviews, answering questions etc.).

To draw up the *evaluation budget* it is also necessary for the various types of cost to be recorded precisely and for the amounts incurred to be estimated as accurately as possible. The following types of cost should be taken into account (cf. Sanders 1983):

- personnel costs for the evaluation team
- costs of any consultants who may need to be called in (e.g. experts, specialists on particular subjects)
- costs of carrying out quantitative surveys (e.g. telephone costs, computer specialists, methods laboratory)
- travel and accommodation costs
- costs of communication media (postage, telephone, EDP etc.)
- printing costs (e.g. for reports, written surveys)
- costs of procuring necessary material (technical equipment, literature, computers etc.)
- costs of possible subcontracts (e.g. for conducting interviews, case studies, procuring material) and
- overheads (office costs etc.)

To sum up, it should be noted that the evaluation conception comprises the objectives and tasks of the evaluation project, the presentation of its implementation in methodological terms and the actual sequence of the individual operations. If a contract is to be awarded for the evaluation project to be carried out, the evaluation conception is, as it were, the tender, forming the basis for the awarding of the contract (cf. Silvestrini 2011: 108ff. on drawing up tenders in detail).

4.3 Implementation phase

Before the implementation of an evaluation can be commenced, the instruments with which the investigative design can be implemented need to be developed (cf. Figure 4.1 in Section 4.1). First, it is advisable to structure the individual evaluation goals. For this, the *guide* developed in Section 2.3 with the aid of various theories for the evaluation of programmes can be used. Furthermore, a *survey plan* needs to be drawn up which documents the procedure of how the information is to be procured for each individual goal, and with which survey instrument (cf. Section 5.2). Then, before the data can be gathered and analysed, the *instruments* need to be developed and tested and the *study population* identified.

The analysis guide serves not only to sort the individual evaluation goals in advance from systematic points of view, but also to structure the data gathered with the aid of the various collection methods. With the aid of the guide introduced in Section 2.3, and others besides, the existing programme structures and contextual conditions, and the changes of mode in the course of the funding, can be recorded and assessed in detail.

To this end, not only the programme, its environment and the intervention process itself (especially planning and implementation), but also the programme provider and the external areas of impact are investigated. Distinctions are made between impacts caused by the programme interventions, planned or unplanned, impacts which occur in the provider (internal impacts) and impacts which go beyond the provider (external impacts). If it is an ex-post evaluation, sustainability can also be determined.

The description and analysis of a programme and of the positive and negative, intended and unintended impacts brought about by it under certain situative conditions pose some major challenges for an evaluation.

Looking at the objectives of a programme, one is – as shown in Section 3.4.1 – confronted with a series of problems that have led some evaluation researchers (cf. Cronbach et al. 1981: 5; Scriven 1991: 180) to make a plea in favour of goal-free evaluations. As goal-free evaluations are – at least in the context of assigned or commissioned research – considered by most evaluators to be a very naive concept (cf. Weiss 1974: 22; Owen & Rogers 1999: 269) and are very unlikely to be practicable, a hypothesis-guided evaluation offers itself as an alternative, seeking to record empirically as many intended and unintended impacts as possible, and then proceeding to clarify the cause-and-effect relationships.

For this, it is necessary to reconstruct the implicit or explicit *programme theory,* in other words the hypotheses on which the network of impacts is based.[1] In order to achieve certain objectives, for example to reduce child mortality, cut unemployment or provide the people in a village with clean drinking-water, various measures are taken, for example a vaccination programme is implemented, an employment programme set up or wells drilled. All these different measures are based on the assumption that their being properly implemented will lead to the desired impacts, i.e. that there is a connection between the objective and the means used to achieve it. As a rule this is not merely a simple cause-and-effect relationship, but an *impact chain.* In an education programme aimed at increasing the knowledge of the pupils, the chain might look something like the following.

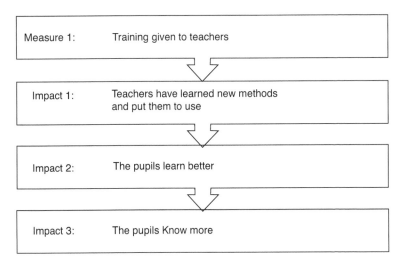

In other words, the *hypotheses* behind this impact chain might be as follows:

(1) If teachers are given methodological and didactic training,
    ⇒then they will change their teaching methods.
(2) If the teaching methods change,
    ⇒then the pupils will learn better.

(3) If the pupils learn better,
    ⇒then they will get to know more.

This sequence of if-then relationships describes the programme-theory concepts, which are intended to lead to the achievement of targets. Another component of the education programme might be that the teachers taking part in the 'model project' are offered more attractive working conditions (e.g. smaller classes, opportunities for advanced training etc.). If that were the case, the hypothesis chain might look like this:

(1) If the teachers are offered better working conditions,
    ⇒then they will be more strongly motivated.
(2) If they are more strongly motivated,
    ⇒then they will give better lessons.
(3) If the lessons improve,
    ⇒then the pupils will learn more.
(4) If the pupils learn more,
    ⇒then they will know more.

Furthermore, impact chains can also be derived for unintended consequences of intervention. Comprehensive knowledge of the programme context is required for this, for example from other studies or evaluations. In relation to an education programme offered in one region only on account of scarcity of funds, the following might occur:

(1) If the programme offers teachers more attractive working conditions,
    ⇒then teachers from other regions will migrate.
(2) If teachers from other regions migrate,
    ⇒then the educational care in those regions will no longer be assured.
(3) If the educational care declines,
    ⇒then the quality of the teaching will also decline.
(4) If the quality of the teaching declines,
    ⇒then the pupils there will know less.

Such a hypothesis-guided search for impacts can be managed with the aid of the guide presented in Section 2.3. Furthermore, the central questions used there for the individual fields of investigation lend themselves to the derivation of assessment criteria. An example of an assessment tableau of this kind is shown in Table 4.1.

Table 4.1 Assessment criteria

---

1. Programme and environment
    1.1 Logic of programme conception
    1.2 Conformity of programme innovation
    1.3 Availability of resources
    1.4 Situative contextual conditions for programme implementation
    1.5 Relevance of programme to target groups

2. Course of programme
    2.1 Quality of programme preparation/planning
    2.2 Quality of programme control
    2.3 Quality of preparation for end of funding period
    2.4 Quality of post-funding support

3. Internal areas of impact (provider)
    3.1 Acceptability of aims to implementing org. and if appropriate in superordinate provider
    3.2 Qualification level of provider's staff
    3.3 Performance ability of organizational structure of provider
    3.4 Financial performance ability of provider
    3.5 Technical level and status of provider's equipment
    3.6 Innovation potential of provider
    3.7 Internal impact balance sheet

4. External areas of impact (audiences, policy fields/fields of practice)
    4.1 Acceptance of aims in target groups
    4.2 Degree of diffusion within target groups
    4.3 Benefit for target groups
    4.4 Diffusion impacts spanning more than one target group
    4.5 Diffusion impacts within policy field
    4.6 Diffusion impacts in neighbouring policy fields
    4.7 External impact balance sheet

5. Sustainability
    At macro level:
    5.1 Efficiency
    5.2 Socio-political relevance
    5.3 Ecological soundness
    At programme level:
    5.4 Programme/output/system/innovation-oriented sustainability

---

It is not sufficient to determine only assessment criteria such as 'acceptability of the aims to the target groups' or 'qualification of the staff in implementation'. *Indicators* must also be developed by which the criteria are to be measured. Indicators are necessary when the circumstance to be recorded cannot be observed directly. For example, an indicator is not as a rule needed for the 'measurement' of a person's income, age, sex etc. But for the examples given above, indicators are absolutely necessary.

The acceptance of the programme objective among the members of the target groups can for example be recorded by finding out what individual members of the target groups are saying about the programme, to what extent they are prepared to stand up for the objectives actively, to what extent they make contributions of their own etc. (cf. Meyer 2011 for a detailed explanation of indicators).

For assessment applying criteria, as well as indicators for 'measurement', it is also necessary to set *threshold values*. This means that target dimensions are stated: dimensions from which the targets will be assumed to have been achieved or for example a positive or negative assessment is to be made. For the criterion 'full employment' one could for example stipulate that it has already been fulfilled if 95 per cent and not 100 per cent are employed, since there will always be a 'statistical base' of job-seekers for reasons which have to do with the job market and the way job-seekers are placed.

For the criterion 'acceptance of aims', measured on a ten-point scale from 0 (no acceptance) to 10 (very high acceptance), the definition might be that a target dimension of 8 would already represent the optimum, since it will never be possible to convince all the people within a given target group without exception etc.

There is no room here for an explanation of how individual assessments can be made and how they can be used to design programme profiles with the aid of which these changes over time can be detected (cf. on this point Stockmann 2008: 186ff.).

In order to examine the investigation questions documented in the evaluation guide and the impact chains developed from them, various different data sources and survey methods need to be used depending on the investigative design of the evaluation, and these are listed in the survey plan.

First, a check needs to be made to see which of the *documents and data* required are actually already on hand. As a rule, project/programme files and statistics exist, and these need to be analysed with regard to the goals. Some programmes also have a monitoring system with which data on the development of the programme are collected continuously, and these are a valuable data source for an evaluation.

In the next step, consideration should be given to the way in which the information still lacking for answering the analysis questions grouped together in the guide can be procured. Here, some thought needs to be given to the question of who might be in possession of such data or competent to provide information on these questions. Then a decision has to be taken on which data gathering methods are to be used for which test group.

Once a selection has been made, the respective *study populations* are to be stipulated, i.e. whether data should be gathered from the respective statistical population as a whole or from a sample drawn from it. If the decision is made in favour of a sample, the selection procedure and the degree of representativeness desired need to be determined (e.g. random selection, conscious or arbitrary selection etc.).

Finally, the issues of who is to gather what data, when, and under what framework conditions need to be resolved. The problems and risks that could occur (e.g. reachability of respondents, their readiness to participate etc.) must be anticipated as early as possible (cf. Section 5.3 on problems in data gathering).

Before actual field work can begin, the selected *instruments* (e.g. questionnaires, guides, observation schemata etc.) still need to be developed and tried out in a *pretest*. Following the participant-oriented model, it is a good idea to discuss difficulties that may occur in data gathering (such as logistical problems, availability of interviewees, their readiness to participate in the evaluation) with the client and if appropriate also with individual stakeholders in order to spot ways of solving these problems or alternatives.

Unlike research work in pure science, the analysis of the data once collected with regard to the issues being investigated is followed by an *assessment* of the results applying the selected assessment criteria (cf. Section 5.5 on data interpretation).

Summing up, it should be noted that in the implementation phase of the evaluation the development of instruments and the procurement and analysis of information are mainly to the fore. This phase often takes up the most time in evaluations (cf. Chapter 5 for more details). To structure the data with regard to the evaluation questions, it is a good idea to develop a guide, which can also be used to derive assessment criteria.

4.4   Utilization phase

4.4.1   Presentation and utilization of findings

Whether or not the findings from an evaluation will be utilized by the various stakeholders, and if so how, depends to a large extent on whether or not the evaluators succeed in getting those findings across convincingly in the communication process. The most important media in this process are the *evaluation report* and the *presentation* of the findings. Great attention must therefore be paid to how the evaluation report is written. It should be preceded by an 'executive summary' that contains the most important insights and recommendations. The main section can be oriented toward the structure of the evaluation guide (cf. Table 2.10 in Section 2.3). It contains all the important findings, interpretations and assessments. The report can be made more interesting and more readable by means of graphics and tables, quotations which are either embedded in the text or highlighted by being placed in small 'boxes', and brief interim summaries. As a rule it ends with concrete recommendations for action for the further development of the programme.

The findings and the data on which they are based need to be presented in a clear and unmistakable way. The assessments built upon them should be such that the rationale can be seen in them intersubjectively, and the recommendations made should follow 'logically' from the analysis and interpretation of those findings. The linguistic style and phraseology should be adapted to suit the audiences. For this reason, by the time they begin to write the evaluation report at the latest, the evaluators should make sure they are quite clear about whom they are actually addressing. The group of audiences is usually closely related to the evaluation objectives: if it is primarily a question of gaining insights, the main audiences might for example be scientists who wish to discover new correlations, or sponsors searching for new, successful strategies with which to implement their political ideas. If the control or legitimation aspect is primary, the findings should be aimed mainly at the sponsor and/or client or at a wider public. If on the other hand the evaluation has aimed to improve programme activities, not only the client but also the organization implementing the programme, the target groups and other stakeholders will be the right audiences for the findings (cf. Rossi et al. 1999: 48; Rossi, Lipsey & Freeman 2004: 42; Fitzpatrick et al. 2012: 458).

Having said that, a well-written evaluation report is no guarantee that the findings will actually be used by the clients and stakeholders: 'In the past decade, evaluators have realized that it isn't enough to draft a good evaluation report. Indeed, evaluators have become increasingly aware that one can work hard to maximize the quality of their report and still find that the impact and influence it has on its stakeholders, programs, or policies is at best negligible and at worst, zero' (Fitzpatrick et al. 2012: 453). For this reason, the evaluation findings should not only be conveyed in written form, but should also definitely include an *oral presentation*. Presentations provide the opportunity to put across the principal findings and recommendations in condensed form and to underline important messages again. Advantage should also be taken of the opportunity to discuss the findings in detail and explain them. Care should however be taken to ensure that the discussion does not get caught up in side issues (such as punctuation or spelling etc.), or minor factual 'errors' or misunderstandings – notes can be made about these in writing – but centres around the essential questions and findings of the evaluation and the recommendations derived from them.

A *'final workshop'* of this kind is at its most effective when the evaluation report has already been distributed in advance and the findings have thus already been made known to all those involved, so that the discussion can be embarked upon without much ado. It is a good idea to structure the discussion according to topics and to draw up a schedule. An atmosphere should be assured in which open communication can take place and all those involved can make comments and give their opinions freely. This is not always easy, for example if the client or sponsor has incisive rights to impose sanctions, i.e. if they can cut or boost funds, or if individual stakeholders (or groups of stakeholders) are economically dependent on the sponsor or client. In such cases it may be a useful idea to hold separate workshops (with the sponsors and clients attending the one and the other stakeholders the other).

In general, final workshops in which the most important stakeholders take part encourage greater acceptance of the evaluation findings and recommendations and thus also (presumably) have a better chance of being implemented than workshops from which the stakeholders are excluded (cf. the 'CEval participant-oriented evaluation approach', developed in the next chapter).

Since the tasks of evaluations include exposing deficiencies and mistakes and rendering them transparent, even if doing so means casting doubt on the strategies and political positions of the stakeholders, especially those of the client, it cannot be assumed – even if all the stakeholders are integrated in the best possible way – that everyone will always be thrilled about the *evaluation's findings:*

> This means that sponsors of evaluation and other stakeholders may turn on the evaluator and harshly criticise the evaluation if the results contradict the policies and perspectives they advocate. Thus, even those evaluators who do a superb job of working with stakeholders and incorporating their views and concerns in the evaluation plan should not expect to be acclaimed as heroes when the results are in. The multiplicity of stakeholder perspectives makes it likely that no matter how the results come out, someone will be unhappy.
>
> (Rossi, Lipsey & Freeman 2004: 43)

It thus happens that stakeholders react negatively to findings that contradict their own positions and expectations. For this reason evaluators ought not to be particularly surprised if their study or they themselves get caught in the crossfire of *criticism*. The following *typical patterns of criticism* have become identifiable in many years of evaluation practice:

(1) *So what's new?*

It sometimes happens that the evaluation clients, evaluees or other stakeholders claim that the findings were already common knowledge before the evaluation and therefore that no one is surprised by them. It is indeed often true that those affected are familiar with deficiencies and problems or have at least developed a feeling for them. However, the task of evaluation goes beyond this, being concerned with delivering empirically sound evidence and robust findings. Regardless of this, an explanation needs to be found in such a case for why, in spite of their knowledge of the existing problems, those responsible have not taken any action and why the 'known' shortcomings were not rectified before the evaluation.

In evaluation research, as in social science as a whole, the observation may also be made that findings that are counter-intuitive, i.e. do not correspond to that which is generally expected, attract the most attention. Having said that, empirically based insights in accord with the mainstream of implicit or explicit suppositions and assumptions are no less significant.

(2) *Methodological deficiencies*

A particularly popular way of casting doubt on the findings of an evaluation is to criticize the investigation design and the methods employed. Time and again, it is astonishing just how many (supposed) 'methodological experts' there are! In view of the fact that there really are many different ways of approaching a problem that needs to be investigated, only the selection of a suitable investigation design and practicable methods can guard against unjustified criticism. For this reason, evaluators must make it clear in a convincing manner that their methodological procedures correspond to the 'state of the art'.

A problem may arise if the client fails to provide the necessary funding to finance an investigation design that is really suitable for the task on hand. That is just where the art of evaluation often lies: in obtaining *an optimum of robust information with a minimum of funding.*

Often, 'second-best' approaches have to be accepted, as the evaluation cannot otherwise be conducted because of a lack of financial resources or time. Nevertheless, there are clients who go ahead and make available low-level funding for an evaluation, magnanimously accepting a 'second-best' solution, only to turn round and criticize the latter's methodological shortcomings at the end of the study. In order to be able to prove that during the preparation of an evaluation attention was drawn to the methodological difficulties and their consequences for the quality of the evaluation, evaluators are advised to document all procedural steps and to agree all reports, records and minutes with the client.

When all is said and done, however, the *quality* of an evaluation is the *responsibility of the evaluators*. For this reason, if they recognize that the conditions for conducting the evaluation in a manner appropriate to the task in hand are not going to be fulfilled and that it will not be possible to meet the appropriate evaluation standards, they should decline the job.

Assessing the feasibility of evaluations is part of the competence of professional evaluators alone and they should make that assessment with all due diligence. (See above all of Section 4.2 on assessment criteria.)

The methodological quality of evaluations is furthermore influenced by the selection procedure used (cf. Section 5.2). For this reason *the interviewees should be selected* with the greatest circumspection. Since representative (random) selections are often not possible, this should be done in a purposeful manner. Care should be taken that, as far as possible, all the relevant perspectives and interests are represented. It is also advisable to agree on the selection with the stakeholders (or at least with the client). Otherwise there is a risk that the evaluators may have to face accusations along the lines of having questioned the 'wrong' people and thus obtained 'wrong' or distorted results; if they had interviewed the 'right people', the accusers will say, the assessment would have turned out completely differently, that is to say more positively.

(3) *What mustn't be true can't be true*

Now and again it happens that findings are plainly denied. If these are facts and circumstances that can be proved beyond doubt with data, the situation can be cleared up quickly. If it is a matter of opinions which have been expressed (e.g. satisfaction with various aspects of a programme), evidence needs to be provided in the form of a number of respondents that is statistically sufficient. The data then 'speak for themselves'. If the findings are interpretations on the part of the evaluator, strict attention must be paid to a logical chain of argument. The more one can avoid making statements that cannot be sufficiently substantiated by existing data, the less an evaluation is open to attack. No evaluation should indulge in speculation.

Especially in the case of very complex evaluands, it may often not be possible to eliminate factual errors completely despite the greatest of care. If these are criticized by those responsible for the programme or those affected by it, who as a rule have much more comprehensive situational knowledge than the evaluators, they are, of course, after having been scrutinized in detail, to be corrected. With substantiated assessment it is quite a different matter. Evaluators have not only the right but also a professional duty to stand by assessments that are adequately backed up by facts, and to resist all possible attempts to influence them.

(4) *Painstaking search for errors*

When the results comprised in the evaluation report are presented, the criticism made by the client or evaluees can sometimes be seen to branch out into innumerable minor details. As the client and the evaluees are always in possession of superior concrete situational knowledge, it is almost always possible for them to discover some mistakes in the presentation, even if they are only marginal. Even grammatical errors or incorrect punctuation in the final report can spark off a debate. In such cases, care should be taken that the main messages and insights of the study are not overshadowed, for there may be method in such actions; those behind them may be attempting not to have to face up to the study's unwelcome conclusions.

(5) *Implementation deficiencies*

Not all evaluations go as planned. If a situation arises in which the client does not provide the support that was agreed – if for example the address data necessary for a survey are not made available, interviewees who have already been nominated can never be found, processes and decisions are subject to delay etc. – these problems are to be documented precisely by the evaluator. It is only in this way that evaluators can defend themselves against later accusations, for example that the number of interviewees was too low or that the report was not completed within the agreed time. It is hardly worth mentioning that the evaluator must draw the attention of the client to problems of this kind before it is too late, and assist – if possible – in solving them. It goes without saying that the inversion of this also applies and it may be necessary for the evaluators to actively demand the support of the clients (or certain stakeholder groups) while the evaluation is being conducted in order to avoid discussions at the end.

This list is certainly not intended to give the impression that criticism of evaluation studies or evaluators is always unfounded, or that errors are always to be sought in omissions on the part of clients, evaluees or other stakeholders or their inability to take criticism and reluctance to learn. *This is a long way from the truth! Studies and evaluators, of course, do give cause for justified criticism, and not all that rarely!* Neither was the section above intended to give the impression that evaluations are always as conflict-laden as that. On the contrary, in most evaluations clients and evaluators probably work together constructively and the clients and evaluees greet the findings with an open mind. Experience also shows that findings and recommendations (provided that the evaluation was sound) have a better chance of being accepted and implemented in organizations in which criticism is generally dealt with in a constructive manner, quality discussions are held openly and an 'evaluation culture' exists, than in organizations in which this is not the case.

Evaluators are best protected against unjustified criticism if

- they have done their work with scientific accuracy, so that their findings will withstand methodological criticism
- professional standards have been taken into account
- optimally the stakeholders were actively integrated in planning and if possible also in conducting the evaluation, and
- the various different interests of the stakeholders were sufficiently taken into account in gathering and analysing the data and interpreting the results.

Having said that, the extensive *integration of the stakeholders* in all the phases of the evaluation process does involve some *risks*. The readiness of an organization or individual stakeholders to learn cannot always be presumed. If an evaluation meets with only low acceptance, for example because it was forced upon those involved, the participant-oriented approach favoured here can lead to massive conflicts that can severely impede its planning and implementation. If the most important stakeholders are already integrated into the design phase of the evaluation but are not interested in working together with the evaluators constructively, it will be difficult to formulate joint evaluation objectives and assessment criteria or come to a consensus on the procedure and the deployment of selected methods. Often enough it is a matter of allaying fears among the evaluees, especially when they are afraid that an institution may be closed or a programme discontinued. In these cases, the evaluators must develop a special empathy for those affected and a high degree of skill in negotiation and persuasiveness. But however much understanding the evaluators may show the stakeholders, it should never be forgotten that the *evaluators bear the responsibility for conducting the evaluation profession-ally*. They must do justice both to the requirements of the clients and the needs of those affected (e.g. the evaluees) and must comply with scientific standards... an undertaking that can sometimes prove difficult.

The implementation of the evaluation findings is no longer the immediate responsibility of the evaluators. For that reason, they are not as a rule involved in drafting a *'management response'*. In such a document the client and if appropriate also the principal stakeholders stipulate which of the evaluation recommendations they intend to implement, in what periods of time, and who is to be responsible for that implementation. For this purpose, some organizations have even established an *implementation monitoring department* in its own right, which scrutinizes follow-up activities. It is also customary in follow-up evaluations to investigate the extent to which prior evaluation recommendations have been implemented and how they have influenced programme events.

4.4.2   Use of evaluations

As already mentioned at the beginning, the worth of an evaluation is determined according to how useful it is: 'In the end, the worth of evaluations must be judged by their utility' (Rossi, Lipsey & Freeman 2004: 411). According to Beywl (2001: 160) the utility of an evaluation manifests itself in insights, information and conclusions being utilized and having an influence on the actions of the audiences in their praxis. In the utility standards of the German Evaluation Society (DeGEval 2002) it is assumed that findings are only used if 'the evaluation is guided by the clarified purposes of the evaluation and the information needs of its intended users'. Special care must therefore already be taken when planning and conducting an evaluation that conditions conducive to the best possible use of the findings are created. This is one of the things the participation model introduced in Section 4.5 aims to assure.

The extent to which evaluations actually create benefit is a matter for debate. In particular, studies carried out in the 1970s and 1980s came to the conclusion that insufficient heed was paid to evaluation findings and recommendations. Later investigations however (cf. Fitzpatrick et al. 2012: 480; Stamm 2003: 183ff.) show that this result can only be confirmed to a certain extent.

There is not only a serious paucity of such studies, so that representative statements can hardly be made for all policy fields, but there is also, in most cases, no differentiated operationalization of use. It therefore makes sense to differentiate between at least three types of use:

(1) *Direct (instrumental) use*

This refers to the direct use of evaluation findings by the management of the client and other stakeholders. For example, this is the case when findings are put to use in decision-making, programmes reorganized in accordance with the evaluation recommendations, or strategies, communication relationships etc. altered.

(2) *Conceptual use*

Conceptual use comes about when evaluation findings influence the general way those involved think about problems. For example, this is the case if it can be shown that the sustainability of programmes is only measurable with the aid of ex-post evaluations and this insight causes an organization to use ex-post evaluations in the future as an additional procedure.

(3) *Persuasive use*

Persuasive use occurs if evaluation findings serve to endorse or refute 'political' positions. This is the case, for example, if they are able to refute positions that were firmly anchored and no longer queried. For example, the evaluation of the sustainability of development projects shows that the participation of the target groups in the planning phase is not – as is often claimed – a decisive variable in the success of the project, but that other variables (such as acceptance of aims, efficiency of the provider etc.) are in fact much more important (cf. Stockmann 1992, 1996).

On the basis of the above distinctions, it becomes clear that the heavy focus on the direct effects of evaluation findings in the early user studies was too narrow. If the term 'use' is defined more broadly, we see that evaluations often have indirect impacts on further-reaching decision-making processes by promoting learning processes (conceptual use) or causing fundamental attitudes and convictions to change in the long term – as in 'constant dripping wears away a stone'.

The following *factors* have been identified in studies of use as decisive *for the practical implementation of evaluation findings* (cf. Fitzpatrick et al. 2012: 485; Rossi, Lipsey & Freeman 2004: 414):

- the relevance of the evaluation for the decision-makers and/or other stakeholders
- the integration of stakeholders into the planning and reporting phases of the evaluation
- the reputation or credibility of the evaluator
- the quality of the communication of the findings (promptness, frequency, methods) and
- the development of back-up procedures for the use of the findings or the making of recommendations for action.

Some organizations attempt to institutionalize the use of evaluation findings. The major German development cooperation implementing organizations (such as the German Society for Technical Cooperation (GTZ) or the Reconstruction Loan Corporation [KfW]) have developed sophisticated knowledge management systems for this, in order to ensure both direct and conceptual use of evaluations (cf. Borrmann & Stockmann 2009). Compliance with the abovementioned factors is intended to ensure instrumental use in particular.

In order to bring about use that persists beyond the individual programme or project, the findings from evaluations are added into knowledge management systems and systematized. Foundations for institutional learning that cover different programmes are thus laid, and such learning can relate to certain programme types, sectors or regions. To ensure this, some organizations even go as far, when new programmes are being planned, as to insist that proof be provided of which evaluation findings have been taken into account.

It must also be noted that many evaluations generate use simply by taking place. Such so-called *process use* comes about when the programme managers and other stakeholders occupy themselves with the programme. For example, workshops that were actually intended to clarify the evaluation objectives and select the indicators with which those objectives can be measured are often seen to mutate into discussions on the programme objectives in general.

In this way, evaluation can already lead to new insights, perspectives and programme corrections while it is being planned and conducted. This form of use is neglected completely in most studies on the subject, as they focus principally on the 'results use' that is concomitant with the findings and recommendations of an evaluation.

4.4.3 Quality of evaluation

The usefulness of an evaluation depends to a large extent on its quality. To ensure that quality, there are – as in other professional and vocational fields – *standards* and *ethical guidelines* that provide a basis for the assessment and orientation of professional behaviour and work. Standards not only define basic quality levels to which the 'experts' in the respective professional or vocational field are supposed to adhere, but also aim to protect customers and the general public against sharp practices and incompetence.

Apart from that, standards offer a basis for control and judgement for providers and their outputs; they can be taken as a basis for decision-making in potential disputes between customers and providers and they promote orientation toward the recognized 'best practices' in a given field of activity (cf. DeGEval 2002; Owen & Rogers 1999; Stufflebeam 2000a; Rossi, Lipsey & Freeman 2004 and others).

The *professionalization of evaluation research* led in the USA of the 1980s to the first attempts to develop evaluation standards. In 1981 the 'Joint Committee on Standards for Educational Evaluation' (JCS 2006) published standards for the educational science sector, which began to be used over the years in more and more sectors (cf. Widmer 2004). In 1994, the so-called 'Joint Committee', meanwhile complemented by the addition of organizations that were not only active in the education sector, presented a revised version entitled 'The Program Evaluation Standards' (cf. Beywl & Widmer 2000: 250). In the German-language areas standards received but little attention for a long time.[2] It was not until the *German Evaluation Society (DeGEval)* had been founded in 1997 that German standards were developed, first being published in 2001.

These standards call for validity for various evaluation approaches, different evaluation purposes and a large number of evaluation fields (DeGEval 2002). They are aimed at 'evaluators as well as individuals and organizations who commission evaluations and evaluand stakeholders' (DeGEval 2002: 12). The DeGEval (2002) sees the *objectives of the standards* as

- helping to assure and promote evaluation quality
- fostering dialogue and providing a specific frame of reference for discussing the quality of professional evaluations
- offering orientation for evaluation planning and implementation
- forming a basis for initial and continuing training in the evaluation field
- forming a basis for the evaluation of evaluations (meta-evaluation) and
- making professional practice more transparent for a wider public.

According to the DeGEval, 'good' evaluations should feature four basic attributes: utility, feasibility, propriety and accuracy. That is to say that

- the *utility standards* are intended to ensure that an evaluation is guided by both the clarified purposes of the evaluation and the information needs of its intended users
- the *feasibility standards* are intended to ensure that an evaluation is planned and conducted in a realistic, thoughtful, diplomatic and cost-effective manner
- the *propriety standards* are intended to ensure that in the course of an evaluation all stakeholders are treated with respect and fairness
- the *accuracy standards* are intended to ensure that an evaluation produces and discloses valid and useful information and findings pertaining to the evaluation questions.

In order to make these four rather abstract concepts clearer, a total of 25 individual standards were formulated. These are allocated to the four superordinate 'guiding standards'. See Table 4.2 for an overview (and www.degeval.de for more detail).

The DeGEval standards are to a large extent a translation of the American ones (cf. DeGEval 2002: 42). As far as their practical applicability goes, it should be noted that they are not of an absolutely binding nature. They rather form a basic orientation framework for determining quality aspects in the planning and conducting of evaluations, by formulating *maximum requirements*. There is no difference in weighting or priority between the four groups or between the various individual standards. Instead, the group headings compete with one another, as do the individual ones. For example, the scientific aspiration expressed in the accuracy standards can easily come into conflict with the requirement of producing useful findings (utility standards) under what are very often severe time and budget constraints (feasibility standards). At the level of individual standards for example, the standards (P2) 'Protection of individual rights' and (P5) 'Disclosure of findings' contradict each other if making the evaluation findings accessible jeopardizes the protection of individual rights (cf. Widmer 2004). In the situative context of any evaluation, the evaluator must therefore once again answer the question of which standards he is going to give priority to, and must, if necessary, document that priority. The relevance and importance of a standard can only be determined in the actual individual case.

As well as these standards, which are intended to ensure the quality of evaluations as a whole, there are guidelines that refer directly to the

Table 4.2   DeGEval standards

Utility	U1 Stakeholder identification
	U2 Clarification of the purposes of the evaluation
	U3 Evaluator credibility and competence
	U4 Information scope and selection
	U5 Transparency of values
	U6 Report comprehensiveness and clarity
	U7 Evaluation timeliness
	U8 Evaluation utilization and use
Feasibility	F1 Appropriate procedures
	F2 Diplomatic conduct
	F3 Evaluation efficiency
Propriety	P1 Formal agreement
	P2 Protection of individual rights
	P3 Complete and fair investigation
	P4 Unbiased conduct and reporting
	P5 Disclosure of findings
Accuracy	A1 Description of the evaluand
	A2 Context analysis
	A3 Described purposes and procedures
	A4 Disclosure of information sources
	A5 Valid and reliable information
	A6 Systematic data review
	A7 Analysis of qualitative and quantitative information
	A8 Justified conclusions
	A9 Meta-evaluation

behaviour of evaluators. In 1994, for example, the American Evaluation Association (AEA) issued so-called *'Guiding Principles for Evaluators'*, which are as it were a code of behaviour and comprise five guiding principles (Beywl & Widmer 2000: 282f.):

- *Systematic inquiry:* evaluators conduct systematic, data-based inquiries
- *Competence:* evaluators provide competent performance to stakeholders
- *Integrity/honesty:* evaluators display honesty and integrity in their own behaviour, and attempt to ensure the honesty and integrity of the entire evaluation process
- *Respect for people:* evaluators respect the security, dignity and self-worth of respondents, program participants, clients and other evaluation stakeholders

- *Responsibility for general and public welfare:* evaluators articulate and take into account the diversity of general and public interests and values that may be related to the evaluation.

There are, moreover, standards that refer to certain policy fields. An example is the OECD's 'DAC Principles for Evaluation of Development Assistance' (1998), which have attained a high degree of importance in the area of development cooperation (cf. http://www.oecd.org/dataoecd/63/50/2065863.pdf). These standards were drawn up by the 'expert group on aid evaluation' of the OECD'S 'Development Assistance Committee', founded in 1988, and first issued in 1991. The DAC principles draw attention to eight main points:

- impartiality and independence
- credibility
- usefulness
- participation of donors and recipients
- donor cooperation
- evaluation programming
- design and implementation of evaluations
- reporting, dissemination and feedback.

All the DAC member states have committed themselves to adhering to these principles, which were reviewed in 1998 (cf. OECD 1998).[3]

It is obvious that the existence of standards is at best a necessary but by no means sufficient requirement for ensuring evaluation quality. For this, it would not only be necessary for the standards to be known to all the actors (or at least the clients and contractors) and evaluations to be aligned and assessed in accordance with those standards, but also for the standards to be of a binding nature anyway. Yet so far, these conditions are hardly fulfilled in the German-speaking areas. A current investigation of the standard of professionalization of evaluation in Germany comes to the conclusion that the standards in the German-speaking areas have a degree of utilization which can be assumed to be rather low (cf. Brandt 2008: 120). Moreover, the DeGEval (2004: 12) points out expressly that the standards it has issued avoid 'laying any binding foundations for accrediting and certifying individuals and organizations offering or conducting evaluations, or for further training in this sphere'.

The standards of the JCS (2006) are much more binding than the German ones. This can in significant measure be explained by the fact that the American standards came about as the result of a lengthy development process supported by a broad base of institutional actors, whilst the DeGEval standards are the result of a working-group within the DeGEval – a result moreover which, when all is said and done, amounted to little more than a translation of the American standards.[4]

Also in contrast to the American evaluation scene, there is in the German-language areas hardly any empirical information in the form of meta-evaluations or other studies from which sound statements could be made about the quality of evaluations (cf. Brandt 2008: 89). Apart from the pioneering work on the subject of meta-evaluation by Thomas Widmer (1996), few fields of practice have been investigated so far (cf. for example Stockmann & Caspari 1998 on the field of development cooperation, and Becher & Kuhlmann 1995 on that of research and technology policy).

It should thus be noted that the usefulness of evaluations depends to a large extent on their quality. All the more astonishing that there have so far been so few meta-evaluations in the German-language areas that investigate this. Efforts to define and develop the quality of evaluation by means of standards are only in their early stages in the German-language areas. The standards issued by the German Evaluation Society (DeGEval) are neither binding to any great extent nor widely circulated (cf. Brandt 2009: 172).

4.5   The CEval participant-oriented evaluation approach

To increase the quality, utility and feasibility of evaluations and ensure a fair investigation (cf. the DeGEval standards in Figure 4.2), a participant-oriented procedure offers numerous advantages. This will be demonstrated by taking the example of the CEval participant-oriented evaluation approach, which has continued to develop systematically in the past 15 years and has proved itself in dozens of studies.

This approach starts from the premise that the involvement of the various stakeholders already leads in the planning phase to a higher degree of acceptance and greater support. This not only ensures that different perspectives and points of view are incorporated in the conception of the evaluation, but also that valuable accumulated knowledge of the various actors can be put to use – for example information on which of the actors are to be interviewed, possibilities for forming control groups, availability of addresses and data etc.

If evaluation is organized as an *interactive process*, which leads to an intensive *dialogue* between the evaluators and the people and institutions involved in it, it is not simply that the various different interests, values and needs of the stakeholders be determined and their knowledge and experience used in the development of the design: acceptance of the evaluation can also be increased as a 'climate of trust' is created. The chance also increases that the evaluation's findings will subsequently be ploughed into development processes, since the stakeholders do not perceive the evaluators as external 'inspectors', but as partners with complementary functions. While the evaluators contribute their *expert knowledge,* the stakeholders provide their *specialized concrete knowledge of the actual situation.*

In view of the fact that a valid assessment of measures and events by the evaluators is often only possible on the basis of the voluntary, proactive cooperation of all those involved, the validity of evaluation findings can be improved by a participant-oriented design.

The *CEval participant-oriented evaluation approach* presented here is oriented toward the critical-rational research model first introduced in Chapter 2 and follows the development schema shown in Figure 4.1. Having said that, it should be noted that the so-called 'research phases' (cf. Figure 4.2) are not identical to the work phases of an evaluation.

The *(I) discovery context* comprises the identification of the evaluand (what is to be evaluated?), the stipulation of the evaluation objectives (what purpose is the evaluation to serve?) and assessment criteria, and the decision as to who (internal or external) is to conduct the evaluation. This process is as a rule determined to a significant extent by the client. In a participant-oriented procedure, however, it is not only the evaluators who are actively involved, but also the evaluees and the various other stakeholders (target groups, participants etc.). Not only are these questions cleared up jointly in such an interaction process; it is also possible to make sure that the views of disadvantaged stakeholder groups receive due attention.

The elaboration of the investigation's hypotheses, the investigative design and the survey methods are part of the research context (II) and are primarily the tasks of the evaluators. Nevertheless, it is important to incorporate the situational knowledge of the evaluees and other stakeholders actively, in order to develop instruments appropriate to the situative context. This applies especially when evaluations are conducted in other socio-cultural contexts. Moreover, a procedure of this kind, agreed with the stakeholders, is open to continual adaptation of the evaluation instruments used, making it possible to react flexibly to changes in contextual conditions in the evaluation process.

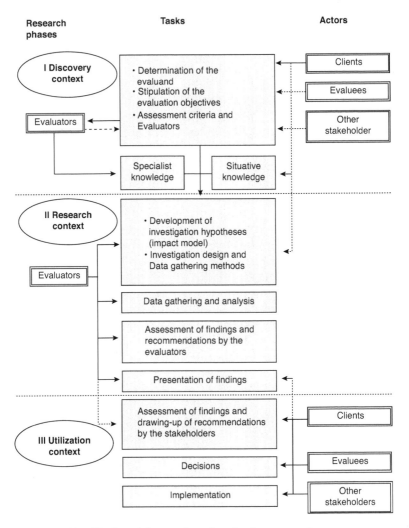

Figure 4.2   The CEval participant-oriented evaluation approach

If evaluators and stakeholders work together closely, this increases their chances of developing hypotheses that are suitable for explaining 'reality' and developing the best possible design and adequate survey methods for the empirical recording of that 'reality'. Having said that, it is the evaluator assigned to conduct the evaluation who bears final responsibility for this.

In *data gathering and analysis* the evaluees above all are important as bearers of information who represent different perspectives and points of view, and these need to be collated in an evaluation in order to obtain as 'objective' a picture as possible of the processes, structures and impacts. For this, as broad a mixture of methods as possible is used for data gathering, whilst the range of procedures familiar from the field of social inquiry is used for data analysis (cf. Sections 5.3 and 5.4 for more details). With information on the progress of the evaluation being disseminated continually, and by means of 'interim' workshops, the integration of the stakeholders can be ensured. But gathering and analysing the data are the tasks of the evaluators, who have the appropriate expert knowledge. Writing the evaluation report and presenting the findings are also the duties of the professional experts.

However, the transition to the *utilization context* (III) of the evaluation can also be organized differently, with the findings being assessed and the recommendations elaborated jointly by the stakeholders depending on the degree of participation desired. In this case, the findings, conclusions and the recommendations derived from them are not merely presented to the client and, if appropriate, to other stakeholders in a workshop, but jointly elaborated first. Now the evaluator limits his role to that of a moderator, presenting the findings from the evaluation and leaving their assessment to the clients and/ or stakeholders.

Whatever the case, the *decision* as to which recommendations are to be implemented finally lies with the client who, in turn, – depending on the degree of participation – can either integrate the affected parties in that decision or not. The management and the affected parties are usually responsible for the *implementation*. The evaluators play only a subordinate role in the *utilization context*. They are as a rule not involved in decisions or their implementation. At most, they may be given the task of observing the progress made in implementation by establishing a monitoring and evaluation system and passing on the information obtained, assessments and recommendations to the management for forthcoming management decisions.

In the approached developed here, *participant-oriented involvement* in an evaluation is concentrated mainly on the *discovery and utilization contexts*. The objectives of an evaluation, the assessment criteria and to a certain degree (as long as the scientific nature of the design is not impaired) the procedure can be determined in a participant-oriented way and then form the specifications for the evaluation. The collection and analysis of information in an empirical-scientific procedure, by contrast, are the tasks of the evaluators alone. The findings can – depending on the degree of participation desired – be *assessed* together with the clients and the various stakeholders. In external evaluations, the *utilization* of the findings and their implementation into activities is exclusively the responsibility of the clients and/or other stakeholders. Other than in quality management systems, the evaluator is, especially if he or she has been recruited externally, not part of the implementation process.

However, it must be emphasized that it is hardly likely to be possible in an evaluation project to do justice to all conceivable interest perspectives or involve all the stakeholders in the process. Particularly *non-organized interests,* such as are often the case with disadvantaged sections of the population, are at risk of not being sufficiently represented. Apropos representation, there is also the problem of who is legitimized to represent the interests of certain groups or at least entitled to articulate the majority opinion of those affected. Such representatives cannot always be found. In this case the suggestion – which comes from 'empowerment evaluation' and 'emancipatory evaluation' – that evaluator sshould represent the interests of disadvantaged parties themseleves, does not help much either. Such a procedure would require evaluators to be familiar with the actual needs and requirements of the disadvantaged sections of the population who were not represented (cf. Mertens 2004: 45ff.; Lee 2004: 135ff.).

To sum up, it should be noted that the *participant-oriented model* developed here is intended to contribute to

- taking into account the interests and perspectives of the various different stakeholders when stipulating the evaluation objectives and assessment criteria
- using their situational knowledge and experience for the development of evaluation design and the selection of the survey methods, in order to develop a set of instruments which does as much justice to the context as possible
- increasing acceptance for the evaluation and its findings among the various stakeholders and
- ensuring the usefulness of the evaluation by having those affected implement the recommendations derived from the insights gained in action.

Notes

1. The Logical Framework approach can be used to structure the programme objectives (intended impacts) and the measures taken to achieve them (interventions) (cf. Section 3.5.3).
2. Beywl (1988: 112ff.) was an early exception.
3. Another set of rules has for example been posted by the United Nations Evaluation Group (UNEG). The 'Standards for Evaluation in the UN System' (2005) are divided into four overriding categories: (1) Institutional Framework and Management of the Evaluation Function, (2) Competencies and Ethics, (3) Conducting Evaluations, (4) Evaluation Reports. At European level, the EU has set standards in the area of structural policy. Cf. for example Evaluation Standards and Good Practice (2003). The current version can be found at http://ec.europa.eu/budget/sound_fin_mgt /eval_framework_En.htm (March 2009). A comparison with the 'standards for quality assurance in market research and social inquiry' (www.adm-ev.de) is also of interest.
4. Comparison with the transformation table in the DeGEval standards booklet (2004: 42) makes this abundantly clear.

5
Gathering and Assessing Information

Wolfgang Meyer

5.1 Introduction

The quality of an evaluation depends to a great extent on the provision of information that is exact and adequate for answering the evaluation question. More than a third of the DeGEval standards relate to accuracy and call for adherence to general scientific standards for empirical data collections and analyses.[1]

This underlines the fact that the scientific ambition of evaluations is revealed most clearly in gathering and assessing information. As already explained in Chapter 2, it is primarily the survey and analysis methods used that distinguish a scientific evaluation from an everyday assessment.

First, it should be noted that with regard to the designs and procedures used for procuring and analysing information, scientifically conducted evaluations resemble fundamental social science research to a considerable degree and, as applied social research, have recourse to the procedures recognized in that field and the methodological insights gained in their application.

There are however restrictions that have to do with the special features of evaluation research. An attempt will be made in the section that follows to illustrate the difference between fundamental research and evaluation in terms of gathering and assessing information.

This is done in four chronological steps, which generally reconstruct the process of gathering and assessing information and have already been referred to in Chapter 4. In the *preparatory phase* (Section 5.2), the investigation design and the survey design, both necessary to high-quality information acquisition, are stipulated on the basis of field explorations. Here, procedures, sets of instruments, analysis procedures and the steps necessary for communicating the findings are selected ahead of the evaluation. Unlike purely scientific investigation designs, evaluation must come to terms to a much greater extent with existing framework conditions and take into account the wishes of clients in its conception. For these reasons, it is often necessary to come to an agreement with the client at this early stage.

The actual *data gathering phase* (Section 5.3), by contrast, largely resembles the procedure in fundamental social science research and can fall back on experience and sets of instruments that have proved useful there too. The interference factors associated with the respective survey procedures need to be taken into account and controlled by means of suitable measures. The special features of evaluation in the development of instruments and data collection are rather to be seen in the demands made on their flexibility as regards the adaptation of the design and the methods deployed.

The *analysis of the data gathered* (Section 5.4) depends to a very considerable extent on the measurement instruments used and above all on the degree of their standardization. The aim is to carry out comparative analyses, in particular on the causal impacts of interventions, by condensing and standardizing, and to draw generalizing conclusions from the individual cases investigated. If it is not so much a matter of evaluation questions as of questions relating to the monitoring of projects, the data analysis can come to focus more on the regular investigation of processes of change.

The mere presentation of empirical findings alone does not enable insights to be gained; it does not become useful to third parties until the *data* have been *interpreted* (Section 5.5). Even if there is a considerable difference here between fundamental and evaluation research on account of the need for data interpretation for target groups, it is necessary to weigh up the findings, critically reflect on one's own procedures, anticipate possible objections and weigh up the pros and cons of chosen procedures in terms of their effects on the quality of the findings in both cases. Furthermore, evaluations involve assessments – that is to say that an assessment of the quality of the evaluand must be carried out by applying rational criteria and adhering strictly to procedural rules, and the assessment must be as independent as possible of the subjective attitudes of the evaluator, the clients and the stakeholders. Here, interpretation techniques from qualitative social research or statistical investigation procedures can provide valuable assistance and at least offer some support in pondering alternative actions with regard to their impacts and impact potential. This scientific foundation of decisions – as has already been explained on several occasions – ultimately helps evaluation to redeem its utility value.

5.2   Preparation for data gathering – from investigation design to survey design

The *design of an evaluation* corresponds largely to the general *design of a research project*. It describes the evaluand, formulates the objectives and tasks, stipulates the manner in which the evaluation is to be conducted, names the people and interest groups who are to participate and determines the audiences for the presentation of the results (cf. Section 4.2.2). The special features of evaluation arise from the orientation of the evaluation process toward its application and in particular from the fact that evaluations are as a rule conducted on behalf of third parties. To a greater or lesser extent, this cut down the freedom of the researchers to make decisions and act on them, and the clients have at least a say in the main planning stages. Furthermore, communication with the clients and the exchange of information with the 'stakeholders' already need to be incorporated into the evaluation design.

A central element in the preparation phase of an evaluation is the drawing-up of the *investigative design* (cf. also Section 4.2.2). Its aim is to plan the empirical procedure by which the identified goal of the evaluation can be pursued. In impact-oriented evaluations it is particularly a matter of realizing the ambition introduced in Section 2.2.2, filtering out the effects of other factors (including interference factors, design effects and measurement errors) from the 'gross outcomes' observed and thus extracting 'net effects' that were actually caused by the interventions (cf. Figure 2.1).

The investigative design governs the necessary steps in data gathering, data processing, data analysis and data interpretation, the deployment of survey and analysis instruments, the selection criteria and modes of drawing samples, the definition of control and / or comparison groups, the creation of framework conditions for obtaining and analysing information, communication of the findings from the evaluators to the clients, target groups, involved parties and other interest groups and deployment of resources during the entire course of the empirical investigation.

Such an investigative design includes a *survey design* of its own for each process of obtaining information that is to be carried out during the evaluation. This data gathering design depends on the survey methods and instruments selected, the methodological problems directly associated with those procedures and instruments, and various different situative factors that come about because of how the group of information bearers is made up, their relationship to the clients of the evaluation and to the evaluators, their availability, the place of implementation and other framework conditions which influence the survey process.

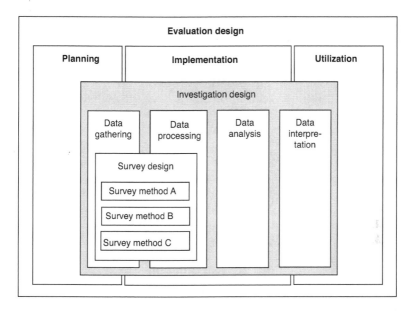

Figure 5.1   Association of various different design forms

The evaluation and investigative design and the various data gathering procedures are *closely linked to one another in an evaluation process* (see Figure 5.1). The quality of the individual findings is ensured by the survey design, and those findings are then brought together in an investigative design, in order to compensate for the weaknesses of individual methods and instruments, shed light on the evaluand from various different angles and answer the evaluation questions as precisely as possible. Finally, the evaluation design incorporates this empirical process into the overall context and also governs communication with the client, the deployment of resources for the various evaluation tasks, the chronological sequence of the evaluation measures, the quality management of the evaluation process, the steps toward the dissemination and utilization of the evaluation findings and all the other tasks of the evaluation that are not directly associated with gaining information (cf. Chapter 4 for more detail).

Because of the central significance of the empirical findings in an evaluation, the survey design is of special importance. With the aid of the findings the intention is to enable rational decisions to be made on the awarding of funding, the core areas of the programme to be assessed or programme control in general. One important prerequisite is thus the *accuracy of the findings (validity)*, which should be as independent as possible of the individual opinions of those involved and those of the evaluators and must not be falsified by special framework conditions either. This applies especially to *impact-oriented evaluations*, which concern themselves with investigating the effects of a social intervention (see for example Caspari & Barbu 2008; CDG 2006; Egger & Lenz 2006; World Bank 2006; Stockmann 2000 on the term 'impact-oriented evaluation'; see also Section 2.2.2).

Evaluation research can have recourse to a number of alternatives for shaping the survey process, and these have proved themselves in fundamental research applications. What these *research designs* have in common is the attempt to eliminate confounding variables, i.e. conscious or unconscious manipulation and influences of framework conditions by means of technical procedures, or at least control of their effects. At this juncture, a systematic list of all the alternatives (cf. the overview in Stockmann 2008: 210) will be forgone; instead, just three central procedures relating to impact investigations and their applicability in evaluation research will be looked at more closely.[2]

As perceived by the public, it is certainly the procedure of experimental intervention research that is most strongly associated with the idea of a scientific research design. These are primarily *laboratory experiments,* which were developed from the natural sciences, but also from social psychology and other sub-fields of social science, and still dominate research practice in these areas (see for example Zimmermann 2006; Kleppmann 2006; Huber 2005; Klauer 2005; Diamond 2001; Graßhoff et al. 2000 on experimental research in the social sciences.) The basic principles of the *field experiments* that are more relevant to evaluation research and that use real action situations instead of an artificially created laboratory environment, will now be explained, taking the example of the most sophisticated experimental design. This will be challenged with regard to its use in the context of evaluations (Section 5.2.1).

The two other research designs came about following criticism of the classical experimental procedure. These are the pragmatic form of 'quasi-experimental designs' (Section 5.2.2), and 'qualitative designs', which follow a different research logic (Section 5.2.3).

5.2.1   Experimental procedure

In general, the examination of a *causal connection* is central in an experiment, and an *effect hypothesis* is thus required – in other words an assumption about the linking of one or more causes to an effect, which is to be tested in the experiment (cf. in particular Graßhoff et al. 2000: 71ff. on the concept of tests of causal hypotheses in experiments). The aim is to control the effects of interference factors by means of multiple comparative measurements on different test groups (cf. for example Meyer 2011a: 136ff.; Bortz & Döring 2002:539f.; Schnell et al. 2008: 224ff. for descriptions of procedures in experiments). The cause-and-effect link in which the experimenters are interested is thus isolated and can be assessed with regard to its strength. The information obtained during an experiment serves this purpose exclusively, which is to say that the data collections (and therefore also the survey designs) become subordinate to the research objective of examining a causal connection. (See Table 5.1 as an example of the way an experiment is set up.)[3]

A further characteristic of the experimental procedure is the *control of the survey situation* by the researcher, who puts together experimental groups according to principles of randomness *('randomization')* and creates stimuli in those groups via purposive intervention (or indeed non-intervention), with the stimuli being intended to trigger measurable effects in accordance with the effect hypothesis. An essential element of the experiment is thus the *random selection* of the subjects. It is important that each person have a calculable (and thus predictable) probability of being selected for the defined test groups.

A further requirement, which is, for example, not normally imposed in socio-psychological experiments, is that of *representativeness;* that is to say that the persons selected should represent a statistical population and thus ensure the transposition of the results to the members of that population (see also Section 5.4.3). Again, random selection takes effect as the central element, whereby it is not now a matter of allocation to

Table 5.1 Experimental procedure (Solomon four-group design) Experimental groups: groups 1 and 3; control groups: groups 2 and 4

	Point in time t1	Point in time t2	Point in time t3
Group 1	Measurement prior to intervention	Intervention	Measurement after completion of intervention
Group 2	Measurement prior to intervention		Measurement after completion of intervention
Group 3		Intervention	Measurement after completion of intervention
Group 4			Measurement after completion of intervention

Source: Meyer (2011a: 138).

test groups but of *drawing the sample*. Especially in large-scale representative surveys, multi-layered selection procedures are used, being intended not only to simplify the sample-drawing process but also to prevent random overemphasis of certain aspects (e.g. regional distribution) (see Haarmann et al. 2006; ADM and AGMA 1999; Althoff 1993 on practices at the opinion research institutes). The two requirements – random allocation to groups and representative selection from a statistical population – can of course also be combined (cf. Gabler & Häder 2006; Merkens 2003; Böltken 1976 for an overview of selection procedures and the drawing of samples).

In the context of evaluations, for methodological and ethical reasons, the high standards of an experimental design can at best be fulfilled to a modest extent, since evaluations, as field studies of socio-political interventions, offer only limited opportunities for manipulation (cf. Lipsey & Cordrey 2000 on the problems of implementing experimental designs in evaluations). One of the first limitations arises from the fact that usually *the evaluation team is only involved for a limited period of time:* whilst in fundamental research the participation of the research team in the entire investigation process is more or less in the nature of things, this only applies to evaluations infrequently (for example in accompanying research or 'ongoing' evaluations). Mostly, the interventions are planned, developed and implemented by third parties without the involvement of the evaluators (and often without even taking their interests into account even potentially). In the conception of the survey design, evaluations are faced with the problem of having to come to terms with the existing framework conditions, only being able to gather information within a (brief) period of time and at best having baseline data at their disposal that are hard to compare.

The fact that evaluations have to be carried out within a certain period of time prevents comparative *before-and-after measurements* from being made that would be of major importance to an experimental design and thus also for examining cause-and-effect relationships. Even if it is not possible to replicate a baseline study (measurement prior to intervention) carried out in the context of project investigations, feasibility studies or ex-ante evaluations, either because there has been no such study or for methodological reasons, it is still possible, as a last resort, to have recourse to matching procedures[4] (cf. Gangl & DiPrete 2006). In 'propensity score matching', for example, a similarity index is generated in an allocation model, and this index reflects a person's conditional probability of being exposed to the impacts of a causal effect (cf. Rosenbaum & Rubin 1983, 1985). Examples of the use of propensity score matching in evaluations can mainly be found in econometric studies by major international providers of development policy (e.g. Augsburg 2006; Shapiro & Trevino 2004; Chen & Ravallion 2003) and in job-market research (e.g. Pessoa e Costa 2007; Bryson et al. 2002; Jaenichen 2002; Lechner 2002; Heckman et al. 1997).

Even if the team of evaluators is given plenty of room for the design, *ethical boundaries* often appear much sooner than in fundamental research (see for example Manski 1995 on the general problems of conducting experiments in the social sciences; see for example Fitzpatrick & Morris 1999 on ethical questions in evaluation research; see for example Panter & Sterba 2011 on ethical issues by using quantitative methodology). In some cases the target groups are legally entitled to the outputs of an intervention programme and it is therefore not possible to form experimental and control groups on a random basis. In clinical pharmacological research, indeed, allocation to an experimental or control group in evaluating the impacts of new medication can be a matter of life and death! This renders extremely strict requirements and controls necessary for investigation and survey designs and these can lead to the premature curtailment of the study (cf. the ICH Guidelines on these requirements, especially ICH 1997).

Generally, the *randomization* of the test groups is the problem in these cases, which is to say that even if random allocation to experimental and control groups were still technically possible in principle, it is not actually feasible on account of social and political constraints. Matching procedures only help here to a certain extent, as selection is as a rule made systematically or perhaps even because all the members of the target group have exercised their right to participate (see Titus 2007; Agodini & Dynarski 2004; Heckman et al. 1996 on the effects of 'propensity score matching' on such a 'selection bias'). It is only extremely seldom that the evaluators have an influence on the decision made during the course of the project or programme as to who may participate in a measure and who may not. Random variations are mostly excluded in the conception of the interventions. At best, in computer simulations or by means of role-playing based on certain framework assumptions, the impacts of an intervention within the experimental group can be compared with a randomly selected control group which simulates the behaviour of that experimental group (for examples see De Zeeuw 2008; Sun & Williamson 2005; De Zeeuw & van der Ploeg 1991; Rohrbach et al. 1987).

Only some of the problems in the implementation of experimental designs have been addressed here, problems which, mostly for pragmatic reasons, can lead to reduced forms (e.g. as pretest/post-test investigations). As a result, 'quasi-experimental' designs have been able to establish themselves alongside the experiment as a group of procedures in their own right. They dispense with some of the latter's strict methodological aspirations, though they are in principle oriented toward its rules of implementation and are not basically different.

5.2.2   Quasi-experimental procedures

The borders with 'quasi-experimental design' have been crossed, at the latest, when instead of there being randomized allocation to control groups the subjects are allocated consciously by the researchers (or any other person) with reference to selected features (or just by chance during a natual development process). (See Greenstone & Gayer 2007; Shadish et al. 2002; Porter & Chibucos 1975; Campbell & Stanley 1963 for the difference between experimental and quasi-experimental designs.) In these cases, the groups are referred to as *'comparison groups'* instead of 'control groups' (cf. Caspari & Barbu 2008). The design of comparison groups calls for selection criteria that make it possible to allocate the subjects unambiguously and avoid self-selection effects.[5] (See Cuppen 2012; Koeber 2005; Spermann & Strotmann 2005; Agha 2002 for examples of quasi-experimental designs in evaluations.)

Ideal-typically, what is striven toward in the design of comparison groups is perfect allocation with the aid of a single, defined dichotomous feature in distribution conditions that are as similar as possible in all other respects and as random as possible. For example, when a group of men is compared with a group of women, this implies the supposition that the variable 'sex' contributes to a differentiation of the effects and that all other features that may perhaps be relevant (e.g. educational background) are distributed more or less similarly in both groups. Only when this is true, and only when the other effects of correlating variables are not superimposed on the feature that links the members of the respective groups (in this case the subjects' sex), will the comparison between the groups provide information about the causal relationship with the measured impacts.[6] In accordance with the effect hypotheses, however, it is possible to use as many distinguishing features as one likes for forming groups (and also for further differentiating between them) and to carry out hypothesis tests in this way via cross-tabulation analyses. However, this makes it necessary to have a much greater number of subjects.

This procedure resembles the (secondary) analysis of cross-sectional data obtained for example from (representative) surveys. (See Glynn et al. 2012; de Vaus 2005; Groves et al. 2002; Peyrot 1996; Biemer et al. 1991; Belson 1986 and others on the *survey method* and its problems.) If interval control variables can be introduced into a multivariate (regression) model instead of grouped data, additional information on the strength of the effects can be obtained in the analysis (see Section 5.4).

Having said that, the necessary statistical prerequisites that need to be fulfilled by such a model include a sufficient number of subjects, with that number increasing sharply with the number of variables. In spite of these constraints, however, the design of causal models on the basis of survey data has established itself as the *'route du roi'* of social science research and, at least in sociology and the political sciences, superseded the experiment in the investigation of impacts.

Representative surveys are used in evaluations too, though it is rare for the population as a whole to be the same as the statistical population. More often, they are limited to certain *target groups* who are supposed to benefit from the project or programme interventions. These interventions are intended to trigger certain expected impacts in the target groups in the framework of the effect hypothesis. A comparison between programme participants and non-participants is intended to provide information on the correctness of this assumption, whereby representative surveys are used for large groups. For example, graduates from a study course are questioned in a survey and comparisons made in the analyses between beneficiaries of a sponsorship scheme and graduates who were not sponsored.

Difficulties often arise in determining the *'risk population'*, i.e. those who may potentially have been exposed to the impacts of a project or programme from the beginning or who actually had the chance of participating anyway. Only if the risk probabilities are known (or can for example be estimated via propensity score matching) can a test be carried out on the differences between groups by means of statistical analysis procedures in a form comparable with experimental design. If it is not possible to determine the risk population or probability values, recourse must be had to other group-forming criteria to determine the comparison groups. An alternative, for example, is to form *extreme groups,* i.e. the results gathered from participants in a programme are compared with the findings from persons of whom it is certain that they were not able to take part.

However, as mentioned above, on account of the lack of randomization, the possibility cannot be excluded that systematic factors other than participation in the programme might explain the measured effects (or non-effects) of the intervention. In methodological terms, a *'theory of error'* is now required: in other words it is now necessary to set up and test alternative effect hypotheses, assuming that it is *not* the intervention that is the cause, but other features unevenly distributed in the test groups. These assumptions too require a theoretical foundation and must at least provide plausible evidence of the alternative causal connection asserted. Whilst selection errors are mathematically controllable with a random selection based on the central axioms of test statistics

Table 5.2   Quasi-experimental multi-group design

Experimental group	Pupils with above-average school performance
Comparison group 1	Other pupils from the same class
Comparison group 2	Pupils with above-average school performance from a parallel class
Comparison group 3	Pupils with above-average school performance from another school

Source: Meyer (2011a: 141).

(cf. Cuddeback et al. 2004), some additional assumptions about the *'selection errors'* are required for a conscious selection. One possibility for controlling these effects is the parallel use of several comparison groups, with different criteria and constructed independently of one another, in a *quasi-experimental multi-group design* (cf. Table 5.2).

The figure shows an example with several potential comparison groups and one experimental group. Funding measures were aimed especially at supporting elite pupils, which meant that not all the pupils in the class in question were intended to benefit from them. The experimental group thus contained part of a school class, whereby its performance could now be compared with that of the remainder of the class (comparison group 1). The problem in such a performance comparison is that there was already a difference between the two groups before the intervention in terms of the comparative feature of school performance, and there is good reason to assume that the further changes in performance now observed have in part been influenced strongly by prior performance. For this reason, a further comparison with elite pupils from another class is a good idea, since they, similarly to the experimental group, produced above-average performances prior to the beginning of the interventions, but have not benefited from the project measures (comparison group 2). However, reduction to the comparison of this group with the experimental group is fraught, since the two groups have been in different classes with different teachers, which means that differences in performance development may have come about for this reason too. This class effect, and the effect of prior performance, can be controlled by combining all three groups. However, if it is also assumed that there may be a diffusion effect on the entire school on account of the implementation of the measures, a further comparison group is required, containing pupils from another school (comparison group 3).

In the example in the figure, not only the effects of prior performance but also the school and class effects can be controlled and thus excluded as explanations of impacts in their own right. With an increasing number of groups, the probability of an evenly distributed distortion of the results in all the groups formed decreases; on the other hand, the cost and effort involved in the survey increase. (In our example, extra data have to be gathered in other classes and other schools.) In principle, this procedure – and thus the number of groups – can be extended at will, and this is necessary if there are appropriate indications about additional interference factors that need to be controlled.

5.2.3 Qualitative procedure

The survey procedures introduced thus far are all based on the fundamental philosophy of 'quantitative' social research, which is in turn based on the theory-of-science basis of critical rationalism (cf. Popper 2005; Albert & Topitsch 1990) and the methodologies derived from the natural sciences (cf. Hempel 1974) (cf. also Section 2.2.6). For many years, however, an alternative understanding of science has been opposed to this natural scientific one, one which focuses more strongly on the individual case and on verstehen of correlations[7] than on 'explaining' them. Partly in fierce criticism of the 'quantitative' mainstream of social science research, a 'qualitative' methodology has developed which meanwhile comprises an equally broad spectrum of procedures (see Flick 2005 for an overview of qualitative social research).

Qualitative social research does not view the experiment as the ideal case to be striven toward in a survey design, but rejects it on account of its artificiality and estrangement from the real social situation (cf. for example Cicourel 1974). The research process is generated as a learning loop and intended, via various in-depth individual case analyses, to help understand real social processes in their natural environment (cf. Figure 5.2). Ideal-typically, this means in qualitative social research that the survey procedure is very much oriented toward the circumstances of the individual case as found and attempts to minimize intervention on the part of the research process. It is not the control of interference factors but the maintenance of 'naturalness' which is to the fore in methodological quality assurance (cf. Miles & Huberman 2007; Helffrich 2005; Seale et al. 2000 and others on the methodological standards of qualitative social research; see in particular Gschwend & Schimmelfennig 2007; Creswell 2012, 2009; Marshall & Rossman 2006; Maxwell 2005; King et al. 1994 on qualitative research designs).

Flick (2002: 68ff.) emphasizes in particular the 'circularity' of the cognitive process[8] in qualitative social research in a *comparison with the procedure of classical quantifying social research*. On account of its orientation toward the individual case, however, findings from qualitative social research can only be replicated with great difficulty.

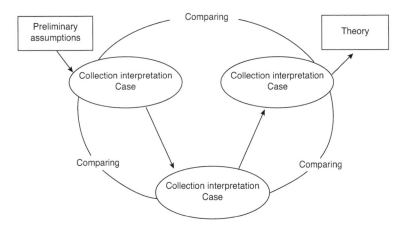

Figure 5.2   Process model of qualitative investigation design
Source: Flick (2002: 73), slightly modified.

Whilst quantitative social research seeks to underpin the existing body of knowledge in this way by failed attempts at refutation, qualitative social research seeks to broaden our perspective by integrating as many individual findings and different interpretations as possible, which can, at the end, be condensed into a generalizable theoretical concept.

Evaluation research distinguishes itself notably by requiring *the two perspectives* to be *combined*. On the one hand, of course, evaluation clients want facts that are as 'hard' as possible and proof of the way the interventions they have introduced have taken effect. On the other, these are mostly innovations, about the effectiveness of which, at least in the actual context of implementation, little is known. Only rarely are there any clearly formulated, verifiable 'programme theories' that can be empirically tested by means of evaluation (cf. Sections 3.3.1 and 4.3). On the contrary, it is in most cases one of the tasks of evaluation to first identify the various potential impact factors by means of exploration, and then, in a second step, to prove their relevance by means of test procedures.

Logically, *mixed-methods approaches* dominate the investigation designs in evaluation; in other words attempts are made to unite the aspirations of qualitative social research with those of the quantitative approach. This has not only the abovementioned advantage of being able to cater to different ambitions that clients might have, but also the methodologically important merit of being able to balance out the weaknesses of individual survey procedures.[9]

Nevertheless, the investigative designs of evaluations not only distinguish themselves by combining different survey methods and corresponding procedures, but also have special features that primarily serve the purpose of *field exploration*. In design-technical terms, the aspirations resulting from this have so far been realized most consistently by Bamberger et al. (2006). Their 'RealWorld' approach sees evaluation as a participant-oriented process, whereby the methodological contribution of experts is primarily made ahead of actual data gathering. The evaluation design envisages the exploration of four main constraints on information acquisition (cf. Figure 5.3). The data should then actually be gathered by the partners independently in situ, i.e. the 'RealWorld' approach is more of an (evaluation) methods consultancy approach for internal evaluations than a procedure for an independently conducted external evaluation in its own right.

The first of the constraints to be investigated relates to the *financial framework conditions* with the aim of ensuring the most efficient acquisition of information possible and precisely determining the minimum necessary survey requirements for an adequate assessment. Often closely associated with the finances is the *time budget available*, which on the one hand depends on the availability of the experts, interviewees and assistants necessary for carrying out the survey, but is on the other hand pre-structured by external factors such as the dates of important project decisions. It is not until the time and budget resources have been taken into account that it is possible to begin actually planning the gathering of the data. For this, the existing *data situation* must be looked at, as must the field conditions that restrict the implementation of individual survey procedures. The result of this step is a rough draft of the investigative design, which cites various information sources and describes the procedure of how to tap them while taking into account the given budget and time resources. The final step attempts to anticipate *possible communication problems* and in particular to eliminate potential opportunities for manipulation by individual stakeholder groups. As well as ensuring that the data collection is methodologically sound, the timely participant-oriented involvement of all stakeholder groups on an equal footing in the process of obtaining the information is very important (see Section 6.4).

To sum up, it should be noted at this point that in social science research a large number of different investigative designs and procedures have been developed for data gathering, and that for most of them a certain amount of experience has now been obtained as regards sources of error and interference factors.[10] The possibility of their being applied in evaluation studies depends on a number of different factors, which,

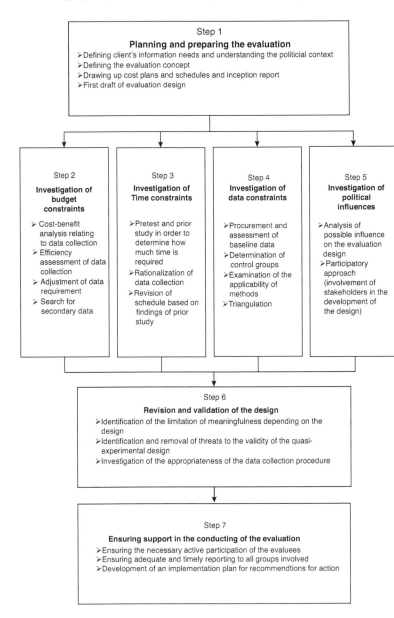

Figure 5.3 Evaluation designs of the 'RealWorld evaluation' approach

even more so than in fundamental research, are beyond the influence of the researchers. Typically, there are special constraints with regard to the amount of time available, the information and data already available, and the requirements of accountability toward third parties (in particular as they relate to obtaining information and the utilization context), and the financial resources made available for the research process. There are also various attempts at manipulation that must be guarded against. The investigative designs in evaluation research are thus distinguished on the one hand by considerably higher costs of field exploration prior to data gathering, and on the other by a more consistent implementation of multi-methods approaches to compensate for the methodological weaknesses in individual procedures.

For this reason, obtaining information in evaluations resembles in many respects the work of detectives, who must avail themselves of as broad an information base as possible and are – sometimes even in the face of determined resistance on the part of the evaluees – committed to obtaining an objective overall picture. In some cases it is necessary to provide multiple support for weak evidence in order not to end up foundering in a marsh of speculative statement and supposition. This means that evaluations (just like criminological investigations) must under no circumstances lose sight of that which is scientific. In contrast to the situation in fundamental research, however, weak evidence and suppositions are, to a certain extent, certainly useful for the practical utilization of the findings, even if evidence underpinned with facts is definitely preferable to a chain of clues, as the latter, however logical it may appear, is not proof.

5.3   Data gathering – from the planning of methods deployment to quality control

Even if there are, with regard to the procedure of obtaining information, some parallels with detective work, this does certainly not mean that evaluations are conducted without a plan and purely intuitively, like the investigative work of many TV detectives. On the contrary, data gathering not only ahead of the survey phase, but also with regard to deploying the various methods, calls for careful planning and – as compared with fundamental research – much more flexibility in the implementation phase. In view of the special features of field research, which cannot without further ado determine its own survey context or change it at will, it is certainly easy to understand that a change of methods, a change of design at short notice or at least a supplementary deployment of methods that was not part of the plan at the outset may become necessary more often. Accordingly, the planning of implementation and the selection of the procedures to be deployed are often not completed in advance, as they are in fundamental research, but must be adapted during implementation to the circumstances, which sometimes undergo major change. This applies particularly to obtaining information in formative evaluations, which are as a rule in a process of dialogue with the project or programme management and therefore have a long-term influence on the course of the programme via their own findings – and thus also on the framework conditions of the evaluation.

5.3.1   Classification of data gathering processes

Similarly to the investigative designs – and of course very much dependent on them – evaluation can have recourse to a wide *variety of different procedures* when it comes to gathering data, but must respect the specific survey-technical features and the methodological problems associated with them and attempt to control them as far as possible by means of appropriate quality assurance measures. Figure 5.4 is a schematic diagram of these various different data gathering methods. It classifies methods mainly by looking at the opportunities the informant and the evaluator interested in obtaining the information have for influencing the data gathering process.

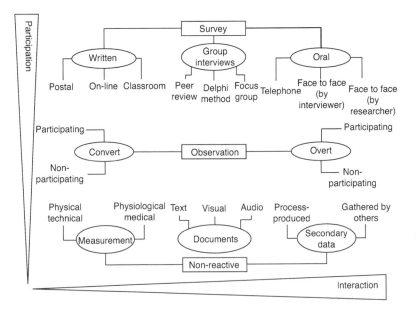

Figure 5.4   Overview of data gathering methods
Source: Meyer (2011b: 223).

In an evaluation it is a question of selectively obtaining *precisely that information which is necessary to answer the action-guiding questions agreed with the client,* by selecting the appropriate survey instruments (cf. Meyer 2011b: 221). Especially from the point of view of the efficiency of the way in which that information is obtained, it is absolutely necessary to handle the individual procedures competently and use them purposively, and to provide the financial means necessary for this. On the other hand, too little competence (or too small a budget for gathering the data) leads inevitably to losses of information or even falsifications, which devalue the information gained in an evaluation as a whole and may thus cause the latter to founder. So cutting corners at the expense of the quality with which the data are gathered is not a good idea at all.

The *quality of data gathering* is inseparably linked to the strengths and weaknesses of the survey procedure used, and there is basically no method which can guarantee that the information will be gained in an error-free way in terms of the procedure itself. The social process of information transfer from a person who is in possession of that information to a recipient is 'filtered' and consciously or unconsciously 'distorted' in one or more different directions on both sides by a complex process of perception and interpretation (cf. Schützeichel 2004 on the various different sociological communication theories; cf. also Meyer 2000 on mass communication). It is of no importance whether this *communication* mainly occurs openly, 'qualitatively', oriented toward the reality of the everyday life of the bearer of information, or 'quantitatively' via more or less well calibrated scales in (quasi-)experimental designs that are controlled as well as they possibly can be by the recipient. Errors already come about through the conscious participation of both parties in a communication process and the opportunities for manipulation afforded by this.

Be that as it may, this need not happen openly and manipulatively in a certain direction, but may transpire, unnoticed by both sides, as a result of *communication problems* such as personal sympathy or antipathy, prefabricated cognitive stereotypes or prejudices, different language skills or forms of expression, situative influences or distracting environmental factors. These effects can occur in one or both of the communication partners, distort the results in the same or different directions, and individual interference factors can cancel each other out or overlap.

Generally, *the more actively the two communication partners are involved in the communication process on data gathering and the greater the extent of their interaction in the transfer of the information, the greater the risk will be that such communication problems will occur and the transfer be flawed.* This can best be illustrated using an example. If neither the researcher nor the guinea pig knew they were participating in an experiment, neither of them would be able to influence that experiment consciously in the way they wanted. However, the specific character of an experiment is that the researcher controls its course and manipulates the experimental conditions. Errors on the part of the researcher in setting up or carrying out an experiment therefore lead to distorted results and can, in the worst case, even devalue it completely. This also applies to experiments on inanimate objects and is thus completely independent of the extent of the interaction between the two information partners: on account of researchers' errors, the history of natural science research is to some extent one of failed experiments – although those experiments did in some cases certainly lead to the gaining of important insights.

The subjects participating in an experiment are not in a position to have any influence on its course until they have also become aware of the fact of their participation and perhaps even guessed the purpose of the experiment. Only in the latter case can they actively manipulate it in a certain direction by changing their behaviour and thus influencing the results. For this too, direct interaction with the researcher (or another person) is not necessary. The *awareness* of one or both partners during an exchange of information that they are involved in such an exchange thus already represents a significant source of error.

The more intensively two people have to communicate directly with one another in order to exchange information, the greater the risk of misunderstanding or misinterpretation that may be triggered by that *interaction* – regardless of the survey design. To the extent that the acquisition of information can manage without interaction (for example in the measurement of body temperature), the source of error in gathering the data is reduced to the quality of the measuring instrument and its functionality *('instrument error')*. However, if – as in an intensive interview – there is an extensive face-to-face exchange, the errors associated with this process of obtaining information *('communication errors')* are significant and mostly have a considerably stronger influence than the instrument errors involved (though the latter also still exist). It is not until this point that the communication problems outlined above begin to take effect as interference factors in the measurement.[11]

The *three main classes of social science data gathering procedure* (survey, observation and non-reactive procedures) differ at first in the *degree to which the bearers and recipients of information actively participate* (cf. again Figure 5.4). Put more simply, both parties are already actively involved in the survey virtually by definition, since answering questions makes both the conscious process of wording the questions on the part of the recipient and that of formulating the answers on the part of the bearer absolutely necessary. This does not apply to observation, as here it is only the (observing) recipients of information who guide the survey process, the bearers being supposed to behave as 'normally' as possible – in other words as in an unobserved situation and thus passively as regards the survey process. Non-reactive procedures, finally, distinguish themselves by obtaining information in a way that is largely independent of the human element. Measurements are made using instruments, whose use is intended to elude not only the influence of the bearer, but also that of the recipient at the time when the information is obtained, thus delivering 'objective' results within the scope of the measuring capabilities of the instrument.

A second dimension of differentiation relates to the *extent of the interaction between the two information partners* and thus the communicative character of the survey process. In a *covert* survey the information is transferred in a largely independent and anonymous way. In a covert observation, for example, the person entrusted with gathering the data notes down exclusively those features that conform to a certain rule and does not communicate in any way at all with the bearers of information. (Indeed, the latter may not even know that they are being observed.) Much the same applies to physical or physiological measurements taken by means of complex auxiliary equipment without any active involvement on the part of either the bearer or the recipient of the information (as in computer tomography, for example). Even in surveys the active exchange can be reduced to the use of an instrument, if for example in postal surveys questionnaires are simply sent out and answered 'covertly' (i.e. without any further interaction with the recipients of the information).

The other end of the scale features narrative interviews, for example, the *'openness'* of the communication situation being one of the very things which distinguishes them, and which are for that reason based on an intensive interaction process between the bearer and the recipient. Even if this interaction does not take place directly between the researcher (or evaluator) and the subjects (or evaluees) (as for example in the secondary analysis of survey data gathered by other researchers in face-to-face interviews), the intensity of the interaction represents considerable potential for error, and this must be looked at more closely.

Even if qualitative social research, on account of its philosophy, does tend to rely more on interaction, whilst quantitative social research relies more on measurements independent of the human element, this does not necessarily mean that the qualitative procedure is more strongly affected by interaction problems than the quantitative one (see for example Cropley 2005; Flick 2006, 2005; Kvale 2001; Wiedemann 1986 on the specific advantages of qualitative procedures). For example, an extremely comprehensive standardized questionnaire in a personal interview can certainly lead to selection and learning processes that are similar to those in an openly conducted narrative interview. The artificiality of the interaction may perhaps even make it more susceptible to problems (for example if the respondents lose interest in the exchange more quickly, perceiving it as unilateral). The methodological problems of interaction as a source of errors are *independent of the degree of standardization* of the survey instruments.

Particularly in evaluations, compensation is made for the methodological disadvantages of manipulability through active participation and intensive communication between bearers and recipients of information by the advantages of the greater amount of information that can be obtained, the greater 'commitment' of the bearers (and thus also the increased acceptance of the survey process) and the accelerated learning process among the recipients that can be expected to result (and the improved basis for assessment this affords). By using several different survey procedures in rotation and in such a way that they complement one another ('triangulation'), it is possible within the investigation design to balance out the various strengths and weaknesses of the survey methods (cf. for example Flick 2008; Stockmann 2008, 1996). However, this does not exempt the evaluator from due diligence in the use of each individual procedure, or to design a procedure which will minimize the interference factors.

5.3.2   Interference factors and survey errors

The interference factors connected with individual survey procedures can of course only be touched on here (cf. Meyer 2011b for a more generous overview; Bryman 2008 also gives an excellent summary). There are also some comprehensive studies available in the methods literature, especially on survey methods and the various problems and sources of interference in survey techniques (cf. for example Nardi 2006; Presser et al. 2004; Groves et al. 2002; Schnell 1997; Lessler & Karlsbeek 1992; Groves 1989; Dijkstra & van der Zouwen 1982). This applies in a much more limited way to observations and non-reactive procedures, though here too the focus is on quantitative procedures strikingly often (cf. Habermehl 1992: 195ff.). Some more recent works, however, approach methods problems specifically from the angle of qualitative social research, so that recently the generally deplored gap by which this branch of methods research is said to be lagging behind has decreased considerably (cf. Helffrich 2005; Steinke 2003, 1999).

The remarks that follow are restricted to a brief overview of the main survey procedures and refer the reader to titles for further reading on implementation and the practical problems associated with it (cf. Table 5.3).

Table 5.3 Overview of the main data gathering procedures

Procedure	Description	Literature
Surveys		
Expert interviews ('guided interviews')	Guided personal interviews with mainly open questions	Bogner et al. (2005); Gläser and Laudel (2004)
Surveys ('face-to-face interviews')	Oral surveys by an interviewer with the help of a standardized questionnaire (mainly closed questions)	Nardi (2006); De Vaus (2005); Mayer (2004); Konrad (2001); Aldrige and Levine (2001)
Computer-aided telephone interviews ('CATI')	Telephone surveys by an interviewer with the aid of a computer-aided survey system (mainly closed questions)	Groves et al. (2001); Hüfken (2000); Gabler et al. (1998)
On-line surveys	Surveys via the Internet (mostly WWW, mostly closed questions) without an interviewer	Das et al. (2010); Couper and Coutts (2006); Welker et al. (2005); Johns et al. (2004); Theobald (2000); Batinic and Bosnjak (1997)
Mail surveys	Surveys by post without an interviewer (mostly closed questions)	Mayer (2004); Bourque and Fielder (2003); Konrad (2001)
'Classroom' interviews	Standardized surveys of a group gathered together in one room, assisted by an interviewer (mostly closed questions)	Gronlund (1959)
Group discussions ('focus groups')	Open but moderated discussions of prescribed questions (the interviewer being more of a moderator, the questions mainly open)	Loos and Schäffer (2006); Lamnek (2005); Stewart and William (2005); Puchta and Potter (2004); Krüger and Casey (2003); Bohnsack (2003); Morgan (2002, 1993, 1988); Bloor (2002)
Multi-loop group interviews ('peer review', 'Delphi' method)	Mixture of standardized and open group interviews with feedback loops (with and without interviewer)	Shatz (2004); Häder (2002); Häder and Häder (2000)
Observation		
Censuses	Quantitative censuses of certain features recorded using a standardized instrument by non-participatory observation (mainly by assistants)	Society for Road and Traffic Research (FGSV) (1995); Stucke (1985); Reuber and Pfaffenbach (2005: 60ff.)

(*continued*)

Table 5.3   Continued

Procedure	Description	Literature
Site visits ('social sphere analyses')	Visits to site and non-standardized recordings with the help of qualitative features (mainly by experts, partly together with subjects)	Boettner (2007); Kessl and Reutlinger (2007); Kirsch (2006, 1999); Urban and Weiser (2006); Riege and Schubert (2005); Orthmann (1999, 1996)
Participating observations	Observation of behavioural patterns in groups by a participant (mainly by researchers)	Faßnacht (2006); Joergensen (2000); Greve and Wentura (1997); Friedrich and Lüdtke (1977)
Covert investigations ('video observations', 'netnography')	Observations of behavioural patterns (mainly by a participating assistant or technical monitoring devices such as cameras), with the subjects not being informed about the observation and not noticing it	Haw and Hadfield (2010); Kozinets (2009); Ackermann et al. (2007); Ludwig (2007); Röwer (2007); Martin and Wawrinowski (2006); Glitza (2005); Ellenbogen (2004); Wallraff (1992, 1977, 1970); Hutt and Hutt (1978)

Non-reactive procedures

Procedure	Description	Literature
Conversations and discourse analyses	Qualitative analyses of conversations, their development, their functions and their linguistic details on the basis of transcriptions (often made during observations)	Hutchby and Wooffitt (2008); Ten Have (2007); Richards and Seedhouse (2006); Wooffitt (2006); Schiffrin (2005); Przyborski (2004); Fairclough (2003); Phillips and Hardy (2002); Wetherell et al. (2001); Dijk (1992); Psathas (1995)
Document analyses and qualitative content analyses	Qualitative analyses of text material with the help of non-standardized features for recording the meaning (mainly by the researchers)	Franzosi (2007); Früh (2007); Krippendorf (2007); Mayring (2007); Mayring and Gläser-Zikuda (2005); Rössler (2005); Glässer and Laudel (2004); Lissmann (2001); Merten (1995)
Computer-aided content analyses	Quantitative analyses of text material with the help of standardized features by computer	Kuckartz et al. (2007); Kuckartz (2007); Rössler (2005); Krippendorff (2004); Lissmann (2001); West (2001a, b); Bos and Tarnai (1998)

(continued)

Table 5.3   Continued

Procedure	Description	Literature
Secondary analyses	Mainly quantitative analyses of data material which is already available (often surveys or statistical data)	Bulmer et al. (2009); Dale et al. (1988); Kiecolt and Nathan (1985)
Process-produced data	Automatic recording of data during the course of the process (e.g. storage of visitors' data on websites)	Schröder (2006); Swart and Ihle (2005); Bergmann and Meier (2003); Schmähl and Fachinger (1990); Schmähl (1984); Clubb and Scheuch (1980)
Technical measurements	Automatic recording of data by technical measuring instruments	Ice and James (2006); Palm (1991); Finsterbusch et al. (1983); Laszlo and Sudlow (1983)

In general, it should be noted that the specific features of the method problems of individual survey procedures have to do with the *path of the information transfer* and the factors that influence it. The focus in the *survey* is accordingly on *question-and-answer* and most methodological works relate to the problems of how to word the questions,[12] which can to a greater or lesser extent provoke response tendencies. Quantitative and qualitative survey forms differ primarily in the pre-structuring of response options, which are intended to facilitate both the response behaviour of the bearers of information and analysis by the recipients, yet in doing so give rise to artificial survey situations[13] and conceivably to response manipulation. The survey ideal is a question that would be perfectly understood by all the respondents as intended by the researchers, and thus correctly answered. Just how difficult this aspiration is to realize can easily be understood, not only in data gathering but also in everyday life.

The focal point of methodological problems in *observations* is somewhat different. Here the crucial problem is the exact *selection* of the aspects to be observed from both a theoretical point of view (i.e. as an instruction from the recipient of information to those gathering the data) and a practical one (i.e. as a decision-making problem of the data gathered in the observation of real objects and their allocation to predetermined categories). On account of the infinite amount of information which could in principle be perceived visually during the observation process – of which it is therefore impossible to keep track – precise specifications and a high degree of concentration are absolutely necessary for the observers if they are to achieve an exact recording. (Cf. Bostrom 2002 for an overview of selection errors in observations and how to deal with them.) The selectivity of perception, for example, leads to survey errors via false allocation or wrong interpretation of the situation. Here again, there is no fundamental difference between qualitative and quantitative forms of observation.

The distinction between covert and overt observation, however, is more significant, for here *methodological aspects can come into conflict with ethical ones*. Such a covert observation prevents the results from being influenced by the bearer and by the observation process itself – cf. the classical study at the Hawthorne Works by Elton Mayo in 1951 as an example of behaviour being influenced by observation; cf. for example Habermehl (1992: 195ff.) on method problems in observations in general – but at the same time it violates the rights of personal possession of information that is laid down in data protection laws in many national contexts. With possibilities for manipulation being excluded and the validity of the findings thus improved, those being observed lose their right to 'participate' voluntarily in the investigation and may thus feel betrayed. This is a major problem, particularly in the context of evaluations, since it means that the control aspect is biased, acceptance of the evaluation process impaired and the processes of learning from the findings impeded (cf. for example Morris 2008: 80ff.).

Such ethical problems can of course also occur when a covert observation is carried out by means of technical aids (e.g. CCTV). However, it is not so much the ethical problems associated with their use that need to be emphasized as a special feature of *non-reactive procedures* as the methodological aspects associated with the *measuring instruments*. If the measurement is carried out independently by means of technical aids and without human intervention, its quality will be determined exclusively by that of the instruments used. This depends on the instrumental precision of the measurement and on external circumstances during the process of measurement.

The amount of effort involved in *calibrating and standardizing* measuring instruments is often underestimated by people without an engineering background (cf. for example Bosch & Wloka 2006; Martens & Næs 2001 on these problems from a technical point of view). No measuring instrument can measure with 100 per cent accuracy. The more precise the measurement needs to be, the greater the trouble that needs to be gone to in order to set up the measuring instruments and measure. On the other hand, in many cases it is not necessary to measure down into the decimal point range and the amount of additional information obtained by such an improvement in measurement accuracy is often small. Much as in the statistical analysis of data (see Section 5.4 for more detail), it is more a question of being familiar with the sources of error and consciously accepting a certain error tolerance (see also Meyer 2011: 201ff. on these problems).

Even when technical aids are used, the sources of error are in many cases co-determined to a considerable extent by the *framework conditions of the measurement*. If for example a thermometer is hung up in the sun instead of the shade, this will influence the measurement results and – if the measurements are carried out in quick succession – also the shape of the curve of measured values. In many cases the sources of error and interference for technical measurements are not that trivial or easy to recognize, which is why attention must be paid to the measurement conditions on the basis of a competent knowledge of how the instruments work (cf. for example Kletz 2001, Müller 1994 on these problems). Here, technical measurement procedures do not differ from social science ones: in a written survey, for example, not only is the wording of the questionnaire very important, but also the environmental conditions in which that questionnaire is answered. In the case of a postal survey the researcher hardly has any control over the latter at all.

As has already been pointed out on several occasions, measurement accuracy is not a question of *'quantitative versus qualitative'*, but depends solely on success in avoiding result distortions due to interference factors. The indisputable advantages of 'qualitative' procedures with a view to how realistic they are and the scope of the information gained are, when all is said and done, methodologically 'bought' with higher risks of result distortion, incurred through information selection on the part of the researcher and the greater number of unknown interference factors. On the other hand, the experimental setup (and the use of standardized survey instruments) in 'quantitative' procedures creates an artificial situation, in which certain information is consciously or unconsciously neglected and the connection to real (everyday) life sacrificed in favour of controlling interference factors. (Cf. Droitcour & Kovar 2008 on the various threats to validity in evaluation studies and the discussion of the pros and cons of qualitative and quantitative procedures.)

Apart from this conflict between 'internal' and 'external' validity, the fact also needs to be considered that *non-standardized survey instruments* by no means measure better than standardized ones merely on account of making fewer or less stringent specifications (and vice versa). For example, the fact that a circumstance has been queried 'openly' and the respondents thus allowed a broad spectrum of interpretation does not necessarily lead to better results than the use of 'closed' questions, which press the interviewees into a mould containing certain response options. Indeed, the 'anchor' provided by those options may be the very thing that helps the respondent to understand the questions correctly and take full account of the desired alternative answers.

Finally, qualitative and quantitative procedures differ primarily in the *different weighting of the interference factors* in the individual phases of the process of obtaining information. In the example above, the problem of anticipating the response behaviour of the respondents is postponed, from a point in time before the data are gathered (standardized survey) to the analysis phase which follows it (non-standardized survey). Whilst with the standardized survey the instrument used is a more likely source of error than with non-standardized surveys, the open interview depends more heavily on the performance of the interviewer and his or her questioning techniques (cf. Maindok 2003 on the importance of interviewer training and the sources of error associated with it). At the same time, allocating the responses to categories by providing fixed scales calls for a greater degree of abstract thinking on the part of the respondents than in a not very highly structured interview; however, those who carry out the analysis then have more freedom to interpret and that, in turn, becomes a further source of error.

Summing up, it should be noted that in general *four distinct sources of interference* need to be considered *in data gathering*. They can occur in different degrees and depend on the actual implementation conditions:

(1) The *measuring instruments*: obtaining the information calls for the use of instruments that record the objects, behavioural patterns, attitudes etc. about which information is being sought with sufficient precision for the information requirements *('validity')* and always lead to largely congruent results when the measurements are repeated under the same conditions *('reliability')*.

(2) The *framework conditions of the measurement:* the process of obtaining the information must on the one hand be as realistic as possible, i.e. must resemble the 'natural' framework conditions of the objects or people being observed, thus enabling the findings to be transposed to everyday situations *('external validity')*. On the other hand, the measurement should take place without any situative influences and not be distorted by environmental factors *('internal validity')*.

(3) The *interests of the recipients of information*: obtaining the information should satisfy the information interests of the recipient (i.e. the evaluator or client respectively) as exactly as possible *('efficiency and effectiveness of obtaining information')*. On the other hand, the results should not be falsified consciously or unconsciously by the activities of the recipients in their efforts to realize this ambition in the context of the survey process *('accuracy of*

information acquisition') since this would, in turn, violate the information interests.

(4) The *interests of the bearers of information:* people in possession of certain information should provide that information as precisely and truthfully as possible so that the evaluation can arrive at exact assessments. If the bearers have at the same time been beneficiaries of outputs provided by the evaluation's clients, there is at least a moral obligation here, for the purpose of the evaluation is to improve those outputs (*'obligation to participate'*). On the other hand, the bearers also have a right to personal security and the freedom to pass on information in a way that is agreeable to them or only selectively (e.g. to prevent it from being abused or to safeguard their own interests) (*'right to refuse to cooperate'*). It may be in the interest of the bearers of information to remain silent on circumstances they consider negative (e.g. abuse of outputs) or to exaggerate aspects they consider positive (e.g. impacts of outputs). Even without assuming that there has been any malicious manipulation by conscious or unconscious selection, the quality of the information transfer may suffer.

5.4   Data analysis – from processing to analysis

Both for the eponymous heroes of classical detective novels and in modern American television series, solving the case centres around the establishment of final proof. Such proof is furnished using (natural) scientific methods, which solidly verify an unambiguous causal connection and eliminate alternative possible explanations logically and beyond all doubt. The classical example is the fingerprint, which, on account of its proven uniqueness – no two people have completely identical fingerprints – makes it possible to allocate a causal connection without any doubt whatsoever between the image left at the scene of the crime and its creator.

What is of course seldom shown in the detective novels and television series are the *analysis processes* carried out by scientific specialists, in some cases extremely painstaking, whose job it is to compare the prints found at the scene of the crime with all the ones which have been put on file during other investigations, systematically recorded and processed for comparison as entries in criminal card files and databases of suspects. Important operations in convicting culprits such as the *processing of information into data*, the systematic comparison of similarities and differences (in other words the actual process of *'analysis'*) or the *interpretation* of the evidence obtained in a way that will withstand critical scrutiny, are skated over for dramaturgical reasons. Moreover, the role of science in fiction is restricted to arriving at *irrefutable proof* – it being, as a rule, unnecessary to calculate probabilities of error in relation to a causal connection once it has been ascertained.

Perhaps it is because of these simplifications of scientific work, circulated as they are on such a massive scale, that many people underestimate the *cost and effort* involved in this phase of gathering and obtaining information. In criminological reality, for example, the fingerprints secured by police officers are often smeared and therefore have to be reconstructed, whereby the poorer 'data quality' thus attained sometimes only makes it possible to allocate them to a given person with a certain degree of probability – even assuming that the culprit was thoughtless enough to leave behind such clearly assignable clues in the first place. Even if the prints secured in the 'survey' are of good quality, they need to be *processed* for comparison with stored data and this procedure will only be successful if the necessary comparative data have been recorded in the respective databases with sufficient quality. The comparison of fingerprints (and thus the actual 'analysis') depends of necessity on these preliminary operations which render the clues gleaned at the scene analysable.

Once information has been recorded in the survey procedures, social science research usually also has to make efforts that are not to be underestimated in order to transform that information into analysable data. Unless the information has been recorded directly electronically, it needs to be *coded* for it to be possible to use statistical analysis procedures at all. Coding enables numerical values to be allocated to the categories and transposed into formats that make it possible for them to be processed by the analysis programmes used (e.g. SAS, SPSS, STATA). Depending on the survey procedure, both the cost of this step and its susceptibility to error may vary. In qualitative procedures the *transcriptions* drawn up in the survey also need to be processed according to the analysis procedure, though it is mostly not numbers but texts which form the basis of the analyses. An interpretation that makes sense is not possible without this interim step of processing for quantitative analysis (also in the form of a 'quantification of qualitative data', e.g. in the context of a computer-aided content analysis) or a systematization and classification of the results that is not based on numbers in preparation for the use of hermeneutic analysis methods (cf. Dankmeier 2006 on coding; Richards 2006; Dittmar 2004; Auerbach & Silverstein 2003 on the handling of qualitative data).

In the social sciences, certain 'proof' cannot be expected, and, for example, in recording attitudes and opinions based on polls, *stochastics* is an inevitable (though extremely useful) companion. Evaluation research too can only rely on solid insights in exceptional cases, especially when it is a matter of linking causes and effects – i.e. a question of whether or not a

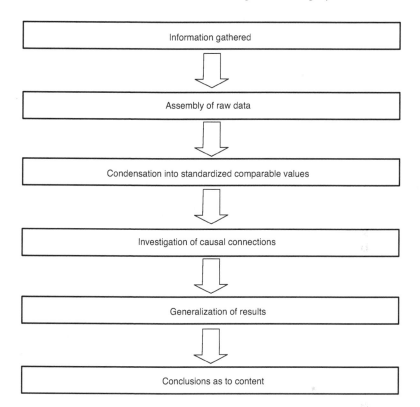

Figure 5.5 General process of data analysis

given intervention has been able to bring about the effects desired by those involved in the programme without causing too many results that are undesired and run counter to the objectives (cf. Section 2.2.2). The task of data analysis, the core of obtaining information in an empirical procedure, is to come up with robust proof of suppositions and pieces of evidence.

5.4.1 The data analysis process

The essential *functions of data analysis* can already be seen in the example of criminological investigation. This can be generalized and shown as a flow diagram of the analysis process, which can be found in similar form in both quantitative-statistical and qualitative-interpretive analyses, independent of the procedures actually used (cf. Figure 5.5). This development is illustrated below by taking the example of statistical analysis. The special features of an interpretive procedure are covered in more detail in the next section (5.5.1).

In a preparatory stage, it is a matter of processing the information into 'raw data', which can then be condensed into *comparable parameters or types* with the aid of statistical or hermeneutic procedures ('coding'). It is thus the aim of this first stage in the analysis to extract a value or meaning which is as universal and meaningful as possible from the information, of which there is, in principle, an infinite quantity. The classical example in descriptive statistics is the mean, a calculated parameter, which is the best way of representing a distribution of values however wide it may be.

However, if the depiction of a group of values is restricted to the mean, important information is lost. At least two *other parameters* are suitable for general use: the standard deviation (or variance) as measures of the statistical dispersion of the values around the mean, and the skewness of a distribution, which shows clustering to the right and/or left of the mean. Each of these numerical measurement values provides information not recorded by the others. Obviously, this by no means completes the list of statistical values[14] used in the description of distributions.

Apart from the pure condensation of information down to a single meaningful value, the *standardization* of that value in order to create comparability in statistics is of the greatest importance. Here too, in the percentage value, there is a calculation which is 'suitable for everyday use': by calculating the values proportional to a maximum and standardizing them on a scale of 0 to 100, it is possible to weigh up different quantities against one another and put them in proportion. For further statistical calculations such as multivariate regression analysis, the Z-transform is helpful. Here, the mean and the standard deviation are used to weight the distribution. The result is a scale with the mean as its natural zero point and the standard deviation as values on the scale (the value +1 corresponding to a positive deviation of a value from the mean by the amount of the standard deviation). Here also, the list of standardized statistical parameters is by no means complete with these examples; a large number of more or less common parameters can be found in the relevant statistics books (cf. Föllinger 2007 for a practical introduction to statistical transformation procedures).

Standardized numerical measurement values are also an essential element in the second step, in which the relations of two or more distributions ('variables') to one another are investigated. The aim is to identify significant *correlations;* that is to say that, applying theoretical assumptions ('hypotheses'), expectations about the relation of (at least) one cause to (at least) one effect are formulated and compared in statistical tests with a 'null hypothesis', i.e. with the assumption that there is no correlation. The classical example here is Pearson's correlation coefficient (Pearson's *r*), a measure of correlation that gauges the empirical relation of two variables in respect of a random distribution and tests them for significance on the basis of the t-distribution.

Like most measures of correlation, Pearson's correlation coefficient provides information not only about the existence of a correlation, but also about its *strength* and *direction*. By standardization, Pearson's coefficient can only assign values between −1 and +1, with +1 reflecting a perfect positive correlation, −1 a perfect negative correlation and 0 no correlation between the two variables being observed. The special appeal of Pearson's correlation coefficient lies in its *simple and rational interpretation:* the square of the sample correlation coefficient estimates the fraction of the variance of the dependent variable as explained by the independent variables.

Few measures of correlation are as convenient as regards their calculation, the scope of the information they provide and their interpretability. This is conditional, among other things, on the *level of measurement* of the variables used for a correlation analysis: Pearson's correlation coefficient assumes an interval scale for both variables, although strictly speaking in the social sciences this prerequisite is only fulfilled for very few aspects under investigation (e.g. an open question on respondents' income or age). In the use of scales for measuring attitudes, which only permit values to be stated stepwise ('discrete distribution'), the acceptance of an interval level of measurement is strictly speaking already impaired/ violated and the calculation of the arithmetic mean (and thus also that of Pearson's correlation coefficient) has already become impossible.

5.4.2 Statistical analysis procedures

Pearson's correlation coefficient also forms the basis of *regression analysis*, the most important and most commonly used bivariate and multivariate *statistical analysis procedure* (cf. Table 5.4 for an overview). Whilst the focus in bivariate analysis as described so far is on the correlation between two variables, in multivariate causal analyses the effects of a random number of independent variables on a single dependent variable are investigated. By this means, the strengths of the effects of various different causes of a common impact can be compared and assessed with regard to their significance for an overall explanation model. With *path analysis*, finally, large-scale impact chains and feedback processes can also be modelled and investigated. More complex procedures such as *multi-level or structural equation models* are also founded, in their basic form, on regression. Even *logit and probit models, longitudinal models* (such as event data, survival and time series analyses) and *factor and cluster analyses* are actually nothing more than derivatives of regression and can be traced back to a common, general linear model (cf. for example Holm 1979, for a comparison of models see Judd et al. 2008).

Table 5.4   Popular linear analysis procedures

Procedure	IV		DV		Description	Literature
	scale	number	scale	number		
Regression procedures						
Linear regression	int,d	rm	int	1	Linear relationship between several independent interval variables and one dependent interval variable	Gordon (2010); Urban (2008); Pedhazur (2006); Weisberg (2005); Groß (2003); Cohen et al. (2002); Aiken and West (1998); Berry and Feldmann (1985)
Analysis of variance ('ANOVA, MCA')	n	rm	int	1	Linear relationship between several non-interval independent variables and one dependent interval variable	Doncaster and Davey (2007); Bray and Maxwell (2003); Iversen and Norpoth (2002); Moosbrugger (2002); Girden (1998); Pokropp (1994)
Path analysis	int	rm	int	rm	Linear relationship between several independent and dependent interval variables	Li (1986); Hermann (1984); Holm (1977); Opp and Schmidt (1976)
Classification procedures						
Factor analysis	int	rm	–	–	Extraction of factors from a set of correlations between interval variables	Brown (2006); Bartholomew and Knott (1999); Kim and Mueller (1994); Geider et al. (1982); Holm (1976); Ritsert et al. (1976)

(*continued*)

Table 5.4   Continued

Procedure	IV scale	IV number	DV scale	DV number	Description	Literature
Cluster analysis	int	rm	–	–	Allocation of a number of objects to homogeneous groups (discovery of empirical classifications and typologies)	Byrne and Uprichard (2012); Schendera (2008); Abonyi and Feil (2007); Aldenderfer and Blashfield (2006); Hoberg (2003); Bacher (1996)
Correspondence analysis	n	rm	–	–	Procedure for the classification of non-interval objects with low numbers of cases	LeRoux and Rouanet (2010); Greenacre (2007); Weller and Romney (2005); Blasius (2001); Greenacre and Blasius (1999)
Network analysis	n	rm	–	–	Procedure for the analysis of structure elements in a social network	Scott (2012); Prell (2011); Scott and Carrington (2011); Stegbauer (2008); Jansen (2006); Trappmann et al. (2005); Carrington et al. (2005); Schnegg and Lang (2002)
Procedures with logarithmic function						
Logit and probit models ('logistic regression')	int,d	rm	n,d	1	Influence of several independent interval variables on a discrete or dichotomous (0–1 coded) dependent variable	Menard (2010); Langer (2008); Pampel (2005); Booroah (2003); De Maris (2003); Aldrich and Nelson (2002); Homer and Lemeshow (2000)

(continued)

Table 5.4   Continued

Procedure	IV		DV		Description	Literature
	scale	number	scale	number		
Survival analysis ('mortality table')	n	1	d	1	Comparison of status change of the values of a nominal variable over time	Cleves et al. (2008); Hosmer et al. (2008); Andersen and Keiding (2006); Martinussen and Scheike (2006)
Event history analysis ('Cox regression', 'non-parametric event-data analysis')	int,d	rm	d	1	Influence of time and several interval covariates on a status change taking into account censored data	Wu (2012); Blossfeld et al. (2007); Blossfeld et al. (1986); Diekmann and Mitter (1984)
Longitudinal analysis ('individual case analyses', 'follow-up examination', 'panel analysis', 'Time series analyses')	n	1	–	–	(trend) Analysis of chronological changes in discrete data, which postulates dependence of the result at a later point in time on the result at the earlier point in time	Newsom et al. (2011); Köhler (2008); Kirchgässer and Wolters (2006); Baur (2005); Jianging and Qiwei (2005); Thome (2005); Janacek (2001); Schlittgen (2001); Schlittgen and Streitling (2001); Engel and Reinecke (1992); Ostrom (1990); Gottmann (1981); Kratochwill (1978)
Combined procedures						
Multi-level models	int	rm	int	rm	Hierarchical regression model for estimating the influence of individual data at aggregate level	Snijders and Boskers (2011); Hox (2010); Skrondal and Rabe-Hesketh (2009); Langer (2004); Engel (1998, 1997); Huinink (1989)

(continued)

Table 5.4   Continued

Procedure	IV		DV		Description	Literature
	scale	number	scale	number		
Structural equation models ('LISREL')	int	rm	int	rm	Influence of several interval variables on a dependent variable using latent, non-observed variables (factor variables)	Kline (2010); Kaplan (2009); Blunch (2008); Reinecke (2006); Langer (2005); Jaccard and Wan (1996)

Notes: IV = independent variable; DV = dependent variable; int = interval; n = nominal; d = dichotomous; rm = random; MCA = multiple classification analysis

In social scientific *fundamental research* the analysis methods presented here have for some time been part of the standard repertoire and thus also of the scientific training canon. Having said that, on account of the core disciplinary areas, some clear differences can be recognized as regards the frequency of their use: whilst for example in sociology linear and logistic regression procedures predominate, in macro-economy it is time series analysis methods that are more common, and in micro-economy, meanwhile, event-data-analytical ones. Psychology, by contrast, occupies itself particularly often with surveying latent constructs such as 'happiness' or 'satisfaction', for which reason factor-analytical procedures play an important role there and structural equation models are used particularly often.

For *evaluation research* as applied social research, the consequence can be drawn from this disciplinary structuring that the competent use of statistical procedures depends more heavily on the training background of the evaluators than on the actual problems concerned, and that many evaluation studies, like fundamental research, restrict themselves to procedures with which the researchers are familiar. Job-market research, for example, is dominated by micro-economic models with the aid of event data on the impacts of interventions on a person's individual risk of unemployment or, as the case may be, the chances of an unemployed person's finding new employment (cf. for example Heise & Meyer 2004; Meyer 1997). Qualitatively oriented analyses, which aim to get to the bottom of selection processes on the job market and the way in which the instruments of active job-market policy work, are by contrast decidedly rare, for example (see Ezzy 2000 for an exception).

Basically, this preference for certain methods does not gainsay the use of one or the other in a given field of application – rather the reverse: data gathering procedures and analysis routines can prevail especially if they have, in the past at least, provided valuable insights. This certainly applies to longitudinal data in job-market research and event analysis, without which a large number of interesting findings could not have been arrived at at all. Having said that, their success does not mean that these procedures are universally superior to other methods or that they should replace them in all the policy fields. At the end of the day, the deployment of methods ought to be oriented exclusively toward the particular problems being investigated, and be appropriate to the evaluand and the research question. This is even more the case in evaluation research than in fundamental research.[15]

5.4.3   Significance tests and representativeness

What the statistical analysis procedures described here have in common is not only that they avail themselves of a derivation of the general linear model, but also that they *test the model as a whole* and assess all the individual factors included in that model for their *significance*. The researcher is thus interested on the one hand in the question of the explanatory power of the model as a whole and on the other in that of the weighting of the contribution of the individual factors for explaining the dependent variables. This centres around the examination of the extent to which these findings are 'significant', i.e. the extent to which they are unlikely not to have come about by virtue of a systematic correlation. Setting a *significance level* as a decision rule determines the risk of such a 'random result' that is still just tolerable, and ensures that only those results are accepted as relevant that have reached that level.

The advantage of using quantitative analysis procedures is thus that the results – at least from a technical point of view – can be interpreted simply and in accordance with clear decision rules. In principle the rationale can be seen in the interpretations of others (if the statistical decision rules are disclosed) and they can be compared easily with one's own. On the other hand, however, 'significant' does not necessarily mean 'relevant', let alone 'correct' or 'good in terms of content'. *Interpreting* the statistical numerical measurement values technically does not release researchers from their responsibility to undertake an interpretation in terms of their content.

One aspect of that *content interpretation* relates to the transposability of the findings examined in relation to one individual case to other individual cases or to a set of cases that includes the case being investigated. In this step too, statistics can provide valuable support under certain conditions. Concluding from an individual case or from a set of individual cases to a population is possible taking into account the rules of stochastics if the cases investigated have been selected randomly. *Random selection* differs from arbitrary selection by the laying down of selection rules, which determine the probability with which an individual case will be included in a sample. As long as each element of the statistical population has a *selection probability* that is calculable and non-zero, it can be used to back-calculate the probability of a transposition of the individual findings to that statistical population. In this case, the individual case represents all the other elements of the statistical population, for which reason the conclusion from the individual case to the set is also known as the *conclusion of representativeness* (cf. Mosler & Schmid 2006; Bourier 2005; Sahner 2005).

Having said that, *statistical representativeness* does not mean representativeness in terms of content; that is to say, selection according to probabilities does not make any meaningful statement about the relevance of the randomly drawn individual case to answering the research questions. It is true that the *probability of error* in the transposition of the results can be calculated using mathematical procedures (and that that probability decreases with the number of cases in the sample), but that implies that all cases have equal weighting inasmuch as they relate to answering the research questions; this fails to take account of the fact that fewer relevant elements may be contained in the random sample. If for example a sample were drawn from all the employees in a company at equal selection probability, the works manager would be very unlikely to be part of it, whilst it may be supposed, on the other hand, that a number of casual workers would be included. If an overall picture of the company were being striven toward, this would certainly not present a problem; if however it was a matter of making corporate decisions, the absence of the manager would be sure to lead to a distortion of the results. Thus a distinction must be made between the statistical representativeness and *representativeness* of selected cases *in terms of content* (cf. Quatember 2005 on these problems). Representativeness can be referred to as related to content if the selected cases precisely reflect the qualities, opinions, statements etc. of the statistical population inasmuch as they relate to the information of interest.

It is the aim of qualitative procedures to select the *typical case* by applying content criteria and, taking that individual case (or the individual cases) as an example (or examples), to depict the decision-making processes, behavioural patterns, thought patterns etc. that usually occur in the statistical population, to see the rationale in them and to understand them in terms of their content. The tool of statistical procedures, which can provide important assistance, especially in the interpretation of results as shown, is dispensed with. Accordingly, qualitative procedures must rely on other interpretation patterns. These will be looked at in the next section.

5.5   Data interpretation – from material to assessment

In the use of qualitative procedures, the two steps illustrated here separately, data analysis and data interpretation, are combined. Whilst statistical analysis, in accordance with rational mathematical criteria, provides clear, *technically interpretable results,* which then have to be reassessed in terms of their content, qualitative social research is based solely on the interpretation of the meaning of the information at hand. For all their diversity in carrying out qualitative analyses, these procedures cannot provide any unambiguous, intersubjectively utilizable decision rules with regard to the relevance, strength or direction of influences. On the contrary: in qualitative analysis there is always a risk that correlations found in an individual case or described by individual persons will be overestimated with regard to their relevance to the total number of cases in which the researcher is interested. What is more, qualitative researchers can be 'dazzled' by their own research work and interests, allowing themselves to be led astray as in a 'self-fulfilling prophecy'.

However, these indisputable disadvantages of qualitative research are balanced by some clear advantages, which relate mainly to interpretation, which goes deeper and penetrates the material being investigated more thoroughly. Whilst in quantitative social research sometimes significances are tested too mechanically and correlations interpreted in terms of their content ad hoc or at least prematurely, qualitative social research devotes much more attention to this step of *understanding correlations and interpreting their meaning* using humanistic methods and their basic theory-of-science principles (cf. in particular Seiffert 2006). This may be of use to evaluations, in particular with regard to assessing the ways individual groups of people act and the recommendations to be derived from this for the improvement of those interactions.

A rational assessment is one of the very things for which such a logically reconstructive *verstehen* of the actions observed is absolutely necessary, for it is only in this way that a *realistic process assessment* is possible while taking into account subjectively perceived compulsions to act and constraints. In this respect, the interpretive procedure is to be preferred, in accompanying and ex-post evaluations, to the assessment procedures (such as multi-criteria analysis) favoured in economics, as it is not based on the artificial model of rational decision-making, carrying out abstract quantifications of individual decision-making alternatives, but oriented strictly toward the actual development of the decision-making processes, consciously taking into account irrational influencing factors and perception errors in its reconstruction of decisional behaviour.

For this reason, we turn our attention in this section to the interpretation of existing data in terms of their content, various different techniques and the corresponding rules for carrying out such scientifically sound interpretation being introduced. In spite of all the differences in detail – what these techniques have in common is above all the baseline of the process. Like the 'numbers' in quantitative analysis, *'words' form the basis of the interpretation:* independent of the procedure selected, the information gathered is converted into a *text* by means of *transcription,* and the text interpreted using certain techniques (on coding procedures in qualitative research cf. Saldana 2012).

5.5.1   Data interpretation as a qualitative process

The individual steps in data interpretation and the conclusions to be drawn from the results are just as hotly debated among the various authors as the objects of interpretation and its objectives. There are a number of *different theoretical approaches* for the foundation of this interpretive phase, and to some extent they either contradict or at least compete with one another. The important point at issue is the 'right' way to interpret, the purpose of which is to deliver intersubjectively comparable, high-quality results.

Just as 'significant' in quantitative social research does not necessarily mean 'correct', it does not necessarily follow from compliance with certain procedures either that the derivation of results observed will be logically correct or that it will be associated with a hidden 'meaning' that is subjectively influenced by the perspectives of the observer. Again, the quality of the results must be assured primarily by the methods used and adherence to the generally accepted rules on which it is based. Alfred Schütz calls these interpretation steps necessary in scientific analysis *'constructions of constructions'* (Schütz 1971: 68), and they are as susceptible to error as the interpretations of people acting in their social environment that serve as the subjects of social science investigations ('first-order constructions'). Only by the conscientious application of interpretation techniques does the scientific procedure differ from these everyday interpretations.

Most qualitative social researchers doubt that an action or situation can have a *'true meaning'*. They assume that ultimately reality can only be reconstructed in the various different interpretations of those involved. Social reality is the product of social constructions, and knowledge acquired about it influences the behavioural patterns of all the members of society in everyday situations (cf. in particular Berger & Luckmann 1999). Thus an object does not become a 'table', until the producer, the vendor and the users have grasped a certain socially traditional concept as to the meaning and utility value of 'tables' and attribute it collectively to a certain object. By contrast, the concept 'table' may be completely unfamiliar to a member of a different culture, or that member may associate a different concept (e.g. 'chair') with the object in question.

This is where the *constructivist theory of science* starts out, postulating an insight logic which is completely different to the classical 'positivist' perspective, the latter being oriented toward the natural scientific cognitive process (cf. for example Zielke 2007; Hibberd 2005; Gergen 2002 for an overview and introduction). Knowledge is not as exact an approach as possible to an (imaginary) 'true value' and it is, accordingly, not a matter of recognizing 'actual', 'objective' and 'stable' reality. In constructivism, (social) reality is not a static condition, but a process (re)produced by human interaction and by people's interpretive knowledge. The task of science is to find the rationale in this process as precisely as possible, recognize its patterns and derive appropriate conclusions. An interpretive analytical methodology is therefore required that does not focus on the truth of the result but the rationale of the interpretation process (for interpreting technics cf. Silverman 2011).

What standards are to be imposed from this perspective on such an *interpretive methodology?* Uwe Flick (2005: 313) put together nine criteria for the selection of an interpretation procedure in the form of a 'checklist':

(1) Question	Can the interpretation procedure and its application get to grips with the main aspects of the question?
(2) Interpretation procedure	Can the interpretation procedure be applied in accordance with the methodological specifications and objectives?
(3) Interpreter	Can the interpreter apply the form of interpretation?
(4) Texts	Is the form of interpretation suitable for the texts to be interpreted?
(5) Survey form	Does the form of interpretation suit the survey material and the survey method?
(6) Room for the case	Is there room for the case and its special features within the framework of the interpretation?
(7) Course of interpretation	Has the interpreter realized the form of interpretation? Has he given the material enough room? Has he come to terms with his role? Was the way the text was to be dealt with clearly defined?
(8) Analysis target	Were clearly defined statements supposed to be investigated as to their frequency distribution, or complex, multi-layer patterns and contexts? Were attempts made to develop a theory or to distribute views in social groups?
(9) Aspiration to generalize	At what level were statements supposed to be made: about the individual case, group-related or generally applicable?

Source: Flick (2005: 313; slightly modified and abridged).

With reference to *conducting evaluation studies,* and with regard to these criteria, it is easy to recognize great possibilities for variation and a corresponding bandwidth of standards for the deployment of interpretation procedures. Thus for example the *goals* of an evaluation are already diverse merely on account of their temporal relationship to the evaluand as ex-ante, ongoing or ex-post. With interpretations, the emphasis will tend to be on the risks potentially expected by experts, the current conflicts of those involved or difficulties actually surmounted in the past, and the techniques used will generally have to concern themselves more openly with the emotionally expressed fears and anxieties of the actors or, more systematically, with the problem cases matter-of-factly described by experts. Much the same also applies to the question of the *interpreters,* who will in a strictly participant-oriented evaluation mainly be novices as regards the interpretation techniques to be used, whilst a scientifically oriented evaluation can presumably have recourse to experts who are experienced in the methods and interpretation techniques used – with appropriate implications for the interpretation and quality control procedures and the manageability of the techniques themselves.

Thus it is not difficult to recognize that there cannot be an interpretation technique that is optimal and suitable for all evaluations, and that the procedures developed in fundamental research may be more or less apt in a given individual case. In evaluations as compared with fundamental social science research, the *decision in favour of a given procedure* therefore depends less on the theoretical position of the researcher and much more heavily on the contextual conditions of the research process (and especially on the specifications of the clients). Unlike quantitative procedures, which can – regardless of the survey and analysis procedures used in assessing the results – begin by referring back to statistical criteria, in the qualitative procedure the interpretation method adopted and the data gathering and analysis strategies are mostly side by side on the test block.

5.5.2   Types of interpretation procedure

In terms of their theoretical foundations, there are in principle three fundamentally different *types of interpretation procedure* (cf. Table 5.5). In the simplest case – which can be compared with the statistical classification procedures (particularly cluster analysis) – individual elements are allocated by virtue of their similarity to groups that differ from one another clearly. The aim of this classification is to form groups which are as homogeneous as possible and whose typical characteristics are intended to segregate individual elements from one another perfectly. Other than with a classification that is oriented toward statistical distance measures,[16] the allocation is now carried out according to content features, and these first needs to be ascertained in the interpretation. The *categorization* is thus not the result of mathematical calculations, but that of an interpretation of content, which is oriented toward certain criteria that still need to be explored.

In the *empirically grounded construction of types* (cf. Kluge 1999), for example, the existing material is first inspected and a common comparison dimension sought (step 1). In step 2, the individual cases are grouped together in that dimension according to the similarity of their features, whereby groups should be formed that can be segregated as

Table 5.5 Overview of interpretive methods (Flick 2005: 311)

Procedure	Description	Literature
Categorizing interpretations		
Coding ('theoretical coding', 'thematic coding')	systematic text interpretation through understanding of the meaning of, and derivation of, the codes and the system of categories used	Böhm (2003); Hildenbrand (2003); Brüsemeister (2000: 189ff.); Strauss and Corbin (1996); Flick (1996)
Typologizations ('empirically grounded construction of types', 'global analysis')	development of categories and types with the aid of the available material by identifying similarities and differences (explorative procedure)	Ecarius and Schäffer (2008); Kluge (1999); Haas and Scheibelhofer (1998); Legewie (1994)
Genre analysis ('conversation analysis', 'consensus analysis')	comparative interpretation of communicative genres (typical patterns which have established themselves socially in interactive exchange)	Hutchby and Wooffitt (2008); Ten Have (2007); Keppler-Seel (2006); Top (2006); Knoblauch and Luckmann (2003); Bergmann (2003)
Linguistic interpretations		
Narratology ('narrative analysis', 'oral history', 'action research')	theoretically sound interpretation of narrative situations (with the aim of typologizing)	Kohler-Riessman (2007); Reason and Bradbury (2007); Herman and Vervaeck (2005); Riley and Hawe (2005); Clandinin and Connelly (2004); Harrison (2002); Jossellson and Lieblich (1993)
Semiotics ('functional linguistics', 'discourse analysis', 'exegesis')	a text is understood as combinations of signs and it is the aim of the analysis to find out what kind of textual meaning they represent…several interpretations are theoretically possible	Jacobsen (2008); Danesi (2007); Eco (2007, 2002); Schmauks (2007); Royce and Bowcher (2007); Young and Fitzgerald (2006); Parker (2003); Glucksberg (2001); Keller et al. (2001); Adam et al. (2000)

(*continued*)

Table 5.5   Continued

Procedure	Description	Literature
Hermeneutic interpretation		
Hermeneutic circles ('symbolic hermeneutics', 'philosophical hermeneutics')	repeated interpretation of a text as a progressive approach toward its meaning (said meaning being assumed to be a product of the author)	Bauman (2010); Joisten (2008); Umlauf (2007); Gadamer (2007); Wiehl (2003)
Deep hermeneutics ('psycho-analytical analysis of culture')	scenic interpretation of life concepts transported into texts or pictures (the meaning being a product of the recipient)	König (2003, 1997)
Objective hermeneutics ('analytical hermeneutics', 'social science hermeneutics')	reconstruction of the 'latent meaning', i.e. the intersubjectively divided understanding of a text...decoding of the 'structural core' by examining each individual sequence (the meaning being a product of society or of the interaction)	Rittelmeyer and Parmentier (2007); Wernet (2006); Danner (2006); Ronald (2004); Reichertz (2003); Soeffner (2003); Hitzler (1997); Oevermann et al. (1979)
Visual analysis	Interpreting pictures, photographies, videos, films for understanding the meaning, the situation, interaction, communication processes etc. by using different kinds of scientific concepts	Reavey (2011)

clearly as possible. In step 3, these newly formed groups are interpreted from the point of view of their content: in other words the correlation of meaning is sought between elements of the same group, which distinguish that group from others. It is the aim of the interpretive analysis in the final step (step 4) to produce a characterization of the individual groups as types with specific, clearly identifiable common properties which are to be distinguished from those of other types on the basis of a certain dimension (or a clearly identified set of dimensions). (Meyer et al. 2002: 73ff., 183ff. give an example of an application which also very clearly illustrates the differences in cognitive gain as compared with cluster analysis.)

What the *philologically sound interpretations* have in common is that they relate to the text and to the linguistic rules and structures associated with it, and avail themselves of the insights of linguistics in interpretation. It is not so much a matter of the comparative classification of the elements as of their allocation to the features that give the text its linguistic character. It is not necessarily the meaning of the text which is to the fore, but rather its symbolic structure and the linguistic aids used in communication (signs, phonemes, morphemes, syntax, semantics and pragmatics, vocabulary and usage, euphemisms and phrases, dialects and articulations etc). Accordingly, heed must be paid in transcription to recording all the linguistic niceties as precisely as possible, and this can as a rule only be done using recording techniques (unless it is an analysis of written texts which have already been completed).

Narrative analysis in particular also emphasizes the significance of the linguistic means used unconsciously in communication and therefore attempts to record acts of speech (and above all narrative situations) as precisely as possible, analyse them in detail and interpret them applying linguistic criteria (see Abell 2004 on the narrative explanation model). Insights gained are intended to come on the one hand from recording communicative skill levels (and any communication problems which may result from it), and on the other via the possibilities of assessing the interactive exchange between various people.[17]

Unlike the linguistically oriented interpretation procedures, *hermeneutics,* which is interested in grasping meaning, has developed as a science of interpretation from philosophy – and in the form of biblical exegesis from divinity – and is in view of that origin probably the oldest form of interpretation technique described here. Differences between the approaches here relate primarily to the allocation of the source in the production of meaning. In 'classical', more philosophically and humanistically oriented hermeneutics, the author of a text (or creator of an object) is at the same time also the producer of its meaning. It is the task of science to reconstruct and interpret the more or less openly disclosed meaning in accordance with the intentions of the author. The scientific discourse is sparked off by the logical reasoning behind such interpretation.

The perspective of *deep hermeneutics,* which was derived from psychoanalysis and has for example been used in aesthetics, turns this view upside down and asks about the effects which indicate the meaning of a text or object to those who interpret it. It is thus a matter of the perception, and the associations connected with that perception, of one of more observers, readers, listeners etc. and of the analysis of the similarities or differences in the ways they perceive (or 'receive') the object.

Social-science-oriented *'objective hermeneutics'* goes yet a step further and sees the meaning as a result of the communication between the producer and the recipient. For understanding to be possible at all, common codes, signs, symbols etc. must be used, which have in turn been passed on down through society and culture. 'Meaning' is therefore a product of society and not a product of the author or recipient alone. With regard to their intentions and perceptions, both are characterized by and dependent on the basic social principles of their common language or perspective in the contemplation of objects. It is a matter of investigating these similarities within the framework of 'objective hermeneutics', adhering to a clearly regulated work plan (Figure 5.6). The combination of research design, survey method, analysis technique and interpretation becomes much stronger than in other procedures.

1st step: *determination of goals* (determination of aims of analysis)

2nd step: *rough analysis of framework conditions* (determination of situative conditions and action problems)

3rd step: *sequential fine analysis* (breakdown into individual, interrelated concrete actions and separate, step-by-step analysis of individual sequences)

4th step: *identification of general structure* (thought-experimental construction of all conceivable action contexts for a concrete action sequence and conclusions about the general structural characteristics of the context)

5th step: *comparison with actual contextual conditions* (comparison between general structural characteristics and actual contextual conditions)

6th step: *analysis of potential consequences* (derivation of possible consequences from one action sequence for the next)

7th step: *comparison with actual consequences* (comparison of the hypothetical action sequence with the real one)

8th step: *structural generalization* (collation of individual results and derivation of general structure hypotheses which are intended to be generally applicable)

Figure 5.6 Procedure in objective hermeneutics

Source: Stockmann and Meyer (2006: 95).

However, it should be noted that none of the hermeneutic procedures described here has so far played any kind of special role in evaluation research. The main reason for this is the high cost of such procedures. Apart from that, hermeneutic interpretation is mostly very subjective and thus relatively unreliable. The appropriate interpersonal confirmation of the findings is difficult, and the measures required to achieve it are obviously not taken even by evaluators who mainly work qualitatively.

5.5.3 Analytical assessment

In general, it is true that an *assessment* is connected with the interpretation of a text, at least implicitly, regardless of the method used. Every reader of a text judges its content, sense, linguistic style, form, layout etc. and forms an opinion as to whether he liked it or not – the same applies to this book itself just as it would to a detective novel and is quite independent of whether the reader is a novice, a student of the evaluation masters course or someone who has been working for many years in an evaluation department. This *normative assessment* of an object is a 'matter of taste' relating to the reader; it is not a result achieved by scientific methods and certainly not an empirically sound evaluation.

An *analytical assessment* differs fundamentally from normative assessments and it does so regardless of whether qualitative or quantitative research logics have been followed, standardized or non-standardized measuring instruments used in the survey, and whether numbers or texts have been analysed and interpreted (cf. Chapter 2 on the distinction between analytical and normative assessment). The analytical assessment stage in empirical research work unites four basic properties (cf. Meyer 2011: 214ff.):

- a common *assessment criterion,* to be followed exclusively, was unambiguously defined at the beginning of the assessment process
- prior to the assessment, *object features* (threshold values) were determined, which unambiguously govern allocation to positive and negative categories
- the object is assessed with the aid of a clearly regulated *procedure* which cannot be manipulated by the researcher or any third parties
- that assessment is exclusively a *comparison* between the features (measurement values) ascertained in the object by means of the procedure and the object features (threshold values) theoretically determined beforehand, which govern the allocation to normatively

assessed categories exclusively by the procedure used, independent of the influence of the researcher or other people.

The interpretation of data thus leads into an assessment when assessment criteria and category features have previously been established theoretically, these being such that the empirically ascertained features can be compared in a strictly regulated analysis procedure. Whether a thing is 'good' or 'bad' is not determined by the assessment procedure per se, and certainly not by the subjective contemplation of the person carrying out the assessment, but by the a priori normative determination of theoretical allocation criteria. (See also the critical remarks by Kromrey 2007 on this kind of 'neutral' procedure in evaluations; see House & Howe 1999 on value problems in general.)

An evaluation must therefore not be 'customer-oriented' to the extent that the evaluators follow the personal predilections of the clients or stakeholders or that the assessment criteria are arbitrarily altered or adapted in retrospect to fit in with (anticipated) attitudes, expectations or hopes. It is the task of the evaluation to *do the groundwork for decisions on alternative actions,* but not to determine them or retrospectively legitimize decisions that have already been made. However, there are differences with regard to the way in which this assignment of doing the groundwork for decision-making is carried out. The spectrum runs from simply elaborating recommendations to working out *procedures that are sound in terms of decision theory*[18] for the selection of alternative actions. Some of these procedures are even suitable for managing the complete process of assessing multi-dimensional decision-making problems in a mixture of qualitative and quantitative procedures and suggesting a choice for alternative action empirically in a *multi-criteria analysis.*

Apart from certain methodological problems that have already been referred to here and are associated with these procedures, it should however be noted that clients are only very rarely prepared to surrender the task of making decisions about their own measures, projects and programmes to evaluators to this degree. Just because the evaluation is conducted on a scientific basis, the evaluators should not presume to degrade the decision-makers to one of lackeys of empirical findings who merely have to follow the 'right' road once it has been ascertained. On the other hand, they must not allow themselves to become the slaves of the personal predilections and attitudes of individual groups of stakeholders either, merely confirming the latter's

prefabricated opinions as being 'right' regardless of their own findings. The utility value of an evaluation consists in just that: a balanced
relationship with the opportunities and limitations of the evaluators'
own scientific procedure and the interpretations of findings associated with it. These must allow sufficient room for a critical methods
discussion, but must not allow it to be used as a 'last-word' argument
against the evaluation. That being so, the joint involvement of clients
and stakeholders in determining and stipulating assessment criteria is
not only a central participant-oriented element but also an important
methodological basis for the acceptance of the assessment process and
the recommendations for action that result from it (cf. Section 4.4).
By now it should be clear that conducting evaluations is more than
just implementing research methods as precisely as possible.

5.6   Summary

The starting-point of every evaluation is the plan of how to proceed
and conduct it, right up to submission of the final report. In most cases,
an *evaluation design* of this kind is already called for by the client in
the invitation to tender and duly represents a general guideline for
cooperation between the parties. Important elements of this design
are the stipulation of the procedures for gathering data and facts on
the evaluand and answering the evaluation questions in an *investigative design*. In contrast to fundamental research, heed must be paid to
specific constraints in developing this investigative design and determining the deployment of research methods for data gathering in evaluation studies, i.e. the *time* available, the existing bodies of data and
information, the interests and *actions of third parties* with regard to the
information gathering process and the *financial framework conditions* of
the evaluation assignment.

   In addition, there may be general problems and sources of interference that also affect fundamental research; these may influence the
quality of the information obtained and must therefore be controlled
adequately. They include the effects of the *measuring instruments* used
(which are inseparably connected with the use of a specific survey
procedure), those of the *framework conditions of the measurement* and
those of the *interests of the recipient* and *bearers of information* affected
by the measurement. By the use of various different survey procedures,
compensation can be made for the respective methodological weaknesses in the investigation design.

Finally, the empirical part of conducting the evaluation is not yet complete when the information has been obtained. That information must first be transposed into analysable numbers or texts *('coding')*, and this is associated with a *condensation of information*. The result is *standardized codes* – e.g. in the form of statistical numerical measurement values – which can then be used to *identify correlations* in causal analyses. A further step is the *generalization* of these results obtained from the individual case, which is what makes it possible for them to be used in future decisions. Analogously to coding, however, the data must still be 'translated' from the 'model logic' to 'everyday practice', i.e. *the results must be interpreted* against the backdrop of the questions being asked and the actual application. *Assessing the quality* of an intervention as called for by an evaluation is only possible independent of normative influences from analytical points of view if there has previously been an *understanding on assessment criteria,* if their *threshold values* have been *stipulated,* and if during the evaluation the *procedural logic for data gathering, allocation* and *interpretation* has been adhered to strictly and correctly (cf. Section 4.3).

Taking into account the *social process of evaluation* is also one of the elements of evaluation design. The social environment of an evaluation is an important interference factor –for example there might be attempts at manipulation – but on the other hand it is also an important information base. Having said that, alongside these rather more technical factors that influence the obtaining of information there are also other important effects of the social environment which influence the course of evaluations and may at the end of the day impede or promote the fulfilment of their purpose. Some of the main actors, who have a special influence on the purposes of the evaluation outlined at the beginning of this book, will now be looked at more closely in the final chapter.

Notes

1. In particular the DeGEval standards A4 – Disclosure of Information Sources, A5 – Valid and Reliable Information and A6 – Systematic Data Review.
2. Longitudinal procedures, which aim to gain information about development processes by means of retrospective or regularly repeated surveys, are not covered here either.
3. The 'Solomon four-group design' shown here is one of the most comprehensive form of experiment. By the formation of four groups (i.e. experimental and control groups), not only are the intervention effects isolated, but the

chronological changes are also controlled during the measurement (by before-and-after measurements). For this reason, this procedure represents the experiment in its optimum form and is thus often used in experimental research in spite of the high cost. Other forms will not be dealt with in any more detail here (see for example Meyer 2011a).

4. In a matching procedure, attempts are made to allocate people who resemble each other in certain key features ('statistical twins'), one to the control group and the other to the experimental group. This can be done retrospectively, for example, people with identical features are selected for the control group by applying the feature combinations of the members of an experimental group. Mostly socio-demographic features (age, sex, educational qualifications etc.) are used for such a selection, with which the assumption is at the same time connected that these attributes may have an (interfering) influence on the correlations to be investigated. The disadvantages of the procedure are similar to those mentioned in the discussion on the formation of comparison groups in quasi-experimental design (Section 5.2.2).

5. The term 'self-selection' denotes a conscious selection decision on the part of the subjects as to which of the groups they wish to be allocated to. Distortions in the investigation results which come about as a result of self-determined allocation are referred to as 'self-selection effects'.

6. The situation is similar with regard to matching procedures: the selection of features posits implicit effect hypotheses on the distorting factors, while other features, which are not taken into account, are classified as not relevant. Whether they are allocated by probability value or absolutely makes no difference (see also Section 5.2.1 on matching procedures).

7. Translator's note: *understanding*

8. This certainly applies if it is only the research design that is looked at, to the neglect of the exchange within the 'scientific community'. The 'learning loops' of quantitative social research are outside the singular research process, and the defence of the methodological procedure, the ability to show how the results presented were arrived at, and above all the potential for obtaining the same results using a similar design are important features in the quality assurance of the quantitative research process.

9. Cf. Morehouse (2011); Yanow and Schwartz-Shea (2011); Creswell (2009); Plano-Clark and Creswell (2008); Creswell and Plano-Clark (2007); Greene (2007); Kelle (2007); Seipel and Rieker (2003); Tashakkori and Teddlie (2003) for an overview of integrative methods approaches; for particular information on their use in evaluations see for example Woltering et al. (2009); Stockmann (2006); Datta (1997); Droitcour (1997); Greene and Caracelli (1997).

10. The examples of the experiment, the quasi-experiment and the qualitative procedure explained here stake no claim to offering a complete overview. For example, panel and time series designs, retrospective investigations and expert models (peer review and the Delphi method) are all missing. An overview can be found in Stockmann (2008: 210), more detailed descriptions of evaluation designs in Meyer (2011a).

11. There are of course also other interfering factors such as the motivations of those involved to manipulate, the complexity of the measurement procedure

(and thus also of the survey design), the methodological competence of the survey staff and the quality of the measuring instruments used, though these will not be taken into account below in classifying the procedures (cf. for example Schnell et al. 2008: 217ff. for an overview of interfering factors).

12. Cf. for example Porst (2008); Mummendey and Grau (2007); Kirchhoff et al. (2006); Gillham (2005); Gubrium and Holstein (2004); Foddy (2001); Peterson (2000) on the wording of questions and the design of questionnaires.

13. Cf. for example Tourangeau et al. (2005); Linden and Hambleton (1997); Schräpler (1997); Scholl (1993); Dijkstra and van der Zouwen (1983); Sudman and Bradburn (1974) on response behaviour and reactions to the interview situation.

14. Cf. for an overview various introductory books on descriptive statistics, for example Privitera (2011); Benninghaus (2007); Toutenburg et al. (2006); Eckey et al. (2005); Pflaumer et al. (2005); Assenmacher (2003); Vogel (2001).

15. On the use of quantitative analysis procedures in evaluation studies, see as a selection from various policy fields for example PISA consortium Germany (2007, 2004); Jacoby et al. (2005); Descy and Tessaring (2004); Stockmann et al. (2001, 2000); Duffy et al. (2001); Bamberg et al. (2000); Maier et al. (2000).

16. When measuring the difference between various objects, distance or similarity measures are calculated. The gaps between the values in multi-dimensional space, shown (mostly) on interval scales, are translated into a distance function (Euclidean distances), the aim being to minimize them in the classification. The exact procedure depends on the statistical procedures used: in cluster and factor analyses, for example, Ward's method is employed.

17. See for example Pottie et al. (2008); Riley and Hawe (2005); McClintock (2004); Rhodes (1996); Mishler (1995); St. John (1985) on the use of the narrative method in evaluations; see Carson 2001 for a special look at the ethical problems associated with it.

18. Cf. Holler and Illing (2000); Eisenführ and Weber (2003) on decision theory; cf. Munda (2004); Stagl (2004); Jansen and Munda (1999) especially on multicriteria analysis.

6
The Evaluation Environment

Wolfgang Meyer

6.1 Introduction

Normative influences from the environment of an evaluation on the process of information gathering cannot – as shown in the previous chapter – be avoided completely. It goes without saying that this also applies to the entire evaluation process. A number of effects that result from this have already been covered at various junctures. The social discourse can, as has been shown, either promote or impede the conducting of evaluations and has a considerable influence on their chances of fulfilling their purpose. In dictatorships, for example, the conditions are lacking that make it possible to govern society rationally at all: without a certain critical faculty on the part of society, deficiencies cannot be relentlessly exposed, and proposals on how to remedy them cannot be discussed with regard to their effectiveness.

At the beginning it was pointed out that evaluations primarily serve three purposes in modern societies. Firstly, in the service of *social enlightenment,* they are supposed to help assess the contribution made by political programmes and projects to solving social problems; secondly, their task as an essential element of *democratic governance* is to make an active contribution to optimizing these very problem-solving processes, which is their bottom line – and thirdly – evaluations should realize an *improved manageability* of the individual measures they bring about. It will only fulfil these purposes if it can avoid being instrumentalized by interest groups and come up with constructive contributions to solving the problems on the basis of its own scientific rationality.

In order for evaluation to fulfil this independent role in modern democracies, *social institutions* are necessary that ensure a professional investigation of the impacts of political programmes and strategies to ensure policy-independent enlightenment in the long-term. Of central importance are first of all the political institutions of democracy, which are intended to prevent abuse in accordance with the principle of the separation of powers and to ensure that funding is used in a way that corresponds to the intentions of the majority of a country's citizens. For example in a country like today's Germany, parliament with its control committees and in its plenary sessions monitors the decisions of government, with the opposition playing a special supervisory role. Above and beyond that, the independent decisional logics of the legal system and the administrative apparatus and their independence from the legislative agencies ensure that political action is safeguarded to a large extent. In accordance with fixed specifications, organizations such as the Federal Court of Auditors investigate the implementation of parliamentary decisions and report irregularities to the supervisory boards and parliamentary control committees. Evaluations, mostly commissioned by ministries or other actors within the political system and conducted by independent scientific organizations, meanwhile fulfil an important function in the network of these institutions of the political system, which are geared to implementing the will of the citizens, ensuring that interests are reconciled and that government stays rational.

For these reasons, the presentation has so far focused on government agencies. At this point, it will be extended to look beyond the political system and shed some light on the *relationship of other, non-governmental actors to evaluations, which are mostly commissioned by government institutions.* The growing complexity of modern societies is leading to a decline in governmental management competence and making it increasingly necessary to involve private organizations and representatives of interests in the process of political control. Nowadays, primarily framework conditions are established through decisions within the political system, with attempts being made to influence the actions of social protagonists by means of incentives and funding programmes. More and more often, civil society organizations are involved as mediators; accordingly evaluating the impacts of such measures also means examining the support they provide.

Civil society, however, sees itself on the other hand as a critical accompanist of government action, which detaches itself to a greater or lesser extent from current government activities and agencies and uses the *public sphere* created via the modern mass media as a central platform on which to present its own positions. As has already been mentioned, this public sphere is by no means without its problems as an ally of evaluation, and the same applies to the actors of civil society. The remarks in Section 6.2 concentrate particularly on the relationship of evaluation to the various civil society actors, who reproduce the public sphere and use it for their exchanges about political control and its impacts.

If evaluations are to make a contribution to *democratic governance,* they not only need to be integrated in the existing social institutions, but also within the organizations in charge of those institutions. This applies particularly to the ministries and their subordinate authorities, which are entrusted with the implementation of political programmes and projects and therefore obliged to take direct responsibility for control. However, with the extension of this responsibility for government in 'good governance' concepts, more and more (mostly charitable) organizations must also be included here and – since the emergence of 'public-private partnerships' – so must private enterprises. Accordingly, the conducting of evaluations concerns a wider and wider range of actors with different constellations of interests. This aspect can be illustrated from two different perspectives, namely the internal and external relationships of organizations.

Modern societies are primarily societies of organizations, and the actors involved in democratic governance and its evaluation are only individuals in very rare or exceptional cases. Accordingly, conducting an evaluation always also relates to organizations and *affects activities and processes within them.* Section 6.3 focuses generally on the integration of evaluations within organizations and emphasizes three potential areas of conflict. In part this is a matter of support for the evaluation on the part of the people involved in the organization, whereby the different forms of integration of those individuals via *membership relationships* can come to have a direct or indirect influence on the course and utilization of the evaluation. As well as this rather informal and in some cases emotionally charged aspect, the *communication structures* implemented between the various hierarchical levels within the organization play a special role. They can represent not only barriers but also bridges for an evaluation, a fact that will be covered here in the appropriate brevity. Whilst the dissemination of information is of central importance for generating and passing on knowledge and thus has a considerable influence on the quality of an evaluation and the utilization of its findings, the question of the formal arrangement of evaluation units within an organization emphasizes the issue of the independence of evaluation interests and their ability to be pushed through. Here it is primarily a question of whether the interests of the evaluation can win out within an organization against other special interests or whether the evaluation must bow to the strategic considerations of third parties within that organization.

Finally, some diverse constellations of actors in the external relationships of organizations will be looked at. Particularly in programmes and projects which, in view of the increasing division of work and responsibility for implementation between governmental and non-governmental organizations, comprise more and more complex constellations of actors, quality assurance in evaluation is becoming increasingly difficult. On account of the considerable influence of these stakeholders (i.e. the actors involved in a programme or project or affected by its impacts) on the conducting of evaluations, this term and the various associated interests of those people and organizations involved in a programme or project will be looked at somewhat more closely. This is the focus of Section 6.4, in which the participant-oriented aspect of evaluation is the central issue.

6.2   Evaluation and the public sphere

As already explained in Chapter 1, evaluations are an important element of modernity and a necessary contribution to ensuring the rationality of political control. At *actor level,* modern societies are essentially characterized by their *plurality,* i.e. the variety of different lifestyles that can be pursued peacefully alongside one another in an open society (cf. Beck 1986; Popper 1992). Accordingly, it is mainly the exchange of various different points of view with the aim of reconciling interests that characterizes modern societies. The central institution here is the *'public sphere',* which is, so to speak, the stage for social communication.

With a view to *political control,* it is above all the element of *citizens' involvement* that is brought to the fore; this goes far beyond merely turning out to vote at an election and emphasizes the active co-shaping of modern society by its members (cf. Holtkamp 2006). Beside the state, which primarily has to cope with the functioning of government as the politically legitimized representative of the citizens for a fixed period of time, modern societies are thus characterized by additional institutions for the participant-oriented involvement of citizens in this process of social shaping. These are first of all the political parties, whose most important task is that of mobilization within the political system. Unlike the parties, *'civil society'* is not concerned with the legal assumption of responsibility for government action, but with organising citizens' interests in social control in a way that is independent of the state.

'The public sphere' and 'civil society' are the main audiences of evaluation when it is a matter of *social enlightenment* and thus of monitoring the effectiveness of government action.[1] As explained in Section 1.1.1, the creation of transparency as regards government by government institutions is essential for social enlightenment. The aim is on the one hand to promote public discourse about values and objectives, but on the other to make it possible to include civil society activities in improving problem-solving competence with regard to the most pressing social issues.

Whilst *civil society* emphasizes the *active and self-determined involvement of individuals*[2] and here evaluation supports the planning and preparation of concrete measures as part of social enlightenment, the *'public sphere'*[3] refers to an *arena* in which *political communication* is intended to take place and for which evaluations merely provide additional information as a basis for discussion.

In modern societies, (mass) media meanwhile dominate this communication arena; in a *controlled dissemination process* journalists, editors, reporters, proof-readers etc. function as specialized 'brokers' of information and opinions, which they convey via specific *media* (e.g. television, radio, the press, specialist journals, conferences etc.) to as many people as possible (cf. Meyer 2000). As a rule, the information disseminated by these *'information brokers'* is in turn supplied by professional press offices or other media specialists within organizations, or recorded and processed in such a way as to be presentable via the media. In other words the producers of information in turn avail themselves of specialists who are familiar with the special 'rules of the game' in *public relations work*.

Having said that, these 'rules of the game' are mostly also created by the interests of the recipients of the information. The mass media are often accused of consciously making scandals out of things and exaggerating them, and even of inventing sensations, rumours or malicious insinuations themselves in order to *'form public opinion'*. And it is indeed the case that this competition for the 'favour of the public', this one-track mind obsessed with viewing-figures and readerships, can lead to a search for that particularly tasty morsel of news which none of the other competitors can offer. (For information about the influence of the media on politics and civil society see Beyme 1994; cf. also Kepplinger 2006; Klingemann & Vollmer 1989.)

If evaluations come up with such 'sensational findings', that is to say unexpected findings with a high level of public interest, they are taken up by the mass media. By contrast, a regular supply of objectively written and factually well-founded reports hardly draws any attention among the public's information brokers (see Chapter 1.3). It is not until the latter get wind, for example, of a scandal involving 'wastage of funds' or perhaps even a suspicion of corruption that the representatives of the media wake up to evaluation findings and become active on their own initiative. When all is said and done, it is not so much the brokers as the purchasers of the information who are to be held ultimately responsible for this behaviour: the vast majority of people are more willing to pay money for 'sensational' information than for good, accurate, matter-of-fact articles.

Thus anyone wishing to reach a wider public via the mass media has better chances if he can at least imbue his information with a semblance of the sensational or – better still – make a scandal out of certain things himself. Evaluations have several problems with this:

(1) The propriety standards, for example, call for all sources of information (i.e. all stakeholders) to be *treated with respect and fairness* – this is particularly important in the case of compliance with data protection legislation – and an unbiased, complete and fair presentation of information (cf. Chapter 4.4.3); i.e. the exact opposite of that which is of particular interest to the information broker.

(2) The information brokers often wish to obtain just the kind of information that the clients (or other stakeholder groups) do not want to see published. Evaluators can thus get caught up in a *conflict of interests,* which is as a rule certain to be decided in favour of the client. This, in turn, is anticipated by representatives of the mass media, so that evaluators can quickly be accused of having 'glossed over' their findings knowingly.

(3) The *utility value* of publications (at least in the mass media) is often greatly overestimated. It is true that a great number of people can be reached in a short time via the mass media, but the sustainability of such an information transfer – again depending on how sensational the nature of the news is – tends to be rather poor. For evaluations this means that even if the mass media are used as a vehicle for conveying the information to the recipients, the message is often perceived by the latter as insufficiently important to be worth remembering. There must be at least some doubt as to whether a broad sweep of enlightenment is possible via the mass media from a sober source such as evaluation. If it is, this is presumably most likely to be a success in a politically explosive or highly topical area (as for example with the PISA evaluation, cf. Chapter 1.3).

If evaluation is to make a contribution to social enlightenment, it can hardly manage without *cooperating with the media*. One prerequisite for such cooperation is of course that the *clients* of evaluations are prepared to have evaluation findings made known to a specialist or wider public. Evaluation contracts often contain clauses that prohibit or at least regulate the passing on of findings. In some cases this happens because the clients themselves wish to reserve the right to disseminate the findings of the evaluation studies they have financed in a way that is suitable for media consumption. Many large organizations (and of course ministries and their subordinate authorities) have press offices of their own, which are in a position to place these in such a way that they attract the greatest possible attention in the mass media, the framework conditions for that placement being well known.

But in this case too, evaluation findings are filtered and can be dressed up in such a way that a particularly positive image is perceived in the public eye. The evaluators no longer have much influence on these processes, which occur in the 'utilization phase' of an evaluation. If evaluation reports are not published in their entirety but merely serve as a kind of quarry from which a *positive selection* is made for press releases or self-presentations in glossy brochures, social enlightenment is served just as little as it would be by a *negative selection* on the part of the media, who expect more attention from a scandal report than from a fair but dull 'not-only-but-also announcement'.

Apart from these direct effects, born of the interaction between mass media and evaluation, a number of indirect impacts passed on by *civil society* can also be assumed. Many civil society organizations see themselves as *critical observers of the state* and its activities. The *state* as the central government authority (and most often also the evaluation client) is in general the anchor point and focus of civil society involvement. It can be assumed that there is a kind of *symbiosis between democratic state and civil society:* 'only in a democratic state will the intrinsically diverse civil society find its necessary unity. ... On the other hand, it is civil society that shapes the constitutional state governance by the rule of law, fills it with life, lends it dynamism and forces it to account for its actions' (Kocka 2002: 30).

Nevertheless, many factions in civil society see the state first and foremost as an 'enemy' or at least primarily as the addressee for the political demands they wish to push through. In this sense, the formation of civil society structures is to be understood as *criticism of existing management and problem-solving competence*. From the point of view of the democratic political system, civil society thus acquires the function of drawing attention to management deficiencies, elaborating alternative proposals for solutions through its own activities and actively arguing in favour of them in the social discourse.

Both the mass media and the evaluation and its findings can be instrumentalized by civil society factions for this criticism. Often, the *campaigns and measures* of civil society organizations aired in the media are of the very kind that make scandals out of certain grievances or at least drag them into the public eye. In this way, evaluation findings can certainly be useful in leading to social enlightenment, but they are also open to abuse and caricature. Conversely, civil society organizations in particular are among those that have good reason to fear that criticism of their own activities resulting from an evaluation could lead to impairments of their image and a loss of credibility (cf. Chapter 6.4).

Apart from the actors of civil society, the political system and the public communication brokers, there is another group that plays a major role: the *'silent majority'*, i.e. those who do not take part actively in political discourse. In a society that makes its decisions on the principle of majority rule, these are the people who really have the power. Accordingly, not only the government and state agencies, but also the other actors in the political system and civil society 'woo' this group for its consent and (passive) support. This in turn can be done by instrumentalizing evaluations and evaluation findings.

Summing up, it can be said that evaluation findings obtained using scientific methods and procedures provide both the state and civil society with means of *monitoring the management impacts* of political programmes. Having said that, evaluation only serves to enlighten when all the principal actors strive toward *a culture of common learning about management impacts* and try to turn it into reality (cf. Chelimsky 2006). If such a culture were lacking, it would mean that one or more groups would have to break out of their immanent system logic and have the courage to act against their usual principles and norms. Such deviant behaviour would be the only way of breaking up 'leagues of silence' and exposing illegal practices.

The price of this would be high, in many cases too high: for example, the *evaluator,* placing full trust in the integrity and responsibility of all those involved, would have to pass on information to the public, and that information could be abused. Regardless of all the consequences for their own governance, *government authorities* would have to face ruthless criticism in the glaring light of the public sphere. *Civil society groups* would have to be prepared to swallow the findings of evaluation studies against their own interests, even if they contradicted their political objectives. And finally, the *information brokers* would have to be prepared to pick up on objects which were difficult to present to the public while depicting them fairly in terms of their content. They would sometimes have to pass on information that was very difficult to get across in an easily comprehensible way. These demands, some of which are somewhat Utopian, make it clear why the enlightenment function, as compared with the other functions, is less well established, and not only in Germany.

6.3 Evaluation and organizations

In the remarks made so far on civil society and the public sphere, the fact that it is not individual citizens but organizations that are the principal actors in these institutions has been neglected. Modern societies are primarily *'societies of organizations'* (cf. Abraham & Büschges 2004: 29ff. for an overview; for the theory see Presthus 1979), in which collective entities (parties, associations, clubs, cooperatives and other forms of interest community) take care of conveying individual interests to the decision-making bodies. This relates not only to the political system and its agencies of social control, but also to civil society, from the political representatives of interests to the voluntary support institutions, and to the entities that convey information between them and the public in the mass and specialist media. Neither are evaluations generally commissioned by individuals – it also being rather rare for them to be conducted by individuals – they are done at the behest of and in the interest of organizations.

One thing governmental and civil society organizations have in common is that they do not strive toward profit but aim to augment public welfare. In other words they are *non-profit organizations,* which differ – on account of a lack of orientation toward profit-making, a lack of competitive drive and a special 'customer' relationship (in the case of government institutions the 'customer' is often entitled to outputs, whereas members of civil society organizations more or less make their own commitments to involvement) – from private enterprises, and also from the administrative authorities, which are oriented solely toward the mission of the state and committed to appropriate outputs vis-à-vis the citizen.

From the beginning, organizations as the central actors in modern societies have been an important evaluand in all social science disciplines, and the diversity of the various theories of organization makes it virtually impossible to keep track of them (cf. for example Abraham & Büschges 2004; Vahs 2003; Kieser 2002; Ortmann, Sydow & Türk 2000; Türk 2000). This also applies to the definition of the term organization itself, though the one cited below is likely to prove widely acceptable on account of its general nature:

That which is referred to as an organization is a collective or corporate social system, which is mainly intended to solve coordination and cooperation problems. There are objectives which characterize the organization, there are members of the organization, there is an internal relationship, which distinguishes itself by featuring a mixture of formalized and informal actions and structures, and there are external relationships with other organizations, and adaptation and exchange relationships with a diverse environment. (Allmendinger & Hinz 2002: 10f.).

Organizations are thus important objects for evaluations, being *providers* of programmes, projects, strategies, policies and the like, and thus directly responsible for conducting them. At the same time, they are affected in that role by the impacts of their own activities, both directly (e.g. by using resources of their own or administering funds raised from outside for the implementation of the project) and indirectly (e.g. by public perception of responsibility for the project or the effects brought about in the target groups with the aid of the funding measures). (See Chapter 2.3 on the role of organizations in an impact-oriented evaluation model; the detailed derivation, which is sound in theory-of-organization terms, is to be found in Stockmann 2008: 102ff. and with reference to vocational training organizations in Stockmann 1996.)

In general, *five elements* can be identified *in characterizing organizations,* and these elements are a starting-point for both organizational analyses and evaluation studies. They are

- the target system of the organization (and thus of its right to exist)
- the formal structure of the organization for the implementation of organizational action
- the financial resources it has at its disposal
- technologies it can deploy for the pursuit of its objectives
- the members of the organization, who contribute to the achievement of its objectives by their individual actions, though the latter is coordinated by the organization.

Certain implications for evaluations are associated with each of these aspects, though they cannot be detailed here due to lack of space (but see Stockmann 2008: 104ff.)

In the section that follows, three aspects will be emphasized as they relate to evaluations: the forms of *membership,* the control of *communication* between the various elements of an organization and the functional position of evaluation within the formal *structure* of an organization. Membership, communication and structure are also core topics in an organizational evaluation and as such focus the interest of the investigation on people's actions. But a distinction needs to be made between the contacts an organization has with people (or other organizations) who (or which) are not part of itself *('external communication')* and the communication processes between its own individual elements *('internal communication')*. Analogously, *external evaluations* are to be distinguished from *internal* ones on account of their institutional independence on the organization (cf. also Chapter 2.2.5 for more detail on this).[4]

6.3.1 Membership of organizations and evaluation

The distinction between what is 'inside' and what is 'outside' an organization is determined first of all by formal, mostly juridically fixed definitions, which govern the *membership relationship* and the associated rights and obligations of the individual in respect of the organization (and vice versa). (See Nassehi 2002: 468ff. on the social function of this inclusion or exclusion by organizations.) In theories of organization, however – and also in the conception of evaluations – the different forms of relationship between individual and organization are often neglected (see Lang & Schmidt 2007 for an exception). A distinction must, for example, be made between *compulsory membership* (as for example that of companies in the Chamber of Industry and Commerce), *voluntary membership* (for example in a sports club), and *involvement without regulated membership* (for example in a citizens' movement or as a voluntary helper in a social institution).

The degree of *interdependence between the individual and the organization* varies considerably. In compulsory membership, the individual member has no freedom of choice, which means that for the organization, at least formally, the unrestricted support of the entire clientele[5] is assured. When an evaluation is being conducted, this may for example have the positive effect that a certain target group can be reached in its entirety via the organization's internal communication structure. Thus craft enterprises can be reached more effectively via the chambers of commerce than via any government register of residents or voluntary affiliations of companies in associations.

Participation in the activities of *organizations without formal membership* happens primarily in non-profit organizations and in civil society.[6] In this case neither the organization nor the individual have any mutual obligation to produce outputs. Support is given in a more or less ad hoc manner and must – depending on the situation – be raised again and again by the organization in the context of 'external communication'. At the same time, the individual must also actively demand the service of the organization in return and renegotiate it in every recurring situation. Examples of such relationships between organizations and individuals are voluntary activities in clubs and voluntary participation in protest campaigns by citizens' movements and other political initiatives.

This special relationship between an organization and its members may affect the conducting of evaluations in a number of ways. On account of the bond between the members and the organizations, which mostly has a much more emotional character, external evaluations are for example more frequently seen as a threat, and criticism of the actions of the organization by evaluators perceived as a personal attack. This can on the other hand lead to much greater support for evaluations, especially when it is internal and in the organization's own interest (cf. Chapter 2).

The range of *voluntary memberships of organizations* runs from private companies to sports clubs, with a corresponding variety of individual regulations and specific features such as cannot be covered here in their entirety (cf. Abraham & Büschges 2004: 100ff. for an overview of various attempts at classification). Just one more form of the distinction regarding membership of organizations, which is also of particular significance to evaluations, will be touched on here: *ownership*. In various degrees, members may have acquired some claim to the resources of the organization and to the profit made by it, as proprietors, investors, sponsors, silent partners and suchlike. This of course applies primarily to private commercial enterprises, whose actions serve to augment the capital of their owners. There is a difference between these and *non-profit organizations*, whose objectives apply to the creation of public goods and in which no distribution of the benefits from joint action to the members is planned. Nevertheless, the members of non-profit organizations can also contribute to the provision of organizational resources via endowment capital or donations.

The effects of a financial commitment of members to their organization may be similar to those described above for voluntary activities. 'Ownership' – here in the truest sense of the word – can tend to promote or impede the conducting of evaluations depending on how they are perceived by the members. The two forms of membership differ here with regard to the emotionality associated with them from the point of view of the members. Often, financial relationships between individual and organization are less affectively charged than voluntary activities, and accordingly the attitude of such individuals to the evaluation of their organizations tends to be more objective. If an evaluation is conducted on behalf of the organization, this does at least mean that the owners have been asked for their agreement and informed about its aims. Often, this also results in a feeling of 'ownership' of the evaluation itself, which is to say that the owners of the organization have an increased interest in that evaluation's leading to meaningful and utilizable findings.

This is however sometimes countered by a possessive mentality, which focuses the assessment of evaluations not so much on the objective tasks of the organization as on the ownership situation (also in the sense of protection of vested rights). Evaluation findings can be interpreted by the owners of an organization as criticisms of their personal decisions and interference in their autonomy as regards decision-making, and duly rejected. Particularly evaluations conducted on behalf of third parties – e.g. a government backer – are confronted with problems of this kind.

Especially in private companies, 'internal communication' was and has continued to be marked by exchanges between the owners and another 'member group' of the organization, namely the *dependent employees,* who have no ownership stake in the organization, but work, and receive remuneration for doing so. The distribution conflict between 'capital' and 'workers' as it relates to their jointly earned surplus has been domi-nating this central internal organizational relationship for more than two centuries. Thanks to the founding of parties and interest groups, this conflict has not remained limited to the individual enterprise either, but has become an essential characteristic of modern society.

This area of tension between capital and workers has multifarious effects on evaluations, at both social and organizational level. Evaluation has certainly benefited both from cooperation and rivalry between employers and employees and their organized lobbies, since these have led to wide-ranging information requirements on many issues relating to employment relationships and thus to evaluation assignments. Having said that, the contractors in these evaluations, which are mostly initi-ated by one side, can easily come under suspicion of being partial and must exercise particular care, especially in the interpretation of their findings, in order not to acquire a reputation for making tendentious presentations. When conducting evaluations within a company this means for example that careful account must be taken of the interests of both the management and the workforce, so that the quality of the information gathered and thus also the utility value of an evaluation can be assured.

For the utilization of the evaluation's findings within an organiza-tion it is necessary to develop the required paths of communication and generate a culture of learning within that organization. Only *learning organizations* with functioning *knowledge management* can benefit from the insights provided by evaluations (cf. for example Argyris & Schön 2002; Gairing 2002). The various forms of membership described and their specific combination within an organization may be both communication barriers and bridges. Compulsory membership, for example, on account of lack of interest and commitment on the part of individual members – a result of coercion perhaps – can impede the exchange of information, although the reachability of the entire clientele is guaranteed by the fact that that membership is institutionally anchored. It is true that a more informal, situative membership may from this point of view offer better motivation toward the exchange of information, but on the other hand a lack of obligation to cooperate also represents a threat to the communication process, because the passing on of information may be interrupted by the fleeting nature of the relationships between this kind of organization and its members. Just how difficult the open exchange of information between owners and dependent employees tends to be is well known and needs no detailed explanation here.

Because of its institutional anchorage as an instrument of organizational control, evaluation gets caught up in the tension among the interests of the different groups of members outlined here. Its main task, that of generating knowledge about organizational action and its impacts, is however characterized not only by the structural component of the membership relationships, but still more so by the developmental aspect of the communication process and its institutionalization. This will be looked at more closely in the section that follows.

6.3.2   Communication within organizations and evaluation

The basis of the concept of a learning organization and the use of knowledge management systems is the existence of a functioning *communication system within the organization*. The problems associated with this do not of course affect organizations in the same way: whilst small ones with few members and close personal contact can mostly control the exchange of experience (information) successfully in an informal way, large organizations with departments, divisions, branches etc. that are physically a long way apart and involve a large, heterogeneous membership must sometimes go to considerable expense and trouble to ensure joint, purposeful action and the exchange of information required for it.

In recent years, the ongoing optimization of communication processes within organizations has become the subject of more lively discussion under the heading of *'knowledge management'* (cf. Chapter 1.1).

The main, common subject of this research work is the question of *how the individual knowledge that exists in organizations (or is obtained via the work processes) can be aggregated in common knowledge in the organization and exploited in the achievement of the latter's objectives* (cf. for example Andrews & Delahaye 2000). *Knowledge* is understood as a 'fluid mix of framed experience, values, contextual information, and expert insights that provide a framework for evaluating and incorporating new experiences and information' (Davenport & Prusak 1998: 5), and it comprises not only 'objective' content but also, above and beyond that, subjective interpretations and endowments of meaning, particularly with a view to the practical implementation of that content. Within organizations knowledge is generated by the interaction of people at different organizational levels (cf. for example Nonaka & Takeuchi 1995) and by being passed on to management committees in a collective context and in a way that is relevant to action (cf. for example Patriotta 2003).

In relation to evaluations, communication within the organization plays a central role, not only in the final dissemination of the evaluation's findings but already in the preparation phase: it must inform the members about the objectives and procedure of the evaluation, try to gain trust and enlist support and open up possibilities for participant-oriented co-shaping of the evaluation process. Once again, the degree of commitment of the individual to the organization is an important factor. The management of the organization for example can place its dependent employees under an obligation to provide the required information to the evaluators, though this does not apply to voluntary helpers who have not made any further commitments to the organization. With owners (e.g. shareholders) too, it is only in rare cases that their participation in evaluations can be ensured via a decree on the part of the organization.

Communication processes within organizations are the main feature of a large number of theoretical and empirical research papers because of their central importance for the development of organizations, the way they function and the effect they have (cf. for example Hiller 2005; Herger 2004; Theis-Berglmair 2003; Tourish & Hargie 2003; Harris 2002, Jablin & Putnam 2000). In general, various different paths of communication can be distinguished, and each has specific qualities and involves different actors. For example, there are differences in terms of the positions of the communication partners in relation to one another in vertical, horizontal and diagonal communications (see for example Hein 1990: 9ff.), the influence of which on evaluations is briefly outlined below.

In *vertical communication* – the exchange of information between those 'giving orders' and those 'receiving orders' across the hierarchical borders – a distinction is to be made between *'top-down'* and *'bottom-up'* communication depending on the main direction of the information transfer. 'Top-down' information transfers from the management executives to the employees convey instructions to act, which are to be carried out by the recipients. Often, the 'orders' are not issued in a personal conversation, but conveyed via formal rules or action routines that are practised and taken for granted, and via compliance through which the hierarchical order is (re)produced. Apart from that they are aimed – mostly by a single sender – at a more or less large and inhomogeneous group of recipients.

In general, passing on information from 'top' to 'bottom' is thus less of a problem for most organizations. This also applies to evaluations: neither the announcement of an evaluation nor the dissemination of its findings poses any difficulties once they have been transformed into appropriate instructions to act and fed into the existing 'top-down' communication networks. For the organization, the evaluation is then a *routine task* that can be processed like any other. A number of organizations have duly developed such evaluation routines, that is to say they conduct evaluations on the basis of stipulated criteria at regular intervals in a standardized way and impart the findings duly arrived at as new instructions to act to the operative units. Examples of this can be found in universities and schools, and in development policy organizations.

The converse path is difficult, in other words communication from 'bottom to top', because of the large number of senders and the imbalance of power between them and the recipients. This influences these 'bottom-up' information transfers, i.e. the passing on of information by employees to their superiors: 'The basic problem is that downward communication is usually a one-way street; it does not provide for feedback from employees. Management assumes that if employees know what their managers know, they will assert themselves to solve the organization's problems (but it doesn't happen that way)' (Lewis 1987: 42). Thus far, far too little attention has been paid to these *'barriers of upward communication'*, both in practice and in scientific research (see for example Green & Knippen 1999 for an exception to this).

Often they are the starting-point of evaluations within organizations, which are concerned with gathering information from employees and systematically processing it for the decision-makers at management level. Here, evaluations are an aid, aiming either to replace the 'bottom-up' communication structures that are lacking, or to complement existing ones by adding external (and, since the evaluators do not belong to the organization, neutral and unprejudiced) views.

In general it is the timely *transfer of information about the impacts* of organizational action from the level at which that action is implemented to the executive positions and committees that is the main task of the 'bottom-up' information transfer. Having said that, it is in the nature of things that impacts occur first 'in situ' – i.e. in the immediate environment of the protagonists – and are therefore perceived by the latter first. The corridors of power, by contrast, are mostly a long way away from the action and often not confronted directly with the consequences of their decisions. Evaluations, which make a contribution to obtaining the appropriate information and passing it on to the levels where decisions are made, are thus an important *instrument of control*, which is often embedded in the context of quality management systems.

Quality management systems seek to ensure quality directly where it is produced and thus promote the decentralization of responsibility (cf. Stockmann 2008, 2002 on the differences and similarities between quality management systems and evaluation).

Horizontal communication is an exchange between different specialist departments at the same hierarchical level. The classical bureaucratic organizational structure does not envisage this form, but it has assumed increasing importance in modern forms of organization. Rarer still is *diagonal communication*, which crosses both departmental and hierarchical borders at the same time. Both these forms are becoming more important for evaluations, rendering them necessary on the one hand because of the exchange of information that is mostly lacking, whilst sometimes causing blockages in organizational effectiveness in the form of rivalry between departments. In the preparation of evaluations and the conveyance of evaluation findings, however, these forms of communication seldom play a significant role.

6.3.3   Structural anchorage of evaluation in organizations

The *implementation of evaluations* within an organization aims primarily to contribute to multiplying organizational knowledge, and is to that extent to be understood as part of knowledge management. If processes are continuously monitored, the consequences of action observed and documented, cause-and-effect relationships investigated and uncertainties as to the effectiveness of implemented measures reduced, the chance of more effective and more efficient collective action will increase. Having said that, the evaluation findings need to be processed in a way that is action-oriented and decision-oriented, and they need to be made available by the time central management decisions are to be made by means of an appropriate knowledge management system. Knowledge management thus governs the utilization of evaluation findings within the organization via the measured impacts of organizational action.

The most important task is to ensure that the information required for decisions arrives in time at the place where those decisions are to be made. This point to the *formal structure* of an organization, in which the various agencies (departments, divisions, offices etc.) are ordered and placed in relation to one another. This gives rise to formal dependences, in which certain departments are authorized to issue directives to others. This in turn raises the question of where in an organization an *evaluation department* is best established – and to what extent it should be linked to other units and tasks.

The answers to these questions are as diverse as the organizations themselves. Whilst some organizations establish their evaluation department as a specialist team directly at management level, there are others which prefer to integrate it in line and associate it with tasks such as quality management, knowledge management, controlling, accounting, project planning etc. Depending on the solution, specific communication problems and power constellations may arise, such as can facilitate or impede the planning, conducting and use of evaluations within an organization. It is thus not possible to provide a general and universal answer to the question of where in an institution evaluation actually belongs.

A further criterion is the *overall control and authority to issue directives* of the evaluation department in all matters relating to the conducting of the evaluation. Only if the evaluation department is empowered to make evaluation-related decisions that are binding on the operative units can it ensure constant quality. If the decisional power remains with the operational units and the evaluation department is not even granted a say in the matter, the evaluations will not be geared to the superordinate interests of the organization but only to those of the department.

Furthermore, the evaluation department is responsible for *quality assurance* for all evaluations conducted or commissioned by an organization. Just as in other organizational tasks, the creation of a specialized department can make it possible to recruit the appropriate expertise and/or generate it from empirical values. This accumulated specialist knowledge is then available to the entire organization and can be put to use by the operational departments. Accordingly, evaluation departments are also service departments.

Even when it is essentially a matter of *self-evaluations,* which are intended to support the operational units in the implementation of their plans, it is advisable to concentrate not only the methodological skill but also the processing and analytical capacities centrally in a single evaluation department. This enables specialist knowledge and experience to be accumulated (and the quality of evaluations to be improved accordingly) and generalizable conclusions can be drawn, which will at the end of the day benefit all the members of the organization.

Beside this *area of tension between evaluation and operational units,* there are other potential divides. For example, there may be competence disputes between the controlling and evaluation departments; quality management functions may come to contradict the requirements of the evaluation; knowledge management may neglect the internal communication of evaluation findings etc. In other words, the evaluation may get caught up in an area of tension between neighbouring *monitoring and communication tasks.* Lastly, there may also be conflicts with the *management,* who may attempt to delegate their own need to control and supervise to the evaluation department.

One last special form of the divide between evaluation and operational units should also be mentioned here because it occurs very often in practice. Projects and measures are not realized as an ongoing task, but designed to run for a certain limited period of time, i.e. they are placed temporarily within the organization. Accordingly, the evaluand is not the relevant operational unit of the organization, but the project for which it is answerable. In many cases the projects run quite autonomously and independently of the organization's operational departments; sometimes, indeed, there is no great interest in the project's progress on the part of these units (if it is not an important project or if it is one that is a long way from the mainstream of the department's usual tasks). Accordingly, conflicts arise in the conducting of the evaluation not with the operational department but with the project management itself. This leads to a number of special features as regards the position of evaluation in the context of a project, and these will be looked at more closely in the next section.

6.4   Evaluation and 'stakeholders'

As we have noted, many activities within organizations are not carried out as routine tasks, and thus not as part of firmly institutionalized processes, but as *projects with limited resources that run for limited periods of time.* Unlike the routine tasks, these projects are innovative undertakings, the aim of which is to develop new concepts, put them to practical tests and finally bring them to the stage where they are 'ready for production'. Accordingly, much less knowledge about the impacts of the individual measures and activities is available to the organization in the case of projects than in the processing of routine tasks. Project management thus makes special (and in some cases much higher) demands on the management of an organization, this being reflected, among other things, in a comprehensive range of specialized literature (cf. for example Kuster et al. 2008; Lessel 2008; Litke 2007; Schelle 2007).

Especially in non-profit organizations, the funding for such projects is often not provided by the organization alone but also by public or private *sponsors*. The project conception may have been very largely fixed by the funding organizations in the form of invitations to tender and may thus only partly correspond to the objectives and ideas of the implementing organization. In some cases the project is not carried out by a provider alone but by a group of organizations that form a project management network. Especially international or European Union development policy projects bring together various different providers in consortia and networks of this kind.

Both project management and project objectives must, in the great majority of cases, take account of various – in some cases extremely diverse – interests of a great variety of organizations, groups and individuals. The term *'stakeholder'* has established itself as a generic term for this heterogeneous constellation of involved parties. It was coined as an offshoot of the term 'shareholder' (cf. also Chapter 1.4), which originated in stock-market parlance. 'Stakeholder' comprises all those people and groups of people who are in one way or another directly or indirectly affected by the activities of a project, involved in it or interested in its outcome. Stakeholders can be members of the organization that is implementing a project, or they can be external people (e.g. target groups) or organizations (e.g. cooperation partners, suppliers, subcontractors and suchlike). An exact distinction and definition of the stakeholders varies depending on the complexity of a project, and the call for participant-oriented involvement on their part is accordingly more or less difficult to meet.

On the other hand, taking into account the various 'stakeholder' interests in time is an important component in the success of a project. Interest groups may boycott measures or cause considerable delay in the development of a project if they feel that they and their interests are not being sufficiently represented or – worse still – if they feel that those interests are threatened by the project. Often enough, a lack of *acceptance* among target groups, social elites or powerful lobby organizations can even lead to the failure and abandonment of projects. The analysis and (long-term) observation of 'stakeholders' and their attitudes to the project and its measures are thus among the main tasks of project management (cf. Chapter 4).

The specific forms of evaluation and the components of *stakeholder involvement* associated with each make it clear that evaluations are interwoven in many different ways with the constellations of stakeholders' interests. Both project providers and funding organizations, for example, are often under considerable pressure to succeed and thus sometimes exert pressure on evaluators to get them to depict their projects in as positive a way as possible.

The motives for this vary, and the direction in which the *presentation of the success of the project might be tweaked* can vary too. For lack of institutional funding, for example, many non-profit organizations are largely dependent on the acquisition of project funds. Consequently, attracting follow-up projects in time becomes a matter of vital necessity, both for the employees concerned and for the organizations themselves. An evaluation that confirms that the project management has made severe errors could have dire consequences; accordingly, in such cases, pressure may be put on the evaluators to point a finger at the funding organizations ('too little funding for project management'), or at the partners or the context. On the opposite side, the funding organizations may be interested in cultivating a positive image in the public eye, which in turn puts pressure on the experts to allocate blame to the project provider ('lack of project management competence'). Depending on the severity of the threat as perceived by those involved, it may become difficult for the evaluators to discern the true circumstances and ensure a correct presentation of them in dialogue with the stakeholders.

It is by no means certain that the stakeholders' interests will be communicated to the evaluators openly and rendered transparent. Indeed, it is to be expected that a critical self-assessment of the project, coupled with expectations that negative evaluation findings will give rise to a highly threatening situation, may lead to cover-ups and obstruction of the evaluation process. Defence mechanisms of this kind can lead to overt or covert *campaigns to discredit* the evaluators with deliberately incorrect information, behaviour designed to damage their reputation, or refusal to cooperate. Accordingly, a project evaluation can at any time be a confrontational process. Building a trusting relationship between evaluators and stakeholders is of great importance. This applies particularly to experts from beyond the project, who may be perceived by the stakeholders as 'outsiders'.

Particularly at the beginning of the evaluation process, evaluators can hardly estimate the *consequences of their assessments* of the project for the stakeholders, and their detachment from the project is one of the very reasons why. The objectively present and subjectively estimated 'threat potential' of an evaluation is an important influencing factor, which can affect the success of a project evaluation considerably and must therefore be recognized early on. For example, the fears of donor organizations that evaluation findings might have a negative influence on revenue from donations once they become known to the public are by no means unfounded, and must be taken seriously.

Finally, evaluations themselves are to be understood as projects in which stakeholders' interests are to be taken up and integrated into the process in order for them to be able to develop successfully. Transparency regarding their own procedures and evaluation criteria, openness with regard to the concerns and wishes of those involved, a readiness to compromise in conflict situations, patience and a certain 'robustness' with regard to accusations made in the heat of emotion, and perseverance with regard to the issue at hand while still paying heed to the justified objections of stakeholders all form part of the social competence of evaluators.

This applies particularly to international cooperation projects, in which cooperating with stakeholder groups also involves crossing different cultural borders. This begins in cooperation with experts from other cultural spheres in the evaluation team, comprising the diplomatic level of governmental agencies and agreements and the organizations and people actually working together within the projects, who represent not only an 'organizational culture' of their own but also different cultural spheres. The larger the number of people involved in a project, the more heterogeneous their number will be with a view to the cultures they belong to; the deeper the relationship of trust between those people and groups needs to be for the successful implementation of the project, the more complex the evaluation and the higher the demands on the evaluation team.

More problems arise on account of the stakeholders' are being oriented more toward practical aspects and details. For example, unlike the evaluation department of the implementing organization, they are more interested in detailed information on the management of the individual project than they are in aggregated, generalizable information. Whilst the evaluation department aims to draw generally applicable conclusions for organizational action from the individual projects, this is precisely one of the things that will not interest the stakeholders. They wish to use the existing knowledge and the insights gained from evaluations to optimize that particular project itself.

6.5 Conclusions and summary

In this final chapter, a number of influencing factors have been addressed that affect the fulfilment of the social purpose of evaluation which was introduced at the beginning of the book (cf. Chapter 1.1). The emphasis was on the control aspect, i.e. the task of evaluation to contribute to improving the impacts of political programmes, projects and measures. By concentrating on (collective) stakeholders, it was possible to point out a number of divides and difficulties in the planning, conducting and utilization of evaluations.

Having said that, the presentation has not claimed to be a complete or systematic analysis. These would have taken up far more space than was available, quite apart from the fact that so far work dealing with the evaluation environment is hardly to be found anywhere in the literature. Several important actors of particular importance in evaluations are therefore missing in this section. These include for example political parties, foundations, associations, scientific institutions, consulting institutes, international organizations and many others besides.

Having said that, the institutions and organizations referred to here have not been selected arbitrarily but with a view to the three evaluation purposes that run through this book as a basic theme. In Chapter 1.1 reference was first of all made to the *contribution made by evaluation to democratic enlightenment;* the importance of modern society and its political institutions for the evolution of an evaluation culture was illustrated systematically, a culture focused mainly on learning about political action and its impacts. As a result, first in the 1970s in the USA, since the 1990s more so in Western Europe and in recent years increasingly also in Latin America, Central and Eastern Europe and to some extent also in Africa and Asia, evaluation communities have come into being; the history of these developments was outlined in Chapter 1.2.

With the growing complexity of modern societies, not only are the demands made on political management increasing, but also the number of social actors involved in the process. Modern societies can no longer be steered meaningfully by government edicts or the individual decisions of lone potentates. Even the complex web of political agencies in modern democracies, which has come about in order to prevent power from being abused, is no longer sufficient to accomplish this, and in recent years there has – under the heading of 'good governance' – been an increasing amount of discussion about the way in which civil society forces can be integrated into the governing process. These *more recent developmental tendencies* were introduced in Chapter 1.3 and the resultant perspectives of evaluation with regard to its three main purposes were discussed in Chapter 1.4.

Even if evaluation has historically been mainly policy-driven and continues to be so, the task of social enlightenment cannot be achieved by the *agencies of the political system* alone. Tribute has been paid to the latter's central role in the emergence, development and future prospects of evaluation at various different junctures in this book, whilst on the other hand the institutions of civil society that are central to social enlightenment and the public (media) sphere have been neglected somewhat on account of their lesser importance for evaluations. This omission has been rectified in this closing chapter, the relationship with evaluation, still fraught up to now, being derived at the same time from the functional principles of these institutions and the action logic of the principal actors that follows from it. Whilst the democratic political system and its agencies meanwhile – very demonstratively – avail themselves of the instrument of evaluation, this is still much less the case with *institutions of social enlightenment*. There too, however, there are definitely some positive development tendencies to be recorded.

Science, and thus the complex *science system,* very strongly marked by international exchange, are without doubt among the social institutions committed to enlightenment. Here, with reference to the development of evaluations, mainly two aspects need to be focused on: firstly, there is the issue of establishing evaluation in the existing research landscape – in other words the relationship between evaluation and science – and secondly the matter of using international research exchanges for social enlightenment within a country – and thus of the relationship between evaluation and politics. These two aspects were covered extensively in Chapter 2.1. It became clear there that, to a certain extent, evaluations fall between two stools. On the one side there are the *instrumental ambitions of politics,* which cannot be eluded simply by a shift to civil society forces or institutionalization within the political system. This influence, also closely connected to the purpose of social enlightenment, is countered by the partly contradictory *technical aspirations of science,* whereby from the point of view of fundamental research, on account of the orientation toward assessment and utilization, the scientific integrity of evaluations is sometimes cast into doubt.

A tense relationship has resulted from this duality of standards, and it has a very clear influence on the evaluation environment. It points at the same time to the second main purpose of evaluation, *the procurement of legitimacy for policy*. In respect of the citizens and in particular civil society, political action can only be justified by an objective, independent and thus credible assessment, and not by (expert) reports written in such a way as to accommodate the wishes of the client or sponsor on the basis of questionable assessment criteria. Accordingly, evaluations can only serve this purpose at all through their scientific integrity. On the other hand, it is of little help in the implementation of political decisions into concrete action if that assessment is made at the wrong time or if it is insufficiently practice-oriented. Evaluations mainly serve to procure legitimacy for policy when they produce meaningful findings adhering to scientific rules on the basis of predetermined criteria in time for rational political management, and provide the decision-makers on that basis with practicable recommendations as to how they should proceed. Ideally, the discovery and utilization contexts of an evaluation are separate from its actual research context: whilst politics continues to be responsible for the former, it assigns the latter to the evaluators in its entirety (see Section 2.1.3).

In view of the diversity of different evaluands, different times at which evaluations are carried out, different evaluation criteria and different evaluation actors, the question of *how evaluations are to be conducted meaningfully* cannot be answered simply, conclusively and unambiguously for all cases. In Chapter 2.2 an attempt was made to provide an overview of forms of evaluation by applying the central questions of what is to be evaluated, to what end, how, by whom and applying what criteria. The form of programme and project evaluation that is most common in practice was mainly considered. Four central functions that guide programme evaluations can be identified: the gaining of insights, the exercising of control, the initiation of development and learning processes and the legitimation of the measures implemented (cf. Section 2.2.3). The various different evaluation conceptions serve these functions to a greater or lesser extent and can accordingly be classified using this schema (cf. Chapter 3.5).

At this point it already becomes clear that for this kind of evaluation the *providers* play a central role. Being responsible for conducting or implementing a programme or project, they are on the one hand the most important audience of evaluation with regard to the management decisions that the evaluation's findings aim to influence. On the other, they are often also initiators or clients of evaluations conducted either internally by in-house evaluation departments or externally by independent experts, consulting firms or scientific institutes. The advantages and disadvantages of these two forms were covered in detail in Section 2.2.5. In this concluding chapter, the divides between the various different actors inside and outside the organizations have also been outlined. Three primary aspects of organization have been emphasized: membership (Chapter 6.3.1), communication (Chapter 6.3.2) and formal structure (Chapter 6.3.3). Each of these areas takes on direct significance for the planning, conducting and utilization of evaluations. Constellations of actors that must be taken into account result from the structural framework conditions within the provider, and they may either assist the evaluation or impede it.

Constellations of actors in the environment of providers and evaluations are, at the end of the day, responsible for the *development of various different evaluation conceptions*, whereby we centre our approach around certain perspectives. For example, a number of evaluators see their own work primarily as applied social research, and hence see the convergence of theoretical and methodological demands in their own discipline as the most important task of evaluation. Others, by contrast, see themselves as advocates of the target groups who are supposed to benefit from the outputs to be investigated. Yet others emphasize the service character of evaluations, having to serve either the clients or the programme directors. Chapter 3 provided an overview of these approaches and some attempts at systematization. Note should be taken of the developmental tendency of evaluation approaches, which increasingly attempt to integrate a larger number of perspectives of the various stakeholder groups and disciplines and have accordingly become more complex, while also gaining in significance in terms of their ambition to explain and the spectrum over which they can be used. One such universally applicable evaluation approach is the CEval concept, explained in detail in Chapter 2.3.

On the one hand it is true to say that evaluations are, as described, policy-driven; yet they are actually primarily implemented in organizations, that implementation affecting the interests of some very diverse groups of actors. By delegating responsibility for political action to organizations via programmes and projects, policy on the one hand improves legitimacy and the citizens' chances of participating, but on the other also enhances the effectiveness of *political management*. If evaluation is implemented early on, in the planning stage, as a fixed element in the course of a project or programme (for example in the form of a closed monitoring and evaluation system), it can at different points in time make an important contribution to this management task. At the same time, it mediates between the interests of the implementer (i.e. the provider involved), the beneficiary from the outputs (i.e.

the target groups of the measures) and the sponsors (mostly the political decision-makers who sponsor programmes and projects in order to achieve certain political aims more effectively and efficiently).

The 'timing' of the evaluation is tricky, as it must, in the course of the programme or project, provide information relevant to upcoming management decisions, and it must do so in time. Since evaluations themselves are a complex *social process,* which calls for a certain amount of work up front not only for methodological reasons, careful planning is necessary that does justice both to management requirements and quality requirements. The steps that are ideal-typically necessary in the preparatory, conducting and utilization phases of evaluations were presented in detail in Chapter 4.

As the quality of an evaluation is very closely associated with the quality of the information it generates, the actual *research process*, i.e. preparing to gather data, actually gathering it, and then analysing and interpreting it, is of special importance. The special framework conditions in an evaluation include time pressures – these are much greater than in fundamental research – which calls for a certain pragmatism and ability to adapt rapidly to extremely diverse framework conditions. Since apart from that the consequences of research errors are far more serious on account of their being used in management processes, mixed-methods concepts have meanwhile established themselves as the *'route du roi'*. An overview of the various social science techniques that can be brought to bear in such evaluations was provided in Chapter 5.

Programmes and projects form a social framework in which their evaluations move (Chapter 6.4). The generic term *'stakeholder'* comprises all the groups of those involved and affected who have a particular interest in the programmes and projects and their results. These interests are affected to a greater or lesser extent by evaluations, which often lead to reactions on the part of the respective interest groups. At the end of the day, the integration of the evaluation into political management also means that the evaluation is tangled up in the political conflicts associated with that management, and yet must search with critical detachment for rational solutions that do justice to everyone. This too is an important contribution made by evaluations in democratic society.

In our society at least, as described in the introduction, evaluations are 'in'. The use of the term is spreading in an inflationary manner, and the order books of consulting firms and university institutes are well filled. More and more government and non-governmental organizations are setting up evaluation departments, or at least regularly purchasing evaluation services on the market. As a direct consequence, the demands made on evaluation are becoming more complex and thus calling for more complex conceptions and more specialized personnel. Knowledge of different empirical social inquiry procedures must therefore be combined with specialist knowledge from different scientific disciplines, including specific experience and social competence in dealing with evaluations.

However, in view of the fact that the term evaluation is not protected, anyone at all has been allowed to offer evaluation services so far. It is not always the case that the complex and unmanageable requirements are actually met by the providers. There is a danger that the term evaluation may fall into disrepute – and indeed there are already examples of this.[7] Professionalization is a matter of necessity; forming evaluation societies and issuing evaluation standards were the first important steps on this road. With the *Zeitschrift für Evaluation* and the 'forum-evaluation' on the Internet, furthermore, opportunities have been created for professional exchange. The establishment of study courses in their own right and proper training opportunities must follow – and here too, some initial successes can be recorded. Nevertheless, the following still holds true: not until evaluation has been anchored in society as a generally recognized professional instrument can it fulfil its purpose and make a contribution to political control, the legitimation of policy and social enlightenment.

Notes

1. This does of course not mean that the institutions of the political systems described at the beginning do not have any interest in (impact) evaluations or that they see them exclusively as an authority for legitimation. On the contrary, government agencies – in particular the ministries and their authorities – are the most frequent clients of evaluations and the impact discussion is coloured by them to a very great extent.

2. Civil society thus represents that part of a society which participates actively and in a self-determining way in its management outside the political system. People who do not make this contribution, or who only do so as a result of governmental coercion, thus cannot be considered part of civil society. According to this very general definition, civil society is not a stable and permanently definable subset of society, but on the contrary distinguishes itself by a high degree of mobility and change in its readiness to participate and the forms of that participation (cf. for example White 2004; Cohen & Arato 1992; Seligman 1992; Wood 1990; Gramsci 1976).

3. Cf. particularly Neidhardt (1994: 7) on the term *öffentlichkeit*; other definitions and conceptional versions of the institution of the public sphere can for

example be found in Imhof (2006); Jarren and Donges (2006, 2004); Habermas (2001); Goffman (1999); Sennett (1998); Peters (1994).

4. The selectivity of the term 'institutional independence' between client and contractor in an evaluation is however often difficult to judge in practice. There may for example be dependencies between organizations that are formally separate as a result of the repeated awarding of contracts. On the other hand, in large-scale organizations the independence of an evaluation department may be ensured by formal rules and may even be greater than that of external implementing organizations that are largely dependent on the client from an economic point of view. As a rule, however, the institutional independence of an evaluation can only be guaranteed by formal segregation of membership.

5. The term 'clientele' is used here to designate the total number of potential members of an organization. That number is limited solely by the organization itself. The trade unions for example would like to represent all employees within a given sector and exclude employers and employees from other sectors from membership by formal rules. Given the individual freedom of choice as regards trade union membership, however, the organized employees form only a subset of this clientele.

6. In a certain sense, the relationship of a company to its regular customers is also to be placed in this category, as long as there are no formal attachments (such as a subscription).

7. For example school or university evaluations are sometimes understood as 'routine exercises' prescribed 'from above', which are treated as more of a burdensome obligation than with any conviction that they may actually be useful to the school or university itself. If as a result the findings are not reflected either and their utilization is not made transparent, this effect of 'reluctance' to participate is exacerbated.

Bibliography

Abell, P. (2004). Narrative Explanation: An Alternative to Variable-Centered Explanation? In: *Annual Review of Sociology* 30, pp. 287–310 (downloadable at http://arjournals.annualreviews.org/doi/pdf/10.1146/annurev.soc.29.010202.100113, as of 15 Aug 2008).

Abonyi, J.; Feil, B. (2007). *Cluster Analysis for Data Mining and System Identification.* Basel; Berlin et al.: Birkhäuser.

Abraham, M.; Büschges, G. (2004). *Einführung in die Organisationssoziologie.* Wiesbaden: VS-Verlag.

Abs, H. J.; Maag Merki, K.; Klieme, E. (2006). Grundlegende Gütekriterien für Schulevaluation. In: Böttcher, W.; Holtappels, H.-G.; Brohm, M. (ed.). *Evaluation im Bildungswesen: eine Einführung in Grundlagen und Praxisbeispiele.* Weinheim: Juventa, pp. 97–108.

Ackermann, R.; Clages, H.; Roll, H. (eds) (2007). *Handbuch der Kriminalistik für Praxis und Ausbildung.* Stuttgart et al.: Boorberg.

Adam, G., Kaiser, O., Kümmel, W. G. und Merk, O. (2000). *Einführung in die exegetische Methode* (LJ sagt exegetischen Methoden (ch)). Gütersloh: Gütersloher Verlagshaus (7).

ADM Arbeitskreis Deutscher Markt- und Sozialforschungsinstitute; AG.MA Arbeitsgemeinschaft Media-Analyse (ed.) (1999). *Stichproben-Verfahren in der Umfrageforschung. Eine Darstellung für die Praxis.* Opladen: Leske + Budrich.

Agha, S. (2002). A Quasi-Experimental Study to Assess the Impact of Four Adolescent Sexual Health Interventions in Sub-Saharan Africa. In: *International Family Planning Perspectives,* 28(2), pp. 67–70 & 113–118 (downloadable at http://www.guttmacher.org/pubs/journals/2806702.pdf, as of 6 June 2008).

Agodini, R.; Dynarski, M. (2004). Are Experiments the Only Option? A Look at Dropout Prevention Programs. In: *The Review of Economics and Statistics,* 86(1), pp. 180–194.

Aiken, L. S.; West, S. G. (1998). *Multiple Regression: Testing and Interpreting Interactions.* Newbury Park et al.: Sage.

Alber, J. (1989). *Der Sozialstaat in der Bundesrepublik Deutschland 1950–1983.* Frankfurt, New York: Campus.

Albert, H.; Topitsch, E.(1990). *Werturteilsstreit.* Darmstadt: Wissenschaftlicher Buchverlag.

Albjerg, G. P. (1966). Joseph Mayer Rice as a Founder of the Progressive Education Movement. In: *Journal of Education Measurement,* 3(2), pp. 129–133.

Aldenderfer, M. S.; Blashfield, R. K. (2006). *Cluster Analysis.* Newbury Park, Calif. et al.: Sage.

Aldrich, J. H.; Nelson, F. D. (2002). *Linear Probability, Logit and Probit Models.* Newbury Park et al.: Sage.

Aldrige, A.; Levine, K. (2001). *Surveying the Social World: Principles and Practice in Survey Research.* Buckingham: Open University Press.

Alkin, M. C. (1969). Evaluation Theory Development. In: *Evaluation Comment,* 2, pp. 2–7.

Alkin, M. C. (ed.) (2004). *Evaluation Roots: Tracing Theorists' Views and Influences.* Thousand Oaks: California.

Alkin, M. C.; Christie, C. A. (2004). An Evaluation Theory Tree. In: Alkin, M. C. (ed.). *Evaluation Roots: Tracing Theorists' Views and Influences.* Thousand Oaks et al.: Sage, pp. 12–66.

Alkin, M.C. (2011). *Evaluation Essentials. From A to Z.* New York, London: Guilford Press.

Alkin, M.C.; Christie, C. A. (2013). An Evaluation Theory Tree. In Alkin, M. C. (ed.). *Evaluation Roots: A Wider Perspective of Theorists' Views and Influences.* Thousand Oaks et al.: Sage (2).

Allmendinger, J.; Hinz, T. (2002). Perspektiven der Organisationssoziologie. In: ibid. (ed.). *Organisationssoziologie.* Wiesbaden: Westdeutscher Verlag, pp. 9–28.

Althoff, S. (1993). *Auswahlverfahren in der Markt-, Meinungs- und Empirischen Sozialforschung.* Pfaffenweiler: Centaurus.

Altschuld, J. W. (1990). The Certification of Evaluators: Highlights from a Report Submitted to the Board of Directors of the American Evaluation Association. In: *American Journal of Evaluation,* 20, pp. 481–493.

Alvesson, M.; Karreman, D. (2001). Odd Couple: Making Sense of the Curious Concept of Knowledge Management. In: *Journal of Management Studies,* 38(7), pp. 995–1018.

Amelingmeyer, J. (2004). *Wissensmanagement. Analyse und Gestaltung der Wissensbasis von Unternehmen.* Wiesbaden: DUV.

Andersen, P. K.; Keiding, N. (ed.) (2006). *Survival and Event History Analysis.* Hoboken, N. J. et al.: Wiley.

Anderson, G.; Gilsig, D. (1998). Participatory Evaluation in Human Resource Development: A Case Study from Southeast Asia. In: Jackson, E. T.; Kassam, Y. (ed.). *Knowledge Shared: Participatory Evaluation in Development Cooperation.* West Hartford, Connecticut: Kumarian, pp. 150–166.

Andrews, K. M.; Delahaye, B. L. (2000). Influences on Knowledge Processes in Organizational Learning. The Psychological Filter. In: *Journal of Management Studies,* 37(6), pp. 2322–2380.

Argyris, C.; Schön, D. A. (2002). *Die Lernende Organisation. Grundlagen, Methode, Praxis.* Stuttgart: Klett-Cotta.

Assenmacher, W. (2003). *Deskriptive Statistik.* Berlin et al.: Springer.

Auerbach, C. F.; Silverstein, L. B. (2003). *Qualitative Data. An Introduction to Coding and Analysis.* New York et al.: New York Univ. Press.

Augsburg, B. (2006). Econometric Evaluation of the SEWA Bank in India. Applying Matching Techniques based on the Propensity Score. *MGSoG Working Paper No. 003.* Maastricht: Maastricht Graduate School of Governance.

Aulinger, A. (ed.) (2008). *Netzwerk-Evaluation. Herausforderungen und Praktiken für Verbundnetzwerke.* Stuttgart: Kohlhammer.

Aurin, K.; Stolz, G. E. (1990). Erfahrungen aus der Aufarbeitung von Evaluationsvorhaben am Beispiel der Projektgruppe 'Gesamtschule' der Bund-Länder-Kommission für Bildungsplanung und Forschungsförderung. In: *Zeitschrift für Pädagogische Psychologie,* 4(4), pp. 268–282.

AUSAID (ed.) (2005). The Logical-Framework Approach. Aus Guideline 3.3, Canberra: Australian Agency for International Development (on the Internet at: http://www.ausaid.gov.au/ausguide/pdf/ausguideline3.3.pdf, as of 1 Jan 2009).

Bacher, J. (1996). *Clusteranalyse: anwendungsorientierte Einführung.* München; Wien: Oldenbourg.

Bamberg, S., Gumbl, H.; Schmidt, P. (2000). *Rational Choice und theoriegeleitete Evaluationsforschung. Am Beispiel der 'Verhaltenswirksamkeit' verkehrspolitischer Maßnahmen.* Opladen: Leske + Budrich.

Bamberger, M.; Rugh, J.; Mabry, L. (2006). *RealWorld Evaluation: Working under Budget, Time, Data, and Political Constraints.* Thousand Oaks et al.: Sage.

Bank, V.; Lames, M. (2000). *Über Evaluation.* Kiel: bajOsch-Hein, Verl. für Berufs- und Wirtschaftspädagogik.

Baringhorst, S. (2004). Sozialintegration durch politische Kampagnen? Gesellschaftssteuerung durch Inszenierung. In: Lange, S.; Schimank, U. (ed.). *Governance und gesellschaftliche Integration,* Wiesbaden: VS-Verlag, pp. 129–146.

Barnard, C. I. (1938). *The Functions of the Executive.* Cambridge, Mass.: Harvard University Press.

Bartholomew, D. J.; Knott, M. (1999). *Latent Variable Models and Factor Analysis.* London et al.: Arnold.

Batinic, B.; Bosnjak, M. (1997). Fragebogenuntersuchungen im Internet. In: Batinic, B. (ed.). *Internet für Psychologen.* Göttingen et al.: Hogrefe, pp. 221–244.

Bauman, Z. (2010). *Hermeneutics and Social Science. Approaches to Understanding.* London et al.: Routledge.

Baumert, J. et al. (ed.) (2001). *PISA 2000. Basiskompetenzen von Schülerinnen und Schülern im internationalen Vergleich.* Opladen: Leske + Budrich.

Bea, F. X.; Göbel, E. (2002). *Organisation: Theorie und Gestaltung.* Stuttgart: Lucius und Lucius.

Becerra-Fernandez, I.; Leidner, D. E. (eds) (2008). *Knowledge Management – An Evolutionary View; Advances in Management Information Systems Vol. 12,* Armonk, NY: M. E. Sharpe.

Beck, U. (1996). Weltrisikogesellschaft, Weltöffentlichkeit und globale Subpolitik. Ökologische Fragen im Bezugsrahmen fabrizierter Unsicherheiten. In: Diekmann, A.; Jaeger, C.C. (ed.). *Umweltsoziologie.* Opladen: Westdeutscher Verlag.

Beck, U. (1999). *The Reinvention of Politics. Rethinking Modernity in the Global Social Order.* Cambridge: Polity Press.

Belson, W. A. (1986). *Validity in Survey Research.* Aldershot, Hants, England: Gower.

Benninghaus, H. (2007). *Deskriptive Statistik. Eine Einführung für Sozialwissenschaftler.* Wiesbaden: VS-Verlag.

Benz, A. (ed.) (2004). *Governance – Regieren in komplexen Regelsystemen. Eine Einführung.* Wiesbaden.

Berger, P. L.; Luckmann, T. (1999). *Die gesellschaftliche Konstruktion der Wirklichkeit. Eine Theorie der Wissenssoziologie.* Frankfurt: Fischer.

Bergmann, J. R. (2003). Konversationsanalyse. In: Flick, U., von Kardorff, E., Steinke, I. (ed.). *Qualitative Forschung. Ein Handbuch.* Reinbek: rororo, pp. 524–537.

Bergmann, J. R.; Meier C. (2003). Elektronische Prozessdaten und ihre Analyse. In: Flick, U., von Kardorff, E., Steinke, I. (ed.). *Qualitative Forschung. Ein Handbuch.* Reinbek: rororo, pp. 429–436.

Berry, W. D.; Feldman, S. (1985). *Multiple Regression in Practice.* Newbury Park, Calif. et al.: Sage.

Beyme, K. von (1994). Die Massenmedien und die Politische Agenda des Parlamentarischen Systems. In: Neidhardt, F. (ed.). *Öffentlichkeit, öffentliche Meinung, soziale Bewegungen*. Opladen: WdV, pp. 320–336.

Beywl, W. (2001). Konfliktfähigkeit der Evaluation und die 'Standards für Evaluationen'. In *Sozialwissenschaften und Berufspraxis*, 24(2), pp. 151–164.

Beywl, W.; Harich, K. (2007). University-Based Continuing Education in Evaluation. The Baseline in Europe. In*: Evaluation*, 13(1), pp. 121–134.

Beywl, W.; Widmer, T. (2000). *Handbuch der Evaluations standards. Die Standards des 'Joint Committee for Educational Evaluation'*. Opladen: Leske + Budrich.

Biemer, P. P. et al. (1991). *Measurement Errors in Surveys*. New York: Wiley.

Bittlingmayer, U. H.; Bauer, U. (ed.) (2006). *Die 'Wissensgesellschaft'. Mythos, Ideologie oder Realität?* Leverkusen: VS-Verlag.

Blasius, J. (2001). *Korrespondenzanalyse*. München et al.: Oldenbourg.

Blau, P. M.; Scott, R. W. (1963). *Formal Organizations: A Comparative Approach*. London: Routledge and Kegan.

Bloor, M. (2002). *Focus Groups in Social Research*. London et al.: Sage.

Blunch, N. J. (2008). *Introduction to Structural Equation Modelling Using SPSS and AMOS*. Thousand Oaks et al.: Sage.

Böhm, A. (2003). *Theoretisches Codieren: Textanalyse in der Grounded Theory*. In: Flick, U.; von Kardorff; E., Steinke, I. (ed.). Qualitative Forschung. Ein Handbuch. Reinbek: rororo, pp. 475–485.

Böltken, F. (1976). *Auswahlverfahren: Eine Einführung für Sozialwissenschaftler*. Stuttgart: Teubner.

Börzel, T. A. (1997). 'What's so special about policy networks?' An exploration of the concept and its usefulness in studying European governance. *European Integration online Papers Vol. 1* (1997), No. 016 (http://eiop.or.at/eiop/texte/1997–016a.htm).

Böttcher, W. et al. (ed.) (2008). *Bildungsmonitoring und Bildungscontrolling in nationaler und internationaler Perspektive. Dokumentation zur Herbsttagung der Kommission Bildungsorganisation, -planung, -recht (KBBB)*. Münster: Waxmann.

Boettner, J. (2007). Sozialraumanalyse – soziale Räume vermessen, erkunden, verstehen. In: Michel-Schwartze, B. (ed.). *Methodenbuch Soziale Arbeit. Basiswissen für die Praxis*. Wiesbaden: VS-Verlag, pp. 259–292.

Bogner, A.; Littig, B.; Menz, W. (ed.) (2005). *Das Experteninterview. Theorie, Methode, Anwendung*. Wiesbaden: VS-Verlag.

Bohnsack, R. (2003). Gruppendiskussion. In: Flick, U.; von Kardorff, E.; Steinke, I. (ed.). *Qualitative Forschung. Ein Handbuch*. Reinbek: rororo, pp. 369–384.

Bol, G. (2004). *Deskriptive Statistik. Lehr- und Arbeitsbuch*. München: Oldenbourg.

Booroah, V. K. (2003). *Logit and Probit. Ordered and Multinomial Models*. Thousand Oaks et al.: Sage.

Borrmann, A. (1999). *Erfolgskontrolle in der Deutschen Entwicklungszusammenarbeit*. Baden-Baden: Nomos.

Borrmann, A.; Gleich, A. v.; Holthus, M.; Shams, R. (2001). *Reform der Erfolgskontrolle in der deutschen Entwicklungszusammenarbeit: eine Zwischenbilanz*. Veröffentlichungen des Hamburgischen Welt-Wirtschafts-Archivs (HWWA), Vol. 63. Baden-Baden: Nomos.

Borrmann, A.; Stockmann, R. (2009). *Evaluation in der deutschen Entwicklungszusammenarbeit. Vol. 1 Systemanalysen, Vol. 2 Fallstudien*. Studie im Auftrag des Bundesministeriums für Wirtschaftliche Zusammenarbeit und Entwicklung – BMZ. Vols. 8 & 9 der Reihe 'Sozialwissenschaftliche Evaluationsforschung'. Münster: Waxmann.

Bortz, J.; Döring, N. (1995). *Forschungsmethoden und Evaluation*. 2nd edition, completely revised and updated, Berlin, Heidelberg, New York: Springer.

Bortz, J.; Döring, N. (2002). *Forschungsmethoden und Evaluation für Human- und Sozialwissenschaftler*, Berlin et al.

Bos, W. et al. (ed.) (2003). *Erste Ergebnisse aus IGLU. Schülerleistungen am Ende der vierten Jahrgangsstufe im internationalen Vergleich*. Münster: Waxmann.

Bos, W. et al. (ed.) (2005). *IGLU. Skalenhandbuch zur Dokumentation der Erhebungsinstrumente*, Münster: Waxann.

Bos, W. et al. (ed.) (2007). *IGLU 2006. Die Lesekompetenz von Grundschulkindern in Deutschland im internationalen Vergleich*. Münster: Waxmann.

Bos, W. et al. (ed.) (2008a). *IGLU-E 2006. Die Länder der Bundesrepublik im nationalen und internationalen Vergleich*. Münster: Waxmann.

Bos, W. et al. (ed.) (2008b). *TIMSS 2007. Mathematische und Naturwissenschaftliche Kompetenzen von Grundschulkindern in Deutschland im internationalen Vergleich*. Münster: Waxmann.

Bos, W.; Gröhlich, C.; Pietsch, M. (2007). *KESS 4. Lehr- und Lernbedingungen in Hamburger Grundschulen*. Münster: Waxmann.

Bos, W.; Pietsch, M. (ed.) (2006). *KESS 4. Kompetenzen und Einstellungen von Schülern und Schülerinnen am Ende der Jahrgangsstufe 4 in Hamburger Grundschulen*. Münster: Waxmann.

Bos, W.; Tarnai, Ch. (ed.) (1998), *Computerunterstützte Inhaltsanalyse in den Empirischen Sozialwissenschaften. Theorie – Anwendung – Software*. Münster et al.: Waxmann.

Bosch, W.; Wloka, M. (2006). *Allgemeine Anforderungen an die Kompetenz von Prüf- und Kalibrierlaboratorien. Kommentar zu DIN EN ISO/IEC 17025*. Berlin et al.: Beuth.

Bostrom, N. (2002). *Anthropic Bias. Observation Selection Effects in Science and Philosophy*. New York et al.: Routledge.

Bourier, G. (2005). *Wahrscheinlichkeitsrechnung und schließende Statistik: praxisorientierte Einführung mit Aufgaben und Lösungen*. Wiesbaden: Gabler.

Bourque, L. B.; Fielder, E. P. (2003). *How to Conduct Self-administrated and Mail Surveys*. Thousand Oaks et al.: Sage.

Bradshaw, J.; Ager, R.; Burge, B.; Wheater, R. (2010a). *PISA 2009: Achievement of 15-year-olds in England*, Slough: NFER.

Bradshaw, J.; Ager, R.; Burge, B.; Wheater, R. (2010b). *PISA 2009: Achievement of 15-year-olds in Wales*, Slough: NFER.

Bradshaw, J.; Ager, R.; Burge, B.; Wheater, R. (2010c). *PISA 2009: Achievement of 15-year-olds in Northern Ireland*, Slough: NFER.

Brägger, G.; Kramis, J.; Teuteberg, H. (2007). Reform der Schulaufsicht und Aufbau der Externen Schulevaluation in der Schweiz. Am Beispiel der Kantone Luzern und Thurgau. In: Böttcher, W.; Kotthoff, H. (ed.). *Schulinspektion: Evaluation, Rechnungslegung und Qualitätsentwicklung vor dem Hintergrund internationaler Erfahrungen*.

Brandt, T. (2009). *Evaluation in Deutschland: Professionalisierungsstand und -perspektiven*. Dissertation. Saarbrücken: Universität des Saarlandes.

Brandtstädter, J. (1990a). Entwicklung im Lebenslauf. Ansätze und Probleme der Lebensspannen-Entwicklungspsychologie. In: Mayer, K. U. (ed.). *Lebensverläufe und Sozialer Wandel*. (Sonderheft der Kölner Zeitschrift für Soziologie und Sozialpsychologie). Opladen: Westdeutscher Verlag.

Brandtstädter, J. (1990b). Evaluationsforschung: Probleme der wissenschaftlichen Bewertung von Interventions- und Reformprojekten. In: *Zeitschrift für Pädagogische Psychologie*. J. 4, H. 4. pp. 215–228.

Braun, D. (2004). Wie nützlich darf Wissenschaft sein? Zur Systemintegration von Wissenschaft, Ökonomie und Politik. In: Lange, S.; Schimank, U. (ed.). *Governance und gesellschaftliche Integration*. Wiesbaden: VS-Verlag, pp. 65–88.

Brauwer, R.; Rumpel, K.-D. (2008). *Bildungscontrolling. Ansätze, Modelle und Kennzahlen*. Aachen: Shaker-Verlag.

Bray, J. H.; Maxwell, S. E. (2003). *Multivariate Analysis of Variance*. Newbury Park, Calif. et al.: Sage.

Brent, R. J. (2008). *Applied Cost-benefit Analysis*. Cheltenham: Edward Elgar.

Brown, D. et al. (2002). *Participatory Methodologies and Participatory Practices: Assessing PRA use in the Gambia* (AgREN Network Papers, No. 124).

Brown, T. A (2006). *Confirmatory Factor Analysis for Applied Research*. New York et al.: Guilford.

Brüsemeister, T. (2000). *Qualitative Forschung. Ein Überblick*. Wiesbaden: Westdeutscher Verlag.

Bryman, A. (2008). *Social Research Methods* Oxford: Oxford University Press.

Bryne, D.; Uprichard, E. (eds., 2012). *Cluster Analysis*. Thousand Oaks et al.: Sage (Sage Benchmarks in Social Research Methods, 4 Vol.).

Bryson, A., Dorsett, R.; Purdon, S. (2002). The use of propensity score matching in the evaluation of active labour market policies. *Department for Work and Pensions Working Paper No. 4*. London: DWP (downloadable at http://www.dwp.gov.uk/asd/asd5/WP4.pdf, as of 4 June 2008).

Bulmer, M.; Sturgis, P.J.; Allum, N. (2009). *The Secondary Analysis of Survey Data*. Thousand Oaks et al.: Sage (Sage Benchmarks in Social Research Methods, 4 Vol.).

Bundesrechnungshof, Präsident des (1989). *Erfolgskontrolle finanzwirksamer Maßnahmen in der öffentlichen Verwaltung*. Stuttgart, Berlin, Köln: Kohlhammer.

Bundesrechnungshof, Präsident des (1998). *Erfolgskontrolle finanzwirksamer Maßnahmen in der öffentlichen Verwaltung*. Stuttgart, Berlin, Köln: Kohlhammer.

Bundesregierung (2001). *Perspektiven für Deutschland: Unsere Strategie für eine nachhaltige Entwicklung*. Zusammenfassung, 19 December 2001, Berlin.

Buschor, E. (2002). Evaluation und New Public Management. In: *Zeitschrift für Evaluation,* 1(2002), pp. 61–74.

Bussmann, W. et al. (ed.) (1997). *Einführung in die Politikevaluation*. Basel, Frankfurt am Main: Helbing & Lichtenhahn.

Campbell, D. T. (1969). Reform as Experiments. In: *American Psychologist*, 24(4), pp. 409–429.

Campbell, D. T. (1975). Assessing the Impact of Planned Social Change. In: Lyons, G. M. (ed.). *Social Research and Public Policies*. Hanover: Dartmouth College, pp. 3–45.

Campbell, D. T. (1991). Methods for the Experimenting Society. In: *Evaluation Practice*, 12(3), pp. 223–260.

Campbell, D. T.; Boruch, R. F. (1975). Making the Case for Randomized Assignment to Treatments by Considering the Alternatives: Six Ways in Which Quasi-Experimental Evaluations in Compensatory Education Tend to Underestimate Effects. In: Bennett, C. A.; Lumsdaine, A. A. (ed.). *Evaluation and Experiment*. New York: Academic Press, pp. 195–296.

Campbell, D. T.; Stanley, J. C. (1963). *Experimental and Quasi-Experimental Designs for Research.* Boston: Houghton-Mifflin.

Carrington, P. J., Scott, J.; Wasserman, S. (ed.) (2005). *Models and Methods in Social Network Analysis.* Cambridge: Cambridge University Press.

Carden, F. & Alkin, M. C. (2012). Evaluation Roots: An International Perspective. In: *Journal of Multidisciplinary Evaluation*, 8, Nr. 17, pp. 102–118.

Carson, A. M. (2001). That's Another Story: narrative methods and ethical practice. In: *Journal of Medical Ethics*, 27, pp. 198–202.

Caspari, A. (2004). *Evaluation der Nachhaltigkeit von Entwicklungszusammenarbeit. Zur Notwendigkeit angemessener Konzepte und Methoden.* Wiesbaden: VS-Verlag.

Caspari, A.; Barbu, R. (2008). Wirkungsevaluierungen: Zum Stand der internationalen Diskussion und dessen Relevanz für Evaluierungen der deutschen Entwicklungszusammenarbeit. *Evaluation Working Papers.* Bonn: Bundesministerium für wirtschaftliche Zusammenarbeit und Entwicklung.

Castells, M. (2002). *Das Informationszeitalter* (3 vols), Leverkusen: VS-Verlag.

CDG (2006). *When Will We Ever Learn? Improving Lives through Impact Evaluation.* Washington, D.C, Centre for Global Development.

Chambers, R. (1994). The origins and practice of participatory rural appraisal. In: *World Development*, 22(7), pp. 953–969.

Chelimsky, E. (1995). New dimensions in evaluation. In: World Bank Operations Evaluations Department (OED). *Evaluation and Development: proceedings of the 1994 World Bank Conference.* Washington D.C., pp. 3–11.

Chelimsky, E. (1997). The Coming Transformation in Evaluation. In: Chelimsky, E.; Shadish, W. R. (ed.). *Evaluation for the 21st Century. A Handbook.* Thousand Oaks et al.: Sage.

Chelimsky, E. (2006). The Purpose of Evaluation in a Democratic Society. In: Shaw, I. F.; Greene, J. C.; Melvin, M. (ed.). *The Sage Handbook of Evaluation.*

Chen, H. (1990). *Theory-Driven Evaluations.* Newbury Park: Sage.

Chen, H.; Rossi, P. (1980). The Multi-Goal, Theory-Driven Approach to Evaluation: A Model Linking Basic and Applied Social Science. In: *Social Forces*, 59, pp. 106–122.

Chen, H.; Rossi, P. (1983). Evaluating with Sense: The Theory-driven Approach. In: *Evaluation Review*, 7, pp. 283–302.

Chen, H.; Rossi, P. (1987). The Theory-driven Approach to Validity. In: *Evaluation and Program Planning*, 10, pp. 95–103.

Chen, H. T.; Donaldson, S. I.; Mark, M. M. (eds) (2011). *Advancing Validity in Outcome Evaluation. Theory and Practice.* San Francisco: Wiley (New Directions for Evaluation no. 130).

Chen, S.; Ravallion, M. (2003). Hidden Impact? Ex-Post Evaluation of an Anti-Poverty Program. *World Bank Policy Research Working Paper 3049*, May 2003 (downloadable at http://www-wds.worldbank.org/external/default/WDSContentServer/IW3P/IB/2003/06/06/000094946_03052804040641/additional/107507322_20041117143515.pdf, as of 4 June 2008).

Christensen, T. (2002). *New Public Management: The Transformation of Ideas and Practice.* Aldershot: Ashgate.

Christie, C. A.; Alkin, M. C. (2008). Evaluation Theory Tree Re-examined. In: *Studies in Educational Evaluation*, 34(2008), pp. 131–135.

Cicourel, A. V. (1974). *Methode und Messung in der Soziologie.* Frankfurt: Suhrkamp.

Clandinin, D. J.; Connelly, F. M. (2004). *Narrative Inquiry. Experience and Story in Qualitative Research.* San Francisco: Jossey-Bass.

Clemens, W. (2000). Angeordnete Sozialforschung und Politikberatung. In: Clemens, W.; Strübing, J. (ed.). *Empirische Sozialforschung und gesellschaftliche Praxis*. Opladen: Leske + Budrich.

Cleves, M. A.; Gould, W. W.; Gutierrez, R. G. (2008). *An Introduction to Survival Analysis Using Stata*. College Station, Tex.: Stata Press.

Clubb, J. M.; Scheuch, E. K. (ed.) (1980). *Historical Social Research: The Use of Historical and Process-Produced Data*. Stuttgart: Klett.

Cohen, J. L.; Arato, A. (1992). *Civil Society and Political Theory*. Cambridge, Mass.: MIT Press.

Cohen, J.; Cohen, P.; West, S. G. (2002). *Applied Multiple Regression/Correlation Analysis for the Behavioral Sciences*. London et al.: Psychology Press (3.).

Cook, T. (1997). Lessons Learned in Evaluation Over the Past 25 Years. In: Chelimsky, E.; Shadish, W. R. (ed.). *Evaluation for the 21st Century: A Handbook*. Thousand Oaks et al.: Sage, pp. 31–68.

Cook, T. D.; Matt, G. E. (1990). Theorien der Programmevaluation. In: Koch, U.; Wittmann, W. (Hg). *Evaluationsforschung: Bewertungsgrundlage von Sozial- und Gesundheitsprogrammen*. Berlin et al.: Springer.

Couper, M. P.; Coutts, E. (2006). Online-Befragung. Probleme und Chancen verschiedener Arten von Online-Erhebungen. In: Diekmann, A. (ed.). *Methoden der Sozialforschung*. Wiesbaden (special edition no. 44 of the Kölner Zeitschrift für Soziologie und Sozialpsychologie), pp. 217–243.

Cousins, J. B.; Earl, L. M. (ed.) (1992). *Participatory Evaluation in Education: Studies in Evaluation Use and Organizational Learning*. London: Falmer Press.

Cousins, J. B.; Earl, L. M. (1995). *Participatory Evaluation in Education: Studies in Evaluation Use and Organizational Learning*. London: Falmer Press.

Cousins, J. B.; Shulha, L. M. (2006). A Comparative Analysis of Evaluation Utilization and Its Cognate Fields of Inquiry: Current Issues and Trends. In: Shaw, I. F.; Mark, M. M.; Greene, J. (eds). *The Sage Handbook of Evaluation: Program, Policy and Practices*. London: Sage.

Creswell, J.W. (2012). *Qualitative Inquiry and Research Design: Choosing Among Five Approaches*. Thousand Oaks et al.: Sage (3.).

Creswell, J. W. (2009). *Research Design. Qualitative, Quantitative, and Mixed Methods Approaches*. Thousand Oaks et al.: Sage (3).

Creswell, J. W.; Plano Clark, V. L. (2007). *Designing and Conducting Mixed Methods Research*. Thousand Oaks et al.: Sage.

Cronbach, L. J. (1982). *Designing Evaluations of Educational and Social Programs*. San Francisco et al.: Jossey-Bass.

Cronbach, L. J. et al. (1980). *Toward Reform of Program Evaluation*. San Francisco et al.: Jossey-Bass.

Cropley, A. J. (2005), *Qualitative Forschungsmethoden: eine praxisnahe Einführung*. Eschborn: Klotz.

Cuddeback, G., Wilson, E., Orme, J. G.; Combs-Orme, T. (2004). Detecting and Statistically Correcting Sample Selection Bias. In: *Journal of Social Service Research*, 30(3), pp. 19–33 (downloadable at http://web.utk.edu/~orme00/articles/Cuddeback_et_al.pdf, as of 6 June 2008)

Cuppen, E. (2012). A Quasi-experimental Evaluation of Learning in a Stakeholder Dialogue on Bio-energy. In: *Research Policy*, 41(3), pp. 624–637.

Dahler-Larsen, P. (2006). Evaluation after Disenchantment? Five Issues Shaping the Role of Evaluation in Society. In: Shaw, I. F.; Mark, M. M.; Greene, J. (eds). *The Sage Handbook of Evaluation: Program, Policy and Practices*. London: Sage.

Dahler-Larsen, P. (2011). *The Evaluating Society*. Stanford University Press: Stanford.

Dale, A.; Arber, S.; Procter, M. (1988). *Doing Secondary Analysis*. London et al.: Unwin Hyman.

Danesi, M. (2007). *The Quest for Meaning. A Guide to Semiotic Theory and Practice*. Toronto: University of Toronto Press.

Das, M.; Ester, P.; Kaczmirek, L. (eds.; 2010). *Socialand Behavioral Research and the Internet. Advances in Applied Methods and Research Strategies*, Hove: Psypress.

Datta, L. (2006). The Practice of Evaluation: Challenges and New Directions. In: Shaw, I. F.; Mark, M. M.; Greene, J. (eds). *The Sage Handbook of Evaluation: Program, Policy and Practices*. London: Sage.

Davenport, T. H.; Prusak, L. (1998). *Working Knowledge: How Organizations Manage What They Know*. Boston: Harvard Business School Press.

De Maris, A. (2003). *Logit Modelling. Practical Applications*. Newbury Park et al.: Sage.

De Vaus, D. (2005). *Surveys in Social Research*. London et al.: Routledge.

De Zeeuw, A. J.; van der Ploeg, F. (1991). Difference Games and Policy Evaluation: A Conceptual Framework. In: *Oxford Economic Papers*, 43, pp. 612–636.

De Zeeuw, A. J. (2008). Dynamic Effects on the Stability of International Environmental Agreements. In: *Journal of Environmental Economics and Management*, 55(2), pp. 163–174.

Degele, N.; Dries, C. (2005). *Modernisierungstheorie*. Eine Einführung. München: Fink (UTB).

Dent, M. (2004). *Questioning the new public management*. Aldershot: Ashgate.

Derlien, H.-U. (1976). *Die Erfolgskontrolle staatlicher Planung. Eine empirische Untersuchung über Organisation, Methode und Politik der Programmevaluation*. Baden-Baden: Nomos.

Derlien, H.-U. (1990). Genesis and Structure of Evaluation Efforts in Comparative Perspective. In: Rist, R. C. (ed.). *Program Evaluation and the Management of Government*. New Brunswick: Transaction.

Derlien, H.-U. (ed.) (1991). *Programmforschung in der öffentlichen Verwaltung*. Werkstattbericht der Gesellschaft für Programmforschung. München.

Derlien, H.-U. (1994). Evaluation zwischen Programm und Budget. In: Hofmeister, A. (ed.). Möglichkeiten und Grenzen der Programmsteuerung: Controlling und Evaluation. Verwaltungspraxis in Ost und West in Zeiten des Wandels. *Schriftenreihe der Schweizerischen Gesellschaft für Verwaltungswissenschaft*. Band 21, pp. 43–61.

Descy, P.; Tessaring, M. (ed.) (2004). Impact of Education and Training. Third report on vocational training research in Europe: background report. Luxembourg: Office for Official Publications of the European Communities (Cedefop Reference series No. 54).

Deutsche Gesellschaft für Evaluation (2002). *Standards für Evaluation*. Köln: DeGEval.

Deutscher, I.; Ostrander, S. A. (1985). Sociology and Evaluation Research: Some Past and Future Links. In: *History of Sociology*, 6, pp. 11–32.

Diamond, W. D. (2001). *Practical Experiment Designs for Engineers and Scientists*. New York: Wiley.

Diekmann, A. (1997). *Empirische Sozialforschung*. Reinbeck: Rowohlt.

Dijk, T. A. v. (ed.) (1992). *Handbook of Discourse Analysis. Vol. 3*. London et al.: Academic Press.

Dijkstra, W.; van der Zouwen, J. (1982). *Response behaviour in the survey-interview.* London et al.: Academic Press.

Dinter, S. (2001). *Netzwerke. Eine Organisationsform moderner Gesellschaften?* Marburg: Tectum.

Dommach, H. (2008). Das Verfahren der Erfolgskontrolle durch die Bundesverwaltung für zuwendungsfinanzierte Projekte und Institutionen. In: *Die Öffentliche Verwaltung.* Heft 7, pp. 282–287.

Donaldson, S. I.; Lipsey, M. W. (2006). Roles for Theory in Contemporary Evaluation Practice: Developing Practical Knowledge. In: Shaw, I. F.; Mark, M. M.; Greene, J. (eds). *The Sage Handbook of Evaluation: Program, Policy and Practices.* London: Sage.

Doncaster, C. P.; Davey, A. J. H. (2007). *Analysis of Variance and Covariance : How to Choose and Construct Models for the Life Sciences.* Cambridge et al.: Cambridge University Press.

Droitcour, J. A. (1997). Cross-Design Synthesis: Concept and application. In: Chelimsky, E.; Shadish, W. R. (ed.). *Evaluation for the 21st century. A handbook.* Thousand Oaks: Sage, pp. 360–372.

Droitcour, J. A.; Kovar, M. G. (2008). Multiple Threats to the Validity of Randomized Studies. In: Smith, N. L.; Brandon, P. R. (ed.). *Fundamental Issues in Evaluation.* New York: Guilford Press, pp. 61–88.

Dror, Y. (1968). *Public policymaking re-examined.* Scranton, Pennsylvania: Chandler.

Drummond, M. F. et al. (2007). *Methods for the Economic Evaluation of Health Care Programmes.* Oxford et al.: Oxford University Press.

Druwe, U. (1987). Politik. In: Görlitz, A.; Prätorius, R. (ed.). *Handbuch Politikwissenschaft. Grundlagen-Forschungsstand-Perspektiven.* Hamburg: Rowohlt. pp. 393–397.

Duffy, S. W., Hill, C. and Estève, J. (ed.) (2001). *Quantitative Methods for the Evaluation of Cancer Screening.* London: Hodder Arnold.

Dunn, W. N. (2004). *Public Policy Analysis: An Introduction.* Prentice-Hall: Pearson.

Dye, T. R. (1978). *Policy-Analysis: What Governments Do, Why They Do It, and What Difference it Makes.* Alabama: University of Alabama.

Eaton, J. S. (2011). *An Overview of U.S. Accreditation.* Washington: Council of Higher Education Accreditation (CHEA).

Ecarius, J.; Schäffer, B. (ed.) (2008). *Typenbildung und Theoriegenerierung: Methoden und Methodologien qualitativer Biographie- und Bildungsforschung.* Wiesbaden: Barbara Budrich.

Eckey, H. F., Kosfeld, R.; Türck, M. (2005). *Deskriptive Statistik. Grundlagen – Methoden – Beispiele.* Wiesbaden: Gabler.

Eco, U. (2007). *Zeichen. Einführung in einen Begriff und seine Geschichte.* Frankfurt: Suhrkamp.

Eco, U. (2002). *Einführung in die Semiotik.* München: Fink.

Egger, M.; Lenz, C. (2006). Wirkungsevaluation der öffentlichen Arbeitsvermittlung. Studie im Auftrag der Aufsichtskommission für den Ausgleichsfonds der Arbeitslosenversicherung. Bern: Staatssekretär für Wirtschaft, *Seco Publikation Arbeitsmarktpolitik No 18* (10. 2006) (downloadable at http://www.seco.admin. ch/dokumentation/publikation/00004/00005/ 01796/index.html?lang=de; as of 3 June 2008).

Eisenführ, F.; Weber, M. (2003). *Rationales Entscheiden.* Berlin et al.. Springer.

Ellenbogen, K. (2004). *Die verdeckte Ermittlungstätigkeit der Strafverfolgungsbehörden durch die Zusammenarbeit mit V-Personen und Informanten.* Berlin: Duncker & Humblot (Schriften zum Prozessrecht 187).

Etzioni, A. (1964). *Modern Organizations.* Englewood Cliffs, N.J.: Prentice-Hall.

Evans, S. M.; Boyte, H. C. (1992). *Free Spaces: The Sources of Democratic Change in America.* Chicago: University of Chicago Press.

Ezzy, D. (2000). Fate and Agency in Job Loss Narratives. In: *Qualitative Sociology,* 23(1), pp. 121–134.

Fairclough, N. (2003). *Analysing Discourse: Textual Analysis for Social Research.* London: Routledge.

Fassnacht, G. (1995). *Systematische Verhaltensbeobachtung,* München: Reinhardt.

Feick, J.; Jann, W. (1988). Nations matter – Vom Eklektizismus zur Integration in der vergleichenden Policy-Forschung? In: Schmidt, M. G. (ed.). *Staatstätigkeit. International und historisch vergleichende Analysen* (PVS-Sonderheft 19). Opladen: Westdeutscher Verlag.

Feinstein, O.; Beck, T. (2006). Evaluation of Development Interventions and Humanitarian Action. In: Shaw, I. F.; Mark, M. M.; Greene, J. (eds). *The Sage Handbook of Evaluation: Program, Policy and Practices.* London: Sage.

Fend, H. (1982). *Gesamtschule im Vergleich. Bilanz der Ergebnisse des Gesamtschulversuchs.* Weinheim: Beltz.

Fetterman, D. M.; Kaftarian, S. J.; Wandersman, A. (eds) (1995). *Empowerment Evaluation. Knowledge and Tools for Self-Assessment and Accountability.* Thousand Oaks: Sage.

Fetterman, D. M. (2000). *Foundations of Empowerment Evaluation.* Thousand Oaks, CA: Sage.

Fetterman, D. M.; Wandersman, A. (eds. 2005). *Empowerment Evaluation Principles in Practice.* New York: Guilford Press.

Finsterbusch, K.; Llewellyn, L. G.; Wolf, C. P. (ed.) (1983). *Social Impact Assessment Methods.* Beverly Hills et al.: Sage.

Fitzpatrick, J. L.; Morris, M. (ed.) (1999). *Current and Emerging Ethical Challenges in Evaluation.* San Francisco: Jossey-Bass.

Fitzpatrick, J. L.; Sanders, J. R.; Worthen, B. R. (2012). *Program Evaluation. Alternative Approaches and Practical Guidelines.* 4th edition. Boston et al.: Pearson.

Fleischmann, H. L.; Hopstock, P. J.; Pelczar, M. P.; Shelley, B. E. (2010). Highlights from PISA 2009: Performance of U.S. 15-year-old Students in Reading, Mathematics and Science Literacy in an International Context (NCES 2011–004). U.S. Department of Education. National Center for Education Statistics. Washington, D.C.: U.S. Government Printing Office.

Flick, U. (ed.) (2006). *Qualitative Evaluationsforschung. Konzepte – Methoden – Umsetzung.* Reinbek: Rowohlt.

Flick, U. (2008). *Triangulation. Eine Einführung.* Wiesbaden: VS-Verlag.

Florio, M. (ed.) (2007). *Cost-Benefit Analysis and Incentives in Evaluation. The Structural-Funds of the European Union.* Cheltenham: Edward Elgar.

Foddy, W. (2001). *Constructing Questions for Interviews and Questionnaires. Theory and practice in social research.* Cambridge et al.: Cambridge Univ. Press.

Föllinger, O. (2007). *Laplace-, Fourier- und z-Transformation.* Heidelberg: Hüthig.

Forschungsgesellschaft für Strassen- und Verkehrswesen (1995). *Hinweise zur Schätzung von Verkehrsbeziehungen mit Hilfe von Querschnittszählungen.* Köln: Forschungsgesellschaft.

Franzosi, R. (ed.) (2007). *Content Analysis*. Vol. 4. Los Angeles et al.: Sage.

Freedman, J. (1997). Accountability in the participatory mode. In: Cummings, H. F. (ed.). *Results-Based Performance*. *Reviews and Evaluations (Canadian Journal of Development Studies*, Vol XVIII, Special Issue). Ottawa: University of Ottawa, pp. 767–784.

Frey, K. et al. (2006). *Evaluationsbericht*. Gutachterkommission zu Evaluation des Centrums für Evaluation (CEval) an der Universität des Saarlandes. Münster.

Friederichs, J.; Lüdtke, H. (1977). *Teilnehmende Beobachtung: Einführung in die sozialwissenschaftliche Feldforschung*. Weinheim et al.: Beltz.

Früh, W. (2007). *Inhaltsanalyse. Theorie und Praxis*. Konstanz: UVK.

Fuchs, D. (1999). Soziale Integration und Politische Institutionen in Modernen Gesellschaften. In: Friedrichs, J.; Jagodzinski, W. (ed.). *Soziale Integration*. *Opladen/Wiesbaden: Westdeutscher Verlag* (Sonderheft 39 der Kölner Zeitschrift für Soziologie und Sozialpsychologie), pp. 147–178.

Furubo, J.-E.; Rist, R. C.; Sandahl, R. (2002) (ed.). *International Atlas of Evaluation*. New Brunswick: Transaction Publishers.

Gabler, S.; Häder, S. (2006). *Auswahlverfahren*. Wiesbaden: VS-Verlag.

Gabler, S.; Häder, S.; Hoffmeyer-Zlotnik, J. H. P. (1998). *Telefonstichproben in Deutschland*. Opladen: WdV.

Gadamer, H. G. (2007). *Wahrheit und Methode* (ed. G. Figal). Berlin: Akademie (new edition).

Gagel, D. (1990). Aktionsforschung – Methoden partizipativer Handwerksförderung. In: Boehm, U.; Kappel, R. (ed.). *Kleinbetriebe des informellen Sektors und Ausbildung im sub-saharischen Afrika*. Hamburg.

Gane, M. (2006). *Auguste Comte. Key Sociologists*. London & New York: Routledge.

Gangl, M.; DiPrete, T. A. (2006). Kausalanalyse durch Matchingverfahren. In: Diekmann, A. (ed.). *Methoden der Sozialforschung*. Wiesbaden: VS-Verlag, pp. 396–420 (special edition no. 44, 2004 of the Kölner Zeitschrift für Soziologie und Sozialpsychologie).

Gairing, F. (2002). *Organisationsentwicklung als Lernprozess von Menschen und Systemen*. München: Beltz.

Geertz, C. (2003). *Dichte Beschreibung. Beiträge zum Verstehen kultureller Systeme*. Frankfurt am Main: Suhrkamp.

Geider, F. J., Rogge, K.-E.; Schaaf, H. P. (1982). *Einstieg in die Faktorenanalyse*. Heidelberg: Quelle & Meyer.

Gergen, K. J. (2002). *Konstruierte Wirklichkeiten. Eine Hinführung zum sozialen Konstruktivismus*. Stuttgart: Kohlhammer.

Gillham, B. (2005). *Research Interviewing. The Range of Techniques*. Maidenhead: Open University Press.

Girden, E. R. (1998). *ANOVA: Repeated Measures*. Newbury Park, Calif. u.a: Sage.

Gläser, J.; Laudel, G. (2009). *Experteninterviews und Qualitative Inhaltsanalyse als Instrumente rekonstruierender Untersuchungen*. Wiesbaden: VS-Verlag.

Glagow, M. (1992). Die Nicht-Regierungsorganisationen in der internationalen Entwicklungszusammenarbeit. In: Nohlen, D.; Nuscheler, F. (ed.). *Handbuch der Dritten Welt. Grundprobleme, Theorien, Strategien*. Bonn: Dietz, pp. 309–326.

Glass, G. and Ellett, F. Jr. (1980). Evaluation Research. In: *Annual Review Psychology*, 31, pp. 211–228.

Glitza, K. H. (2005). *Observation. Praxisleitfaden für private und behördliche Ermittlungen.* Stuttgart et al.: Boorberg.

Glucksberg, S. (2001). *Understanding Figurative Language. From Metaphor to Idioms.* Oxford: Oxford University Press.

Glynn, J. R.; Dube, A.; Kayuni, N.; Floyd, S.; Molesworth, A.; Parrott, F.; French, N.; Crampin, A. C. (2012). Measuring concurrency: an empirical study of different methods in a large population-based survey and evaluation of the UNAIDS guidelines. In: *AIDS,* 26 (8), pp. 977–985.

Gölz, N. (2002). *Soll-Ist-Vergleich und Abweichungsanalyse in der Grenzplankostenrechnung.* Norderstedt: Grin.

Götz, K.; Schmid, M. (2004a). *Theorien des Wissensmanagement.* Frankfurt et al.: Lang.

Götz, K.; Schmid, M. (2004b). *Praxis des Wissensmanagement.* München: Vahlen.

Goffman, E. (1999). *Das Individuum im öffentlichen Austausch. Mikrostudien zur öffentlichen Ordnung.* Frankfurt: Suhrkamp (3rd edition).

Gollwitzer, M.; Jäger, R. S. (2007). *Evaluation. Workbook.* Weinheim, Basel: Beltz.

Gordon, R.A. (2010). *Regression Analysis for the Social Sciences,* Abingdon: Routledge.

Gramsci, A. (1976). *Selections from the Prison Notebooks.* London: Lawrence & Wishart.

Graßhoff, G., Casties, R.; Nickelsen, K. (2000). *Zur Theorie des Experiments. Untersuchungen am Beispiel der Entdeckung des Harnstoffzyklus.* Bern: Bern Studies in the History and Philosophy Sciences.

Green, T. B.; Knippen, J. T. (1999). *Breaking the Barrier to Upward Communication. Strategies and Skills for Employees, Managers, and HR Specialists.* New York: Quorum Books.

Greenacre, M. J.; Blasius, J. (ed.) (1999). *Correspondence Analysis in the Social Sciences. Recent developments and applications.* San Diego: Academic Press.

Greenacre, M. J. (2007). *Correspondence Analysis in Practice.* Boca Raton: Chapman & Hall.

Greene, J. C. (2006). *Evaluation, Democracy, and Social Change.* In: Shaw, I. F., Greene, J. C.; Mark, M. M. (ed.). *Handbook of Evaluation. Policies, Programs and Practices.* London et al.: Sage, pp. 56–75.

Greene, J. C. (2007). *Mixed Methods in Social Inquiry.* San Francisco: Jossey-Bass.

Greene, J. C.; Caracelli, V. J. (ed.) (1997). *Advances in Mixed-Method Evaluation. The Challenges and Benefits of Integrating Diverse Paradigms.* San Francisco: Jossey-Bass.

Greenstone, M.; Gayer, T. (2007). Quasi-Experimental and Experimental Approaches to Environmental Economics. Resources for the Future Discussion. paper RFF-DP-07-22 (downloadable at http://www.rff.org/Documents/RFF-DP-07-22.pdf, as of 4 June 2008).

Greve, W.; Wentura, D. (1997). *Wissenschaftliche Beobachtung. Eine Einführung,* Weinheim et al.: Beltz.

Gronlund, N. E. (1959). *Sociometry in the Class Room.* New York: Harper.

Groß, J. (2003). *Linear Regression.* Berlin; Heidelberg et al.: Springer.

Groves, R. M. (1989). *Survey Errors and Survey Costs.* New York et al.: Wiley.

Groves, R. M., Dillman, D. A., Eltinge, J. L.; Little, R. J. A. (ed.) (2002). *Survey Nonresponse.* New York: John Wiley and Sons.

Groves, R. M. et al. (ed.) (2001). *Telephone Survey Methodology.* New York et al.: Wiley.

Gruschka, A. (ed.) (1967). *Ein Schulversuch wird überprüft. Das Evaluationsdesign für die Kollegstufe NW als Konzept handlungsorientierter Begleitforschung.* Kronberg.

Gschwend, T.; Schimmelfennig, F. (ed.) (2007). *Research Design in Political Science. How to practice what they preach.* Basingstoke et al.: Palgrave Macmillan.

Guba, E. G. (1981). Investigative reporting. In: Smith, N. L. (ed.). *Metaphors for Evaluation: Sources of New Methods.* New Perspectives in Evaluation (Vol. 1). Beverly Hills, CA: Sage.

Guba, E. G.; Lincoln, Y. S. (1989). *Fourth Generation Evaluation,* Newbury Park et al.: Sage.

Gubrium, J. F.; Holstein, J. A. (ed.) (2004). *Handbook of Interview Research. Context and Method.* Thousand Oaks et al.: Sage.

Haarmann, A.; Schulz, E.; Wasmer, M.; Blohm, M.; Harkness, J. (2006). Konzeption und Durchführung der 'Allgemeinen Bevölkerungsumfrage der Sozialwissenschaften' (ALLBUS) 2004. Mannheim: ZUMA (ZUMA-Methodenbericht 2006/06).

Haas, B.; Scheibelhofer, E. (1998). *Typenbildung in der qualitativen Sozialforschung.* Wien: IHS.

Habermas, J. (2001). *Strukturwandel der Öffentlichkeit.* Frankfurt am Main: Suhrkamp (7th edition).

Habermehl, W. (1992), *Angewandte Sozialforschung,* München/Wien.

Häder, M. (2002). *Delphi-Befragungen. Ein Arbeitsbuch.* Wiesbaden: Westdeutscher Verlag.

Häder, M.; Häder, S. (ed.) (2000). *Die Delphi-Technik in den Sozialwissenschaften. Methodische Forschungen und innovative Anwendungen.* Wiesbaden: Westdeutscher Verlag.

Hage, G.; Aiken, M. (1969). Routine Technology, Social Structure, and Organization Goals. In: *ASQ,* 14, pp. 366–376.

Hanf, K.; Toole, L. J. Jr. (1992). Revisiting Old Friends. Networks, Implementation Structures and the Management of Inter-organisational Relations. In: Jordan, G.; Schubert, K. (ed.) *Policy Networks. European Journal of Political Research,* Special Issue 21, 1–2, pp. 163–180.

Harris, T. W. (ed.) (2002). *Applied Organizational Communication. Principles and Pragmatics for Future Practice.* Mahwah: Erlbaum.

Harrison, M. D. (2002). *Narrative Based Evaluation. Wording toward the Light.* New York et al.: Lang.

Hartwich, H. H. (ed.) (1985). *Policy-Forschung in der Bundesrepublik Deutschland. Ihr Selbstverständnis und ihr Verhältnis zu den Grundfragen der Politikwissenschaft.* Opladen.

Haw, K.; Hadfield, M. (2010). *Video in Social Science Research. Functions and Forms,* Abingdon: Routledge.

Haun, M. (2005). *Handbuch Wissensmanagement. Grundlagen und Umsetzung, Systeme und Praxisbeispiele.* Berlin: Springer.

Heckman, J. J., Ichimura, H.; Smith, J.; Todd, P. E. (1996). Sources of selection bias in evaluating social programs: An interpretation of conventional measures and evidence on the effectiveness of matching as a program evaluation method. In: *Proceedings of the National Academy of Sciences USA,* 93, pp. 13416–13420, November 1996

(downloadable at http://www.pnas.org/cgi/reprint/93/23/13416.pdf?ck=nck, as of 6 June 2008).

Heckman, J. J., Ichimura, H.; Todd, P. E. (1997). Matching as an Econometric Evaluation Estimator: Evidence from Evaluating a Job Training Programme. In: *Review of Economic Studies*, 64, pp. 605–654.

Hein, M. R. (1990). *Organisationskommunikation und Organisationskultur. Führungskräfte – Kommunikatoren und Kulturmanager. Eine empirische Analyse.* Bonn: BDW.

Heiner, M. (1998). Lernende Organisation und Experimentierende Evaluation. In: Heiner, M. (ed.). *Experimentierende Evaluation. Ansätze zur Entwicklung lernender Organisationen.* Weinheim und München: Juventa, pp. 11–53.

Heise, M.; Meyer, W. (2004). The benefits of education, training and skills from an individual life-course perspective with particular focus on life-course and biographical research. In: Descy, P.; Tessaring, M. (ed.). *Impact of Education and Training. Third Report on Vocational Training Research in Europe: Background Report.* Luxembourg: Office for Official Publications of the European Communities, pp. 321–381.

Helffrich, C. (2005). *Die Qualität qualitativer Daten. Manual für die Durchführung qualitativer Interviews.* Wiesbaden: VS-Verlag.

Hellstern, G.-M.; Wollmann, H. (1983). Bilanz-Reformexperimente, wissenschaftliche Begleitung und politische Realität. In: Hellstern, G.-M.; Wollmann, H. (ed.). *Experimentelle Politik – Reformstrohfeuer oder Lernstrategie.* Opladen: Westdeutscher Verlag.

Hellstern, G.-M.; Wollmann, H. (ed.) (1984). *Handbuch zur Evaluierungsforschung Vol. 1.* Opladen: Westdeutscher Verlag.

Hempel, C. G. (1974). *Philosophie der Naturwissenschaften.* München: dtv.

Hempel, C. G.; Oppenheim, P. C. (1948). Studies in the Logic of Explanation. In: *Philosophy and Science*, 15, pp. 135–175.

Henry, G. T.; Julnes, G. and Mark, M. M. (ed.) (1998). *Realist Evaluation. An Emerging Theory in Support of Practice.* San Francisco: Jossey-Bass.

Henry, G. T. (1996). Does the Public have a Role in Evaluation? Surveys and Democratic Discourse. In: Braverman, M. T.; Slater, J. K. (ed.). *Advances in Survey Research.* San Francisco: Jossey-Bass (New Directions for Evaluation 70), pp. 3–15.

Herger, N. (2004). *Organisationskommunikation. Beobachtung und Steuerung eines organisationalen Risikos.* Wiesbaden: VS-Verlag.

Hermann, D. (1984). *Ausgewählte Probleme bei der Anwendung der Pfadanalyse.* Frankfurt am Main et al.: Lang.

Herman, L.; Vervaeck, B. (2005). *Handbook of Narrative Analysis.* Lincoln et al.: University of Nebraska.

Hibberd, F. J. (2005). *Unfolding Social Constructivism.* Berlin et al.: Springer.

Hildenbrand, B. (2003). Anselm Strauss. In: Flick, U.; von Kardorff, E.; Steinke, I. (ed.). *Qualitative Forschung. Ein Handbuch.* Reinbek: rororo, pp. 32–42.

Hill, H. (ed.) (2001). *Modernisierung – Prozesse oder Entwicklungsstrategie?* Frankfurt: Campus.

Hiller, P. (2005). *Organisationswissen. Eine wissenssoziologische Neubeschreibung der Organisation,* Wiesbaden: VS-Verlag.

Hitzler, R. (ed.) (1997). *Sozialwissenschaftliche Hermeneutik. Eine Einführung.* Opladen: Leske + Budrich.

Hoberg, R. (2003). *Clusteranalyse, Klassifikation und Datentiefe.* Köln: Eul (series: Quantitative Ökonomie 129).

Holler, M. J.; Illing, G. (2000). *Einführung in die Spieltheorie.* Berlin et al..

Holm, K. (ed.) (1976). *Die Befragung. Vol. 3, Faktorenanalyse.* München: Francke.

Holm, K. (ed.) (1977). *Die Befragung. Vol. 5, Pfadanalyse,* Coleman-Verfahren. Tübingen: Francke

Holtkamp, L. (2006). Bürgerbeteiligung in Deutschland. In: *Alternative Kommunalpolitik* 01/06, pp. 54–59.

Hosmer, D. W.; Lemeshow, S.; May, S. (2008). *Applied Survival Analysis: Regression Modelling of Time-to-Event Data.* Hoboken, NJ : Wiley.

Hosmer, D. W.; Lemeshow, S. (2000). *Applied Logistic Regression.* New York: Wiley & Sons.

House, E. (1978). Assumptions underlying evaluation models. In: *Educational Researcher,* 8, pp. 4–12.

House, E. R. (2006). Democracy an Evaluation. In: *Evaluation,* 12(1), pp. 119–127.

House, E. H.; Howe, K. R. (1999). *Values in Evaluation and Social Research.* California: Thousand Oaks.

House, E. H.; Howe, K. R. (2000). Deliberative Democratic Evaluation in Practice. In: Stufflebeam, D. L.; Madaus, G. F.; Kellaghan, T. (ed.). *Evaluation Models: Viewpoints on Educational and Human Services Evaluation.* Kluwer Academic Publ., pp. 409–422.

Hox, J. (2010). *Multilevel Analysis. Techniques and Aplications,* Hove: Psypress.

Huber, O. (2005). *Das psychologische Experiment. Eine Einführung.* Bern: Huber.

Hüfken, V. (ed.) (2000). *Methoden in Telefonumfragen,* Wiesbaden: WdV.

Hutchby, I.; Wooffitt, R. (2008). *Conversation Analysis. Principles, Practice, and Applications.* Cambridge et al.: Polity.

Hutt, S. J.; Hutt, C. (1978). *Direct Observation and Measurement of Behavior.* Springfield: Thomas.

Ice, G. H.; James, G. (ed.) (2006). *Measuring Stress in Humans: a practical guide for the field.* Cambridge et al.: Cambridge University Press.

ICH – INTERNATIONAL CONFERENCE ON HARMONISATION OF TECHNICAL REQUIREMENTS FOR REGISTRATION OF PHARMACEUTICALS FOR HUMAN USE (1997). ICH Harmonized Tripartite Guideline. General Considerations for Clinical Trials E8, Current Step 4 (17 July 1997), Genf: ICH (downloadable at http://www.ich.org/LOB/media/MEDIA484.pdf, as of 4 June 2008).

Imhof, K. (2006). Öffentlichkeitstheorien. In: Bentele, G.; Brosius, H.-B.; Jarren, O. (ed.). *Lexikon Kommunikations- und Medienwissenschaft.* Wiesbaden: VS-Verlag (2nd edition), pp. 193–209.

Ipe, M. (2003). Knowledge Sharing in Organizations: A Conceptual Framework. In. *Human Resource Development Review,* 2(4), pp. 337–359.

Iversen, G. R.; Norpoth, H. (2002). *Analysis of Variance.* Newbury Park et al.: Sage.

Jablin, F. M.; Putnam, L. L. (ed.) (2000). *The New Handbook of Organizational Communication. Advances in Theory, Research, and Methods.* Thousand Oaks: Sage.

Jacobsen, A. (2008). *Semiotik. Ausgewählte Texte 1919–1982.* Frankfurt: Suhrkamp.

Jacoby, K. P., Schneider, V., Meyer, W.; Stockmann, R. (2005). *Umweltkommunikation im Handwerk. Bestandsaufnahme – Vergleichende Analyse – Entwicklungsperspektiven.* Münster: Waxmann

Jaenichen, U. (2002). Mikroevaluationen: Bildung von Vergleichsgruppen zur Schätzung individueller Förderwirkungen. In: Kleinhenz, G. (ed.) (2002).

IAB-Kompendium Arbeitsmarkt- und Berufsforschung. Beiträge zur Arbeitsmarkt- und Berufsforschung, BeitrAB 250, Nürnberg: IAB, pp. 387–397.

Jann, W. (1994). Politikfeldanalyse. In: Nohler, D. (ed.). *Lexikon der Politik. Vol. 2: Politikwissenschaftliche Methoden* (ed. Jürgen Kuz, Dieter Nohlen, Rainer-Olaf Schulze) München: Beck. pp. 308–314.

Jansen, D. (2006). *Einführung in die Netwerkanalyse. Grundlagen, Methoden, Forschungsbeispiele.* Wiesbaden: VS-Verlag.

Janssen, R.; Munda, G. (1999). Multi-criteria Methods for Quantitative, Qualitative and Fuzzy Evaluation Problems. In: van den Bergh, J. C. J. M. (ed.). *Handbook of Environmental and Resource Economics.* Cheltenham: Edward Elgar, pp. 837–852.

Jarren, O.; Donges, P. (2006). *Politische Kommunikation in der Mediengesellschaft. Eine Einführung.* Wiesbaden: VS-Verlag (2nd edition).

Jarren, O.; Donges, P. (2004). Staatliche Medienpolitik und die Politik der Massenmedien: Institutionelle und symbolische Steuerung im Mediensystem. In: Lange, S.; Schimank, U. (ed.). *Governance und gesellschaftliche Integration.* Wiesbaden: VS-Verlag, pp. 4–64.

JCS, Joint Committee on Standards for Educational Evaluation; Sanders, J.R. (ed.) (2006). *Handbuch der Evaluationsstandards. Die Standards des 'Joint Committee on Standards for Educational Evaluation'.* (3rd edition). Opladen: Leske + Budrich.

Joergensen, D. L. (2000). *Participant Observation: A Methodology for Human Studies.* Newbury Park et al.: Sage.

Johns, M. D.; Chen, S.-L. S.; Hall, G. J. (ed.) (2004). *Online Social Research.* New York: Peter Lang.

Joisten, K. (2008). *Philosophische Hermeneutik.* Berlin: Akademie.

Jones, S. C.; Worthen, B. R. (1990). AEA Members' Opinions Concerning Evaluator Certification. In: *American Journal of Evaluation*, 20, pp. 495–506.

Josselson, R.; Lieblich, A. (ed.) (1993). *The Narrative Studies of Live.* Newbury Park et al.: Sage.

Judd, C. M.; McClelland, G.H.; Ryan, C.S. (2008). *Data Analysis. A Model Comparison Approach*, Abidon: Psypress (2.).

Julnes, G.; Mark, M. M.; Henry, G. T. (1998). Promoting Realism in Evaluation. Realistic Evaluation and the Broader Context. In: *Evaluation*, 4, pp. 483–504.

Julnes, G. (ed. 2012). *Promoting Valuation in the Public Interest: Informing Policies for Judging Value in Evaluation.* San Francisco: Wiley (New Directions for Evaluation no. 133).

Kaplan, D. (2009). *Structural Equation Modelling. Foundations and Extensions.* Thousand Oaks et al.: Sage (2.).

Karlsson, V., Ove, C., Ross, F. (2006). The Relationship Between Evaluation and Politics. In: Shaw, I. F.; Mark, M. M.; Greene, J. (eds). *The Sage Handbook of Evaluation: Program, Policy and Practices.* London: Sage.

Kelle, U. (2007). *Die Integration qualitativer und quantitativer Methoden in der empirischen Sozialforschung. Theoretische Grundlagen und methodologische Konzepte.* Wiesbaden: VS-Verlag.

Keller, R; Hirseland, A.; Schneider, W.; Viehöver, A. (ed.) (2001). *Handbuch Sozialwissenschaftliche Diskursanalyse Vol. 1: Theorien und Methoden.* Opladen: Leske + Budrich.

Kenis, P.; Schneider, V. (1996). *Organisation und Netzwerk. Institutionelle Steuerung in Wirtschaft und Politik.* Frankfurt/New York: Campus.

Keppler-Seel, A. (2006). Konversations- und Gattungsanalyse. In: Ayaß, R.; Bergmann, J. (ed.). *Qualitative Methoden der Medienforschung.* Reinbek: rororo, pp. 293–323.

Kepplinger, H. M. (2006). *Die Mechanismen der Skandalierung. Die Macht der Medien und die Möglichkeiten der Betroffenen.* München: Olzog-Verlag.

Kessl, F.; Reutlinger, Ch. (2007). *Sozialraum: eine Einführung.* Wiesbaden: VS-Verlag.

Kiecolt, K. J.; Nathan, L. E. (1985). *Secondary Analysis of Survey Data.* Beverley Hills et al.: Sage.

Kieser, A. (ed.) (2002). *Organisationstheorien.* 5th edition. Stuttgart: Kohlhammer.

Kieser, A.; Kubicek, H. (1992). *Organisation.* Berlin et al.: de Gruyter.

Kieser, A.; Walgenbach, P. (2003). *Organisation* (4th edition, revised and extended). Stuttgart: Schäffer-Poeschel.

Kim, J.-O.; Mueller, C. W. (1994). *Introduction to Factor Analysis: What It is and How to do it.* Newbury Park, Calif. et al.: Sage.

King, G., Keohane, R. O.; Verba, S. (1994). *Designing Social Inquiry: Scientific Inference in Qualitative Research.* Princeton: Princeton Univ. Press.

Kirsch, R. (2006). Methoden einer sozialräumlichen Lebensweltanalyse. In: Deinet, U.; Kirsch, R. (ed.). *Der sozialräumliche Blick der Jugendarbeit. Methoden und Bausteine zur Konzeptentwicklung und Qualifizierung.* Wiesbaden: VS-Verlag, pp. 87–154.

Kirsch, R. (1999). Strukturierte Stadtteilbegehung. In: Deinet, U. (ed.). *Sozialräumliche Jugendarbeit. Eine praxisbezogene Anleitung zur Konzeptentwicklung in der offenen Kinder- und Jugendarbeit.* Opladen: WdV, pp. 82ff.

Kirchhoff, S., Kuhnt, S., Lipp, P.; Schlawin, S. (2006). *Der Fragebogen. Datenbasis, Konstruktion und Auswertung.* Wiesbaden: VS-Verlag.

Kissling-Näf, I.; Knoepfel, P.; Marek, D. (1997). *Lernen in öffentlichen Politiken.* Basel: Helbing & Lichtenhahn.

Klauer, K. J. (2005). *Das Experiment in der pädagogisch-psychologischen Forschung. Eine Einführung.* Münster: Waxmann.

Kleppmann, W. (2006). *Taschenbuch Versuchsplanung: Produkte und Prozesse optimieren.* München/Wien: Hanser.

Kletz, T. (2001). *An Engineer's View of Human Error.* New York et al.: Taylor & Francis.

Klieme, E.; Artelt, C.; Hartig, J.; Jude, N.; Köller, O.; Prenzel, M.; Schneider, W.; Stanat, P. (2010). *PISA 2009. Bilanz nach einem Jahrzehnt.* Münster et al.: Waxmann.

Kline, R. B. (2010). *Principles and Practice of Structural Equation Modeling.* London et al.: Taylor & Francis (3.).

Klingemann, H.-D.; Voltmer, K. (1989). Massenmedien als Brücke zur Welt der Politik. Nachrichtennutzung und private Beteiligungsbereitschaft. In: Kaase, M.; Schulz, W. (ed.). *Massenkommunikation. Theorie, Methoden, Befunde.* Opladen: WdV (special edition no. 30 of the Kölner Zeitschrift für Soziologie und Sozialpsychologie), pp. 221–258.

Kluge, S. (1999). *Empirisch begründete Typenbildung. Zur Konstruktion von Typen und Typologien in der qualitativen Sozialforschung.* Opladen: Leske + Budrich.

Knoblauch, H.; Luckmann, T. (2003). Gattungsanalyse. In: Flick, U., von Kardorff, E.; Steinke, I. (ed.). *Qualitative Forschung. Ein Handbuch.* Reinbek: rororo, pp. 538–546.

Koch, R. (2004a). New Public Management als Referenzmodell für Verwaltungsmodernisierungen. In: Strohmer, M. F. (ed.). *Management im Staat.* Frankfurt am Main: Lang.

Koch, R. (2004b). *Umbau öffentlicher Dienste: internationale Trends in der Anpassung öffentlicher Dienste an ein New Public Management.* Wiesbaden: Deutscher Universitäts-Verlag.

Kocka, J. (2002). Civil Society and the Role of Politics. In: Schröder, Gerhard (ed.). *Progressive Governance for the XXIst Century. Contributions to the Berlin Conference.* München et al.: Ch. Beck et al., pp. 27–35.

Koerber, C. (2005). Introducing Multimedia Presentations and a Course Website to an Introductory Sociology Course. How Technology Affects Student Perceptions of Teaching Effectiveness. In: *Teaching Sociology* 33: 285–300.

König, H. D. (1997). Tiefenhermeneutik als Methode kultursoziologischer Forschung. In: Hitzler, R.; Honer, A. (ed.). *Sozialwissenschaftliche Hermeneutik. Eine Einführung.* Opladen: Leske + Budrich, pp. 213–241.

König, H. D. (2003). Tiefenhermeneutik. In: Flick, U., von Kardorff, E.; Steinke, I. (ed.). *Qualitative Forschung. Ein Handbuch.* Reinbek: rororo, pp. 556–569.

Kohler-Koch, B. (1991). Insellillusion und Interdependenz: Nationales Regieren unter den Bedingungen von 'international governance'. In: Blanke, B.; Wollmann, H. (ed.). *Die alte Bundesrepublik.* Opladen: Westdeutscher Verlag. pp. 45–67.

Kohler-Riessman, C. (2007). *Narrative Methods for the Human Sciences.* Thousand Oaks et al.: Sage.

Konrad, K. (2001). *Mündliche und schriftliche Befragung: ein Lehrbuch.* Landau: Verlag Empirische Pädagogik.

Konzendorf, G. (2009). Institutionelle Einbettung der Evaluationsfunktion in Politik und Verwaltung in Deutschland. In: Widmer, T.; Beywl, W.; Fabian, C. (ed.). *Evaluation. Ein systematisches Handbuch.* Wiesbaden: VS-Verlag.

Kortman, W. (1995). *Diffusion, Marktentwicklung und Wettbewerb: Eine Untersuchung über die Bestimmungsgründe zu Beginn des Ausbreitungsprozesses technologischer Produkte.* Frankfurt am Main.: Europäische Hochschulschriften.

Kozinets, R.V. (2009). *Netnography. Doing Ethongraphic Research Online.* Thousand Oaks et al.: Sage.

Krippendorff, K. (2007). *Content Analysis. An Introduction to its Methodology.* Thousand Oaks et al.: Sage.

Kromrey, H. (1995). *Empirische Sozialforschung. Modelle und Methoden der Datenerhebung und Datenverarbeitung.* Opladen: Leske + Budrich.

Kromrey, H. (2001). Evaluation – Ein vielschichtiges Konzept. Begriff und Methodik von Evaluierung und Evaluationsforschung. Empfehlungen für die Praxis. In: *Sozialwissenschaften und Berufspraxis,* 24(2), pp. 105–31.

Kromrey, H. (2002). *Empirische Sozialforschung: Modelle und Methoden der standard-isierten Datenerhebung und Datenauswertung.* Opladen: Leske + Budrich.

Kromrey, H. (2007). Wissenschaftstheoretische Anforderungen an empirische Forschung und die Problematik ihrer Beachtung in der Evaluation – Oder: Wie sich die Evaluationsforschung um das Evaluieren drückt. In: *Zeitschrift für Evaluation,* 1/2007, pp. 113–124.

Krüger, R. A.; Casey, M. A. (2003); *Focus Groups: A Practical Guide for Applied Research.* Thousand Oaks et al.: Sage.

Kuckartz, U. (2007). *Einführung in die computergestützte Analyse qualitativer Daten.* Wiesbaden: VS-Verlag.

Kuckartz, U. et al. (2007). *Qualitative Evaluation. Der Einstieg in die Praxis.* Wiesbaden: VS-Verlag.

Kuhlmann, S.; Bogumil, J.; Wollmann, H. (ed.) (2004). *Leistungsmessung und -vergleich in Politik und Verwaltung: Konzepte und Praxis* (Stadtforschung aktuell Vol. 96). Wiesbaden: VS-Verlag.

Kuhlmann, S.; Holland, D. (1995). *Evaluation von Technologiepolitik in Deutschland. Konzepte, Anwendung, Perspektiven.* Heidelberg: Physika.

Kunter, M. et al. (2002). *PISA 2000: Dokumentation der Erhebungsinstrumente. Berlin: Max-Planck-Institut für Bildungsforschung* (Materialien aus der Bildungsforschung Nr. 72; on the Internet at edoc.mpg.de, as of 1 Jan 2009).

Kuster, J. et al. (2008). *Handbuch Projektmanagement.* Berlin/Heidelberg: Springer.

Kvale, S. (2001). *InterViews: An Introduction to Qualitative Research Interviewing.* Thousand Oaks et al.: Sage.

Lachenmann, G. (1977). Evaluierungsforschung: Historische Hintergründe, sozial-politische Zusammenhänge und wissenschaftliche Einordnung. In: Kantowsky, D. (ed.). *Evaluierungsforschung und -praxis in der Entwicklungshilfe.* Zürich: Verlag der Fachvereine.

Ladechi, C. R. (2001). Participatory Methods in the Analysis of Poverty: A critical Review. (*QEH Working Paper Series, no. 62*). Oxford University: Queen Elizabeth House (QEH), URL: http://www2.qeh.ox.ac.uk/pdf/qehwp/qehwps62.pdf – 09/02.

Lamnek, S. (2005). *Gruppendiskussion. Theorie und Praxis.* Weinheim/Basel: Beltz.

Landwehr, N.; Steiner, P. (2007). *Grundlagen der externen Schulevaluation: Verfahrensschritte, Standards und Instrumente zur Evaluation des Qualitätsmanagements.* Bern: h.e.p. Verlag.

Lange, E. (1983). Zur Entwicklung und Methodik der Evaluationsforschung in der Bundesrepublik Deutschland. In: *Zeitschrift für Soziologie,* 12(3), pp. 253–270.

Langer, W. (2008). *Logitmodelle. Eine Einführung für die Forschungspraxis.* Wiesbaden: VS-Verlag.

Laszlo, G.; Sudlow, M. F. (1983). *Measurement in Clinical Respiratory Physiology.* London: Academic Press.

Lechner, M. (2002). Program Heterogeneity and Propensity Score Matching: An Application to the Evaluation of Active Labor Market Policies. In: *Review of Economics and Statistics,* 84, pp. 205–220 (Download unter http://faculty.smu.edu/millimet/classes/eco7321/papers/lechner02.pdf, as of 4 June 2008)

Lee, B. (2004). Theories of Evaluation. In: Stockmann, R. (ed.). *Evaluationsforschung. Grundlagen und ausgewählte Forschungsfelder* (2nd edition). Opladen: Leske + Budrich, pp. 135–173.

Leeuw, F. L. (2004). Evaluation in Europe. In: Stockmann, R. (ed.). *Evaluationsforschung: Grundlagen und ausgewählte Forschungsfelder.* 3rd edition. Münster et al.: Waxmann.

Leeuw, F. L. (2006). Evaluation in Europe. In: Stockmann, R. (ed.). *Evaluationsforschung: Grundlagen und ausgewählte Forschungsfelder.* 2nd edition. Münster et al.: Waxmann.

Leeuw, F. L.; Toulemonde, J.; Brouwers, A. (1999). Evaluation Activities in Europe: A Quick Scan of the Market. In: *Evaluation,* 5(4), pp. 487–496.

Lege, J. (2006). Akkreditierung als rechtswidrige Parallelverwaltung. In: *Forschung und Lehre*, 5/2006, pp. 8–10.

Legewie, H. (1994). Globalauswertung von Dokumenten. In: Boehme, A., Mengel, A.; Muhr, T. (ed.). *Texte verstehen. Konzepte, Methoden, Werkzeuge*. Konstanz: Univ. Konstanz, pp. 177–182 (downloadable at http://www.ssoar.info/ssoar/files/2008/405/legewieglobal.pdf, as of 1 Sep 2008).

Lehmann, R. H., Venter, G. Y., Van Buer, J., Seeber, S.; Peek, R. (ed.) (1997). Erweiterte Autonomie für Schule – Bildungscontrolling und Evaluation. 2nd concluding volume from the summer academy of the same name from 31 August to 6 September 1997 in Nyíregyháza (Hungary). Berlin und Nyíregyháza: HU Berlin.

Lerner, D. (1968). Modernization. Social Aspects. In: *International Encyclopaedia of the Social Sciences*, 10.

LeRoux, B.; Rouanet, H. (2010). *Multiple Correspondence Analysis*. Quantitative Applications in the Social Sciences 163. Thousand Oaks et al.: Sage.

Lessel, W. (2008). *Projektmanagement. Projekte effizient planen und erfolgreich umsetzen*. Berlin: Cornelsen.

Lessler, J. T.; Kalsbeek, W. D. (1992). *Nonsampling Errors in Surveys*. New York et al.: Wiley.

Levin, H. M.; McEwan, P. J. (2007). *Cost-effectiveness Analysis. Methods and Applications*. Thousand Oaks et al.: Sage.

Lewin, K. (1951). *Field Theory in social sciences*. New York: Harper. Deutsch: Feldtheorie in den Sozialwissenschaften. Bern: Huber, 1963.

Lewis, P. V. (1987). *Organizational Communication. The Essence of Effective Management*, New York et al.: Wiley.

Li, C. C. (1986). *Path analysis : a primer*, Pacific Grove. Calif.: Boxwood Press.

Lienhard, A. (2005). *10 Jahre New Public Management in der Schweiz: Bilanz, Irrtümer, Erfolgsfaktoren*. Bern: Haupt.

Lincoln, Y.; Guba, E. (1985). *Naturalistic Inquiry*. New York: Sage.

Lincoln, Y.; Guba, E. (1986). Research, Evaluation and Policy Analysis: Heuristics and Disciplined Inquiry. In: *Policy Studies Review*, 5(3), pp. 546–566.

Lincoln, Y.; Guba, E. (2000). Paradigmatic Controversies, Contradictions, and Emerging Confluences. In: Denzin, N. K.; Lincoln, Y. S. (ed.). *Handbook of Qualitative Research*. Thousand Oaks, CA: Sage.

Lincoln, Y.; Guba, E. (2004). The Roots of Fourth Generation Evaluation. In: Alkin, M. (ed.). *Evaluation Roots: Tracing Theorists' Views and Influences*. Thousand Oaks, CA: Sage Publications.

Lippitt, R. (1940). An Experimental Study of Authoritarian and Democratic Group Atmospheres. *Univ. Iowa. Stud. Child. Welf.*, 16, pp. 45–195.

Lipsey, M. W.; Cordray, D. S. (2000). Evaluation Methods for Social Intervention. In: *Annual Review of Psychology 2000*, Bd: 51. pp. 345–375 (downloadable at http://arjournals.annualreviews.org/doi/pdf/10.1146/annurev.psych.51.1.345?cookieSet=1, as of 6 June 2008).

Lissmann, U. (2001). *Inhaltsanalyse von Texten. Ein Lehrbuch zur computerunterstützten und konventionellen Inhaltsanalyse*. Landau: Verlag Empirische Pädagogik.

Litke, H.-D. (2004). *Projektmanagement. Methoden, Techniken, Verhaltensweisen – Evolutionäres Projektmanagement*, München: Hanser.

Littré, É. (2005 [1877]). *Auguste Comte et la Philosophie Positive*. Elibron Classics, facsimile of the 1877 edition published in Paris, Boston: Adamant Media Corporation.

Löffelholz, J. (1993). *Kontrollieren und steuern mit Plankostenrechnung: Normalkostenrechnung, Plankostenrechnung, Soll-Ist-Vergleich, Kostenartenrechnung, Kostenstellenrechnung, Kostenträgerrechnung, Grenzkostenrechnung, Gemeinkostenplan, Plankalkulation, kurzfristige Erfolgsrechnung.* Wiesbaden: Gabler.

Loos, P.; Schäffer, B. (2006). *Das Gruppendiskussionsverfahren. Theoretische Grundlagen und empirische Anwendung.* Wiesbaden: VS-Verlag.

Ludwig, J. (2007). *Investigativer Journalismus.* Konstanz: UVK.

Madaus, G. F.; Kellaghan, T. (2000). Models, Metaphors, and Definitions in Evaluation. In: Stufflebeam, D. L.; Madaus, G. F.; Kellaghan, T. (ed.). *Evaluation Models. Viewpoints on Educational and Human Services Evaluation.* Norwell: Kluwer, pp. 19–32.

Madaus, G. F.; Stufflebeam, D. L. (2000). Program Evaluation: A Historical Overview In: Stufflebeam, D. L.; Madaus, G. F.; Kellaghan, T. (ed.). *Evaluation Models. Viewpoints on Educational and Human Services Evaluation.* Norwell: Kluwer, pp. 3–18.

Madaus, G. F.; Stufflebeam, D. L. (2000). *Evaluation Models. Viewpoints on Educational and Human Services Evaluation. Second Edition.* Boston et al.: Kluwer Academic Publishers.

Madaus, G. F.; Stufflebeam, D. L. (2002). *Evaluation Models. Viewpoints on Educational and Human Services Evaluation.* Second Edition. eBook. New York.

Maier, W.; Engel, R. R.; Möller, H. J. (ed.) (2000). *Methodik von Verlaufs- und Therapiestudien in Psychiatrie und Psychotherapie.* Bern et al.: Hogrefe.

Maindok, H. (2003). *Professionelle Interviewführung in der Sozialforschung. Interviewtraining: Bedarf, Stand und Perspektiven.* Herbolzheim: Centaurus-Verlag.

Mannheim, K. (1964). Das Problem der Generation. In: *Karl Mannheim, Wissenssoziologie. Auswahl aus dem Werk.* ed. Kurt H. Wolff. Luchterhand: Neuwied/Berlin, pp. 509–565.

Manski, C. F. (1995). *Identification Problems in the Social Sciences.* Cambridge: Harvard University Press.

March, J. G.; Simon, H. A. (1958). *Organizations.* New York: John Wiley.

Mark, M. M. (2005). Evaluation Theory or What are Evaluation Methods for? In: *The Evaluation Exchange* XI(2) (Summer 2005), pp. 2–3.

Mark, M. M.; Henry, G. T.; Julnes, G. (2000). *Evaluation: An Integrated Framework for Understanding, Guiding and Improving Public and Nonprofit Policies and Programs.* San Francisco: Jossey-Bass.

Mark, M. M.; Henry, G. T., Julnes, G. (1999). Toward an Integrative Framework for Evaluation Practice In: *American Journal of Evaluation,* 20(2), pp. 177–198.

Marshall, C.; Rossman, G. B. (2006). *Designing Qualitative Research.* Thousand Oaks et al.: Sage.

Martens, H.; Næs, T. (2001). *Multivariate Calibration.* Chichester et al.: Wiley.

Martin, E.; Wawrinowski, U. (2006). *Beobachtungslehre: Theorie und Praxis reflektierter Beobachtung und Beurteilung.* Weinheim; München: Juventa.

Martinussen, T.; Scheike, T. H. (2006). *Dynamic Regression Models for Survival Data,* New York, NY: Springer.

Mastronardi, P. (2004). *New Public Management in Staat und Recht: ein Diskurs.* Bern et al.: Haupt.

Matthison, S. (ed.) (2006). *Encyclopedia of Evaluation.* London et al.: Sage.

Maxwell, J. A. (2005). *Qualitative Research Design. An interactive approach.* Thousand Oaks et al.: Sage.

Mayer, H. O. (2004). *Interview und schriftliche Befragung. Entwicklung, Durchführung und Auswertung.* München/Wien.

Mayntz, R. (1994). *Modernization and the Logic of Interorganizational Networks.* Köln: Max-Planck-Institut für Gesellschaftsforschung.

Mayntz, R. (1997). *Soziologie in der Öffentlichen Verwaltung.* Heidelberg: C. F. Müller.

Mayntz, R. (ed.) (1980c). *Implementation politischer Programme.* Königsstein: Athenäum.

Mayntz, R.; Scharpf, F. W. (1995). Steuerung und Selbstorganisation in staatsnahen Sektoren. In: Mayntz, R.; Scharpf, F. W. (ed.). *Gesellschaftliche Selbstregelung und politische Steuerung.* Frankfurt/New York: Campus, pp. 9–38.

Mayntz, R.; Ziegler, R. (1976). Soziologie der Organisation. In: König, R. (ed.). *Handbuch der empirischen Sozialforschung. Vol. 9.* Stuttgart: Enke.

Mayo, E. (1951). *Probleme industrieller Arbeitsbeziehungen.* Frankfurt: Verlag der Frankfurter Hefte.

Mayring, P.; Gläser-Zikuda, M. (ed.) (2005). *Die Praxis der Qualitativen Inhaltsanalyse.* Weinheim et al.: Beltz.

Mayring, P. (2007). *Qualitative Inhaltsanalyse. Grundlagen und Techniken.* Weinheim et al.: Beltz.

McClintock, C. (2004). Using Narrative Methods to Link Program Evaluation and Organisation Development. In: *The Evaluation Exchange,* 9(4), pp. 14–15.

McLaughlin, K. (ed.) (2002). *New Public Management: current trends and future prospects.* London: Routledge.

Melvin, M.; Greene, J. C.; Shaw, I. F. (2006). The Evaluation of Policies, Programs, and Practices. In: Shaw, I. F.; Mark, M. M.; Greene, J. (eds). *The Sage Handbook of Evaluation: Program, Policy and Practices.* London: Sage.

Menard, S. (2010). *Logistic Regression: From Introductory to Advanced Concepts and Applications.* Thousand Oaks et al.: Sage.

Merkens, H. (2003). Auswahlverfahren, Sampling, Fallkonstruktion. In: Flick, U., von Kardorff, E.; Steinke, I. (ed.). *Qualitative Forschung. Ein Handbuch.* Reinbek: rororo, pp. 286–298.

Merten, K. (1995). *Inhaltsanalyse. Einführung in Theorie, Methode und Praxis.* Opladen: WdV .

Mertens, D. M. (1998). *Research Methods in Education and Psychology: Integrating Diversity with Quantitative and Qualitative Approaches.* Thousand Oaks, CA: Sage.

Mertens, D. M. (2004). Institutionalizing Evaluation in the United States of America. In: Stockmann, R. (ed.). *Evaluationsforschung.* Opladen: Leske + Budrich. pp. 45–60.

Mertens, D. M. (2006). Institutionalizing Evaluation in the United States of Amerika. In: Stockmann, R. (ed.). *Evaluationsforschung: Grundlagen und ausgewählte Forschungsfelder.* 3rd edition. Münster et al.: Waxmann.

Meyer, W. (1997). *Individuelle Erwerbschancen in Ostdeutschland. Auswirkungen des wirtschaftsstrukturellen Wandels.* Wiesbaden: Deutscher Universitätsverlag.

Meyer, W. (2000). Wegweiser zur 'nachhaltigen' Gesellschaft? Die Evaluationspraxis im Umweltbereich. Vortrag in der Ad-hoc Gruppe 'Gute Gesellschaft gestalten: Der Beitrag von Evaluationen' am Soziologie-Kongress 26 Sep 2000 in Cologne. Lecture manuscript. Saarbrücken: Universität des Saarlandes.

Meyer W. (2002a). Regulating Environmental Action of Non-Governmental Actors. The impact of communication support programs in Germany. In: Biermann, F.; Brohm, R.; Dingwerth, K. (ed.). *Global Environmental Change and the Nation State: Proceedings of the 2001 Berlin Conference of the Human Dimensions of Global Environmental Change.* Potsdam: Potsdam Institute for Climate Impact Research (forthcoming).

Meyer, W. (2002b). *Sociology Theory and Evaluation Research. An Application and its Usability for Evaluation Sustainable Development.* Paper presented on EASY-Eco-Conference, Vienna 23–25 May 2002 (downloadable at http://www.ceval.de).

Meyer, W. (2002c). Die Entwicklung der Soziologie im Spiegel der amtlichen Statistik. In: Stockmann, R.; Meyer, W.; Knoll, T. (ed.). *Soziologie im Wandel. Universitäre Ausbildung und Arbeitsmarktchancen in Deutschland.* Opladen: Leske + Budrich, pp. 45–116.

Meyer, W. (2003a). Evaluation als Thema in sozialwissenschaftlichen Berufs- und Fachverbänden. Teil I: Soziologie und Psychologie. In: *Zeitschrift für Evaluation* (ZfEv) 1/2003, pp. 131–142.

Meyer, W. (2003b). Evaluation als Thema in sozialwissenschaftlichen Berufs- und Fachverbänden. Teil II: Erziehungs- und Politikwissenschaften. In: *Zeitschrift für Evaluation* (ZfEv) 2/2003, pp. 323–336.

Meyer, W. (2006). Evaluation von Netzwerksteuerung. In: *Zeitschrift für Evaluation* ZfEv 2/2006, pp. 317–332.

Meyer, W. (2011). Measuring: indicators – scales – indices – interpretations. In: Stockmann, R. (ed.). *A Practitioner Handbook on Evaluation.* Cheltenham / Northampton: Edward Elgar, pp. 189–219.

Meyer, W. (2011a). Evaluation Designs. In: Stockmann, R. (ed.). *A Practitioner Handbook on Evaluation.* Cheltenham/Northampton: Edward Elgar, pp. 135–157.

Meyer, W. (2011). Data collection: surveys – observations – non-reactive procedures. In: Stockmann, R. (ed.). *A Practitioner Handbook on Evaluation.* Cheltenham/Northampton: Edward Elgar, pp. 220–279.

Meyer, W.; Baltes, K. (2004). Network Failures. How realistic is durable cooperation in global governance? In: Jacob, K.; Binder, M. & Wieczorek, A. (ed.). *Governance for Industrial Transformation. Proceedings of the 2003 Berlin Conference on the Human Dimension of Global Environmental Change.* Berlin: Environmental Policy Research Centre, pp. 31–51.

Meyer, W.; Elbe, S. (2007a). Initiating Network Governance through Competition. Experiences from Eighteen German Regions. In: Cheshire, L., Higgins, V.; Lawrence, G. (ed.). *Rural Governance: International Perspectives,* Abingdon: Routledge, pp. 81–97.

Meyer, W.; Elbe, S. (2007b). Evaluation of Local Network Governance in Germany. In: George, C.; Kirkpatrick, C. (ed.). *Impact Assessment and Sustainable Development. European Practice and Experience.* Cheltenham: Edward Elgar (Evaluating Sustainable Development Vol. 2), pp. 45–64.

Meyer, W.; Elbe, S. (2004). Local Network Governance. Perspectives and Problems in the German Rural Sector. Paper prepared for the *XIth World Congress of Rural Sociology – Globalisation, Risks and Resistance in rural economics and societies, Trondheim 25–30 July 2004* (published on-line at http://www.irsa-world.org/XI/papers/2–1.pdf).

Meyer, W., Jacoby, K.P.; Stockmann, R. (2002). Evaluation der Umweltberatungsprojekte des Bundesumweltministeriums und des Umweltbundesamtes. *Nachhaltige Wirkungen der Förderung von Bundesverbänden,* Berlin: UBA (UBA Texte 36/02).

Meyer, W.; Jacoby, K.-P.; Stockmann, R. (2003). Umweltkommunikation in Verbänden: Von der Aufklärungsarbeit zur institutionellen Steuerung nachhaltiger Entwicklung. In: Linne, G.; Schwarz, M. (ed.). *Ein Handbuch für nachhaltige Entwicklung.* Opladen: Leske + Budrich.

Meyer, W.; Stockmann, R. (2006). Comment on the Paper: An Evaluation Tree for Europe. Vortragsmanuskript zur EES-Tagung: *Evaluation in Society: Critical Connection.*

Miles, M. B.; Huberman, A. M. (2007). *Qualitative Data Analysis. An Expanded Sourcebook,* Thousand Oaks et al.: Sage.

Mishan, E. J.; Quah, E. T. E. (2007). *Cost-Benefit Analysis,* London: Routledge.

Mishler, E. (1995). Models of Narrative Analysis: A Typology. In: *Journal of Narrative and Life History,* Vol. 5(2), pp. 87–123.

Mohr, H.-W. (1977). *Bestimmungsgründe für die Verbreitung von neuen Technologien.* Berlin: Duncker & Humblot.

Moosbrugger, H. (2002). *Lineare Modelle: Regressions- und Varianzanalysen,* Bern, Göttingen et al.: Huber.

Morehouse, R. (2011). *Beginning Interpretative Inquiry. A Step-by-Step Approach to Research and Evaluation,* Abingdon: Routledge.

Morgan, D. L. (1988). *Focus Groups as Qualitative Research.* Newbury Park et al.: Sage.

Morgan, D. L. (ed.) (1993). *Successful Focus Groups.* Newbury Park: Sage.

Morgan, D. L. (2002). Focus Group Interviewing. In: Gubrium, J. F.; Holstein, J. A. (ed.). *Handbook of Interview Research: Context and Methods.* Thousand Oaks: Sage, pp. 141–160.

Morris, M. (ed.) (2008). *Evaluation Ethics for Best Practice. Cases and Commentaries.* New York: Guilford Press.

Mosler, K.; Schmid, F. (2006). *Wahrscheinlichkeitsrechnung und schließende Statistik.* Berlin/Heidelberg: Springer.

Mühlenkamp, H. (2008). *Kosten-Nutzen Analyse.* München: Oldenbourg.

Mülbert, T. (2002). *New Public Management: ein Vergleich der Diskussionen zwischen Deutschland und Großbritannien.* Universität Konstanz: Diplomarbeit.

Müller, H. (1994). *Einführung in die Theorie der Messfehler,* Dresden: Hochschule für Technik und Wirtschaft (Fernstudiengang Vermessungswesen, Lehrbrief Fehler- und Ausgleichsrechnung).

Müller-Jentsch, W. (2003). *Organisationssoziologie. Eine Einführung.* Frankfurt am Main: Campus.

Mullis, I. et al. (2003). PIRLS 2001 International Report. IEA's Study of Reading Literacy Achievement in Primary School in 35 Countries, Chestnut Hill: IEA International Association for the Evaluation of Educational Achievement (on the Internet at http://timssandpirls.bc.edu/pirls2001i/pdf/p1_IR_book.pdf, as of 1 Jan 2009).

Mummendey, H. D.; Grau, I. (2007). *Die Fragebogen-Methode.* Göttingen: Hogrefe-Verlag (5).

Munda, G. (2004). Social Multi-criteria Evaluation. Methodological Foundations and Operational Consequences. In: *European Journal of Operational Research,* 158(3), pp. 662–677.

Nardi, P. M. (2006). *Doing Survey Research: A Guide to Quantitative Methods,* Boston et al.: Allyn and Bacon.

Naschold, F.; Bogumil, J. (2000). *Modernisierung des Staates. New Public Management in deutscher und internationaler Perspektive.* Opladen: Leske + Budrich.

Nassehi, A. (2002). Die Organisationen der Gesellschaft. Skizze einer Organisationssoziologie in gesellschaftstheoretischer Absicht. In: Allmendinger, J.; Hinz, T. (ed.). *Organisationssoziologie*. Wiesbaden: WdV (Sonderheft 42 der Kölner Zeitschrift für Soziologie und Sozialpsychologie), pp. 443–478.

Neidhardt, F. (1994). Öffentlichkeit, Öffentliche Meinung, Soziale Bewegungen. In: ibid. (ed.). *Öffentlichkeit, Öffentliche Meinung, Soziale Bewegungen*. Opladen: WdV (Sonderheft 34 der Kölner Zeitschrift für Soziologie und Sozialpsychologie), pp. 7–41.

Neugebauer, U.; Bewyl, W. (2006). Methoden zur Netzwerkanalyse In: *Zeitschrift für Evaluation*, 2(2006), pp. 249–286.

Newson, J.; Jones, R.N.; Hofer, M. (eds., 2011). *Longitudinal Data Analysis. A Practical Guide for Researchers in Aging, Health, and Social Sciences*, Hove: Psypress.

Nonaka, I.; Takeuchi, H. (1995). *The Knowledge Creating Company. How Japanese Companies Create the Dynamics of Innovation*. New York: Oxford University Press.

Nöthen, J. (2004). New Public Management: Aufgaben, Erfahrungen und Grenzen der Verwaltungsmodernisierung in Deutschland. In: Moldaschl, M. (ed.). *Reorganisation im Non-Profit-Sektor*. München: Hampp.

Nolte, R. (2005). Changemanagement in der öffentlichen Verwaltung: 'Management des Wandels' – Veränderungsprozesse im Kontext der Reformbewegung des New Public Management und des neuen Steuerungsmodells. In: *Verwaltungsarchiv, Zeitschrift für Verwaltungslehre, Verwaltungsrecht und Verwaltungspolitik*, 96. pp. 243–266.

NORAD [Norwegian Agency for Development Cooperation] (1999). The Logical Framework Approach (LFA). *Handbook for Objectives-oriented Planning*. Oslo: NORAD.

OECD (ed.) (1991). DAC Principles for Evaluation of Development Assistance. Paris: OECD / DAC (verified download February 2012: http://www.oecd.org/dataoecd/31/12/2755284.pdf)

OECD (ed.) (1998). *Review of the DAC Principles for Evaluation of Development Assistance*. Paris: OECD/DAC.

OECD (ed.) (2006). *Assessing Scientific, Reading and Mathematical Literacy. A Framework for PISA 2006*. Paris: OECD (verified download January 2009 www.pisa.oecd.org).

OECD (ed.) (2007). *PISA – die internationale Schulleistungsstudie der OECD*. Paris: OECD (on the Internet at www.pisa.oecd.org; as of 1 Jan 2009).

OECD (ed.) (2009). *PISA 2009 Assessment Framework. Key Competencies in Reading, Mathematics and Science*. Paris: OECD (verified download May 2012: http://www.oecd.org/dataoecd/11/40/44455820.pdf).

OECD (ed.) (2010). *PISA 2009 Results: What Students Know and Can Do – Student Performance in Reading, Mathematics and Science (Volume 1)*. Paris: OECD (verified download May 2012: http://dx.doi.org/10.1787/9789264091450-en.pdf).

Oelkers, J. (2008). Erfahrungen mit Schulevaluation in der Schweiz, Vortrag in der Landesakademie für Fortbildung und Personalentwicklung an Schulen am 25 June 2008 in Comburg (on the Internet at http://www.paed.uzh.ch/ap/downloads/oelkers/Vortraege/323_Comburg.pdf, as of 1 Jan 2009).

Oevermann, U., Allert, T.; Konau, W. (1979). Die Methodologie einer 'objektiven' Hermeneutik und ihre allgemeine forschungslogische Bedeutung in den Sozialwissenschaften. In: Soeffner, H. G. (ed.). *Interpretative Verfahren in den Sozial- und Textwissenschaften*. Stuttgart: Metzler, pp. 352–433.

Opp, K.-D.; Schmidt, P. (1976). *Einführung in die Mehrvariablenanalyse: Grundlagen der Formulierung und Prüfung komplexer sozialwissenschaftlicher Aussagen.* Reinbek : Rowohlt.

Ortmann, N. (1996). Methoden zur Erkundung von Lebenswelten. In: Deinet, U.; Sturzenhecker, B (ed.). *Konzepte entwickeln. Anregungen und Arbeitshilfen zur Klärung und Legitimation.* Weinheim: Beltz. pp. 26 – 34.

Ortmann, N. (1999). Die Stadtteilerkundung und Schlüsselpersonen. In: Deinet, U. (ed.). *Sozialräumliche Jugendarbeit. Eine praxisbezogene Anleitung zur Konzeptentwicklung in der offenen Kinder- und Jugendarbeit.* Opladen: WdV, pp.74–81.

Ortmann, G.; Sydow, J.; Türk, K. (ed.) (2000). *Theorien der Organisation. Die Rückkehr der Gesellschaft.* Opladen: Westdeutscher Verlag.

Owen, J. M.; Rogers, P. J. (1999). *Program Evaluation. Forms and Approaches.* London et al.: Sage.

Palm, W. (1991). *Zur Validität psychologischer und physikalischer Messprozesse: Untersuchungen über das Problem der Reproduzierbarkeit psychologischer Messdaten.* Frankfurt am Main: Haag und Herchen.

Pampel, F. C. (2005). *Logistic Regression. A Primer.* Thousand Oaks et al.: Sage.

Panter, A.T.; Sterba, S.K. (eds., 2011). *Handbook of Ethics in Quantitative Methodology,* Abidon: Psypress.

Paran-Woolfe, L.; M. Krüger (2001). *Report of Working Group Consultation or Participation of Civil Society.* Brussels: EU.

Parker. I. (2003). Die diskursanalytische Methode. In: Flick, U., von Kardorff, E.; Steinke, I. (ed.). *Qualitative Forschung. Ein Handbuch.* Reinbek: rororo, pp. 546–556.

Parnes, O.; Vedder, U.; Willer, S. (2008). *Generation. Eine Geschichte der Wissenschaft und der Kultur.* Frankfurt: Suhrkamp.

Patriotta, G. (2003). *Organizational Knowledge in the Making. How Firms Create, Use, and Institutionalize Knowledge.* New York: Oxford University Press.

Patton, M. Q. (1986). *Utilization-focused Evaluation.* Beverly Hills, CA: Sage.

Patton, M. Q. (1988). *How to Use Qualitative Methods in Evaluation.* Thousand Oaks: Sage.

Patton, M. Q. (1990). *Qualitative Evaluation and Research Methods,* Thousand Oaks: Sage.

Patton, M. Q. (1994). Development Evaluation. In: *American Journal of Evaluation,* 15(3), pp. 311–319.

Patton, M. Q. (1996). *Utilization-Focused Evaluation: The New Century Text.* Thousand Oaks, CA: Sage.

Patton, M. Q. (1997). *Utilization-focused Evaluation: The New Century Text.* Thousand Oaks: Sage.

Patton, M. Q. (2003). Utilization-focused Evaluation. In: T. Kellaghan; Stufflebeam, D. L. (ed.). *International Handbook of Educational Evaluation.* Norwell: Kluwer, pp. 223–244.

Patton, M. Q. (2012). *Essentials of Utilization-Focused Evaluation.* Thousand Oaks: Sage.

Pede, L. (2000). *Wirkungsorientierte Prüfung der öffentlichen Verwaltung.* Bern: Haupt.

Pedhazur, E. J. (2006). *Multiple Regression in Behavioral Research: Explanation and Prediction.* London et al.: Wadsworth Thomson Learning.

Pessoa e Costa, S. (2007). Using propensity score matching to evaluate two French active labour market programmes, paper presented at *XXIst Annual*

Conference of the European Society for Population Economics, 14–16 June 2007, Department of Economics, University of Illinois at Chicago, Chicago, Illinois, USA (downloadable at http://web.econ.uic.edu/espe2007/paper/A31.pdf, as of 4 June 2008).

Peters, B. (1994). *Der Sinn von Öffentlichkeit.* In: Neidhardt, F. (ed.). Öffentlichkeit, öffentliche Meinung, soziale Bewegungen. (special edition no. 34 of the Kölner Zeitschrift für Soziologie und Sozialpsychologie.) Opladen: Westdeutscher Verlag, pp. 42–76.

Peterson, G. J.; Vestman, O. K. (2007). *Conceptions of Evaluation.* Myndigheten för Nätverk och Samarbete inom Högre Utbildning Rapport 08/2007. Stockholm: Mälardalen Universitet.

Peyrot, M. (1996). Causal Analysis: Theory and Application. In: *Journal of Pediatric Psychology*, 21(1), pp. 3–24. (downloadable at http://jpepsy.oxfordjournals.org/cgi/reprint/21/1/3.pdf, as of 6 June 2008).

Pflaumer, P.; Heine, B.; Hartung, J. (2005). *Statistik für Wirtschafts- und Sozialwissenschaften: Deskriptive Statistik.* München: Oldenbourg.

Phillips, N.; Hardy, C. (2002). *Discourse Analysis. Integrating Processes of Social Construction.* London: Sage.

Picciotto, R. (2002). Evaluation in the World Bank: Antecedents, Methods, and Instruments. In: Furubo, J.-E.; Rist, R. C.; Sandahl, R. (ed.). *International Atlas of Evaluation.* New Brunswick: Transaction Publishers.

PISA-Konsortium Deutschland (ed.) (2008). *PISA 2006 in Deutschland. Die Kompetenzen der Jugendlichen im Dritten Ländervergleich.* Münster: Waxmann.

PISA-Konsortium Deutschland (ed.) (2007). *PISA 2006. Die Ergebnisse der dritten internationalen Vergleichsstudie.* Münster: Waxmann.

PISA-Konsortium Deutschland (ed.) (2006). *PISA 2003. Dokumentation der Erhebungsinstrumente.* Münster: Waxmann.

PISA-Konsortium Deutschland (ed.) (2000). Schülerleistungen im internationalen Vergleich. Eine neue Rahmenkonzeption für die Erfassung von Wissen und Fähigkeiten, Berlin: Max-Planck-Institut für Bildungsforschung (on the Internet at http://www.mpib-berlin.mpg.de/pisa/Rahmenkonzeptiondt.pdf, as of 1 Jan 2009).

Pitschas, R. (2004). *Looking behind New Public Management: 'new' values of public administration and the dimensions of personnel management in the beginning of the 21st century.* Speyer: Forschungsinstitut für Öffentliche Verwaltung bei der Deutschen Hochschule für Verwaltungswissenschaft.

Plano-Clark, V. L.; Creswell, J. W. (ed.) (2008). *The Mixed Methods Reader.* Los Angeles et al.: Sage.

Provus, M. M. (1971). *Discrepancy Evaluation.* Berkeley, CA: McCutchan.

Pollitt, C. (1998). Evaluation in Europe: Boom or Bubble? In: *Evaluation*, 4(2), pp. 214–224.

Popham, W. (1975). *Educational Evaluation.* Englewood Clifs: Prentice Hall.

Popper, K. R. (1992). *Die offene Gesellschaft und ihre Feinde* (2 vols.). Stuttgart: UTB.

Popper, K. R. (2005). *Lesebuch: ausgewählte Texte zu Erkenntnistheorie, Philosophie der Naturwissenschaften, Metaphysik, Sozialphilosophie* (ed. by D. Miller). Tübingen: Mohr.

Porst, R. (2008). *Fragebogen: Ein Arbeitsbuch.* Wiesbaden: VS-Verlag.

Porter, A. C.; Chibucos, T. R. (1975). Common Problems of Design and Analysis in Evaluative Research. In: *Sociological Methods Research*, 3; p. 235.

Posavac, E. J.; Carey, R. G. (1997). *Program Evaluation: Methods and Case Studies.* NJ: Prentice-Hall.

Pokropp, F. (1994). *Lineare Regression und Varianzanalyse.* München, Wien: Oldenbourg.

Pottie, K. et al. (2008). Narrative Reports to Monitor and Evaluate the Integration of Pharmacists Into Family Practice Settings. In: *Annals of Family Medicine,* 6(2), pp. 161–164.

Prakash, A.; Hart, J. A. (ed.) (2001). *Globalization and Governance.* London/New York: Routledge.

Prell, C. (2011). *Social Network Analysis. History, Theory and Methodology.* Thousand Oaks et al.: Sage.

Prenzel, M.; Kobarg, M.; Schöps, K.; Rönnebeck, S. (eds. 2012). *Research on PISA: Research Outcomes of the PISA Research Conference 2009.* Dordrecht: Springer Netherlands.

Presser, S. et al. (ed.) (2004). *Methods for Testing and Evaluating Survey Questionnaires.* New York et al.: Wiley.

Presthus, R. (1979). *The Organizational Society. An Analysis and A Theory.* London: Macmillan (2.).

Privitera, G. J. (2011). *Statistics for the Behavioral Sciences,* Thousand Oaks et al.: Sage.

Przyborski, A. (2004). *Gesprächsanalyse und dokumentarische Methode. Qualitative Auswertung von Gesprächen, Gruppendiskussionen und anderen Diskursen.* Wiesbaden: VS-Verlag.

Psathas, G. (1995). *Conversation Analysis. The Study of Talk-in-Interaction.* Thousand Oaks: Sage.

Puchta, C.; Potter, J. (2004). *Focus Group Practice.* London et al.: Sage.

Rat der Europäischen Gemeinschaft (1992). *Vertrag über die Europäische Union.* Luxembourg: Amt für amtliche Veröffentlichungen der Europäischen Gemeinschaften.

Reade, N. (2004). *Der Government Performance and Results Act – Funktionsweise und Wirkungen. Magisterarbeit in der Fachrichtung Soziologie.* Saarbrücken: Universität des Saarlandes.

Reason, P.; Bradbury, H. (2007). *The Sage Handbook of Action Research. Participative Inquiry and Practice.* Thousand Oaks et al.: Sage (2.).

Reavey, P. (ed., 2011). *Visual Methods in Psychology. Using and Interpreting Images in Qualitative Research,* Abingdon: Psypress.

Rehbinder, M. (2002). New Public Management: Rückblick, Kritik und Ausblick. In: Eberle, C.-E. (ed.). *Der Wandel des Staates vor den Herausforderungen der Gegenwart.* München: Beck.

Reichard, C. (2002). Institutionenökonomische Ansätze und New Public Management. In: König, K. (ed.). *Deutsche Verwaltung an der Wende zum 21. Jahrhundert.* Baden-Baden: Nomos.

Reichard, C. (2004). New Public Management als Reformdoktrin für Entwicklungsverwaltungen. In: Benz, A. (ed.). *Institutionenwandel in Regierung und Verwaltung.* Berlin: Duncker & Humblot.

Reichertz, J. (2003). Objektive Hermeneutik und hermeneutische Wissenssoziologie. In: Flick, U., von Kardorff, E.; Steinke, I. (ed.). *Qualitative Forschung. Ein Handbuch.* Reinbek: rororo, pp. 514–524.

Rein, M. (1984). Umfassende Programmevaluierungen. In: Hellstern, G.-M.; Wollmann, H. (ed.). *Handbuch zur Evaluierungsforschung Vol. 1.* Opladen: Westdeutscher Verlag.

Reuber, P.; Pfaffenbach, C. (2005). *Methoden der empirischen Humangeographie.* Braunschweig: Westermann.

Rice, J. M. (1893). *The Public-School System of the United States.* New York: Century.

Rice, J. M. (1897). The Futility of the Spelling Grind. In: *Forum*, 23, pp. 163–172.

Richards, K.; Seedhouse, P. (ed.) (2006) *Applying Conversation Analysis.* Basingstoke et al.: Palgrave Macmillan.

Richards, L. (2006). *Handling Qualitative Data. A practical guide.* London et al.: Sage.

Riege, M.; Schubert, H. (ed.) (2005). *Sozialraumanalyse. Grundlagen – Methoden – Praxis.* Wiesbaden: VS-Verlag.

Riley, T.; Hawe, P. (2005). Researching Practice. The methodological Case for Narrative Inquiry. In: *Health Education Research*, 20: 226–236 (downloadable at: http://her.oxfordjournals.org/cgi/reprint/20/2/226?ck=nck, as of 15 Aug 2008).

Rist, R. C. (1990) (ed.). *Program Evaluation and the Management of Government.* New Brunswick: Transaction.

Ritsert, J.; Stracke, E.; Heider, F. (1976). *Grundzüge der Varianz- und Faktorenanalyse.* Frankfurt am Main et al.: Campus Verl.

Rittelmeyer, C.; Parmentier, M. (2007). *Einführung in die pädagogische Hermeneutik.* Darmstadt: Wissenschaftliche Buchgesellschaft.

Ritz, A. (2003). *Evaluation von New Public Management: Grundlagen und Empirische Ergebnisse der Bewertung von Verwaltungsreformen in der schweizerischen Bundesverwaltung.* Bern: Haupt.

Rössler, P. (2005). *Inhaltsanalyse.* Konstanz: UVK.

Roethlisberger, F. J.; Dickson, W. J. (1934). *Management and the Worker.* Cambridge.

Röwer, B. (2007). *Erscheinungsformen und Zulässigkeit heimlicher Ermittlungen.* Duisburg: Wiku-Verlag.

Rogers, E. M (1995). *Diffusion of Innovations.* 4th edition. New York.

Rogers, E. M.; Jouong-Im K. (1985). Diffusion of Innovations in Public Organizations. In: Merritt, R. L.; Merritt, A. J. (ed.). *Innovations in the Public Sector.* Beverly Hills etc.: Sage. pp. 85–107.

Rohrbach, L. A. et al. (1987). Evaluation of Resistance Skills Training using Multitrait-multimethod role play skill assessments. In: *Health Education Research*, 2(4), pp. 401–407.

Ronald, K. (2004). *Hermeneutik. Eine sozialwissenschaftliche Einführung.* Konstanz: UVK.

Rondinelli, D. A. (1983). *Secondary Cities in Developing Countries: Policies for Diffusing Urbanization.* Beverly Hills: Sage.

Rosenbaum, P. R.; Rubin, D. B. (1983). The Central Role of the Propensity Score in Observational Studies for Causal Effects. In: *Biometrika*, 70, pp. 41–55.

Rosenbaum, P. R.; Rubin, D. B. (1985). Constructing a Control Group Using Multivariate Matched Sampling Methods that Incorporate the Propensity Score. In: *The American Statistician*, 39, pp. 33–38.

Rossi, P. H.; Freeman, H. E.; Hofmann, G. (1988). *Programm Evaluation: Einführung in die Methoden angewandter Sozialforschung* Stuttgart: Enke.

Rossi, P. H.; Lipsey, M. W.; Freeman, H. E. (1999). *Evaluation. A Systematic Approach.* 6th edition, Thousand Oaks et al.: Sage.

Rossi, P. H.; Lipsey, M. W.; Freeman, H. E. (2004). *Evaluation. A systematic Approach.* Thousand Oaks et al.: Sage.

Roth, R. (2004). Reden Sie mit dem Pferd. Bedingungen, Möglichkeiten und Grenzen Demokratischer Evaluationskultur in Deutschland. In: *Soziale Arbeit und Sozialpolitik. Sozial Extra*, 28(6).

Royce, T. D.; Bowcher, W. L. (ed.) (2007). *New Directions in the Analysis of Multi-Modal Discourse.* Mahwah et al.: Erlbaum.

Royse, D. et al. (2001). *Program Evaluation. An Introduction.* Australia: Brooks/Cole

Ruep, M.; Keller, G. (2007). *Schulevaluation. Grundlagen, Methoden, Wirksamkeit.* Frankfurt et al.: Lang.

Sahner, H. (2005). *Schließende Statistik. Eine Einführung für Sozialwissenschaftler.* Wiesbaden: VS-Verlag.

Saldana, J. (2012). *The Coding Manual for Qualitative Researchers.* Thousand Oaks et al.: Sage (2.).

Sanders, J. R.; Cunningham, D. J. (1973). A Structure for Formative Evaluation in Product Development. In: *Review of Educational Research*, 43, pp. 217–236.

Sanders, J. R.; Cunningham, D. J. (1974). Techniques and Procedures for Formative Evaluation. In: Borich, G. D. (ed.). *Evaluation educational programs and products.* Englewood Cliffs, NJ: Educational Technology.

Saner, R. (2002). Quality Assurance for Public Administration: A Consensus Building Vehicle. In: *Public Organization Review: A Global Journal.* Netherlands: Kluwer. pp. 407–414.

Scharpf, F. W. (1993). Coordination in Hierarchies and Networks. In: Scharpf, F. W. (ed.). *Games and Hierarchies and Networks. Analytical and Theoretical Approaches to the Study of Governance Institutions.* Frankfurt/New York: Campus, pp. 125–165.

Schedler, K.; Proeller, I. (2003). *New Public Management* (2nd edition, revised). Bern: Haupt.

Schelle, H. (2007). *Projekte zum Erfolg führen. Projektmanagement – systematisch und kompakt.* München: DTV-Beck.

Schendera, C. (2008). *Clusteranalyse mit SPSS*, München: Oldenbourg (due to appear).

Schiffrin, D. (ed.) (2005). *Handbook of Discourse Analysis.* Malden: Blackwell.

Schmähl, W.; Fachinger, U. (1990). Prozeßproduzierte Daten als Grundlage für sozial- und verteilungspolitische Analysen: einige Erfahrungen mit Daten der Rentenversicherungsträger für Längsschnittanalysen. Bremen: Zentrum für Sozialpolitik (ZeS-Arbeitspapier 1990,6)

Schmähl, W. (1984). 'Prozessproduzierte' Längsschnittinformationen zur Einkommensanalyse: Anmerkung zu den Datenquellen. Frankfurt/Mannheim: Sonderforschungsbereich 3 (Sfb3-Arbeitspapier 130).

Schmauks, D. (2007). *Semiotische Streifzüge. Essays aus der Welt der Zeichen.* Berlin: Lit.

Schmidt, M. G. (ed.) (1988). *Staatstätigkeit. International und historisch vergleichende Analysen (PVS-Sonderheft 19).* Opladen: Westdeutscher Verlag.

Schnegg, M.; Lang, M. (2002). *Netzwerkanalyse. Eine praxisorientierte Einführung.* Hamburg: Universität (Methoden der Ethnographie Heft 1, downloadable at: http://www.methoden-der-ethnographie.de/heft1/Netzwerkanalyse.pdf).

Schneider, V.; Kenis, P. (1996). Verteilte Kontrolle: Institutionelle Steuerung in modernen Gesellschaften. In: Kenis, P.; Schneider, V. (ed.). *Organisation und Netzwerk. Institutionelle Steuerung in Wirtschaft und Politik.* Frankfurt/New York: Campus, pp. 9–44.

Schneider-Barthold, W. (1992). Zur Angemessenheit von quantitativen und qualitativen Erhebungsmethoden in der Entwicklungsländerforschung. Vorzüge und Probleme der Aktionsforschung. In: Reichert, C.; Scheuch, E. K.; Seibel, H. D. (ed.). *Empirische Sozialforschung über Entwicklungsländer. Methodenprobleme und Praxisbezug*. Saarbrücken: Breitenbach.

Schnell, R. (1997). *Nonresponse in Bevölkerungsumfragen*. Ausmaß, Entwicklung und Ursachen. Opladen: Leske + Budrich.

Schnell, R.; Hill, P. B.; Esser, E. (1992). *Methoden der empirischen Sozialforschung*. München, Wien: Oldenbourg.

Schnell, R., Hill, P. B. und Esser, E. (2008). *Methoden der empirischen Sozialforschung*. München/Wien: Oldenbourg.

Schönig, W. (ed.) (2007). *Spuren der Schulevaluation: zur Bedeutung und Wirksamkeit von Evaluationskonzepten im Schulalltag*. Bad Heilbronn: Klinkhardt.

Scholl, A. (1993). *Die Befragung als Kommunikationssituation. Zur Reaktivität im Forschungsinterview*. Opladen: Westdeutscher Verlag.

Schräpler, J.-P. (1997). Eine empirische Erklärung von formalen Antwortstilen: Stereotypes Antwortverhalten und Zustimmungstendenzen im Sozioökonomischen Panel (SOEP). In: *Kölner Zeitschrift für Soziologie und Sozialpsychologie*, 49, pp. 728–746.

Schröder, W. H. (ed.) (2006). *Historisch-sozialwissenschaftliche Forschungen: quantitative sozialwissenschaftliche Analysen von historischen und prozess-produzierten Daten; eine Buchreihe: 1977 – 1991*. Köln: Zentrum für Historische Sozialforschung (Historical social research 18).

Schröter, E.; Wollmann, H. (1998). New Public Management. In: Bandemer, S. (ed.). *Handbuch zur Verwaltungsreform*. Opladen.

Schubert, K. (1991). *Politikfeldanalyse*. Opladen: Westdeutscher Verlag.

Schubert, K.; Bandelow, N. C. (2003). *Lehrbuch der Politikfeldanalyse*. München: Oldenbourg.

Schütz, A. (1971). *Gesammelte Aufsätze, Vol. 1: Das Problem der sozialen Wirklichkeit*. Den Haag: Nijhoff.

Schützeichel, R. (2004). *Soziologische Kommunikationstheorien*. Konstanz: UVK.

Schultz, B. (2006). Möglichkeiten und Grenzen des Matching-Ansatzes – am Beispiel der betrieblichen Mitbestimmung, IWH-Diskussionspapier Nr. 15, Halle: IWH (downloadable at http://www.iwh.uni-halle.de/d/publik/disc/15–06.pdf, as of 4 June 2008).

Scott, J. (2012). *Social Network Analysis*. London et al.: Sage (3.).

Scott, J.; Carrington, P. (2011). *The Sage Handbook of Social Network Analysis*. Thousand Oaks et al.: Sage.

Scott, R. W. (2003). *Organizations: Rational, Natural, and Open Systems*. New Jersey: Prentice Hall.

Scriven, M. (1967). *The methodology of evaluation*. In Stake, R. E. (ed.). Curriculum evaluation. Chicago: Rand McNally.

Scriven, Michael (1974). Evaluation Perspectives and Procedures. In: J. W. Popham (ed.). *Evaluation in Education. Current Applications*. Berkeley: McCutcheon, pp. 3–93.

Scriven, M. (1980). *The Logic of Evaluation*. California: Edgepress.

Scriven, M. (1983). Evaluation Ideologies. In: Madaus, G. F.; Scriven, M.; Stufflebeam, D. L. (ed.). *Evaluation Models: Viewpoints on Educational and Human Services Evaluation*. Boston: Kluwe-Nijhoff.

Scriven, M. (1991). *Evaluation Thesaurus*. Thousand Oaks, CA: Sage.

Scriven, M. (1994). Product Evaluation: The State of the Art. In: *Evaluation Practice*, 15, pp. 45–62.

Scriven, M. (1997). Minimalist Theory. The least Theory that Practice Requires. In: *American Journal of Evaluation*, 19(1), pp. 57–70.

Scriven, M. (2002). *Evaluation Thesaurus* (4th edition). Newbury Park et al.: Sage.

Seale, C., Gobo, G.; Gubrium, J. (2000). *The Quality of Qualitative Research*. London et al.: Sage.

Seiffert, H. (2006). *Einführung in die Wissenschaftstheorie, Vol. 2: Geisteswissenschaftliche Methoden*. Phänomenologie, Hermeneutik und historische Methode, Dialektik. München: Beck.

Seipel, C.; Rieker, P. (2003). *Integrative Sozialforschung. Konzepte und Methoden der qualitativen und quantitativen empirischen Forschung*. Weinheim, München: Juventa.

Seligman, A. B. (1992). *The Idea of Civil Society*. New York, Free Press

Sennett, R. (1998). *Verfall und Ende des öffentlichen Lebens. Die Tyrannei der Intimität*. Frankfurt: Fischer (14th edition).

Sensi, D.; Cracknell, B. (1991). Inquiry into Evaluation Practices in the Commission. In: MONITOR Collection. Luxembourg: Office for Official Publications of the EC.

Silverman, D. (2011). *Interpreting Qualitative Data*. Thousand Oaks et al.: Sage (4.).

Silvestrini, S. (2011). Organizational Aspects of Evaluations. In: Stockmann, R. (ed.). *A Practitioner Handbook on Evaluation*. Cheltenham/Northampton: Edward Elgar, pp. 99–134.

Shadish, W. R.; Cook, T. D.; Leviton, L. C. (1991). *Foundations of Program Evaluation: Theory and Practice*. London: Sage.

Shadish, W. R.; Cook, T. D.; Campbell, D. T. (2002). *Experimental and Quasi-experimental Designs for Generalized Causal Inference*. Boston: Houghton Mifflin.

Shapiro, J.; Trevino, J. M. (2004). Compensatory Education for Disadvantaged Mexican Students: An Impact Evaluation Using Propensity Score Matching, World Bank Policy Research Working Paper 3334, June 2004 (downloadable at: http://www-wds.worldbank.org/servlet/WDSContentServer/WDSP/IB/2004/0 8/02/000160016_20040802152704/Rendered/PDF/WPS3334.pdf, as of 4 June 2008).

Shatz, D. (2004). *Peer Review: A Critical Inquiry*. Lanham: Rowman & Littlefield Publ.

Skrondal, A.; Rabe-Hesketh, S. (2009). *Multilevel Modelling* (4 vols). Thousand Oaks et al.: Sage.

Smith, E. R.; Taylor, R. W. (1942). *Appraising and Recording Student Progress*. New York: Harper and Row.

Smith, M. F. (1990). Should AEA Begin a Process for Restricting Membership in the Profession of Evaluation? In: *American Journal of Evaluation*, 20, pp. 521–531.

Snijders, T. A. B.; Bosker, R. (2011). *Multilevel Analysis: An Introduction to Basic and Advanced Multilevel Modeling*. Thousand Oaks et al.: Sage (2.).

Soeffner, H.-G. (2003). Sozialwissenschaftliche Hermeneutik. In: Flick, U., von Kardorff, E.; Steinke, I. (ed.). *Qualitative Forschung. Ein Handbuch*. Reinbek: rororo, pp. 164–175.

Spermann, A.; Strotmann, H. (2005). The Targeted Negative Income Tax (TNIT) in Germany: Evidence from a Quasi Experiment, ZEW Discussion Paper No. 05–68, Mannheim: ZEW. (downloadable at ftp://ftp.zew.de/pub/zew-docs/dp/dp0568.pdf, as of 6 June 2008).

Stagl, S. (2004). Valuation for Sustainable Development – The Role of Multicriteria Evaluation. In: *Vierteljahreshefte zur Wirtschaftsforschung*, 73(1), pp. 53–62.

Stake, R. E. (1967). The countenance of educational evaluaton. *Teachers College Record*, 68, pp. 523–540.

Stake, R. E. (1972). Responsive Evaluation. *Unpublished Manuscript*.

Stake, R. E.. (1975). *Program Evaluation, Particularly Responsive Evaluation* (Occasional Paper No. 5) Kalamazoo: Western Michigan University Evaluation Center.

Stake, R. E. (1980). Program Evaluation, Particularly Responsive Evaluation. In: Dockrell, W. B.; Hamilton, D. (ed.). *Rethinking Educational Research*. London: Hodder & Stoughton.

Stake, R. E. (1983). The Case Study Method in Social Inquiry. In: Madaus, G. F. et al. (ed.). *Evaluation Models*. Boston: Kluwer-Nijhoff.

Stake, R. E.; Schwandt, T. A. (2006). On Discerning Quality in Evaluation. In: Shaw, I. F.; Mark, M. M., Greene, J. (eds). *The Sage Handbook of Evaluation: Program, Policy and Practices*. London: Sage.

Stamm, M. (2003). Evaluation im Spiegel ihrer Nutzung: Grande idée oder grande illusion des 21. Jahrhunderts?. In: *Zeitschrift für Evaluation*, 2, pp.183–200.

Stanley, J. C. (1966). Rice as a Pioneer Educational Researcher. In: *Journal of Educational Measurement*, 3(2), pp. 135–139.

Stanat, P. et al. (2002). PISA 2000: Die Studie im Überblick. Grundlagen, Methoden, Ergebnisse, Berlin: Max-Planck-Institut für Bildungsforschung (on the Internet at www.mpib-berlin.mpg.de/pisa/PISA_im_Ueberblick.pdf, as of 1 Jan 2009).

Staudt, E.; Hefkesbrink, J.; Treichel, H.-R. (1988). *Forschungsmanagement durch Evaluation: Das Beispiel Arbeitsschwerpunkt Druckindustrie*. Frankfurt am Main: Campus.

Stegbauer, C. (ed.) (2008). *Netzwerkanalyse und Netzwerktheorie. Ein neues Paradigma in den Sozialwissenschaften*. Wiesbaden: VS-Verlag.

Steinke, I. (2003). Gütekriterien qualitativer Forschung. In: Flick, U.; von Kardorff, E.; Steinke, I. (ed.). *Qualitative Forschung. Ein Handbuch*. Reinbek: rororo, pp. 319–331.

Steinke, I. (1999). *Kriterien qualitativer Forschung. Ansätze zur Bewertung qualitativ-empirischer Sozialforschung*, Weinheim/München: Beltz.

Stewart, K.; William, M. (2005), Researching Online Populations. The Use of Online Focus Groups for Social Research. In: *Qualitative Research* 5: pp. 395–416.

Stockmann, R. (1996). *Die Wirksamkeit der Entwicklungshilfe. Eine Evaluation der Nachhaltigkeit von Programmen und Projekten der Berufsbildung*. Opladen: Westdeutscher Verlag.

Stockmann, R. (2000). Wirkungsevaluation in der Entwicklungspolitik. In: *Vierteljahrshefte zur Wirtschaftsforschung*, 69(3), pp. 438–452.

Stockmann, R. (2002). Zur Notwendigkeit und Konzeption einer deutschsprachigen 'Zeitschrift für Evaluation'. In: *Zeitschrift für Evaluation*, 1(1), pp. 3–10.

Stockmann, R. (2006) (ed.). *Evaluationsforschung: Grundlagen und ausgewählte Forschungsfelder*. 3rd edition. Münster et al.: Waxmann.

Stockmann, R. (2008). *Evaluation and Quality Development: Principles of Impact-Based Quality Management*. Frankfurt et al.: Peter Lang.

Stockmann, R. (ed. 2011). *A Practitioner Handbook on Evaluation*. Cheltenham / Northampton: Edward Elgar.

Stockmann, R.; Caspari, A. (1998). Ex-post Evaluation als Instrument des Qualitätsmanagements in der Entwicklungszusammenarbeit. Eschborn:

Gutachten im Auftrag der Deutschen Gesellschaft für Technische Zusammenarbeit (GTZ).

Stockmann, R.; Meyer, W. (2006). Evaluation von Nachhaltigkeit. Studienbrief EZ0400 des Fernstudiengangs Nachhaltige Entwicklungszusammenarbeit der TU Kaiserslautern. Kaiserslautern: Zentrum für Fernstudien und universitäre Weiterbildung.

Stockmann, R., Meyer, W., Gaus, H., Urbahn, J.; Kohlmann, U. (2001). *Nachhaltige Umweltberatung. Evaluation eines Förderprogramms der Deutschen Bundesstiftung Umwelt.* Opladen: Leske + Budrich.

Stockmann, R., Meyer, W., Krapp, S.; Köhne, G. (2000). *Wirksamkeit deutscher Berufsbildungszusammenarbeit. Ein Vergleich zwischen staatlichen und nicht-staatlichen Programmen in der Volksrepublik China.* Opladen: Westdeutscher Verlag.

Stouffer, S.A. et al. (1949). *The American Soldier. Vol. II: Combat and its Aftermath.* Princeton, NJ: Princeton University Press.

Strauss, A. L.; Corbin J. M. (1996). *Grounded Theory.* Grundlagen Qualitativer Sozialforschung. Weinheim: PVU.

Streeck, W. (2001). Tarifautonomie und Politik: Von der Konzertierten Aktion zum Bündnis für Arbeit. In: Gesamtverband der metallindustriellen Arbeitgeberverbände (ed.). *Die deutschen Arbeitsbeziehungen am Anfang des 20. Jahrhunderts. Wissenschaftliches Kolloquium aus Anlass des Ausscheidens von Dr. Werner Stumpfe als Präsident von Gesamtmetall.* Köln: Deutscher Institutsverlag, pp. 76–102

Stucke, G. (1985). *Bestimmung der städtischen Fahrtenmatrix durch Verkehrszählungen.* Karlsruhe: Universität.

Stufflebeam, D. L. (1971). The Relevance of the CIPP Evaluation Model for Educational Accountability. In: *Journal of Research and Development in Education,* 5, pp. 19–25.

Stufflebeam, D. L. (1973). In Introduction to the PDK Book: Educational Evaluation and Decision-Making. In: Worthen, B. R.; Sanders, J. R. (ed.). *Educational Evaluation: Theory and practice.* Belmont, CA: Wadsworth.

Stufflebeam, D. L. (1983). The CIPP Model for Program Evaluation. In: Madaus, G. F.; Scriven, M. S.; Stufflebeam, D. L. (ed.). *Evaluation Models: Viewpoints on Educational and Human Services Evaluation.* Boston: Kluwer: Nijhoff, pp. 117–141.

Stufflebeam, D. L. (2000). Foundational Models for 21st Century Program Evaluation. In: Stufflebeam, D. L.; Madaus, G. F.; Kellaghan, T. (ed.). *Evaluation Models. Viewpoints on Educational and Human Services Evaluation.* Boston et al.: Kluwer Academics, pp. 33–84.

Stufflebeam, D. L.; Madaus, G. F.; Kellaghan, T. (2000). *Evaluation Models: Viewpoints on Educational and Human Services Evaluation.* Boston: Kluwer Academic Publisher Group.

Stufflebeam, D. L.; Shinkfield, A. J. (2007). *Evaluation. Theory, Models and Applications.* San Francisco: John Wiley & Son.

Suchman, E. (1967). *Evaluative Research: Principles and Practice in Public Service and Social Action Programs.* New York: Russell Sage.

Sudman, S.; Bradburn, N. M. (1974). *Response Effects in Surveys. A Review and Synthesis.* Chicago: Aldine.

Summa, H.; Toulemonde, J. (2002). Evaluation in the European Union: Addressing Complexity and Ambiguity. In: Furubo J. E., Rist R. C., Sandahl R. (ed.). *International Atlas of Evaluation.* New Brunswick: Transaction Publishers.

Sun, H.; Williamson, C. (2005). *Simulation Evaluation of Call Dropping Policies for Stochastic Capacity Networks*. In: Proceedings of the SCS Symposium on the Performance Evaluation of Computer and Telecommunication Systems (SPECTS), Philadelphia, PA, pp. 327–336, July 2005 (downloadable at http://pages.cpsc.ucalgary.ca/~carey/papers/2005/CallDropping.pdf, as of 6 June 2008).

Swart, E.; Ihle, P. (ed.) (2005). *Routinedaten im Gesundheitswesen. Handbuch Sekundärdatenanalyse: Grundlagen, Methoden und Perspektiven*. Bern: Huber.

Sydow, J.; Windeler, A. (ed.) (2000). *Steuerung von Netzwerken. Konzepte und Praktiken*. Opladen: Westdeutscher Verlag.

Tashakkori, A.; Teddlie, C. (ed.) (2003). *Handbook of Mixed Methods in Social and Behavioural Research*. Thousand Oaks: Sage.

Ten Have, P. (2007). *Doing Conversation Analysis. A Practical Guide*. Los Angeles: Sage.

Tews, K. (2004). Diffusion als Motor globalen Politikwandels: Potentiale und Grenzen. *FU-Report 01–2004*. Berlin: Freie Universität.

Theis-Berglmair, A.-M. (2003). *Organisationskommunikation. Theoretische Grundlagen und empirische Forschungen*. Münster: Lit.

Theobald, A. (2000). *Das World Wide Web als Befragungsinstrument*. Wiesbaden: Gabler.

Thompson, J. D. (1967). *Organizations in Action*. New York: McGraw-Hill.

Thüringer Rechnungshof (2008). *Jahresbericht 2008 mit Bemerkungen zur Haushalts- und Wirtschaftsführung und zur Haushaltsrechnung 2006*. Rudolstadt: Thüringer Rechnungshof.

Titus, M. A. (2007). Detecting Selection Bias, Using Propensity Score Matching, and Estimating Treatment Effects: An Application to the Private Returns to a Master's Degree. In: *Research in Higher Education*, 48(4).

Top, J. (2006). *Konsensanalyse. Ein neues Instrument der Inhaltsanalyse. Theoretische Fundierung und empirische Kalibrierung*. Norderstedt: Books on Demand.

Tourangeau, R.; Rips, L. J.; Rasinski, K. A. (2005). *The Psychology of Survey Response*. Cambridge et al.: Cambridge Univ. Press.

Tourish, D.; Hargie, O. (ed.) (2003). *Key Issues in Organizational Communication*. London: Routledge.

Toutenburg, H.; Heumann, C.; Schomaker, M. (2006). *Deskriptive Statistik. Eine Einführung in Methoden und Anwendungen mit SPSS*. Berlin et al.: Springer.

Trappmann, M.; Hummell, H. J.; Sodeur, W. (2005). *Strukturanalyse Sozialer Netzwerke. Konzepte, Modelle, Methoden*. Wiesbaden: VS-Verlag.

Türk, K. (ed.) (2000). *Hauptwerke der Organisationstheorie*. Wiesbaden: Westdeutscher Verlag.

Tyler, R. W. (1935). Evaluation: A Challenge to Progressive Education. In: *Educational Research Bulletin*, 14, pp. 9–16.

Tyler, R. W. (1938). The Specific Techniques on Investigation: Examining and Testing Acquired Knowledge, Skill and Ability. In: Freeman, F. (ed.). *The scientific movement in education* (37th yearbook of the National Society for the Study of Education, Part II), Bloomington: Public School Publishing Company, pp. 341–356.

Tyler, R. W. (1942). General Statement on Evaluation. In: *Journal of Educational Research*, 35, pp. 492–501.

Tyler, R. W. (1950). *Basic Principles of Curriculum and Instruction*. Chicago: University of Chicago Press.

Umlauf, V. (2007). *Hermeneutik nach Gadamer.* Freiburg/München: Alber.
Uphoff, N. (2002). Why NGOs are not a Third Sector. A Sectoral Analysis with Some Thoughts on Accountability, Sustainability and Evaluation. In: Edwards, M.; Hulme, D. (ed.). *Non-Governmental Organisations. Performance and Accountability beyond the magic bullet.* London: Earthscan, pp. 17–30.
Urban, D.; Mayerl, J. (2008). *Regressionsanalyse: Theorie, Technik und Anwendung.* Wiesbaden: VS-Verlag.
Urban, M.; Weiser, U. (2006). *Kleinräumige Sozialraumanalyse. Theoretische Grundlagen und praktische Durchführung. Identifikation und Beschreibung von Sozialräumen mit quantitativen Daten.* Dresden: Saxonia.
Vahs, D. (2003). *Organisation. Einführung in die Organisationstheorie und –praxis.* Stuttgart: Schäffer-Poeschel (4th edition).
van der Linden, W. J.; Hambleton, R. K. (ed.) (1997). *Handbook of Modern Item Response Theory.* New York; Berlin, Heidelberg: Springer.
Vedung, E. (1999). *Evaluation im öffentlichen Sektor.* Wien, Köln, Graz: Böhlau.
Vedung, E. (2000). Evaluation Research and Fundamental Research. In: Stockmann, R. (ed.). *Evaluationsforschung.* Opladen: Leske + Budrich. pp. 103–127.
Vedung, E. (2004). Evaluation Research and Fundamental Research. In: Stockmann, R. (ed.). *Evaluationsforschung.* 2nd edition. Opladen: Leske + Budrich. pp. 111–134.
Vogel, F. (2001). *Beschreibende und schließende Statistik.* München: Oldenbourg.
Wallraff, G. (1970). *Industriereportagen. Als Arbeiter in deutschen Großbetrieben.* Köln: Kiepenheuer & Witsch.
Wallraff, G. (1977). *Der Aufmacher. Der Mann, der bei 'Bild' Hans Esser war.* Köln: Kiepenheuer & Witsch.
Wallraff, G. (1992). *Ganz Unten. Mit einer Dokumentation der Folgen.* Köln: Kiepenheuer & Witsch.
Weber, M. (1968). *Methodologische Schriften.* Frankfurt: Fischer.
Weick, K. E. (1995). *Sense-making in Organizations.* Thousand Oaks et al.: Sage.
Weick, K. E. (1985). *Der Prozess des Organisierens.* Frankfurt: Suhrkamp.
Weinert, F. E. (ed.) (2001). *Leistungsmessungen in Schulen.* Weinheim und Basel: Beltz Verlag.
Weisberg, S. (2005). *Applied Linear Regression.* Hoboken, New Jersey: Wiley-Interscience.
Weiss, C. H. (1992). *Evaluation.* 2nd edition. Upper Saddle River, USA: Prentice-Hall Inc.
Weiss, C. H. (1974). *Evaluierungsforschung.* Opladen: Westdeutscher Verlag.
Weiss, C. H. (1998). *Evaluation,* New Jersey: Prentice Hall.
Welker, M.; Werner, A.; Scholz, J. (2005). *Online-Research. Markt- und Sozialforschung mit dem Internet.* Heidelberg: dpunkt.verlag.
Weller, S. C.; Romney, A. K. (2003). *Metric Scaling: Correspondence Analysis.* Newbury Park et al.: Sage.
Wernet, A. (2006). *Einführung in die Interpretationstechnik der Objektiven Hermeneutik.* Wiesbaden.
West, M. D. (ed.) (2001a). *Application of Computer Content Analysis.* Westport: Ablex. Publ.
West, M. D. (ed.) (2001b). *Theory, Method and Practice in Computer Content Analysis.* Westport: Ablex. Publ.

Wetherell, M.; Taylor, S.; Yates, S. J. (ed.) (2001). *Discourse as Data. A guide for analysis.* London et al.: Sage.

Weyer, J. (ed.) (2000). *Soziale Netzwerke. Konzepte und Methoden der sozialwissenschaftlichen Netzwerkforschung.* München/Wien: Oldenbourg.

White, G. (2004). Civil Society, Democratization and Development: Cleaning the Analytical Ground. In: Burnell, P.; Calvert, P. (ed.). *Civil Society in Democratization.* London/Portland: Frank Cass, pp. 6–21.

White, R.; Lippitt, R. (1953). Leader Behavior and Member Reaction in Three 'Social Climates'. In: Cartwright, D.; Zander, A. (ed.). *Group Dynamics, Research and Theory.* Evanston, Ill.: Row, Peterson and Company.

Widmer, T. (2000). Qualität der Evaluation – Wenn Wissenschaft zur praktischen Kunst wird. In: Stockmann, R. (ed.) *Evaluationsforschung.* Opladen: Leske + Budrich.

Widmer, T. (2001). Qualitätssicherung in der Evaluation – Instrumente und Verfahren. In: *LeGES-Gesetzgebung und Evaluation,* 12, pp. 9–41.

Widmer, T. (2002). Staatsreformen und Evaluation: Konzeptionelle Grundlagen und Praxis bei Schweizer Kantonen. In: *Zeitschrift für Evaluation,* 1/2002. pp. 101–114.

Widmer, T. (2004). Qualität der Evaluation – Wenn Wissenschaft zur praktischen Kunst wird. In: Stockmann, R. (ed.). *Evaluationsforschung. Grundlagen und ausgewählte Forschungsfelder.* Opladen: Leske + Budrich.

Widmer, T.; Beywl, W.; Fabian, C. (ed.) (2009). *Evaluation. Ein systematisches Handbuch.* Wiesbaden: VS-Verlag.

Widmer, T.; Frey, K. (2006). Evaluation von Mehrebenen-Netzwerkstrategien. In: *Zeitschrift für Evaluation,* 2(2006), pp. 287–316.

Wiedemann, P. M. (1986). *Erzählte Wirklichkeit: Zur Theorie und Auswertung narrativer Interviews.* Weinheim et al.: Beltz.

Wiehl, R. (2003). Gadamers philosophische Hermeneutik und die begriffsgeschichtliche Methode. In: *Archiv für Begriffsgeschichte,* 45, pp. 10–20

Will, H.; Winteler, A.; Krapp, A. (ed.) (1987). *Evaluation in der beruflichen Aus- und Weiterbildung.* Heidelberg: Sauer.

Willke, H. (2004). *Einführung in das systematische Wissensmanagement.* Heidelberg: Carl-Auer-Systeme-Verlag.

Windhoff-Héritier, A. (1983). *Policyanalyse. Eine Einführung.* Frankfurt am Main: Campus.

Winkler, K. (2004). *Wissensmanagementprozesse in face-to-face und virtuellen communities. Konzepte, Gestaltungsprinzipien und Erfolgsfaktoren.* Berlin: Logos.

Wittmann, W. W. (1985). *Evaluationsforschung. Aufgaben, Probleme und Anwendungen.* Berlin et al.: Springer.

Wittmann, W. W. (1990). Aufgaben und Möglichkeiten der Evaluationsforschung in der Bundesrepublik Deutschland. In: Koch, U.; Wittman, W. W. (ed.). *Evaluationsforschung: Bewertungsgrundlage von Sozial- und Gesundheitsprogrammen.* Berlin: Springer.

Wollmann, H. (1994). Evaluierungsansätze und -institutionen in Kommunalpolitik und -verwaltung. Stationen der Planungs- und Steuerungsdiskussion. In: Schulze-Böing, M.; Johrendt, N. (ed.). *Wirkungen kommunaler Beschäftigungsprogramme. Methoden, Instrumente und Ergebnisse der Evaluation kommunaler Arbeitsmarktpolitik.* Basel, Boston, Berlin: Birkhäuser.

Wollmann, H. (1997). Evaluation in Germany. In: *European Evaluation Society. Newsletter*, 3, pp. 4–5.

Wollmann, H. (1998). Modernisierung der kommunalen Politik- und Verwaltungswelt – Zwischen Demokratie und Managementschub. In: Grunow, D.; Wollmann, H. (ed.). *Lokale Verwaltungsreform in Aktion: Fortschritte und Fallstricke*. Basel et al.: Birkhäuser. pp. 400–439.

Wollmann, H. (1999). *Politik- und Verwaltungsmodernisierung in den Kommunen: Zwischen Managementlehre und Demokratiegebot*. Die Verwaltung (Schwerpunktheft 3).

Wollmann, H. (2000). Staat und Verwaltung in den 90er Jahren: Kontinuität oder Veränderungswelle? In: Czada, R.; Wollmann, H. (ed.). *Von der Bonner zur Berliner Republik. 10 Jahre Deutsche Einheit*, (Leviathan-Sonderheft 19/1999). Opladen: Westdeutscher Verlag.

Wollmann, H. (2002). Verwaltungspolitik und Evaluierung. Ansätze, Phasen und Beispiele im Ausland und in Deutschland. In: *Zeitschrift für Evaluation*, 1(2002), pp. 75–100.

Wollmann, H. (ed.) (2003). *Evaluation in the Public Sector: Reform Concepts and Practice in International Perspective*. Cheltenham: Edward Elgar.

Wollmann, H. (2004). Leistungsmessung ('performance measurement') in Politik und Verwaltung: Phasen, Typen und Ansätze im internationalen Überblick. In: Kuhlmann, S.; Bogumil, J.; Wollmann, H. (ed.). *Leistungsmessung und -vergleich in Politik und Verwaltung. Konzepte und Praxis*. Wiesbaden: VS-Verlag.

Wollmann, H. (2005). Evaluierung von Verwaltungsmodernisierung. In: Blanke, B.; von Bandemer, S.; Nullmeier, F.; Wewer, G. (ed.). *Handbuch zur Verwaltungsreform*. Wiesbaden: VS-Verlag, pp. 502–510.

Woltering, V.; Herrler, A.; Spitzer, K.; Spreckelsen, C. (2009). Blended Learning Positively Affects Students' Satisfaction and the Role of the Tutor in the Problem-based Learning Process: Results of a Mixed-method Evaluation. In: *Advances in Health Sciences Education*, 14(5), pp. 725–738.

Wood, E. M. (1990). The Uses and Abuses of 'Civil Society'. In: Miliband, R.; Panitch, L. (ed.). The Retreat of the Intellectuals. *Socialist Register*. London: Merlin Press, pp. 60–84.

Wooffitt, R. (2006), *Conversation Analysis and Discourse Analysis. A comparative and critical introduction*, London et al.: Sage.

World Bank (publication date unknown). *The LogFrame Handbook. A Logical Framework Approach to Project Cycle Management*. Washington: World Bank (on the Internet at www.wau.boku.ac.at/fileadmin/_/H81/H811/ Skripten/811332/811332_G3_log-framehandbook.pdf, as of 1 Jan 2009).

World Bank – Independent Evaluation Group (2006). *Impact Evaluation – The Experience of the Independent Evaluation Group of the World Bank*. Washington: World Bank (downloadable at: http://lnweb18.worldbank.org/oed/oeddoclib. nsf/DocUNIDViewForJavaSearch/35BC420995BF58F8852571E00068C6BD/$fil e/impact_evaluation.pdf, as of 3 June 2008).

Worthen, B.; Sanders, J. (1973). Educational Evaluation. Theory and Practice. In: *Evaluation Review*, 13(1), pp. 18–31.

Wottawa, H.; Thierau, H. (1990). *Evaluation*. Bern et al.: Hans Huber.

Wottawa, H.; Thierau, H. (1998). *Lehrbuch Evaluation*. 2nd edition. Bern: Huber.

Wottawa, H.; Thierau, H. (2003). *Lehrbuch Evaluation*. 3rd edition, revised. Bern: Huber.

Wu, L. (ed., 2011). *Event History Analysis*. Thousand Oaks et al.: Sage (Sage Benchmarks in Social Research Methods, 4 Vol.).

Yanow, D.; Schwartz-Shea, P. (2011). *Interpretive Approaches to Research Design. Concepts and Processes*, Abingdon: Routledge.

Young, L.; Fitzgerald, B. (2006). *The Power of Language. How Discourse influences Society*. London: Equinox.

Zapf, W. (ed.) (1991). *Die Modernisierung moderner Gesellschaften. Verhandlungen des 25. Deutschen Soziologentages*. Frankfurt: Campus.

Zielke, B. (2007). *Sozialer Konstruktivismus. Psychologische Diskurse*. Göttingen: Vandenhoeck und Ruprecht.

Zimmermann, E. (2006). *Das Experiment in den Sozialwissenschaften*. Wiesbaden: VS-Verlag.

Zohlnhöfer, W. (ed.) (1996). *Die Tarifautonomie auf dem Prüfstand*. Berlin: Duncker & Humblot.

Index